Law and Disaster

On the 11th of March 2011, an earthquake registering 9.0 on the Richter scale (the most powerful to ever strike Japan) hit the Tohoku Region in northern Japan. The earthquake produced a devastating tsunami that wiped out coastal cities and towns, leaving 18,561 people dead or classified as missing. Due to the disaster, the capability of the Fukushima Nuclear Power Plant, operated by Tokyo Electric Power Company (TEPCO), was compromised, causing nuclear meltdown. The hydrogen blast destroyed the facilities, resulting in a spread of radioactive materials, and, subsequently, serious nuclear contamination. This combined event – earthquake, tsunami, and nuclear meltdown – became known as the Great East Japan Earthquake Disaster.

This book examines the response of the Japanese government to the disaster, and its attempts to answer the legal questions posed by the combination of earthquake, tsunami, and nuclear meltdown. Japanese law, policy, and infrastructure were insufficiently prepared for these disasters, and the country's weaknesses were brutally exposed. This book analyses these failings, and discusses what Japan, and other countries, can learn from these events.

Professor Shigenori Matsui is Director of Japanese Legal Studies, Peter A. Allard School of Law, University of British Columbia, Canada. He is an internationally renowned expert in the fields of Constitutional Law, Mass Media Law, and Internet Law. Before joining the UBC Law School, he was a professor of Osaka University Law School. He has served for the Japanese government as a member of the National Freedom of Information Review Board, and as an examiner for the National Bar Examination Commission.

Law and Disaster

Earthquake, Tsunami and Nuclear Meltdown in Japan

Shigenori Matsui

Routledge
Taylor & Francis Group
LONDON AND NEW YORK

First published 2019 by Routledge

2 Park Square, Milton Park, Abingdon, Oxfordshire OX14 4RN
52 Vanderbilt Avenue, New York, NY 10017

Routledge is an imprint of the Taylor & Francis Group, an informa business

First issued in paperback 2019

British Library Cataloguing-in-Publication Data
A catalogue record for this book is available from the British Library

Library of Congress Cataloging-in-Publication Data
Names: Matsui, Shigenori, author.
Title: Law and disaster : earthquake, tsunami and nuclear meltdown in Japan / By Shigenori Matsui.
Description: New York : Routledge, 2018.
Identifiers: LCCN 2018015567| ISBN 9781138481947 (hbk) | ISBN 9781351059343 (web pdf) | ISBN 9781351059336 (epub) | ISBN 9781351059329 (mobipocket)
Subjects: LCSH: Disaster relief—Law and legislation—Japan—Tåohoku Region | Tohoku Earthquake and Tsunami, Japan, 2011. | Earthquakes—Government policy—Japan—Tåohoku Region. | Nuclear power plants—Law and legislation—Japan. | Liability for nuclear damages—Japan.
Classification: LCC KNX3037 .M38 2018 | DDC 344.5205/34—dc23
LC record available at https://lccn.loc.gov/2018015567

ISBN: 978-1-138-48194-7 (hbk)
ISBN: 978-0-367-48132-2 (pbk)

Typeset in Galliard
by Swales & Willis Ltd, Exeter, Devon, UK

Contents

Preface

The Tohoku Earthquake and powerful tsunami on 11 March 2011 brought tremendous loss and damages to Japan. Moreover, it triggered a serious nuclear disaster in the Fukushima Nuclear Power Plant. This is a study of law for the preparation of disaster, the response to the disaster, and the reconstruction after the disaster. Right after I learned about the devastation inflicted by the Tohoku Earthquake, I began to research the role that law played in order to prepare for the disaster, to respond to the disaster, and to reconstruct the disaster areas. This book is a result of my seven years research on disaster law in Japan.

Many people helped me in the writing of this book. Foremost is my family, who supported me throughout my research. I am indebted to the support from my colleague, Professor Yves Tiberghien and the encouragement of my colleague Professor David Edgington for the publication of this book. I would like to thank my students, Jason Hughes, Hisayo Saito, Natasha Fox, and Jonathan Wearing, for their help with citation checking and editing. Finally, I would like to thank everyone who gave me useful insights and helpful comments through all of the seminars and conferences hosted by the Centre for Japanese Research, Institute of Asian Research, University of British Columbia.

This book cites many Japanese statutes, regulations and associated terms for which there is no official English translation. I consulted various sources to find the most common English translation but, in the end, I chose the one that I believe most appropriately fits the original Japanese terms and phrases. Some of these are very peculiar to Japan and may be difficult for foreign observers to understand. I hope the glossary which appears in the appendices will be helpful to readers in this respect. Traditional English style has been used for names with the first name followed by the family name although the reverse is customary in Japan.

This book is dedicated to all the victims of natural disaster everywhere in the world.

Shigenori Matsui
Professor of Law, University of British Columbia,
Peter A. Allard School of Law
11 March 2018

Introduction

0.1 Earthquake, tsunami, and nuclear meltdown

0.1.1 The Tohoku Earthquake and tsunami

On Friday, 11 March 2011, at 2:46 pm, a massive earthquake hit the eastern part of Japan, referred to as the Tohoku Region (which translates literally as the "Northeastern" region).[1] It was the most powerful earthquake to hit Japan since the modern earthquake measurement system was first introduced. It was also one of the strongest earthquakes in recorded history all around the world.[2] The earthquake has generally come to be known as the Tohoku Earthquake.[3]

The earthquake caused extensive and serious damage to thousands of buildings and homes. It was, however, the tsunami triggered by the earthquake, not the earthquake itself, that caused further extraordinary loss and damage. The massive tsunami created by this earthquake inundated Tohoku's coastline cities immediately. Many coastal cities in the Tohoku Region, including several in Iwate, Miyagi, and Fukushima Prefectures, were literally swept away by the tsunami. In the end, 18,561 people people were either killed or remain missing. The Japanese government named the disaster caused by this earthquake the "Great East Japan Earthquake Disaster (*Higashinihon daishinsai*)."[4]

1 USGS, The M9.1 near the east coast of Honshu, Japan (USGS) https://earthquake.usgs.gov/earthquakes/eventpage/official20110311054624120_30#executive accessed 25 December 2017.

2 It was the fourth largest earthquake ever recorded in the world. USGS, 20 Largest Earthquakes in the World (USGS) https://earthquake.usgs.gov/earthquakes/browse/largest-world.php accessed 25 December 2017.

3 The Japan Meteorological Agency (JMA) officially named this earthquake "The off the Pacific Coast of Tohoku Earthquake." Japan Meteorological Agency, Tohoku chihō taiheiyōoki jishin [The off the Pacific Coast of Tohoku Earthquake] (JMA) www.jma.go.jp/jma/menu/jishin-portal.html accessed 25 December 2017. See also JMA, Heisei 23nen (2011nen) Touhoku chihō taiheiyōoki jishin [The 2011 off the Pacific Coast of Tohoku Earthquake] (JMA) www.data.jma.go.jp/svd/eqev/data/2011_03_11_tohoku/ accessed 25 December 2017. This word is also often used in statutes passed by the Japanese legislature. But the Tohoku Earthquake is more commonly used in the media to refer to this earthquake. n 1.

4 Prime Minister Kan's Press Interview (kantei, 1 April 2011) www.kantei.go.jp/jp/kan/statement/201104/01kaiken.html accessed 25 December 2017.

The Japanese government engaged in rescue response, ordering the Self Defense Forces (SDF) to locate and assist survivors and to transport necessary aid. SDF officers rescued survivors trapped in the rubble and transported them along with other survivors to shelters and hospitals. Numerous shelters were set up as hundreds of thousands were in dire need of water, food, and blankets. At one stage, more than 450,000 people had been evacuated and were forced to spend days, weeks, or even months in emergency shelters. All electricity, water, and LP gas had been cut off. Many survivors waited days before receiving any help at all because transportation systems, including public roads, railroads, and airports had been so severely damaged. Moreover, in some cases, entire communities were wiped out, including the municipal government itself, further inhibiting coordinated efforts at providing aid. After several days, the focus of government efforts shifted from rescue to recovery and restoration. Local governments began to collect dead bodies, clear debris, establish temporary housing for those who had lost their homes, and provide assistance to affected residents. Then, the central government started to assist municipal governments in reconstructing their communities.

The government needs to rebuild all the infrastructures, rebuild the communities, and restore and further facilitate the economic recovery of Tohoku. At the same time, the government needs to make sure that the same kind of disaster does not happen again if another massive earthquake and tsunami strikes in the future.

0.1.2 Meltdown at the nuclear power plant in Fukushima

Unfortunately, the disaster inflicted by the powerful tsunami was not limited to the carnage discussed above. The nuclear power plants in Fukushima prefecture, operated by the Tokyo Electric Power Co. (*Tokyo denryoku*) (TEPCO), threatened health and safety in Japan but also gave rise to grave concern worldwide.[5] Though there were two nuclear power plants operated by TEPCO at Fukushima, it was the No 1 (Daiichi) Nuclear Power Plant that had the most dire impacts. Although the reactors in the power plant were shut down automatically following the earthquake, the plant lost electricity due to the earthquake and the emergency generators were also lost as a result of the tsunami. Consequently, the power plant lost its capacity to cool the fuel rods in the reactor's core along with those stored in the fuel ponds. Nuclear fuel rods, normally submerged in, and cooled by, circulating water, evaporated the water with their heat in the absence of a cooling system. The fuel rods overheated and began to melt, generating dangerous levels of hydrogen within the containment building, and eventually triggering the hydrogen blasts that seriously damaged the facility and allowed

5 International Atomic Energy Agency (IAEA), The Fukushima Daiichi Accident: Report by the Director General (2015) (IAEA) www-pub.iaea.org/MTCD/Publications/PDF/Pub1710-ReportByTheDG-Web.pdf accessed 25 December 2017. *See also* Prime Minister of Japan and His Cabinet, Report of Japanese Government to the IAEA Ministerial Conference on Nuclear Safety—The Accident at TEPCO's Fukushima Nuclear Power Stations (kantei, June 2011) http://japan.kantei.go.jp/kan/topics/201106/iaea_houkokusho_e.html accessed 25 December 2017.

radioactive materials to contaminate the surrounding environment. The prime minister instructed all people living within a 20 km radius of the power plant to evacuate and issued instructions to all people living within a 30 km radius to remain indoors. The Japanese government then scrambled to restore the power and supply the water necessary for cooling the fuel rods in the reactors and in the fuel ponds.

The accident had very serious impacts on the local residents. With the expansion of evacuation instructions, at one point, some 165,000 residents evacuated because of this accident together with the damage from the tsunami in Fukushima where some 52,000 residents were evacuees. Many local residents were forced to stay away from their homes in unfamiliar communities and stayed in temporary places to wait for their return. The government needed to provide varying assistance to these evacuees.

Contamination had also had serious effects on agricultural products in neighboring communities. Spinach, cabbage, broccoli, cauliflower, and other vegetables showed extremely high levels of radioactive contamination with the central government banning the marketing and consumption of vegetables produced in affected prefectures. Highly contaminated water also ran from the nuclear power plant into the sea, raising concerns over the safety of seafood harvested nearby. Further, the soil was also contaminated resulting in the abandonment of staple rice crop planting.

Even after TEPCO and the government managed to control the damaged nuclear power plants, it had to provide assistance to those evacuees, pay damage awards and compensation, dispose of all the nuclear waste contaminated by the accident, and decontaminate the affected areas for evacuees to return. The government also needs to reconstruct Fukushima.

0.2 The Great East Japan Earthquake Disaster and failures of law and politics

0.2.1 Failures of law and politics

All these developments revealed that Japan's "disaster law," a legal system for a disaster, was clearly unprepared for a disaster of this magnitude. Surely, Japan's preparation for the powerful earthquake proved that it could save many residents from the disaster. But it was not able to save 18,561 residents from the tsunami nor was it able to prevent the nuclear meltdown accident in Fukushima. There are simply so many things that should have been done in advance and there are so many things that should have been done more appropriately after the disaster. In other words, the disaster revealed various failures of law.

Moreover, the disaster revealed that there are certain characteristics of Japanese law that had prevented the successful preparation for this kind of disaster, much more effective responses to the disaster, or much better reconstruction measures toward disaster areas. The problems they produced are not simply a result of the careless oversight or absence of careful preparation; they are much more foundational. In other words, the incidents manifested the much deeper failures of law in disaster-struck Japan.

They also revealed that one of the reasons for these failures of law is the inability of politics in Japan to introduce better legal preparation and government counter-disaster policy, and the incapacity to offer better responses to the disaster. In other words, certain characteristics of Japanese politics prevented the Japanese government from introducing better legal as well as non-legal disaster preparation measures, and also prevented the Japanese government from adopting better countermeasures against the Great East Japan Earthquake Disaster. In short, the incidents also manifested failures of politics.

This book was written to highlight the inadequacies of disaster law in Japan. Moreover, it will expose the failures of law and politics in Japan, confounding these inadequacies and arguing for the necessity to overcome them in order to prepare for, respond to, and reconstruct the disaster area after a massive natural disaster and serious nuclear disaster more effectively.

This is a study of law and politics and government policymaking. It is a study on how disaster law was prepared before the disaster, how this disaster law worked or failed against the disaster, and what kinds of measures are necessary to build much better disaster law. It is also a study on what had been preventing the government from introducing much better disaster laws and how the government could change these to prepare better countermeasures.

0.2.2 Why law and politics?

One may wonder why this book is focusing on law and politics. In order to prepare for a massive disaster, it is necessary to:

1. prevent the disaster (prevent the loss and damages and reduce the loss and damages);
2. prepare for countermeasures to be implemented (provide rescue, assistance, and emergency restoration); and
3. prepare for the reconstruction of the disaster area.[6]

Every step requires a legal scheme to accomplish the corresponding goals; the law cannot be ignored for the discussion of disaster preparation. Moreover, it is imperative to have adequate counter-disaster legal systems in place for providing adequate response to the disaster. In other words, disaster law needs to be carefully prepared and adequately implemented.[7]

6 Luke Nottage, Hitoshi Nasu, & Simon Butt, "Disaster Management: Socio-Legal and Asia-Pacific Perspectives," in Simon Butt, Hitoshi Nasu, & Luke Nottage (eds), *Asia-Pacific Disaster Management: Comparative and Socio-Legal Perspectives* (Springer 2014) 1, 9.

7 As a result, increasing attention came to be paid to "disaster and law" or "disaster law." Daniel A. Farber & Michael G. Faure, *Disaster Law* (Elgar 2010); Daniel A. Farber & James Ming Chen, *Disaster Law and Policy* (Aspen 2015); Kritian Cedervall Lauta, *Disaster Law* (Routledge 2016); Amita Singh, *Disaster Law: Emerging Thresholds* (Routledge 2017). See also BerkeleyLaw, Disaster Law (UC Berkeley School of Law) www.law.berkeley.edu/research/clee/research/past-research-initiatives/disaster-law/ accessed 25 December 2017.

This book will examine what went wrong with the Japanese disaster law during the Great East Japan Earthquake Disaster to find what was missing and what needs to be introduced in order to prepare for a massive natural disaster or serious nuclear accident.[8] These problems are what this book calls "failures of law." This examination will provide a picture of what needs to be adopted as a part of better disaster law.

But the book will also reveal that there are certain characteristics of Japanese law that had been preventing sufficient preparation and adequate response to a massive natural disaster or serious nuclear disaster. They are manifestations of much deeper problems of the legal system. The failures of law also include these deeper flaws.

The book will further find that there are political reasons for these failures of law. In other words, there is a political reason why some critical laws are missing or why the details of the legal system are inadequate. These are what this book calls "failures of politics." This book thus reveals that these failures of politics were preventing Japan from preparing for a massive natural disaster or serious nuclear disaster, and providing the effective response to that kind of disaster.

The failures of law and failures of politics are often intertwined, but they are not necessarily the same. The legislature might commit error without realization or without sufficiently knowing the underlying issues. Then, the error is merely a careless error or a result of lack of careful observation or solid prediction. The legislature could learn important lessons and remedy these deficiencies. But sometimes, if the failures are more deeply ingrained in the legal system, then it would require more radical change. Moreover, there might be a political reason for the government to pay a blind eye to the necessity of sufficient preparation or appropriate response. Then, that is a manifestation of the failure of politics. If that is the case, it would take much more radical changes to politics in order to correct the failures of law.

Some of these characteristics that this book will find as preventing effective preparation and response to massive disaster have already been pointed out by other Japan studies researchers. This book confirms that these problems are manifested in the preparation for natural disasters or nuclear disasters. The book will thus confirm that these problems are not simply things of the past but rather inherent problems of the Japanese legal and political systems. Moreover, this book will reveal that these problems led to calamity in the wake of the Great East Japan Earthquake Disaster. Therefore, there is an urgent need to reconsider these problems and revise them, especially in order to face the next massive disaster, which is sure to come within the near future.

0.3 Roadmap of the book

0.3.1 Path to the disaster

Following this Introduction, Chapter 1 examines the state of Japanese law before the disaster. Japan is famous for its susceptibility to natural disasters, including

8 For a similar attempt after Hurricane Katrina in the United States, see Daniel A. Farber & Jim Chen, *Disasters and the Law: Katrina and beyond* (Aspen 2006); Robin Malloy (ed.), *Law and Recovery from Disaster: Hurricane Katrina* (Routledge 2016).

very powerful earthquakes. Indeed, the Japanese government has made strident efforts to prepare for powerful earthquakes and tsunamis. This chapter outlines the legal system as it relates to natural disaster response, disaster-related insurance, earthquake preparation, and prediction systems. It also discusses many lessons learned by the Japanese government in the wake of the Hanshin Awaji Earthquake in 1995. This is followed by a detailed look at the state of disaster-related law and the legal system's capacity for responding to disasters. Chapter 1 aims to assess governmental preparedness for massive earthquakes and tsunamis.

0.3.2 Disaster

Chapter 2 deals with the Great East Japan Earthquake Disaster and its aftermath. The discussion focuses on rescue and recovery operations and examines governmental response to many of the unprecedented legal questions that arose from this calamity. Some of these questions pertained to burial of such huge numbers of disaster victims while others centered on disposal of unprecedented quantities of debris and other disaster waste. Other questions relate to procedures for providing exceptional legal treatment to assist disaster survivors. This chapter concludes by asserting that the legal system was not prepared for this disaster and that governmental response was woefully inadequate.

Chapter 3 outlines the progression of events leading to the nuclear meltdown in Fukushima along with the Japanese government's attempts to contain the disaster. This chapter examines the legal system as it relates to nuclear emergency and legal deficiencies hampering response to the accident in Fukushima. It explores how the Japanese government intervened at the Fukushima plant, ordered the evacuation of local residents, prohibited the marketing and consumption of contaminated agricultural products and fish, and responded to electricity shortages following the accident. Consideration is given to some of the legal questions posed by the Fukushima accident and the manner in which the government addressed them. Chapter 3 shows that the Japanese legal system failed to prepare for serious nuclear disaster and that governmental response to the Fukushima accident was grossly inappropriate.

0.3.3 After the disaster

Chapter 4 canvasses the reconstruction process following the disaster in the Tohoku Region, exploring legal responses and legal failures to appropriately facilitate reconstruction. It examines what kind of assistance was provided to victims of the disaster, how the basic plan for reconstruction was adopted, how the Reconstruction Agency, the government agency charged with facilitating reconstruction, was created and what kinds of measures were adopted to promote reconstruction. It will conclude that the reconstruction continues to lag at a pace far behind what is necessary, leaving many disaster victims frustrated by prolonged delays and inconveniences. This frustration is a manifestation of the inadequacy of the reconstruction process.

Chapter 5 explores the aftermath of the Fukushima accident and the reconstruction of Fukushima. It outlines the roadmap to final containment and examines a number of legal questions to be resolved, including how to dispose of nuclear waste and how to facilitate the environmental decontamination. This chapter also addresses damage awards and compensation issues as they relate to TEPCO as well as mechanisms for supporting TEPCO in the future. Finally, the prospects of and timeline for allowing residents to return to their homes, along with various measures related to reconstruction in Fukushima, is explored. Chapter 5 concludes by demonstrating how the above measures are ultimately unsatisfactory, fraught with difficulty, and have done little to assuage the deep frustrations of Fukushima residents.

0.3.4 Future

Chapter 6 explores the future of law and politics in Japan seven years after the Tohoku Earthquake. This chapter will examine what earthquake and tsunami preparations have been introduced since the Tohoku Earthquake, especially as they pertain to the future Kanto Earthquake, Tokai Earthquake, and possible triple mega earthquakes consisting of the Tokai Earthquake, Nankai Earthquake, and Tohnankai Earthquake, the so-called Nankai Trough Megathrust Earthquake. Included are fundamental revisions to disaster countermeasure legislations and various new measures to be adopted in the disaster countermeasure plans. Also included are new nuclear power plant regulations and a new organization to ensure the safety of the plant. Consideration will also be given to the overall energy policy for Japan, the future of nuclear power, and methods for ensuring its safety. This chapter thus shows the lessons the Japanese government learned from this experience and incorporated into the disaster law system. The chapter further explores to what extent the Japanese people have learned lessons from the failures of law and politics and critically examines whether there are significant changes to the fundamental problems of Japanese law and politics.

0.3.5 Conclusions and lessons to be learned

The book concludes with a summary of the main arguments presented herein along with lessons the Japanese people would do well to internalize.

The Tohoku Earthquake proves that the Japanese legal system for the preparation of massive natural disasters and serious nuclear disasters was shamefully inadequate. We now know what should have been adopted and prepared. The Tohoku Earthquake also manifested much deeper problems in Japanese law and politics that demands radical change if the country is to avert a similar disaster in the future. Addressing these fundamental problems is nothing short of an absolute necessity for Japan.

The lessons from this experience could prove very useful for other countries as well, since a massive disaster such as that wrought by the Tohoku Earthquake could strike anywhere in the world. Also, where there is a nuclear power plant, there is always a risk that a serious nuclear accident might happen. It might be tempting to believe that other countries are much better prepared for the disaster and do not have to learn lessons from Japan. Such a belief is often mistaken. No matter how completely you believe you are ready to face a massive natural disaster and serious nuclear disaster, you will always find some inadequacies. Moreover, it surely is tempting to believe that Japan is unique and other countries are so different that they don't have any problems. But who could honestly conclude that other countries are totally devoid of all the drawbacks pointed out in this book with respect to Japan, and confidently assert that their countries are perfectly prepared for a massive natural disaster or nuclear disaster? This book ultimately will ask everyone the same question: are you ready to face a massive natural disaster or serious nuclear disaster?

1 Japan and earthquakes

Before the Tohoku Earthquake

Japan is a country plagued by natural disasters. Accordingly, the Japanese government has prepared for natural disasters by enacting numerous statutes and introducing a variety of countermeasures. This chapter examines the history of earthquake preparedness in Japan and outlines various countermeasures as they relate to earthquakes, including the framework of Japan's legal system on disasters, the earthquake insurance system, the earthquake preparation system, and earthquake prediction systems. It will also examine significant lessons learned in the wake of the Hanshin Awaji Earthquake of 1995. The chapter will also discuss the details of the legal system as related to disaster preparedness for earthquakes prior to the Tohoku Earthquake, in order to show the steps the Japanese government had taken to prepare for massive earthquakes and tsunamis.

1.1 Japan and earthquakes

Japan has experienced countless powerful earthquakes. Before examination of the legal system on earthquake disaster preparation, this chapter briefly outlines the history of powerful earthquakes in Japan and the basic structures of government.

1.1.1 Powerful earthquakes in Japan

Japan is subject to all manner of natural disasters. In addition to powerful hurricanes battering the country every autumn, strong, recurring earthquakes have been known to strike periodically. The island nation is surrounded by four tectonic plates; the North American, the Pacific, the Philippine Sea, and the Eurasian plates.[1] Pressure from these four plates and the subduction occurring when they butt up against one another causes forceful tremors. Historic records compiled

1 Japan Meteorological Agency, Jishin hassei no shikumi [Mechanism of Earthquake] (JMA) www.data.jma.go.jp/svd/eqev/data/jishin/about_eq.html accessed 20 January 2018.

over the past 2,000 years reveal a steady trend of recurring and extremely powerful earthquakes throughout the Japanese archipelago.[2]

The Kanto Earthquake (*Kanto daishinsai*) of 1 September 1923 was especially destructive.[3] This earthquake struck the capital, Tokyo, shortly before noon at a magnitude of 7.9 on the Richter scale. It destroyed countless houses and buildings, including many government and office buildings, crushing untold numbers of people beneath rubble. Moreover, as many families had been cooking lunch at the time, widespread fires broke out causing fierce firestorms across the city. All told, some 1.9 million people were rendered homeless while more than 100,000 lost their lives or were classified as missing in one of the deadliest earthquakes in the nation's history.[4]

However, the Kanto Earthquake is only one of many devastating earthquakes to have ravaged Japan. In 1854, the Tokai (Eastern Sea) Earthquake (*Tokai jishin*) (formally known as the Ansei Tokai Earthquake) struck central Japan, at a magnitude of 8.4 on the Richter scale, killing some 2,000 to 3,000.[5] The epicenter was believed to be off the coast of Shizuoka Prefecture, just southeast of Tokyo. It is a well-known fact that strong earthquakes assail this area every 100 to 150 years. Merely one day later, an immensely powerful quake, known as the Ansei Nankai (Southern Sea) Earthquake hit yet another area in central Japan at an estimated Richter scale magnitude of 8.5, with more than 3,000 people losing their lives in the ensuing tsunami.[6]

Almost one hundred years later, on 7 December 1944, another destructive temblor bombarded central Japan. This earthquake came to be known as the Tohnankai (Southeastern Sea) Earthquake.[7] The epicenter was off the coast of

2 The number of earthquakes per year with moment magnitude greater than or equal to 7 varies year to year, but there have been approximately 3 magnitude-7 or greater earthquakes per year (compared to about 0.2 magnitude-8 or greater earthquake) in Japan. Japan Meteorological Agency, Jishin nitsuite [On Earthquake] (JMA) www.jma.go.jp/jma/kishou/know/faq/faq7.html accessed June 20, 2018. Japan is a country where most earthquakes can be located. USGS, Which Country Has the Most Earthquakes? (USGS) www.usgs.gov/faqs/which-country-has-most-earthquakes?qt-news_science_products=7#qt-news_science_products accessed 20 January 2018.

3 USGS, M 8.1—near the south coast of Honshu, Japan (USGS) https://earthquake.usgs.gov/earthquakes/eventpage/iscgem911526#executive accessed 25 December 2017.

4 Richard J. Samuels, *3.11: Disaster and Change in Japan* (Cornell 2013) 47, 50–57. For more on the impact of this earthquake on the culture and society of Japan, *see* Joshua Hammer, "The Great Kanto Earthquake of 1923" (*Smithsonian Magazine*, May 2011) www.smithsonianmag.com/history/the-great-japan-earthquake-of-1923-1764539/ accessed 25 December 25, 2017; Charles J. Schencking, "The Great Kanto Earthquake and the Culture of Catastrophe and Reconstruction in 1920s Japan," (2008) 34:2 *Journal of Japanese Studies* 295.

5 Cabinet Office, Houkokusho (1854 Ansei Tokai jishin/Ansei Nankai jishin) [Report (1854 Ansei Tokai Earthquake/Ansei Nankai Earthquake)] (Cabinet Office) www.bousai.go.jp/kyoiku/kyokun/kyoukunnokeishou/rep/1854_ansei_toukai_nankai_jishin/index.html accessed 25 December 2017.

6 Ibid.

7 USGS, M 8.1—near the south coast of western Honshu, Japan (USGS) https://earthquake.usgs.gov/earthquakes/eventpage/iscgem899647#executive accessed 25 December 2017.

Mie Prefecture and the magnitude was estimated at 7.9 on the Richter scale. More than 1,000 people were killed or classified as missing. On 21 December 1946, yet another massive earthquake (the Shouwa Nankai Earthquake) struck off the coast of Wakayama Prefecture, registering at 8.3 on the Richter scale.[8] Subsequently, a massive tsunami inundated several coastal cities in Kochi, Wakayama, and Tokushima Prefectures leaving more than 1,400 people dead or missing. These areas are also famously prone to violent earthquakes every 100 to 150 years.

Another massive earthquake is expected to hit Tokyo and the Kanto Region in the near future (another Kanto Earthquake). Still, there is broad consensus that the likelihood of a powerful earthquake assailing the Tokai area in central Japan is even more likely. Some sources put the likelihood of another Tokai Earthquake striking again within 30 years at more than 87%.[9] Others predict that another Tokai Earthquake will hit together with another Nankai earthquake and Tohnankai earthquake, a triple mega earthquake also known as the Nankai Trough Megathrust Earthquake, and will inflict even more extensive damage.[10]

1.1.2 Preparing for earthquakes

Owing to Japan's susceptibility to powerful earthquakes, the Japanese government has an imperative responsibility to prepare for these disasters. Thus, in 1961, the Diet (Japan's national legislature), enacted the Basic Act on Disaster Countermeasures (*saigai taisaku kihonhō*).[11] This Act was concerned with enabling a governmental response to natural disasters, including earthquakes. The Diet also enacted the Special Measures Act on Large-Scale Earthquake Countermeasures (*daikibo jishin taisaku tokusohō*) in 1978.[12] This statute was premised upon the assumption that with close monitoring of the movement of faults and land, it is possible to predict powerful earthquakes, enabling a "warning" in advance of an earthquake, and prompting the central government as well as local governments to prepare countermeasures.

8 USGS, M 8.3—near the south coast of western Honshu, Japan (USGS) https://earthquake.usgs.gov/earthquakes/eventpage/iscgem898698#executive accessed 25 December 2017.

9 Ministry of Education, Culture, Sports, Science, and Technology, Zenkoku jishindō yosoku chizu 2010 [2010 National Map of Predicted Earthquakes] (MEXT) www.jishin.go.jp/main/pamphlet/leaflet/leaflet.pdf accessed 25 December 2017.

10 Central Disaster Prevention Council, Nankai trough kyodai jishin taisaku nitsuite [On Countermeasures against the Nankai Trough Megathrust Earthquake] (Cabinet Office May 2013) www.bousai.go.jp/jishin/nankai/taisaku_wg/pdf/20130528_honbun.pdf accessed 25 December 2017.

11 Saigai taisaku kihonhō [Basic Act on Disaster Countermeasures], Law no 223 of 1961. See n. 138. What triggered the enactment of this statute was the serious damage caused by the Isewan Typhoon in 1959, leaving more than 5,000 persons dead because of the high tide and collapse of river dikes. Taizo Hosoda, "Isewan taifu to saigai taisaku kihonhō no seitei [Isewan Typhoon and the Enactment of the Basic Act on Disaster Countermeasures]" (2009) 98 *Shobobosai no Kagaku*.

12 Daikibojishin taisaku tokubetsusochihō [Special Measures Act on Large-Scale Earthquake Countermeasures], Law no 73 of 1978. See n 216.

The primary responsibility to prepare and respond to natural disaster lies with the municipal government whereas the prefecture has a responsibility to assist the municipal government and the central government in primary disaster prevention planning and overall coordination of various countermeasures.[13] With respect to emergency rescue operations resulting from natural disaster, it is primarily considered the job of rescue teams inside the fire department of the municipal government[14] and the rescue team inside the mobile police force of the prefectural police force.[15] These groups can provide assistance to those injured or trapped inside collapsed houses. It is the job of the fire department of the municipal government to extinguish any fires caused.[16] If the disaster is more serious, Japan's Self-Defense Forces (*jieitai*) (SDF) officers could be dispatched as an emergency rescue mission.[17] With respect to normal natural disasters, including minor earthquakes, this is the system that is supposed to be employed.

The Basic Act on Disaster Countermeasures introduced a system designed for serious natural disasters such as more serious earthquakes.[18] Therefore, the Japanese government has at least prepared for earthquakes.

1.1.3 Intensifying construction standards

The Japanese government is also attempting to reduce the damage resulting from the collapse of houses due to powerful earthquakes. After the 1923 Kanto Earthquake, the government first introduced safety standards for all houses against powerful earthquakes.[19] In 1950, the Construction Standard Act was enacted to statutorily mandate the safety standard against earthquakes.[20] The government gradually intensified safety standards to withstand powerful tremors. Especially, in 1980, the government also amended the Construction Standards Act Enforcement Order[21] in order to beef-up construction standards with the aim of enabling homes and buildings to withstand powerful earthquakes and the new construction standard was adopted in 1981.[22] It was designed to make

13 Basic Act on Disaster Countermeasures (n 11), art 3–art 5.
14 Shoubouhō [Fire Fighters Act], Law no 186 of 1948.
15 Keisatsuhō [Police Act], Law no 162 of 1954; Keisatukan shokumu shikkohō [Police Officer Job Execution Act] Law no 136 of 1948.
16 Fire Fighters Act (n 14) art 1.
17 Jieitaihō [Self Defense Forces Act], Law no 165 of 1954, art 83(2).
18 See nn 153–215.
19 Toshiyuki Tanaka, Taishinkijun hensen no rekishi [History of Seismic Safety Standard] (Okayama University of Science) www.archi.ous.ac.jp/column/fpdf/17_tanaka.pdf accessed 25 December 2017.
20 Kenchiku kijunhō [Construction Standards Act], Law no 201 of 1950.
21 Kenchiku kijunhō sekorei no ichibuwo kaiseisuru seirei [Cabinet Order to Amend Parts of the Construction Standard Act Enforcement Order], Cabinet Order no 196 of 1980.
22 Ministry of Land, Infrastructure and Transport, Jutaku, tatemonotō no taishinka nitsuite [On Safety Standard against Earthquake of the Houses and Constructions] (MLIT) www.mlit.go.jp/jutakukentiku/house/jutakukentiku_house_fr_000043.html.

sure that all the newly constructed houses could withstand regular earthquakes and provide minimal protection from death for those living inside in the case of the most powerful earthquakes, which are less frequent but possible.[23] The basis of the legal system's response to earthquakes was thus created.

1.1.4 Earthquake insurance

The Japanese government also introduced the earthquake insurance (*jishin hoken*) system in 1966 to enable homeowners to receive insurance coverage in the event that their houses were destroyed.[24] Prior to 1966, there was no earthquake insurance for homes. Previously, homeowners could buy fire insurance, which covered damage only in the event that the house was destroyed by fire. However, fire insurance contracts had limitation clauses, excluding liability for damage caused by fire triggered by earthquakes or even volcanic eruptions. As a result, there was no insurance when homes were destroyed by earthquakes or tsunamis and insurance companies were not liable for fire damage if the fire had been triggered by an earthquake. This prompted the central government to implement insurance reform. Now, when homeowners buy earthquake insurance as coverage in addition to fire insurance, insurance companies pay out against damage to homes caused by earthquake, tsunami, or volcanic eruption.[25] Owing to the risk of insurance payouts becoming too large for private insurance companies to absorb, the central government assumes responsibility for covering insurance payouts as a form of reinsurance.[26]

Earthquake insurance is, however, optional coverage and can only be purchased together with fire insurance.[27] Insurance premiums are set based on the

23 Ministry of Land, Infrastructure, and Transport, Manshon no taishinseitō nitsuite no Q&A [Q&A on the Seismic Safety Standard of Condominiums] (MLIT) www.mlit.go.jp/kisha/kisha05/07/071208_2_.html accessed 25 December 2017.

24 Songaihoken ryouritsu sanshutsu kikō [General Insurance Rating Organization of Japan], Earthquake Insurance in Japan (GIROJ July 2014) www.giroj.or.jp/english/pdf/Earthquake.pdf accessed 25 December 2017.

25 Jishinhoken nikansuru hōristu [Act concerning Earthquake Insurance], Law no 73 of 1966 (Earthquake Insurance Act). Basically, this earthquake insurance could be contracted with domestic or foreign liability insurance companies licensed by the prime minister. Ibid art 2(1). For general description of the earthquake insurance, *see* Nihon songaihoken kyoukai [General Insurance Association of Japan], Jishinhoken no gaiyo [Summary of Earthquake Insurance] (SONPO) www.sonpo.or.jp/insurance/commentary/jishin/pdf/index/05gaiyo.pdf accessed 25 December 2017. See Nihon jishin saihoken kabushiki gaisha [Japan Earthquake Reinsurance Co.] Earthquake Insurance in Japan (JER) www.nihonjishin.co.jp/english/2017/en_04.pdf accessed 25 December 2017; Ministry of Finance, Jishinhoken seido no gaiyo [Summary of the Earthquake Insurance System] (MOF) www.mof.go.jp/financial_system/earthquake_insurance/jisin.htm accessed 25 December 2017.

26 Earthquake Insurance Act (n 25) art 3. The Japan Earthquake Reinsurance Co. Ltd, takes over all liability based on the reinsurance from all insurance companies and has reinsurance contract with the government to cover payment over the limit. Nihon jishin saihoken kabusiki gaisha [Japan Earthquake Reinsurance Co.] www.nihonjishin.co.jp/top.html accessed 25 December 2017.

27 Earthquake Insurance Act (n 25) art 2(2).

risk of an earthquake, requiring residents in higher risk areas to pay higher premiums.[28] As a result, insurance premiums are often too costly for homeowners. Furthermore, there are limitations on insurance payouts with only 30–50% of a home's market value covered by the earthquake insurance even when it is totally destroyed, with an upper limit payout maximum of 50 million JPY (450,000 USD at the exchange rate of 1USD to 110 JPY).[29] Under this scheme, insurance payouts are not sufficient for covering the costs of building a new home. Moreover, cumulative insurance payouts per earthquake are limited by government order with payments reduced if cumulative damages exceed that limit.[30] Due to all of these limitations, the number of homeowners purchasing earthquake insurance remains quite low with many declining it altogether.[31]

1.1.5 Earthquake preparedness measures

Based on the Basic Act on Disaster Countermeasures, the Central Disaster Prevention Council (*chuo bosai kaigi*) adopted the Basic Disaster Prevention Plan in 1963[32] and local governments adopted their local disaster prevention plans based on this Plan. The government updated this Plan in accordance with new lessons or new insights to strengthen the disaster prevention measures.

The Japanese government introduced various earthquake and tsunami preparedness measures. For example, the government intensified the seismic resistance of public buildings and public infrastructure, especially public schools because they would be used as shelters for local residents.[33] They also established

28 Standard premium rate is calculated by the General Insurance Rating Organization of Japan (*Songai hoken ryouritsu sanshutsu kikō*), collecting all of the data supplied by the insurance companies, and approved by the director of the Financial Services Agency and insurance companies will adopt the rate. Songai hoken ryouritsu sanshutsu kikō [General Insurance Rating Organization of Japan], Jishinhoken kijunryouritsu [Standard Earthquake Insurance Premium Rate] (GIROJ) www.giroj.or.jp/service/ryoritsu/quake/quake.html accessed 25 December 2017. All of the insurance companies thus use the same rate. The premium rate is higher in prefectures that are likely to be hit by the Tokai Earthquake than others. There is a discount for buildings built after 1981 or for buildings with capability to withstand powerful earthquakes. Ibid.

29 Earthquake Insurance Act (n 25) art 2(2); Jishinhoken nikansuru hōristu sekourei [Earthquake Insurance Act Enforcement Order], Cabinet Order no 164 of 1966, art 2.

30 Earthquake Insurance Act (n 25) art 4. Currently 11.3 trillion JPY [103 billion USD] is the limit. Ministry of Finance (n 25).

31 As at the end of 2010, only 23.7% of all households took out earthquake insurance. Nihon songaihoken kyoukai [General Insurance Association of Japan], Jishinhoken: Todouhukenbetsu setaikanyuritsu no suii [Change in the Participation Ratio of the Earthquake Insurance] (SONPO) www.sonpo.or.jp/news/statistics/syumoku/pdf/index/kanyu_jishin.pdf accessed 25 December 2017. Even after the Tohoku Earthquake, only 30.5% of all residents are covered by the earthquake insurance as of end of 2016. Ibid.

32 Central Disaster Prevention Council, Bousai kihon keikaku [Basic Disaster Prevention Plan] (Cabinet Office) www.bousai.go.jp/taisaku/keikaku/kihon.html accessed 17 January 2018. The Plan was revised after the Hanshin Awaji Earthquake and also after the Great East Japan Earthquake Disaster. See Chapter 6 n 72.

33 Cabinet Office, Disaster Management in Japan (Cabinet Office) www.bousai.go.jp/1info/pdf/saigaipanf_e.pdf accessed 17 January 2018 19.

numerous robust barriers to fend off tsunamis in locations where a tsunami disaster is likely to occur.[34]

Moreover, the Japanese government introduced an earthquake measuring and reporting system and a tsunami warning system. When an earthquake strikes, many seismic measurement devices established all over Japan will detect the movement and the Japan Meteorological Agency (JMA) quickly issues earthquake information (*jishin jōhō*).[35] Then, major broadcasters immediately report its occurrence, along with its magnitude, and epicenter, as provided by the JMA. When an earthquake occurs at sea and there is a possibility that a tsunami will affect coastline cities, the JMA issues a tsunami warning (*tsunami keihō*).[36] The Nihon Housou Kyoukai (NHK), Japan's national public broadcaster, and other broadcasters broadcast tsunami warnings that are transmitted to the public with special emphasis on those residing in coastline cities and for municipal governments in these areas, prompting immediate evacuation. Municipal governments in coastal municipalities have also established public warning systems to call for evacuation by loudspeaker.[37] Municipal governments have also established shelters capable of withstanding tsunamis. Furthermore, emergency earthquake alert systems detect the early movement of the earthquake and transmit a warning as to the main tremor, emergency earthquake early report/emergency earthquake warning (*kinkyu jishin sokuhō/kinkyu jishin keihō*), if the tremor is expected to be strong through television and radio (now through some smartphones as well).[38]

The Japanese government has attempted to educate the public on the necessity for preparation for a powerful earthquake. September 1 has been designated as Disaster Prevention Day, a day for disseminating disaster prevention knowledge and raising public awareness, in commemoration of the Great Kanto Earthquake.[39] The government and schools provide earthquake drills on

34 Ibid 16.

35 Ibid 14; Japan Meteorological Agency, Jishin jōhō [Earthquake Information] (JMA) www.data.jma.go.jp/svd/eqev/data/joho/seisinfo.html accessed 17 January 2018.

36 Japan Meteorological Agency, Tsunami keihō/chuihō, tsunami jōhō, tsunami yosoku nitsuite [Tsunami Warning/Alert, Tsunami Information and Tsunami Estimate System] (JMA) www.data.jma.go.jp/svd/eqev/data/joho/seisinfo.html accessed 17 January 2018. If the expected tsunami is not very strong, the JMA issues tsunami advisory (*tsunami chuihō*).

37 According to the Kisho gyoumuhō [Weather Business Act], Law no 165 of 1952, art 13(1), the JMA is mandated to issue warnings of expected tsunami. The JMA is obliged to provide notification of that warning to the National Police Agency (NPA), the Ministry of Land, Infrastructure, Transport and Tourism, the Maritime Police Agency, the prefectures, the NHK, and major telecommunications companies. Ibid art 15(1). The NPA, the prefectural government, and telecommunication companies are obliged to attempt to transmit that warning to relevant municipal governments. The municipal governments are mandated to make a public announcement and to inform the administrative agencies inside the municipalities. The NHK is obliged to broadcast that warning to the public. Ibid art 15(3)–(6). The tsunami warning is used to indicate the possible height of expected tsunami and the expected time of arrival onshore. The warning is either a "tsunami warning" or an "extremely high tsunami warning."

38 Japan Meteorological Agency, Kinkyu jishin sokuhō nitsuite [Emergency Earthquake Warning] (JMA) www.jma.go.jp/jma/kishou/know/faq/faq25.html accessed 17 January 2018.

39 Cabinet Office, Bousai no hi oyobi bousai shukan nitsuite [Disaster Prevention Day and Disaster Prevention Week] (Cabinet Office) www.bousai.go.jp/kyoiku/week/bousaiweek.html accessed 17 January 2018.

this Disaster Prevention Day. Municipal governments are also required to run evacuation drills every year. The public is urged to plan ahead for evacuation routes and meeting locations in times of emergency. The government has also encouraged the public to prepare emergency food and drink together with first aid kits to survive for at least the first three days after a massive earthquake.

The Japanese government has further introduced an earthquake prediction program. This program measures tectonic plate movements, primarily in anticipation of a future Tokai Earthquake. This program is enforced by a committee within the JMA (specifically, the Earthquake Assessment Committee for Earthquake Disaster (*jishin bousai taisaku kyouka chiiki hanteikai*)), which aims to allow a warning to be issued to residents when the JMA determines that a powerful earthquake is imminent.[40] The Coordinating Committee for Earthquake Prediction (*jishin yochi renrakukai*) was also established within the Geospatial Information Authority of Japan, Ministry of Land, Infrastructure, Transport and Tourism,[41] and is composed of government officials and university researchers collaborating to predict earthquakes. This program is founded on the belief that by collecting large amounts of information, it may be possible to predict powerful earthquakes and, as a result, to facilitate more effective preparation.

1.1.6 Earthquakes and tsunamis in the Sanriku region

The Tohoku Region,[42] literally the northeast region, is located north of the Kanto Region, which includes Tokyo. It consists of six prefectures, including the Miyagi, Iwate, and Fukushima Prefectures on the Pacific side. The latitude of Sendai city, the most populous city in the Tohoku Region is roughly equal to Washington D.C. The west side of the Tohoku Region, facing the Sea of Japan, tends to be mostly cold during the winter and sometimes accumulates heavy snow. The Pacific side is not as cold but is still chilly during the winter (85% of the land of

40 Japan Meteorological Agency, Jishin bousai taisaku kyokachiiki hanteikai [Earthquake Assessment Committee for Earthquake Disaster] (JMA) www.data.jma.go.jp/svd/eqev/data/tokai/hanteikai.html accessed 25 December 2017. It consists of six experts on earthquakes and holds regular sessions every month on the possibility of a massive Tokai Earthquake. If there is an unusual movement or sign of a possible massive earthquake, a meeting is urgently called and the meeting can issue prediction information regarding a possible Tokai Earthquake, which would lead the prime minister to issue an "emergency warning" (*keikai sengen*). n 222.

41 Coordinating Committee for Earthquake Prediction (GSI) http://cais.gsi.go.jp/YOCHIREN/index.e.html accessed 25 December 2017. This organization is designed to exchange information on earthquake prediction, especially the observation data, and facilitate academic discussion on it and issue a report twice a year.

42 For a general description of the Tohoku Region, see Ministry of Land, Infrastructure, and Transport, Tohoku chihō no genjō to kadai [Current Situation and Agenda of the Tohoku Region] (MLIT) www.thr.mlit.go.jp/road/sesaku/chuki/04_honpen_genjou_to_kadai.pdf accessed 25 December 2017; Tohoku chihō kasseika kenkyu center [Research Center for the Revitalization of Tohoku], Tohoku no shakai keizai no gaiyō [Summary of the Society and Industry of Tohoku] (Kasseiken) www.kasseiken.jp/pdf/library/guide/26fy-chosa-02-01.pdf accessed 25 December 2017.

the Tohoku Region is classified as a heavy snow area). The total population of the Tohoku Region is roughly 10 million and many people leave the Tohoku Region for Tokyo, seeking university education and the chance of a better job. As a result, there are many residents in Tokyo who were originally born in the Tohoku Region. Meanwhile, the Tohoku Region has been suffering from population loss and a rapidly aging demographic.

The land covered by the Tohoku Region occupies roughly 20% of the whole of Japan but 68 percent of that land is forest. The major industry in the Tohoku Region is agriculture, producing, for instance, 35% of the rice for the whole of Japan. This success of agricultural production owes a great deal to the proximity to Tokyo, the largest metropolitan city, with a total population of over 13 million. But gradually, high tech industries and automobile industries came to establish their factories on the Pacific side of the Tohoku Region. It is well known that the residents in the Tohoku Region have a very strong sense of community-belonging and maintain close personal relationships.

The Tohoku Region sits on the North American tectonic plate and the Pacific plate is pushing it from the east side, slowly moving it beneath the North American plate into the Japan Trench. As a result, there have been a series of powerful earthquakes off the Pacific coast of Tohoku, especially in the region generally referred to as the "Sanriku" region, that have inflicted serious damage. The Tohoku coast is dotted with small fishing cities and port towns in which most residents are clustered in-between the coastline and steep mountains, making residents especially vulnerable to tsunamis.

An earlier historic record indicated that there was a massively powerful earthquake in this region in 869AD, generally called Jogan Earthquake.[43] It is said that the earthquake was so powerful, estimated to be roughly 8.4 on the Richter scale, that it caused over one thousand deaths and produced a very powerful tsunami, sweeping through the Sendai Plain, and reaching 3 km inland. But the description is so ambiguous that it is hard to estimate the magnitude of the earthquake and precisely evaluate the loss and damage. Virtually no one mentioned this Jogan Earthquake prior to the Tohoku Earthquake.

In 1896, the powerful Meiji Sanriku-oki Earthquake struck off the coast of Kamaishi, at an estimated magnitude of 8.5 on the Richter scale.[44] Shortly after, a powerful tsunami hit the coastline villages reaching as far as 38.2 meters up the coastal mountains. This was the highest reaching tsunami recorded in Japan prior to 2011. Roughly 22,000 people were killed or missing as a result of this

43 Yuichi Namegaya & Kenji Satake, "Reexamination of the 869AD Jogan Earthquake Size from Tsunami Deposit Distribution, Simulated Flow Depth, and Velocity" (2014) 41:7 *AN AGU Journal* 2297; Daisuke Sugawara, Kazuhisa Goto, Fumihiko Imamura, Hideaki Matsumoto, & Koji Minoura, "Assessing the Magnitude of the 869AD Jogan Tsunami Using Sedimentary Deposits: Prediction and Consequence of the 2011 Tohoku-oki Tsunami," (2012) 282 *Sedimentary Geology* 14.

44 USGS, M8.5—Sanriku, Japan, 1896 (USGS) https://earthquake.usgs.gov/learn/today/index.php?month=6&day=15 accessed 25 December 2017.

powerful tsunami. Another very powerful earthquake, the Showa Sanriku-oki Earthquake, hit just off the coast of Kamaishi in 1933 at a magnitude of 8.4.[45] Again a powerful tsunami followed, inundating the coastline cities. More than 3,000 people were killed or classified as missing as a result of this earthquake and tsunami. When a very powerful earthquake hit Chile in 1960,[46] the resulting tsunami crossed the Pacific Ocean to reach the Sanriku region, almost one full day after the earthquake in Chile, killing 142 people while causing extensive damage. Also, a moderately powerful earthquake struck off the Coast of Miyagi in 1978 at a magnitude of 7.4, bringing a relatively minor tsunami and resulting in 28 deaths and 1,325 persons injured (off the Miyagi Prefecture Earthquake).[47]

The central government, local governments, municipal governments, and local residents in the Sanriku region were definitely aware of tsunami risks. After the Basic Act on Disaster Countermeasures was enacted, each of the prefectures in the Tohoku Region established damage estimates for powerful earthquakes and tsunamis as well as local disaster prevention plans.[48] Especially, after the off Miyagi Prefecture Earthquake in 1978, Miyagi prefecture and Fukushima prefecture were included in one of the eight close attention areas for powerful earthquakes.[49] Basically, the local government facilitated the seismic upgrade of buildings and infrastructure. The local government also adopted the tsunami damage estimate and distributed a tsunami hazard map to local residents.[50] At that time, it was anticipated that the most powerful earthquake to hit this region would be 8.0 in magnitude and could lead at most to a 10m tsunami. The Japanese government built strong tsunami barriers (sea walls) to safeguard these ports and cities.[51] A tsunami warning system was introduced. When a tsunami warning was issued, residents were told to evacuate as soon as possible. Ships were advised to vacate the coast and head for the open ocean to avoid the tsunami. But aside from these general countermeasures, no special countermeasures were introduced in the Tohoku Region despite the repeated powerful

45 USGS, 8.4—off the east coast of Honshu, Japan (USGS) https://earthquake.usgs.gov/earthquakes/eventpage/official19330302173100_30#executive accessed 25 December 2017.

46 USGS, M 9.5—Bio-Bio, Chile (USGS) https://earthquake.usgs.gov/earthquakes/eventpage/official19600522191120_30#executive accessed 25 December 2017.

47 Facts and Details, Major Earthquakes in Japan in the 2000s (Facts and Details) http://factsanddetails.com/japan/cat26/sub160/item862.html accessed 25 December 2017.

48 The earthquake countermeasures of the Miyagi Prefecture before the Tohoku Earthquake are summarized in Miyagi Prefecture, Higashinihon daishinsai izen no jizentaisaku [Countermeasures prior to the Great East Japan Earthquake Disaster], (Miyagi Prefecture) www.pref.miyagi.jp/uploaded/attachment/297640.pdf accessed 25 December 2017.

49 Ibid 66.

50 Ibid 66–67.

51 Tarou Town of Miyako City, Iwate Prefecture built a 10-meter high tsunami barrier of 2,433 meters in length, proudly the highest and mightiest tsunami barrier in Japan, comparable to the "Great Wall of China." Federica Ranghieri & Mikio Ishiwatari (eds.), *Learning from Megadisasters: Lessons from the Great East Japan Earthquake* (World Bank 2014) 26.

earthquakes off the Pacific Coast.[52] It was believed that residents in this area were well prepared to face possible tsunamis.

However, governmental focus was placed predominately on prediction of a Tokai Earthquake and thus, it may be said that the vulnerability of the Sanriku region has gone virtually ignored despite repeated and extensive tsunami damage. No serious attempt to collect information on potentially powerful earthquakes in this region was made and there were no attempts to predict earthquakes in this area. Most people did not consider that an earthquake as massive as the Tohoku Earthquake would strike in this region or that such a massive tsunami would breach these shores to cause such extensive casualties and damage.

1.2 Hanshin Awaji Earthquake

Despite a variety of preparatory measures being in place, in some cases particularly strong earthquakes have revealed problems in existing prevention and relief systems. One of the deadliest earthquakes in recent history was the Hanshin Awaji Earthquake of 1995.[53] This earthquake was especially illustrative of this point. What kinds of lessons did the government learn from its experience of the Hanshin Awaji Earthquake?

1.2.1 Hanshin Awaji Earthquake

The Hanshin Awaji Earthquake, which hit the Western city of Kobe in 1995, inflicted massive damage on the city. The epicenter of the Hanshin Awaji Earthquake was the northern part of Awaji Island, very close to Kobe, directly below the land's surface.[54] Striking at a magnitude of 6.9 on the Richter scale, at 5:36am in the early morning of 17 January 1995, this earthquake destroyed vast

52 After the Hanshin Awaji Earthquake, discussed below, the central government intensified the earthquake countermeasures and the local government in the Tohoku Region also upgraded the earthquake and tsunami countermeasures. In 2004, Nihon kaiko/chishima kaiko shuuhen kaikougata jishin nikakawaru jishin bousai taisaku no suishin nikansuru tokubetsu sochihō [Special Measures Act on the Promotion of Earthquake Disaster Prevention Measures against the Deep Sea Earthquake in the Vicinity of the Japan Trench and the Chishima Trench], Law no 27 of 2004, was enacted. It authorized the government to designate the "special countermeasures promotion areas," establish a "special disaster prevention measures promotion plan," install earthquake measuring devices, and provide for special assistance to the buildings upgrade. The Pacific Coast parts of Tohoku were designated as a promotion area and the government promoted the seismic upgrade and intensified the warning system and preparation for the evacuation. Miyagi Prefecture (n 48) 68–69. In 2009, the Miyagi Prefecture enacted the Earthquake Disaster Countermeasures Promotion Ordinance and attempted to mobilize all residents for the preparation of an earthquake and tsunami. Ibid 71.

53 USGS, M 6.9—Kobe, Japan, 1995 (USGS) https://earthquake.usgs.gov/learn/today/index.php?month=1&day=16 accessed 25 December 2017.

54 Hyogo Prefecture, Hanshin Awaji daishinsai no hukyuu, hukkou no joukyo nitsuite [On Reconstruction from Hanshin Awaji Earthquake] (Hyogo Prefecture January 2017) https://web.pref.hyogo.lg.jp/kk41/documents/fukkyuufukkou.pdf accessed 25 December 2017.

numbers of homes, buildings, department stores, hospitals, and even overhead highways, killing more than 6,400 people.[55] The number of casualties was so high because the earthquake occurred directly below one of Japan's most densely populated urban centers, Kobe.

Immediately after the earthquake, municipal governments as well as Hyogo Prefecture began the emergency response. But it was only after 10am that the central government decided to establish the Extraordinary Disaster Response Headquarters, headed by the Director General of National Land Agency, based on a cabinet decision in accordance with the Basic Act on Disaster Countermeasures as described below.[56] At 11:30am, the Headquarters held the first meeting and decided to take inventory of the loss and damage, rescue survivors, provide emergency help, extinguish fires, and provide emergency repairs to infrastructure and lifelines.[57] The government response was more or less in line with the statutory provisions of the Basic Act on Disaster Countermeasures.

1.2.2 Lessons from the Hanshin Awaji Earthquake

The Hanshin Awaji Earthquake was especially noteworthy because it offered several very important lessons from a legal standpoint. First, it was the first major earthquake triggered by the movement of active faults, unlike most of Japan's earthquakes, which are triggered by the movement of oceanic plates. The earthquake drew attention to the fact that many of Japan's buildings and cities were constructed right along active faults; there was simply nothing in place to prohibit development right above fault lines.[58]

Second, many of the buildings constructed after the 1981 building code amendments withstood the earthquake. This earthquake proved that the standard was sufficient to withstand powerful earthquakes.[59] However, many of the wooden homes built before the 1981 amendment simply collapsed, crushing and killing scores of residents.[60] This earthquake thus revealed that many buildings

55 Samuels (n 4) 57–63; Cabinet Office, Hanshin Awaji daishinsai, kyoukun jouhou shiryoshuu [Hanshin Awaji Earthquake Lesson Information], Jinteki higai [Human Casualties] (Cabinet Office) www.bousai.go.jp/kyoiku/kyokun/hanshin_awaji/data/detail/1-1-2.html accessed 25 December 2017.

56 Cabinet Office, Hanshin Awaji daishinsai no soukatsu/kenshō ni kakawaru chousa [Check on the Countermeasures toward the Hanshin Awaji Earthquake Disaster] (Cabinet Office) www.bousai.go.jp/kyoiku/kyokun/hanshin_awaji/chosa/pdf/002.pdf accessed 25 December 2017. On 19 January 1995, the government decided to establish the Emergency Disaster Response Headquarters, headed by the prime minister, based on the cabinet decision and not based on the Basic Act on Disaster Countermeasures. Ibid.

57 Ibid.

58 Yoshiaki Hisada, "Active Fault and Mitigation of Building Damages" (2008) 28 *Katsudansō Kenkyu* 77.

59 Cabinet Office, Juutakutō no taishinka no suishin nitsuite [On Promotion of Seismic Upgrade] (Cabinet Office) www.bousai.go.jp/kohou/oshirase/h15/pdf/sankou1-1.pdf accessed 25 December 2017.

60 Ibid. *See also* Cabinet Office, Hanshin Awaji daishinsai, kyoukun jouhou shiryoshuu [Hanshin Awaji Earthquake Lesson Information], Tatemono no higai [Building Damages] (Cabinet Office) www.bousai.go.jp/kyoiku/kyokun/hanshin_awaji/data/detail/1-1-3.html (Building Damages).

needed seismic upgrade in order to withstand strong earthquakes. Unfortunately, the safer standards only applied to newly constructed buildings.

Third, even though the earthquake hit Kobe shortly before 6:00am, it took several hours before the prime minister and the cabinet, sitting in Tokyo, became aware of the extent of the damage.[61] Sitting Prime Minister Tomiichi Murayama became aware of the earthquake through television news but it took several more hours before relevant information was transmitted to him through official channels with the result that the government simply did not respond to the earthquake at all until then.[62] There was no systematic reporting system to collect and report information on the earthquake to the prime minister and the cabinet swiftly. As a result, it took about four hours to establish countermeasure headquarters and start the response.

Fourth, the governor of Hyogo Prefecture (where Kobe is located) was not immediately informed of the seriousness of the damage and thus it took four hours before he requested Japan's SDF's deployment in rescue operations.[63] At the time of this earthquake, only the governor had the authority to request that SDF move in. As a result, SDF had no option but to stand by idly until the official request was delivered.[64] Needless to say, many people died before SDF were deployed.

Fifth, immediately after the earthquake, police did not cordon off traffic coming into the city.[65] This caused tremendous traffic congestion, preventing ambulances and firefighters from moving in smoothly. Many houses and buildings had collapsed. Fire quickly spread and burned many affected areas.[66] There were insufficient numbers of fire engines and firefighters and effective backup assistance from neighboring fire departments were prevented by traffic congestion and difficulty of communication.[67] There was a lack of sufficient vehicles and machinery for removing debris and collapsed buildings to save the lives of survivors. Many of the people trapped under collapsed buildings were not rescued. This earthquake thus revealed the necessity of regulating traffic in affected areas and also the necessity for cooperation between neighboring local governments and local municipalities in order to cope with large-scale disasters.

61 "Hanshin Awaji daijishin: Shinsai 20 shunen [Hanshin Awaji Earthquake: 20 Years Later]" (*Kobe Shimbun* 15 January 2015) www.kobe-np.co.jp/rentoku/sinsai/20/rensai/201501/0007660539.shtml (interview with then prime minister Murayama).

62 Ibid. *See also* Samuels (n 4) 58.

63 Cabinet Office, Hanshin Awaji daishinsai: Soukatsu, kenshō chousa sheet [Hanshin Awaji Earthquake: Recap] (Cabinet Office) www.bousai.go.jp/kensho-hanshinawaji/chosa/sheet/010.pdf accessed 25 December 2017.

64 Samuels (n 4) 59.

65 Akinori Ebara, "Disasters and Traffic Regulation" (1995) 21 *Kokusai Koutsu Anzengaku Kaishi* 22.

66 Cabinet Office, Hanshin Awaji daishinsai, kyoukun jouhou shiryoshuu [Hanshin Awaji Earthquake Lesson Information], Kasai no hassei to enshokakudai [Fire Damages] (Cabinet Office) www.bousai.go.jp/kyoiku/kyokun/hanshin_awaji/data/detail/1-1-4.html accessed 25 December 2017 (Fire Damages).

67 Cabinet Office, Hanshin Awaji daishinsai, kyoukun jouhou shiryoshuu [Hanshin Awaji Earthquake Lesson Information], Kouikiouen [Backup Assistance] (Cabinet Office) www.bousai.go.jp/kyoiku/kyokun/hanshin_awaji/data/detail/1-5-4.html accessed 25 December 2017.

Sixth, more than 540,000 houses were seriously damaged or burned down.[68] Over 310,000 evacuees were forced to scramble into various shelters.[69] This was the first earthquake to produce such a large volume of shelter seeking evacuees. Isolated because of serious damage to trains and major roads, evacuees faced tremendous barriers to receiving help. This experience showed that adequate earthquake preparation must include provision of numerous emergency shelters along with sufficient quantities of emergency food and supplies for evacuees.

Seventh, this earthquake convinced the public that everyday citizens had a necessary role to play in actual rescue efforts as well as in providing assistance as volunteers.[70] This was the first earthquake in which citizens volunteered *en masse* in order to provide assistance to evacuees.[71] With so many volunteers the government had to establish a system for enlisting volunteers and organizing their work, which did not exist before the earthquake.

Eighth, the Hanshin Awaji Earthquake wrought considerable damage upon many condominiums in the affected areas.[72] Some were totally destroyed and needed rebuilding. On the other hand, some suffered serious damage but could still be repaired. Nevertheless, many owners preferred rebuilding because they were not confident that repaired condominiums would withstand subsequent powerful earthquakes and also because repaired condominiums would have less market value. Under the Condominium Act, the decision to rebuild a condominium building was available only when the condominium had become too old, and thus required unreasonably high expenses to maintain, ***and*** when four-fifths of unit owners approved of rebuilding.[73] There were some ambiguities over whether a decision to rebuild was possible in cases where a condominium building had been seriously damaged by an earthquake but could still be repaired. Due to split opinions, owners struggled to make collective decisions on whether

68 Building Damages (n 60).

69 Cabinet Office, Hanshin Awaji daishinsai, kyoukun jouhou shiryoshuu [Hanshin Awaji Earthquake Lesson Information], Hinansho no kaisetsu [Establishment of Shelters] (Cabinet Office) www.bousai.go.jp/kyoiku/kyokun/hanshin_awaji/data/detail/1-3-2.html accessed 25 December 2017.

70 A total number of 1.8 million people participated as volunteers. Cabinet Office, Hanshin Awaji daishinsai, kyoukun jouhou shiryoshuu [Hanshin Awaji Earthquake Lesson Information], Volunteers (Cabinet Office) www.bousai.go.jp/kyoiku/kyokun/hanshin_awaji/data/detail/2-4-1.html accessed 25 December 2017.

71 Samuels (n 4) 61.

72 Hanshin Awaji daishinsai mansion hukko mondai tokubetsu iinkai [Special Committee on Rebuilding Condominium Suffered by the Hanshin Awaji Earthquake], Hanshin Awaji daishinsai niyoru bunjo mansion no hukkyu katei to kanrikumiai no taiou [Rebuilding Process of Condominium Suffered by the Hanshin Awaji Earthquake and the Role of Management Corporation], Bunjo mansion no hisai jokyo [Damages to Condominium] (Kobe University 1996) www.lib.kobe-u.ac.jp/directory/eqb/book/6-301/pdf/06_chapter2.pdf accessed 25 December 2017 (among 2935 condominium surveyed, 122 suffered extreme serious damages and 189 condominium suffered serious damages).

73 Tatemono no kubunshoyutō nikansuru hōritsu [Act concerning Ownership of Condominiums], Law no 69 of 1962, art 62 (amended in 2002) (Condominium Act).

to rebuild or repair and thus many damaged condominiums were left untouched for several years.[74]

Ninth, the Hanshin Awaji Earthquake destroyed many houses and condominiums. At that time, the participation ratio for earthquake insurance was at an all-time low and the participation ratio among the residents of Hyogo prefecture was far lower than the national average. Only 78 billion JPY (711 million USD) was paid out from earthquake insurance.[75] Many houses were burnt down as a result of the earthquake but the residents were not able to receive fire insurance payments either, because of the exemption clause. Many residents were thus left without any property or financial resources with which to restart their lives, and called for government support in re-establishing themselves.[76] Moreover, many homeowners lost their homes but still faced responsibilities for outstanding mortgages on their destroyed homes. Many borrowed again from banks in order to finance new homes while still paying off mortgages for homes destroyed in the earthquake, a situation called "double loans" (*niju loan*).[77] This put great financial stress on many homeowners. However, the Japanese government adopted the position that it could not help private citizens acquire property.[78] The central government was thus unwilling to assist residents in rebuilding their houses.

Tenth, the Japanese government needed some kind of government organization to lead reconstruction efforts in the affected areas. Moreover, some communities suffered serious damage because so many old wooden houses had been clustered along very narrow roads, contributing to the spread of fire.[79] The municipal government thus had to redevelop these affected areas so that

74 Cabinet Office, Hanshin Awaji daishinsai, kyoukun jouhou shiryoshuu [Hanshin Awaji Earthquake Lesson Information], Juutaku no saiken [Rebuilding Suffered Houses] (Cabinet Office) www.bousai.go.jp/kyoiku/kyokun/hanshin_awaji/data/detail/3-2-2.html accessed 25 December 2017; Hanshin Awaji daishinsai mansion hukko mondai tokubetsu iinkai [Special Committee on Rebuilding Condominium Suffered by the Hanshin Awaji Earthquake], Hanshin Awaji daishinsai niyoru bunjo mansion no hukkyu katei to kanrikumiai no taiou [Rebuilding Process of Condominium Suffered by the Hanshin Awaji Earthquake and the Role of Management Corporation], Mansion no hukko katei niokeru shomondai [Various Problems for Rebuilding Suffered Condominium] (Kobe University) www.lib.kobe-u.ac.jp/directory/eqb/book/6-301/pdf/08_chapter4.pdf.

75 Hoken News, Jishin hoken tanjoukara 50nen: Seido no kadai to kongowo kangaeru [50Years from the Birth of the Earthquake Insurance: Agenda and Future] (Hoken News 1 September 2016), http://hoken.ne.jp/news_wp/2016/09/01/2016-09-01-地震保険誕生から５０年%E3%80%80制度の課題と今後を/.

76 Ryosuke Aota, "Consideration on Public Support to Housing and Livelihood Reconstruction for Disaster Victims—Transition of Public Support to Private Property of Victims," (2011) 14 *Chiiki Anzen Gakkai Ronbunshu* 141; Michiko Otsuka & Takashi Ozawa, "Hisaisha seikatsu saiken shien [Disaster Victim Life Rebuilding Assistance]" (2004) 437 *Chousa to Jouho* 1.

77 Hyogoken Bengoshikai [Hyogo Bar Association], Saigai hisaisha nitaisuru kouteki shienhouan nitsuite no youbousho [Request on Public Assistance Bill for Disaster Victims] (Hyogo Bar Association 7 May 1998) www.hyogoben.or.jp/about/index-03-10-05.html accessed 25 December 2017.

78 Otsuka & Ozawa (n 76) 2.

79 Fire Damages (n 66) (indicating the Nagata ward of the Kobe City suffered most extended fire damages).

new homes would be built according to an established city development plan with wide public streets sufficient to prevent the spread of fires. All of these reconstruction and large-scale redevelopment projects only came about after the disaster.

1.2.3 Lessons learned

The Japanese government learned many lessons from this earthquake. The cabinet established a system for quickly collecting post-earthquake information and reporting it to the prime minister immediately.[80] The cabinet also established the Cabinet Crisis Management Center attached to the Cabinet House, the prime minister's office and residence.[81] The Diet also introduced statutory amendments to the Basic Act on Disaster Countermeasures to allow SDF to move in without a governor's request.[82] The central government also organized a system to facilitate cooperation between firefighters and rescue teams beyond municipal borders.[83] Governments at all levels were required to prepare measures for accepting volunteers and promoting their participation.[84] The government also drove the Diet to pass the Earthquake Disaster Prevention Countermeasures Special Measures Act[85] to supplement the countermeasures against the earthquake.

The Diet fortified building standards under the Construction Standards Act again.[86] The government also introduced the Act concerning the Facilitation of Seismic Upgrades for Buildings,[87] mandating that owners of certain buildings, namely owners of buildings that had been constructed prior to the introduction of

80 See n 159.
81 Samuels (n 4) 62.
82 See n 186.
83 Shōbō soshikihō [Fire Department Organization Act], Law no 226 of 1947, art 44. Local fire departments established a system of cooperation in the event of a large-scale fire or disaster. At present, the head of the National Fire and Disaster Management Agency can request that local fire departments mobilize their personnel and equipment in order to cooperate with their counterparts in affected municipalities.
84 See n 148; Basic Act on Disaster Countermeasures (n 11) art 8(2)(xiii). See also chapter 6 n 25; Central Disaster Prevention Council, Bosai kihon keikaku [Basic Disaster Prevention Plan] 77–78 (April 2017), Cabinet Office www.bousai.go.jp/taisaku/keikaku/pdf/kihon_basic_plan170411.pdf accessed 25 December 2017.
85 Jishin bousai taisaku tokubetsu sochihō [Earthquake Disaster Prevention Countermeasures Special Measures Act], Law no 111 of 1995. See n 235.
86 Kenchiku kijunhō no ichibuwo kaiseisuru hōritsu [Act to Amend Parts of the Construction Standards Act], Law no 100 of 1998. Standards were further elevated by the Kenchikubutsu no anzensei no kakuho wo hakarutameno kenchiku kijunhōtō no ichibuwo kaiseisuru hōritsu [Act to Amend Parts of the Construction Standards Act in order to Secure the Safety of Buildings], Law no 92 of 2006.
87 Tatemono no taishinkaishu no sokushin nikansuru hōritsu [Act concerning Facilitation of Seismic Upgrades for Buildings], Law no 123 of 1995. The proposal to prohibit the construction of buildings right above active fault lines was not accepted, because there are so many active faults in Japan and it is simply unfeasible to prohibit all construction in these areas. Moreover, many active faults remain unidentified as yet.

the 1981 building code amendments, have their properties evaluated for capacity to withstand powerful earthquakes, and undergo seismic upgrading if necessary.[88]

In order to facilitate community recovery and rebuilding in Kobe, the Diet enacted the Act concerning Basic Policy and Organization for Reconstruction after the Hanshin Awaji Earthquake Disaster[89] only one month after the disaster. The statute established the Hanshin Awaji Earthquake Disaster Reconstruction Headquarters (*Hanshin Awaji daishinsai hukkou honbu*), headed by the prime minister, to coordinate implementation of rebuilding policies by various government departments.[90] Six months later, the Hanshin Awaji Earthquake Disaster Reconstruction Plan was adopted to lead the reconstruction works.[91]

The Diet passed the special measures act to allow the co-owners of affected condominiums to rebuild easily[92] and also decided to amend the Condominium Act[93] to give more discretion to owners intent on rebuilding damaged condominiums. Under the amended Condominium Act, a four-fifths majority of owners can elect to rebuild a condominium regardless of the reason for doing so[94] and also the four-fifths majority of the condominium complex can decide to rebuild the entire complex if two-thirds of each building's owners agree to this rebuilding.[95] As a result of these reforms, rebuilding condominiums seriously damaged by earthquakes has become a much more streamlined process.[96]

88 All these changes proved to be effective after the 2004 Niigata Chuetsu Earthquake, USGS, M 6.6—near the west coast of Honshu, Japan (USGS) https://earthquake.usgs.gov/earthquakes/eventpage/usp000d6vk#executive accessed 25 December 2017. The earthquake registered 6.8 on the Richter scale, killing 68 while inflicting injury on more than 4,800, destroying the homes of more than 10,000, and forcing more than 100,000 to evacuate. Four minutes after the initial earthquake, the Cabinet had established a response room, as had the Ministry of Defense. SDF officers were deployed immediately.

89 Hanshin Awaji daishinsai hukkou no kihon houshin oyobi soshiki nikansuru hōritsu [Act concerning Basic Policy and Organization for Reconstruction after the Hanshin Awaji Earthquake Disaster], Law no 12 of 1995.

90 For the process of reconstruction after the Hanshin Awaji Earthquake, see David W. Edgington, *Reconstructing Kobe: The Geography of Crisis and Opportunity* (UBC Press 2010).

91 Hanshin Awaji shinsai hukko keikaku [Hanshin Awaji Earthquake Disaster Reconstruction Plan] (Hyogo Prefecture) https://web.pref.hyogo.lg.jp/kk41/wd33_000000043.html accessed 24 January 2018.

92 Hisai kubun shoyuu tatemono no saikentō nikansuru tokubetsu sochihō [Special Measures Act on Rebuilding of Condominium Suffered from Damages], Law no 43, 1995.

93 Tatemono no kubun shoyutō nikansuru hōritsu oyobi manshion no tatekae no enkatsukatō nikansuru hōritsu no ichibuwo kaiseisuru hōritsu [Act to Amend Parts of the Condominium Act and the Act concerning Smooth Rebuilding of Condominium], Law no 140 of 2002.

94 Condominium Act (n 73) art 62.

95 Ibid art 70(1). *See* Mark D. West & Emily M. Morris, "The Tragedy of the Condominiums: Legal Responses to Collective Action Problems After the Kobe Earthquake" (2003) 51 *American Journal of Comparative Law* 903.

96 The Diet also enacted Misshu shigaichi niokeru bousai gaiku no seibi no sokushin nikansuru hōritsu [Act concerning Facilitation of Redevelopment to Create Parts with Sufficient Disaster Prevention Capacity within the Highly Clustered Urban Areas], Law no 49 of 1997, to facilitate the redevelopment in urban areas clustered by age-old wooden houses with insufficient disaster prevention capacity.

Strong public demand for government assistance also culminated in the enactment of the Disaster Victim Life Rebuilding Support Act,[97] which provided prefectural financial support, disaster victim life rebuilding support benefit (*hisaisha seikatsu saiken shienkin*), to those who had suffered tremendous loss as a result of natural disaster and faced financial difficulty rebuilding their lives. The bill was submitted by individual House members and was not supported by the cabinet. However, the Diet passed the bill.[98] The Act granted financial support of up to one million JPY (9,000 USD) for relocation and everyday necessity for those victims of natural disaster who had lost their homes completely or whose homes had been so seriously damaged that they required demolition or large-scale renovation.[99] In order to receive this government aid, the victims required a certificate of damage (*risai shoumeisho*) from the municipal government. The amount of aid was decided based on the extent of the damage. The Act was amended in 2004 after the Niigata Chuetsu Earthquake to provide an additional 2 million JPY (18,000 USD) for the costs of debris disposal and for paying down interest on a home loan.[100] The Act was further amended in 2007 to allow victims of disaster to apply this aid money to any purpose related to rebuilding a new life.[101] Therefore, after 2007, victims could receive up to 3 million JPY (27,000 USD) and this government aid could be used to build a new home.

Thanks to various reconstruction measures, all of the infrastructures as well as all of the damaged buildings have now been rebuilt and residents have returned to begin the recovery of the economy in Kobe.[102]

1.3 Legal framework relating to earthquakes

What was the legal system in place with respect to natural disasters? Who had a responsibility to respond? What was the relationship between the central government and the local government? What kinds of countermeasures were contemplated? Were there any special procedures or countermeasures against the powerful earthquake?

97 Hisaisha seikatsu saiken shienhō [Disaster Victim Life Rebuilding Support Act], Law no 66 of 1998.

98 Otsuka & Ozawa (n 76).

99 Disaster Victim Life Rebuilding Support Act (n 97) art 3.

100 Hisaisha seikatsu saiken shienhō no ichibuwo kaiseisuru hōritsu [Act to Amend Parts of the Disaster Victim Life Rebuilding Support Act], Law no 13 of 2004.

101 Hisaisha seikatsu saiken shienhō no ichibuwo kaiseisuru hōritsu [Act to Amend Parts of the Disaster Victim Life Rebuilding Support Act], Law no 114 of 2007. The benefit is paid from the fund run by the Disaster Victim Life Rebuilding Supporting Organization (*Hisaisha seikatsu saiken shien hōjin*) with the support of the central government.

102 Mizuho Sougō Kenkyusho [Mizuho Research Institute], Kakono Shinsaiji no hukko kara eta kyoukun [Lessons Learned from Past Disasters] (Mizuho Research Institute 1 June 2011) www.mizuho-ri.co.jp/publication/research/pdf/policy-insight/MSI110601.pdf accessed 25 December 2017. However, some areas, such as the Nagata ward, are still suffering from the economic effects, because the major industry in the Nagata ward used to be chemical shoes production which was not able to keep up with the competition even before the disaster. Ibid.

1.3.1 Constitutional basis for the government powers in time of emergency

The Constitution of Japan of 1946, the current constitution in Japan, does not have any provision on emergencies caused by natural disasters. Indeed, unlike the Basic Law of Germany, which now contains provisions for military emergency, the Constitution of Japan does not have any provision for emergency even against foreign attacks. Moreover, unlike the United States,[103] it is generally believed that the Emperor or the prime minister or the cabinet does not have inherent unwritten power such as martial law to suspend the civil government and form a military government in times of emergency. Therefore, it is no wonder that the Constitution does not have any provision for emergencies resulting from natural disaster.

Based on the popular sovereignty principle,[104] the Constitution of Japan established the liberal democratic government structure. All the legislative powers are granted to the Diet, the national legislature.[105] Executive power is granted to the cabinet, a collective body,[106] consisting of the prime minister and ministers of state chosen by the prime minister.[107] Based on the separation of powers principle, the executive power is distinguished from the legislative power and the cabinet only has a power to execute the law passed by the legislature.[108] This means that the cabinet does not have any power to make an order or to restrict the civil rights and civil liberties of the public unless authorized by the statute. Therefore, in order to find an authorization to prepare for the disaster or to respond to the disaster, attention must be placed upon whether there is any statute passed by the Diet and what kind of powers are authorized by these statutes to the government.

It is important to note, in this regard, that there is no emergency legislation that authorizes the government or the prime minister to respond and exercise broad power even in times of emergency. Even for an emergency resulting from attack by a foreign power, there is no statute that authorizes the prime minister to order the SDF to use powers that ignore all the regulatory statutes or authorize the prime minister to restrict the civil rights and civil liberties of the public.[109]

103 Cornell University Law School, Legal Information Institute, CRS Annotated Constitution, Article II, Martial Law and Constitutional Limitations (Cornell) www.law.cornell.edu/anncon/html/art2frag11_user.html accessed 25 December 2017; Major Kirk L. Davies, "The Imposition of Martial Law in the United States" (2000) 49 *Air Force Law Review* 67.

104 Nihonkoku kenpō [CONSTITUTION OF JAPAN], 1946, preamble & art 1.

105 Ibid art 41.

106 Ibid art 65.

107 Ibid art 66(1).

108 Ibid art 73(i). For a structure of the government in Japan, see Shigenori Matsui, *The Constitution of Japan: A Contextual Analysis* (Hart 2011).

109 See for instance, the UK Civil Contingencies Act of 2004, 2004 c. 36. The Constitution of Japan renounced war power and prohibited the maintenance of armed forces. Constitution of Japan (n 104) art 9. The Japanese government established the SDF and justifies them as a minimum force to defend Japan as distinct from armed forces. However, if Japan were to be attacked and SDF deployed for defense, there would be no emergency legislation granting sweeping exceptions to the defense activities of the SDF. Therefore, legally speaking, the SDF's tanks may need to keep the speed limit and stop at the red light even when engaging in defense actions.

There is also no statute authorizing the government or the prime minister to exercise power in times of emergency resulting from a massive natural disaster. Therefore, the focus must be placed on specific legislation dealing with natural disasters.

1.3.2 Framework for natural disaster countermeasures

As stated above, various statutes have been enacted by the Diet to respond to natural disasters such as powerful earthquakes and tsunamis. Two of the most important statutes are the Disaster Assistance Act[110] and the Basic Act on Disaster Countermeasures.[111] Taken together, these statutes provide for government actions to be adopted in the event of serious natural disasters. Moreover, the Diet has enacted the Special Measures Act on Large-Scale Earthquake Countermeasures[112] to prepare for large-scale, powerful earthquakes. The Earthquake Disaster Prevention Countermeasures Special Measures Act[113] was also enacted to supplement the countermeasures against earthquakes.

Before examining the government response to the Tohoku Earthquake, it is important to take a look at the details of these legal measures in place for responding to earthquakes and tsunamis. The examination will show that these statutes grant very specific power to the central government and the local government and that there is a very precise division of power between the central and local governments. Authority for responding to natural disaster basically rests with local government and the power of the central government is very limited in this respect.

In order to understand the significance of the division of powers, it is necessary to understand the structure of the government in Japan. Japan is not a federal state. However, the Constitution of Japan of 1946, adopted after the end of the Pacific War during the occupation and enacted under strong ideological influence from the Constitution of the United States, guaranteed local autonomy. In a chapter on "local self-government," the Constitution of Japan thus proclaims that "[r]egulations concerning organization and operations of local public entities shall be fixed by law in accordance with the principle of local autonomy."[114] Following constitutional provisions such as this, the Diet passed the Local Government Act of 1947[115] to establish the fundamental organizations, powers, and relationship between local governments and the central government. According to the Local Government Act, "local public entities" referred to in the Constitution are divided into "general local government" and "special local government."[116] The "general local governments" are further divided into cities, towns, and villages

110 Saigai kyujohō [Disaster Assistance Act], Law no 118 of 1947.
111 Basic Act on Disaster Countermeasures (n 11).
112 Special Measures Act on Large-Scale Earthquake Countermeasures (n 12).
113 Earthquake Disaster Prevention Countermeasures Special Measures Act (n 85).
114 Constitution of Japan (n 104) art 92.
115 Chihou jichihō [Local Government Act], Law no 67 of 1947.
116 Ibid art 1–3(1). The "special local government" includes a "ward," as will be explained later (n 120), union of local public entities and the property district. Ibid art 1–3(3).

(generally called municipal governments) and prefectures.[117] Cities, towns, and villages are the most fundamental units of local government[118] and prefectures are broader units, responsible for handling matters with impacts on more than a single city, town, or village.[119] There are 47 prefectures in Japan. Population density is the basic distinction for determining a city, town, or village.[120] Japan has 791 cities, 744 towns, and 183 villages as of 10 October 2016.[121] Therefore, the governmental structure in Japan is divided into the central government, prefectural governments, and municipal governments.

The power of local governments under the Constitution is somewhat ambiguous. The Constitution grants local governments the "right to manage their property, affairs and administration and to enact their own regulations within the law"[122] but the precise scope of local power is not clear. Unlike the Constitution of the United States, which granted only listed powers to the federal government and left everything else to the states and the people,[123] the Constitution of Japan does not have any provision limiting the power of the central government. Therefore, it is not clear whether there is a limit on the power of the central government (that is to say, whether there are some powers that must be reserved for local government, with any interference from the central government being unconstitutional). It is a predominant understanding that the power of local government is derived from the central government and must be defined by the Diet and that local government can only exercise powers duly granted by the Diet. According to the Local Government Act, local government can handle "local matters" and other matters that are delegated to it by statutes or cabinet orders.[124]

Moreover, local governments can enact ordinances only "within law." This means that local governments cannot violate statutes passed by the Diet. National law trumps local law. In practice, this supremacy of national law together with the unlimited powers of the national government deprives local governments of their inherent, unrestrained powers to manage purely local matters.

117 Ibid art 1–3(2).

118 Ibid art 2(3).

119 Ibid art 2(5).

120 For instance, in order for a town to become a city, the community must have a population of no less than 50,000, no less than 60% of all residents living in urban areas, no less than 60 percent of the population engaged in professions in commercial or industrial fields or belonging to the same family of those engaged in such professions, and satisfy the requirements to become a city including the existence of vital urban facilities. Ibid art 8(1).

121 Ministry of Internal Affairs and Communications, Shichosonsu no suii [Changes in the Number of City, Town and Village] (MIAC) www.soumu.go.jp/main_content/000283329.pdf accessed 25 December 2017. The Tokyo Metropolitan Government, which is one of 47 prefectures and is the capital city of Japan, is special since most of its area is divided into 23 wards and these wards are the most basic units of local government. These wards are special local government as distinguished from general local government but in reality they are not much different from regular cities.

122 Constitution of Japan (n 104) art 94.

123 Constitution of the United States, 10th Amendment.

124 Local Government Act (n 115) art 2(2).

As a result, local governments can exercise inherent powers over local matters subject to statutory regulation and powers delegated under the supervision of the central government. It is important to note that the SDF is managed by the Ministry of Defense (MOD) of the central government, police are managed by prefectural governments under the heavy supervision of the central government via the National Police Agency (NPA), located inside the Cabinet Office, and firefighters and rescue personnel are managed by municipal governments under the supervision of the National Fire and Disaster Management Agency (NFDMA), located inside the Ministry of Internal Affairs and Communications (MIC).

1.3.3 Disaster Assistance Act

The Disaster Assistance Act enables prefectural governments to provide assistance to disaster victims and to secure social order by providing necessary assistance in cooperation with local governments, public organizations, and the public.[125] This statute applied to natural disasters where a large-scale fire has destroyed a certain percentage of homes within a municipality, where a certain percentage of homes have been destroyed in a prefecture, where there are special difficulties in providing assistance (such as when large numbers of destroyed homes are located in isolated communities), or where there are many casualties or the possibility of injury.[126] When a natural disaster occurred, the prefectural government was supposed to provide various assistance, including provision of shelter and temporary housing, food and water, clothing, medical services, rescue, temporary repair of damaged homes, and financing for necessities of life, school supplies, and burial.[127]

If assistance was necessary, the heads of the designated administrative agencies, explained below, could order business operators engaged in the production, collection, sale, distribution, storage and transportation of necessary materials to store those materials; they even reserved authority to expropriate those materials.[128] In order to give effect to these storage or expropriation orders, government officials could enter properties where these materials are stored or located.[129]

125 Disaster Assistance Act (n 110) art 1. The Disaster Assistance Act was substantially revised in 2014 after the Tohoku Earthquake. *See* Chapter 6 n 48. It needs to be noted that the matters under the Disaster Assistance Act are national matters delegated to local government, while the matters under the Basic Act on Disaster Countermeasures are local matters.

126 Disaster Assistance Act (n 110) art 2 (under the current Act, the designation of disaster to trigger the application of the Act is delegated to cabinet order); Saigai kyujohō sekourei [Disaster Assistance Act Enforcement Order], Cabinet Order 225 of 1947, art 1.

127 Disaster Assistance Act (n 110) art 23 (under the current Act, art 4).

128 Ibid art 23–2(1) (under the current Act, art 5(1)). Appropriate compensation must be paid. Ibid art 23–2(3) (under the current Act, art 5(3)). Criminal punishment was possible for those in contravention of this storage order. Ibid art 45(ii) (under the current Act, art 31(ii)). For a meaning of "designated administrative agencies," see n 142.

129 Ibid art 23–3(1) (under the current Act, art 6(1)).

Prefectural governors could also order medical professionals, construction workers, and transportation workers to engage in assistance operations if necessary.[130] Governors could even order the cooperation of victims in need or any persons in the vicinity.[131] If providing disaster assistance, governors could also assume management of hospitals, clinics, hotels and other facilities designated by cabinet order, use lands, houses or materials, or order business operators engaged in production, collection, sale, distribution, storage, and transportation of necessary materials to store them or to expropriate them.[132] These governors could also delegate their powers to heads of municipal government.[133] Further, the Health, Labor, and Welfare Minister could instruct governors of other prefectures to assist the operations of governors in the affected area(s).[134]

Basically, prefectural governments of the places where disasters occurred had to pay for all costs associated with disaster assistance.[135] In order to prepare for such spending, prefectural governments had to pay into a disaster assistance fund (*saigai kyujo kikin*).[136] However, if expenditures exceeded certain limits set out in the statute, the central government was supposed to bear a portion of the burden.[137]

1.3.4 Basic Act on Disaster Countermeasures

The basic legal framework applicable to more serious natural disasters is established by the Basic Act on Disaster Countermeasures.[138] It aims to promote the facilitation of comprehensive and well-planned disaster prevention measures and thereby contribute to the maintenance of social order and attainment of public welfare by clarifying the responsibility of the central and local governments and by providing the basics of disaster prevention countermeasures.[139]

Disasters include extreme winds, rain, and snow, flooding, high tides, earthquakes, tsunami, volcanic eruptions and other extraordinary natural disasters,

130 Ibid art 24(1) (under the current Act, art 7(1)). Criminal punishment was possible for those in contravention of this order. Ibid art 45(i) (under the current Act, art 31(i)).

131 Ibid art 25 (under the current Act, art 8).

132 Ibid art 26(1) (under the current Act, art 9(1)). In order to implement this power, governors could permit officials to enter into places where these materials are stored or located. Ibid art 27(1) (under the current Act, art 10(1)). Criminal punishment was possible for those who contravene this storage order. Ibid art 45(ii) (under the current Act, art 31(ii)).

133 Ibid art 30(1) (under the current Act, art 13(1)).

134 Ibid art 31 (under the current Act, this power is granted with the prime minister. art 14).

135 Ibid art 33(1) (under the current Act, art 18(1)).

136 Ibid art 37 (under the current Act, art 22).

137 Ibid art 36 (under the current Act, art 21). See n 193.

138 Basic Act on Disaster Countermeasures (n 11) art. 1. The Basic Act on Disaster Countermeasures was amended twice after the Tohoku Earthquake to respond to various lessons the government had learned from its experience. *See* Chapter 6 nn 4–46.

139 Basic Act on Disaster Countermeasures (n 11) art 1. The 2013 amendment also clarified the fundamental principles of disaster prevention measures. Ibid art 2-2. Chapter 6 n 18.

large-scale fires, and explosions causing extreme damage, as defined by the cabinet order.[140] The Act then delineates the responsibilities of the central government,[141] designated administrative agencies (*shitei gyousei kikan*),[142] along with those of prefectural,[143] and municipal governments,[144] designated public organizations (*shitei koukyo kikan*),[145] and even those of local residents.[146] The Act obliges the central government and local governments to make coordinated efforts to contribute to the prevention of damage to land, life, and property of the people.[147] In order to prevent disasters or expansion of damage, the central government and local governments must make efforts to fortify infrastructure, strengthen buildings, improve transportation and telecommunication systems, improve warning systems, promote earthquake prediction systems, prepare to accept and manage volunteers and provide information to the public.[148]

The Act established the Central Disaster Prevention Council presided over by the prime minister in the Cabinet Office and authorized the Council for the establishment of the Basic Disaster Prevention Plan.[149] The Council is also tasked with deliberation and advice on important matters on disaster prevention based on the solicitation of the prime minister, and the Act mandated the prime minister to seek advice on basic policy for disaster prevention, important coordination of disaster prevention measures, outline of emergency measures to be adopted during disaster emergencies, and others.

Each designated administrative agency is mandated to establish the disaster prevention business plan based on the Basic Disaster Prevention Plan and update it every year if necessary.[150] Each prefecture must establish its own prefectural disaster prevention council and make a prefectural disaster prevention plan based upon the Basic Disaster Prevention Plan.[151] Each municipality must also establish a municipal disaster prevention council and make a municipal disaster prevention plan.[152]

140 Basic Act on Disaster Countermeasures (n 11) art 2(i).
141 Ibid art 3.
142 Ibid art 3(3). Designated administrative agencies are agencies of the central government designated by the prime minister in order to carry out the responsibilities of the central government in performing its disaster prevention duties. Ibid art 2(iii).
143 Ibid art 4.
144 Ibid art 5.
145 Ibid art 6. Designated public organizations include designated national public organizations, such as independent public corporations, the Bank of Japan, Japan Red Cross, NHK, and other private organizations such as electrical, gas, transportation, and telecommunication companies performing public functions designated by the prime minister (ibid art 2(v)). Designated local public organizations include local public independent corporations and other local private organizations engaging in the provision of electricity, gas, transportation, and telecommunication that are so designated by governors (ibid art 2(vi)).
146 Ibid art 7.
147 Ibid art 8(1).
148 Ibid art 8(2). The 2013 amendment also mandated the moral obligation to promote the cooperation between the central and local government with volunteers. Ibid art 5–3.
149 Ibid art 11 & art 12. See Central Disaster Prevention Council (n 32).
150 Basic Act on Disaster Countermeasures (n 11) art 36.
151 Ibid art 14(1) & (2). The council must be presided over by the governor. Ibid art 15(1) & (2).
152 Ibid art 16(1).

The Act thereafter provides in detail on countermeasures against disaster, starting from disaster prevention, disaster emergency countermeasures, and disaster restoration.

1.3.5 Disaster prevention

The Basic Act on Disaster Countermeasures first provides for the disaster prevention measures. It thus listed the matters to be prepared as disaster prevention measures and obliged the heads of the designated administrative agencies, heads of the local government and designated public organizations to implement the disaster prevention measures according to disaster prevention plans.[153] For instance, they are mandated to create organizations to estimate the damages from the disaster, predict the disaster, and promptly transmit the information on the disaster and constantly improve the system.[154] They are also mandated to conduct disaster prevention drills[155] and to store the necessary goods and materials for disaster emergency countermeasures or for disaster restoration, organize them, and check them.[156,157]

1.3.6 "Disaster emergency countermeasures"

When a disaster is likely to happen or when a disaster has occurred, heads of designated administrative agencies, local governments, and designated public organizations have a responsibility to implement various "disaster emergency countermeasures" (*saigai oukyu taisaku*): to issue and transmit warnings, advise or instruct evacuation, extinguish fires, rescue and protect disaster victims, make temporary repairs to damaged facilities and equipment, clean up and prevent disease, prevent crime, regulate traffic, maintain social order, secure emergency transportation, and adopt other necessary measures to prevent and contain the disaster.[158] When the disaster caused damages, the municipal government is also mandated to report the damages and countermeasures adopted to the prefectures promptly and the prefectures are mandated to transmit that information to the prime minister promptly.[159]

153 Ibid art 46.

154 Ibid art 47(1). The 2012 amendment also added the responsibility to conduct disaster prevention education (ibid art 47–2).

155 Ibid art 48.

156 Ibid art 49. The 2013 amendment also added the obligation to make necessary arrangements with suppliers in order to ensure the smooth cooperation for disaster emergency countermeasures or disaster restoration. Ibid art 49–3.

157 The 2013 amendment further added the obligation to designate the "designated emergency evacuation spots" (*shitei kinkyu hinan basho*), designated places to gather when the specific disaster occurs, and "designated shelters" (*shitei hinansho*) (ibid art 49–4, 49–7), shelters to stay when the disaster occurs, and publicize the information to the residents (ibid art 49–9) as well as the obligation to create the list of residents who need assistance for smooth and swift evacuation (ibid art 49–10) and provide that list and information to agencies and organizations that would provide assistance to these residents for evacuation (ibid art 49–11).

158 Ibid art 50.

159 Ibid art 53.

When anyone notices any unusual signs indicating the possibility of disaster, that person must immediately notify the heads of the municipal government or police officers.[160] When so notified, heads of the municipal government must, in turn, notify the JMA and other relevant agencies,[161] while police detachments must notify heads of municipal governments.[162] When a prefectural governor is notified by the JMA as to a disaster prediction or warning, he/she must notify heads of municipal governments and other relevant agencies, requesting that necessary measures be undertaken.[163]

When a disaster is imminent, heads of municipal government must order firefighters to prepare and dispatch and/or request that police take like measures as necessary.[164] If there is a facility that might pose special damage risks in the event of a disaster, municipal government heads can instruct the owner, occupant, or manager of that facility to remove hazards or adopt necessary security measures.[165] When a disaster has occurred or is imminent, municipal government heads are authorized to issue an "evacuation recommendation" or "evacuation instruction" to residents and visitors[166] and to issue an instruction as to where residents and visitors should evacuate to.[167]

1.3.7 Establishment of Disaster Response Headquarters

When a disaster occurs within the boundaries of a municipality, the affected municipal government is empowered to establish a municipal disaster response headquarters.[168] Further, governors of disaster-affected prefectures have the authority to establish a prefectural disaster response headquarters.[169]

In cases where an "extraordinary disaster" (*hijō saigai*) occurs, the prime minister is empowered to establish an Extraordinary Disaster Response Headquarters (*hijō saigai taisaku honbu*) to be presided over by one of the ministers of state.[170] The Extraordinary Disaster Response Headquarters is authorized to make general adjustments to the implementation of "extraordinary disaster" response measures undertaken by heads of designated administrative agencies, governors, heads of municipal government and other designated public organizations.[171] The director

160 Ibid art 54(1).
161 Ibid art 54(4).
162 Ibid art 54(3).
163 Ibid art 55. The 2013 amendment added the obligation of the heads of municipal government to publicize the warning to the residents and transmit the warning to various relevant organization. Ibid art 56.
164 Ibid art 58.
165 Ibid art 59.
166 Ibid art 60(1). An evacuation instruction is a bit stronger than an evacuation recommendation but both are advisory and not mandatory.
167 Ibid art 60(2).
168 Ibid art 23–2.
169 Ibid art 23.
170 Ibid art 24 & art 25(1).
171 Ibid art 26.

of the Headquarters is authorized to issue necessary instructions to governors and heads of municipal governments in order to implement "extraordinary disaster" response adequately and promptly.[172]

In the event of responding to an "emergency disaster" (***kinkyu saigai***) the prime minister has the authority to establish and preside over an Emergency Disaster Response Headquarters (***kinkyu saigai taisaku honbu***).[173] The prime minister, as director of the Emergency Disaster Response Headquarters, is similarly authorized to adjust implementation of disaster response undertaken by heads of designated administrative agencies, governors, heads of the municipal governments, and other designated public organizations[174] and to issue the necessary instructions to them if it is necessary to ensure that countermeasures are put in place adequately and promptly.[175]

1.3.8 "Emergency measures"

The Basic Act on Disaster Countermeasures lists various "emergency measures" (***oukyu taisaku***) to be adopted. It is the responsibility of the municipal government heads to implement these emergency measures to prevent the spread of damage by deploying firefighters and rescue personnel.[176]

The municipal government heads can designate the affected area as a "hazard zone" (***keikai kuiki***) and restrict or prohibit the entry of any persons aside from emergency personnel and/or order people in the affected area to vacate in the interests of preventing harm to human life or person.[177] They can use land, buildings, and other properties owned by private persons or take possession of them if necessary.[178] Additionally, they have the authority to remove structures and other properties if necessary when they inhibit emergency measures.[179] If necessary, they can even order residents to participate in emergency response.[180] The heads of the municipal government can of course request the assistance of other municipal government heads[181] in addition to that of prefectural governors.[182]

Municipal government heads can request that governors ask for the deployment of the SDF[183] under article 83, paragraph 1 of the Self Defense Forces Act, which authorized the governors to ask for the deployment,[184] and can otherwise

172 Ibid art 28(2).
173 Ibid art 28-2 & art 28-3(1).
174 Ibid art 28-4.
175 Ibid art 28-6(2).
176 Ibid art 62(1).
177 Ibid art 63(1). The violator could be punished by a fine of 100,000 JPY (9,000 USD). Ibid art 116(ii).
178 Ibid art 64(1).
179 Ibid art 64(2).
180 Ibid art 65(1).
181 Ibid art 67(1).
182 Ibid art 68(1).
183 Ibid art 68-2(1).
184 Self Defense Forces Act (n 17) art 83(1).

inform the Defense Minister or officers designated by the Defense Minister as to damages sustained in the event the request for deployment cannot be accommodated.[185] Alternatively, the Defense Minister or officials designated by the Minister are at liberty to deploy the SDF absent an official request for the purposes of protecting human life and property in the event of an emergency.[186]

The governors also must implement emergency measures according to statute and the local disaster prevention plan.[187] The governors can issue engagement orders, cooperation orders, or storage orders to residents under the Disaster Assistance Act,[188] or store, use, or expropriate private property for public use.[189] The governor can also substitute the emergency measures to be implemented by the municipal government if the municipal government is paralyzed[190] and ask for assistance from the governors of other prefectures as well.[191] Prefectural public safety commissions can prohibit vehicular traffic, if necessary, aside from emergency vehicles on designated emergency road (*kinkyu kotsusoro*).[192] When such prohibitions are issued, police can order owners or operators of vehicles and other property to remove vehicles or property or take other appropriate measures to secure unfettered passage for emergency vehicles.[193] If vehicle owners or operators refuse to abide by these orders or are not available to receive such orders, police are authorized to have such property removed and even to inflict damage on said property, if necessary.[194] Deployed SDF officers as well as firefighters have these same powers if police officers are not present.[195,196]

185 Basic Act on Disaster Countermeasures (n 11) art 68–2(2).
186 Ibid; Self Defense Forces Act (n 17) art 83(2).
187 Basic Act on Disaster Countermeasures (n 11) art 70.
188 Disaster Assistance Act (n 110). See nn 125–34.
189 Basic Act on Disaster Countermeasures (n 11) art. 71.
190 Ibid art 73.
191 Ibid art 74. The 2012 amendment also added a request for assistance from the prime minister. Ibid art 74–2.
192 Ibid art 76.
193 Ibid art 76–3(1).
194 Ibid art 76–3(2).
195 Ibid art 76–3(3) & (4).
196 The 2013 amendment added various exceptional treatments for emergency measures: the designation of "highly unusual and extremely serious extraordinary disaster" (*ichijirushiku ijo katsu gekijinna hijo saigai*) and exclusion of the fire safety regulation on shelters or temporary housings (ibid art 86–2), exclusion of the hospital regulation to medical facilities during emergency (ibid art 86–3), exception to burial and cremation of victims (ibid art 86–4), special treatment for disposal of disaster waste (ibid art 86–5). The 2013 amendment also added the obligation to provide shelters for residents and provide emergency goods to evacuees (ibid art 86–6) and to make sure to care for victims who were unable to stay in the shelters (ibid art 86–7). Furthermore, the 2012 amendment authorized the municipal government to secure the places for temporary stay for residents outside of the municipalities (ibid art 86–8) and outside of the prefecture (ibid art 86–9). Also the 2013 amendment allowed the governors to request the transportation of victims from the designated public organizations providing transportation services (ibid art 86–14) and the 2012 amendment allowed the heads of the designated administrative agencies and governors to request the transportation of goods and materials for implementation of disaster emergency countermeasures (ibid art 86–18). Finally, the 2013 amendment added several important mandates for the assistance to disaster victims: the mandate for the heads of the municipal government to investigate the extent of the damage and issue a certificate of damage without delay (ibid art 90–2), and to create a list of disaster victims (ibid art 90–3) and use it (ibid art 90–4).

Generally speaking, the municipal government(s) or the prefecture(s), depending upon their responsibility, must pay costs for disaster prevention and disaster emergency countermeasures.[197] However, the central government can assist with all or portions of costs within the budget.[198] Especially in the event of an "extremely serious disaster" (*gekijin saigai*) that causes massive damage, the central government must designate the disaster as such and take responsibility for implementing emergency measures and reducing the financial burden on affected local governments.[199]

1.3.9 "Disaster emergency situation" declaration

When an extraordinary disaster occurs and its effects are exceptional and serious enough to have grave impacts on the economy and public welfare of the country, the prime minister can declare a "disaster emergency situation" (*saigai kinkyu jitai*) with cabinet approval.[200] The prime minister must receive Diet approval for the declaration within 20 days.[201] The prime minister must establish the Emergency Disaster Response Headquarters once this declaration is issued.[202] When there is an urgent necessity to take measures to maintain the order of the national economy or to secure the public welfare, the prime minister can adopt the following cabinet orders if the Diet is in recess and there is no time to ask for an extraordinary session or if the House of Representatives has been dissolved and there is no time to ask for an emergency session of the House of Councilors:

1. an order that stipulates on the distribution of everyday necessities or restricts or prohibits their sale or transfer, in the event of critical shortage;
2. an order setting a maximum price for goods and services related to emergency response, restoration, or the stability of the national economy; or
3. an order allowing for the extension of payment due dates related to debts or the duration of rights.[203]

If a "disaster emergency situation" is declared and it is difficult to accept foreign rescue teams due to statutory restrictions, the prime minister can issue a cabinet order permitting the adoption of adequate measures in situations where the Diet is in recess and there is no time to request an extraordinary session or if the House of Representatives has been dissolved and there is no time to ask for an emergency session of the House of Councilors.[204]

197 Ibid art 91.
198 Ibid art 94.
199 Ibid art 97. Gekijin saigai ni taisho surutameno tokubetsu no zaisei enjōtō nikansuru hōritsu [Act concerning Special Financial Assistance in order to Cope with Extremely Serious Disaster], Law no 150 of 1962 (Extremely Serious Disaster Act).
200 Basic Act on Disaster Countermeasures (n 11) art 105(1).
201 Ibid art 106(1).
202 Ibid art 107.
203 Ibid art 109(1).
204 Ibid art 109–2.

It must be emphasized that these orders can be issued only when the Diet is in recess and there is no time to request an extraordinary session or if the House of Representatives has been dissolved and there is no time to ask for an emergency session of the House of Councilors and the power that can be exercised by the prime minister is quite limited.[205]

1.3.10 "Emergency" declaration

Moreover, the prime minister can issue an "emergency" (***kinkyu jitai***) declaration based upon a recommendation of the National Public Safety Commission on the whole country or a part of it when facing a large-scale disaster, riot, or other emergency situation and finding the declaration necessary in order to maintain the public safety.[206] When this emergency declaration is issued, the prime minister can temporarily take control of the police and direct and supervise the director of the police.[207]

Police officers can temporarily protect injured persons in need of immediate attention,[208] issue a necessary warning to anyone present or other relevant persons when there is a danger such as natural disaster causing danger to human life or serious damages to the property, detain or order evacuation of a person in danger if immediate response is necessary to avoid injury or damages, order a person present or any other persons to adopt necessary measures to avoid injury or damage or adopt such measures by himself/herself.[209] Moreover, if a police officer finds someone is going to commit the crime, he/she can issue a warning to avoid the crime, and prevent such conduct if there is a danger to human life, if injury might occur, or if property could be seriously damaged and there is an immediate need to take action.[210] Therefore, if such an emergency declaration is issued and when the prime minister takes over the police temporarily, the prime minister will be able to order the police officer to take these measures. Moreover, in such circumstances, the prime minister can issue legal orders to and direct the head of the prefectural police forces inside the areas that are covered by the emergency declaration, order the head of the prefectural police forces that are not covered by the declaration to dispatch police officers to places inside the declared area, so the dispatched police officers can exercise their powers inside the declared areas.[211] In other words, the prime minister can order the police officers to exercise their power outside of their jurisdictions.

205 This declaration has never been issued in Japan since the Basic Act on Disaster Countermeasures was enacted.

206 Police Act (n 15) art 71(1). When the prime minister issued the emergency declaration, he/she must seek approval from the Diet within 20 days and if the Diet disapproved it, he/she needs to repeal it as soon as possible. Ibid art 74(1) & (2).

207 Ibid art 72(1).

208 Police Officer Job Execution Act (n 15) art 3.

209 Ibid art 4

210 Ibid art 5.

211 Police Act (n 15) art 73.

However, the power the prime minister can exercise under this circumstance is limited to the power that can be exercised by police officers. Moreover, this declaration can be issued only when such action is necessary to maintain public safety.[212]

1.3.11 Disaster restoration

The heads of the designated administrative agencies, the heads of the local government and designated public organizations are tasked with restoration from the disaster in accordance with the disaster prevention plan.[213] The central government is supposed to assist the restoration work by distributing the "local tax distribution grants" (*chihokouhuzei kouhukin*) or other grants or providing the necessary financial support.[214] The central government is also to bear part of the costs of the restoration tasks.[215]

1.3.12 Special Measures Act on Large-Scale Earthquake Countermeasures

The Special Measures Act on Large-Scale Earthquake Countermeasures was enacted in 1978 to provide for the prevention of damage due to powerful earthquakes.[216]

First, this Act allowed the prime minister to designate the areas where intensified earthquake countermeasures are necessary because of the possibility of a very powerful earthquake ("earthquake countermeasure reinforcement areas") (*jisin bosai taisaku kyouka chiki*).[217] The government is mandated to closely monitor the areas to predict a very powerful earthquake,[218] and the Central Disaster Prevention Council is mandated to prepare the Earthquake Disaster Prevention Basic Plan for the designated areas.[219] Each designated administrative agency and designated public organization is mandated to prepare an earthquake disaster prevention reinforcement plan based on the Earthquake Disaster Prevention Basic Plan[220] and the managers of certain facilities, such as hospitals, hotels,

212 This declaration has never been issued in Japan since the Police Act was enacted.

213 Basic Act on Disaster Countermeasures (n 11) art 87.

214 Ibid art 90. The "local tax distribution grant" is allocated by the central government to local governments from the revenue collected by national taxes in order to supplant the local tax revenue. In addition to the annual grant, the central government can add an additional special grant when the local government is hit by a serious disaster.

215 Ibid art 96.

216 Special Measures Act on Large-Scale Earthquake Countermeasures (n 12) art 1.

217 Ibid art 3(1). The Diet enacted the Special Measures Act to provide for financial support for seismic upgrade in these designated areas. Jishin bousai taisaku kyouka chiiki niokeru jishin taisaku kinkyu seibi jigyou nikakawaru kunino zaiseijo no tokubetsusochi ni kansuru hōritsu [Special Measures Act on the Financial Support for Earthquake Countermeasures Facilitation Tasks in the Earthquake Countermeasure Intensification Areas], Law no 63 of 1980.

218 Special Measures Act on Large-Scale Earthquake Countermeasures (n 12) art 4.

219 Ibid art 5(1).

220 Ibid art 6(1).

railroad companies, or managers of facilities storing oil or natural gas inside the designated areas are required to prepare an earthquake disaster prevention emergency plan.[221]

Second, the prime minister is mandated to issue an "emergency warning" (*keikai sengen*) if the head of the JMA predicts a massive earthquake[222] and publicizes this prediction to the public.[223] The prime minister also has to notify the residents and visitors inside the designated areas to take precautionary measures and tell the local governors and others to engage in earthquake disaster prevention emergency countermeasures.[224] The prime minister is then mandated to establish the "Earthquake Disaster Preparation Headquarters" (*jishin saigai keikai honbu*), presided over by the prime minister as a director.[225] The headquarters basically fulfills the general coordination of all earthquake disaster prevention emergency countermeasures.[226] If it is necessary to adequately and promptly enforce the earthquake disaster prevention emergency countermeasures, the director can instruct the heads of the designated administrative agencies or local governments[227] and request the deployment of the SDF officers.[228] The earthquake disaster prevention countermeasures could include anything related to public notification of prediction, evacuation recommendation and instruction, fire extinguishment, emergency rescue, emergency transport, emergency food and medical supplies, and even maintenance of social order.[229] When the emergency warning is issued, the local residents are obliged to adopt measures to prevent and mitigate the damage and to cooperate with the earthquake disaster prevention countermeasures to be adopted by the head of local government, the police officers and others.[230] The head of the relevant local government can instruct the enforcement of the earthquake disaster prevention countermeasures and request or recommend the adoption of other necessary measures.[231] Local public safety commissions of the relevant local government can ban or restrict the passage of pedestrians and motor vehicles if necessary[232] and police officers could issue warnings or instructions if needed to secure safe evacuation, and even ban or restrict the entry into dangerous places, order people to leave, or take other necessary measures such as removal of blocking motor vehicles.[233]

221 Ibid art 7(1).
222 Ibid art 9(1).
223 Ibid art 9(2).
224 Ibid art 9(1).
225 Ibid art 10(1) & art 11(1). Both prefectural government and the municipal government need to establish headquarters separately. Ibid art 16.
226 Ibid art 12.
227 Ibid art 13(1).
228 Ibid art 13(2).
229 Ibid art 21(1).
230 Ibid art 22.
231 Ibid art 23.
232 Ibid art 24.
233 Ibid art 25.

Together with the earthquake prediction system, this Act was chiefly designed for the purposes of government preparation in anticipation of a future Tokai Earthquake.[234]

1.3.13 Earthquake Disaster Prevention Countermeasures Special Measures Act

The Earthquake Disaster Prevention Countermeasures Special Measures Act[235] was enacted after the Hanshin Awaji Earthquake to intensify the earthquake disaster prevention countermeasures and to contribute to the maintenance of the social order and attainment of public welfare by providing for the goal of earthquake disaster prevention countermeasures and establishment of a five-year earthquake disaster prevention plan.[236] It mandated the local government to strive to establish the goal of implementation of earthquake disaster prevention countermeasures by clarifying the anticipated earthquake disaster in their local disaster prevention plans.[237] It authorized the governor to establish the five-year plan on facilities to be upgraded for earthquake disaster prevention in areas where there is a possibility of serious earthquake disaster.[238] The facilities to be upgraded include evacuation place, evacuation routes, firefighter facilities, roads necessary for emergency transportation, hospitals, public schools, hub facilities for emergency countermeasures, emergency wireless communication network, storage for emergency water, and storage for emergency food and goods.[239] There is a special central government support for the activities included in the five-year plan.[240] The Act also mandated the central government to strive to provide financial support for intensification of earthquake disaster prevention measures.[241]

Moreover, it specifically mandated the seismic diagnosis for public school facilities that do not satisfy the standards of the Construction Standard Act[242] and also mandated the central government and local government to provide financial support for private schools for seismic upgrade.[243] It also attempts to

234 Some 260 municipalities are designated as an "earthquake disaster countermeasures reinforcement area" in anticipation of the Tokai Earthquake. All municipalities in Shizuoka Prefectures are included, as are many municipalities along the Pacific Coastline, including those in Aichi and Kanagawa Prefectures. Central Disaster Prevention Council, Jishin bousai taisaku kyouka chiiki no shitei ni tsuite [On Designation of Areas Where Intensified Measures Are Needed to Prevent Earthquake Disaster] (Cabinet Office) www.bousai.go.jp/kaigirep/chuobou/4/pdf/20020423siryou-1-1.pdf accessed 25 December 2017. No municipalities on the Sanriku Coast were included.

235 Earthquake Disaster Prevention Countermeasures Special Measure Act (n 85).

236 Ibid art 1.

237 Ibid art 1–2.

238 Ibid art 2.

239 Ibid art 3.

240 Ibid art 4.

241 Ibid art 6.

242 Ibid art 6–2.

243 Ibid art 6–3.

facilitate earthquake research by establishing the earthquake research facilitation headquarters[244] and mandating the central government to strive to promote the science and technology on earthquake research.[245] It further mandated the prefectures to strive to circulate documents describing the expected tremor of the earthquake, the areas to be submerged under water by the tsunami, and the degree of earthquake damage to local residents.[246]

***

The Japanese government has gone to great lengths to prepare for natural disasters. However, there is no statute granting broad and comprehensive powers to the central government, even during times of emergency. The prime minister does not have the authority to declare an "emergency" and order mandatory evacuation or otherwise exercise legal orders directly against citizens, nor is the prime minister authorized to suspend or ignore statutes, even in times of emergency. He or she is allowed to exercise only those powers granted to them by statute. And as the next chapter vividly illustrates, these restrictions raised various serious difficulties in the aftermath of the Tohoku Earthquake.

Moreover, the earthquake preparation and prediction systems were created with a focus on the possibility of a future Tokai Earthquake in mind. No similar efforts were ever undertaken with respect to preparation for another massive earthquake in the Sanriku region or other places. On 12 July 1993, a powerful earthquake struck the western part of Hokkaido with a magnitude of 7.8 on the Richter scale.[247] The Okushiri Island west of Hokkaido suffered devastating loss and damage, with 201 persons dead and 28 persons missing (Okushiri Island Earthquake or off the Southwestern Coast of Hokkaido Earthquake).[248] The Okushiri Island was located quite close to the epicenter and a huge tsunami hit the island within minutes before local residents could evacuate to higher ground, even before the tsunami warning. In such circumstances, it may be difficult to avoid such massive damage.[249] But there was no earthquake measurement device on the island and in retrospect some precursors to the earthquake were ignored. This earthquake showed the limits of earthquake preparation in areas other than the Tokai region.

244 Ibid art 7.

245 Ibid art 13.

246 Ibid art 14.

247 Hokkaido, Hokkaido nansei oki jishin no gaiyo [Summary of the off the Southwestern Coast of Hokkaido Earthquake] (Hokkaido) www.pref.hokkaido.lg.jp/sm/ktk/nanseiokikiroku/05nansEiokikiroku_1syou.pdf accessed 25 December 2017.

248 Ibid 16.

249 After this earthquake, the JMA came to issue the initial tsunami warning within three minutes in order to notify the local residents about the risk of tsunami as soon as possible. Japan Meteorological Agency, Press release: Kinkyu jishin sokuhō no gijutsu wo katsuyoushita tsunami keihō/chuihō no jinsokuka nitsuite [On Speeding up the Tsunami Warning Using the Technology of Early Emergency Earthquake Report] (JMA 7 September 2006) www.jma.go.jp/jma/press/0609/07b/20060907EEW.pdf accessed 25 December 2017.

Furthermore, the overall emphasis of disaster prevention is placed on the prediction of a disaster and not on the reduction of damages. And the Japanese government has placed emphasis on improving the structural resilience against earthquakes.[250] Also, no preparation was given to planning on what should be done after a serious disaster or what kind of reconstruction activities need to be implemented. As the next chapter graphically demonstrates, the absence of preparation for the aftermath of a natural disaster has proven to create grave challenges in the case of the Tohoku Earthquake.

250 Ranghieri & Ishiwatari (n 51) 25.

2 Tohoku Earthquake, tsunami, and aftermath

The Tohoku Earthquake and the subsequent tsunami inflicted tremendous loss and damage. The government engaged in rescue and assistance operations for all victims. Various legal questions have been raised in the aftermath of the earthquake. They include questions on how to dispose of the remains of such a huge number of disaster victims, how to dispose of post-disaster debris, and how to dispose of automobiles and home electronic devices damaged by the tsunami. The aftermath of the earthquake and tsunami have also raised various questions relating to how assistance should be provided and what types of exceptional treatments can and should be extended to disaster victims. This chapter examines governmental response to these legal questions. It also examines why such devastating loss and damage had to happen and what was wrong with the preparation for the powerful earthquake and tsunami in Japan. This examination will show the serious failures of law in the preparation for and in response to the disaster and the deep-rooted failures of politics behind these failures of law.

2.1 The Tohoku Earthquake and tsunami

2.1.1 The Tohoku Earthquake

At 2:46 pm on 11 March 2011, an extraordinarily powerful earthquake rocked the Tohoku Region. The epicenter was 130 km off the Sanriku Coast, 24 km below the ocean's surface.[1] Its strength was unprecedented. The Japan Meteorological Agency (JMA) initially reported the magnitude of the earthquake at 8.4 on the Richter scale but then upgraded it to 8.8 and, ultimately, to 9.0.[2] Western research

1 Japan Meteorological Agency, Heisei23nen (2011nen) Tohoku chihō taiheiyōoki jishin [The 2011 off the Pacific Coast of Tohoku Earthquake] (JMA) www.data.jma.go.jp/svd/eqev/data/2011_03_11_tohoku/ accessed 12 January 2018.

2 Ibid. Reconstruction Agency, Hukkou no torikumi to kanren shoseido [Reconstruction Measures and Related Systems] (Reconstruction Agency 6 November 2017) www.reconstruction.go.jp/topics/main-cat1/sub-cat1-1/20171106_torikumitoshoseido.pdf accessed 12 January 2018, 2; Japan Meteorological Agency, Heisei 23nen (2011nen) Tohoku chihō taiheiyōoki jishin nitsuite [The 2011 off the Pacific Coast of Tohoku Earthquake] (JMA 13 March 2011) www.jma.go.jp/jma/press/1103/13b/201103131255.html accessed 17 January 2018.

institutions now believe that the earthquake's magnitude was 9.1.[3] Many buildings were destroyed or seriously damaged. The earthquake was very powerful and was felt in many parts of Japan, even at great distances from the epicenter. Earthquake-triggered deaths even incurred in distant Tokyo and Kanagawa as well.[4]

Despite its sheer power, the loss and damage brought by this earthquake was less serious than that suffered in the Hanshin Awaji Earthquake of 1995. Once again, the Tohoku Earthquake proved that construction standards are sufficient to withstand even the most powerful earthquakes. Nonetheless, few anticipated the unprecedented loss and damage that would be brought by the ensuing tsunami.

2.1.2 Tsunami

In the wake of the earthquake, a tsunami warning was issued immediately by the JMA. An evacuation recommendation and then an evacuation instruction was issued by the municipal governments. Warning and evacuation systems have been proven to save the lives of hundreds of thousands. Without them, an even greater number of people would have been swept away in the tsunami following the earthquake. However, in the case of the Tohoku Earthquake, the earthquake occurred very close to the coastline and was extraordinarily powerful. Given its proximity to the coast, it did not take long for the tsunami to hit the coast. The first wave was not as strong as the second and subsequent waves, which battered the coastline between 30 minutes to one hour after the earthquake, and were so powerful that many people, houses, buildings, automobiles, and ships were simply swept away.[5] In some areas, the tsunami reached heights of more than 17 meters above sea level, the same height as the rooftops of three-storied buildings and waves reached heights of more than 40 meters in the

3 USGS, M9.1—near the east coast of Honshu, Japan, USGS https://earthquake.usgs.gov/earthquakes/eventpage/official20110311054624120_30#executive accessed 12 January 2018.

4 Seven people died in Tokyo and four people died in Kanagawa Prefecture. However, all commuter trains in Tokyo halted operations making it impossible for workers to return home. All major streets in Tokyo were filled with people attempting to return home on foot. Some spent several hours on foot before reaching home. All roads were filled with cars attempting to return home, bringing traffic to a stand-still for an extended period of time. Many gave up hope of returning home and spent the night in the shelters or at their companies' facilities because hotel rooms had quickly filled up. This experience indicated vulnerabilities associated with urban life and the need to urge downtown companies to discourage their employees from returning home and to stock emergency supplies for their employees, such as blankets, emergency water, and emergency food. See Chapter 6 nn 87–89.

5 Tsunami higher than 8.6m arrived at Ishinomaki, Miyagi Prefecture, at 15:26 pm and tsunami higher than 9.3m arrived at Souma, Fukushima Prefecture, at 15:51 pm. Japan Meteorological Agency, Jishin/tsunami gaiyo [Summary of the Earthquake and Tsunami] (JMA) www.jma.go.jp/jma/kishou/books/saigaiji/saigaiji_201101/saigaiji_201101_01.pdf accessed 20 January 2018, 10. The tsunami measurement devices were not able to measure the exact height of such high tsunami.

mountains, setting a new record.[6] These powerful waves breached the mighty tsunami barriers and reached six kilometers inland in some places.

As of 1 September 2017, 15,984 persons had been found dead with an additional 2,577 persons still missing.[7] The total number of casualties was, thus, 18,561. According to one survey, more than 90% of those killed in the disaster were drowned, and the remains contained bruises, scars, and fractured bones—which is consistent with being washed away among debris.[8] This is a clear indication that victims of tsunami significantly outnumber victims of the earthquake itself.[9]

2.2 Rescue

The earthquake was so powerful it could be felt in Tokyo as well. Prime Minister Naoto Kan and other government officials must have realized how powerful the earthquake was and how devastating the damage was going to be. The central government followed the statutory countermeasures to respond to the earthquake.

2.2.1 Establishment of the headquarters

When the earthquake struck, the Diet was in session and Kan was in attendance at a Diet hearing. He returned to the Cabinet House and immediately established a Cabinet Response Room within the Cabinet Crisis Management Center at 2:50 pm and issued orders for damage assessment, along with instructions to ensure the safety of residents and their prompt evacuation.[10] At 3:14 pm, less than 25 minutes after the earthquake and even before the devastation by

6 Tohoku chihō taiheiyōoki jishin tsunami goudou chousa group [The off the Pacific Coast of Tohoku Earthquake Tsunami Research Group] (the 2011 off the Pacific Coast of Tohoku Earthquake Tsunami Information) www.coastal.jp/ttjt/ accessed 12 January 2018. JMA estimates based on the traces that the tsunami that struck Ohunato, Iwate Prefecture, was 16.7m high. Japan Meteorological Agency, Heisei23nen3gatsu jishin/Kazan geppou [Monthly Report on Earthquake and Volcano, March 2011] (JMA) www.data.jma.go.jp/svd/eqev/data/gaikyo/monthly/201103/monthly201103.pdf accessed 20 January 2018, 122. Some researchers estimate that some places were hit by much higher tsunami. University of Tokyo, Earthquake Research Institute, Tsunami chousa kekka [Result of Tsunami Research] (University of Tokyo) www.eri.u-tokyo.ac.jp/PREV_HP/outreach/eqvolc/201103_tohoku/tsunami/#miyakotaro accessed 20 January 2018.

7 Reconstruction Agency (n 2) 2. In addition to this, an additional 3,591 persons died from earthquake related causes. Ibid. The grand total number of casualties thus reached 22,152. Ibid. Chapter 4 n 1.

8 Cabinet Office, Heisei23nenban bousai hakusho [2011 Disaster Prevention Whitepaper] (Cabinet Office) www.bousai.go.jp/kaigirep/hakusho/h23/bousai2011/html/honbun/1b_1h_1s_2.htm accessed 12 January 2018.

9 In addition, 121,776 houses were totally destroyed and 280,326 houses were half destroyed. Reconstruction Agency (n 2) 2. 744,269 houses suffered partial damage. Ibid.

10 Emergency Disaster Response Headquarters, Heisei 23 (2011) nen Tohoku chihō taiheiyōoki jishin (Higashinihon daishinsai) ni tsuite [On the 2011 off the Pacific Coast of Tohoku Earthquake (Great East Japan Earthquake Disaster)] (kantei 25 September 2012) www.kantei.go.jp/saigai/pdf/201209251700jisin.pdf accessed 12 January 2018, 8.

the tsunami, Kan established the Emergency Disaster Response Headquarters, headed by himself as prime minister.[11] This was the first time that an Emergency Disaster Response Headquarters had ever been established based on the Basic Act on Disaster Countermeasures in Japan.

Apparently, the prime minister realized the possibility of extraordinary disaster in the wake of this earthquake even before the tsunami had struck. But he did not anticipate that such a massive disaster would be followed by such a powerful tsunami. Much of the public watched on television the terrifying scenes showing the tsunami reaching deep inland and sweeping away houses, ships, automobiles, together with residents. When the sun set and it became impossible to see, the people saw many fires caused by the earthquake and tsunami burning down the remaining buildings. Many residents rushed to the shelters or to higher ground and escaped tragedy, but many others fell victim to this disaster. Many were left behind in the buildings surrounded by the water, and many others were left trapped and wounded in collapsed buildings.

2.2.2 Deployment of the Self Defense Forces

Upon receiving requests from the governors of Iwate, Miyagi, and Fukushima prefectures, Kan ordered the deployment of the Self Defense Forces (SDF). SDF officers arrived in the Tohoku Region in the early morning of 12 March and started rescue and assistance.

Initially 20,000 SDF officers were deployed but this increased to 50,000[12] and then to 100,000.[13] They were ordered to engage in an emergency rescue mission as per article 83 of the Self Defense Forces Act.[14] SDF officers searched for survivors among demolished homes, debris, and rubble, transporting any lucky enough to be found to shelters or to hospitals.

Technically, in order to search for survivors, these officers necessarily had to enter private property. Theoretically, questions could have been raised over their non-consensual entry into private property. When SDF officers are deployed for emergency rescue missions, however, they can exercise the same powers as police officers, if none are present.[15] They can thus issue a warning to the person present or manager of the property if there are dangers to human life or body or to property because of the natural disaster, stop them or order evacuation to prevent danger if it is urgent, order them to take necessary measures to prevent danger, or to take such measures by him/herself[16] and also enter into privately

11 Ibid.

12 Message from Prime Minister Naoto Kan (kantei 12 March 2011) www.kantei.go.jp/jp/kan/statement/201103/12message.html accessed 12 January 2018.

13 Message from Prime Minister Naoto Kan (kantei 13 March 2011) www.kantei.go.jp/jp/kan/statement/201103/13message.html accessed 12 January 2018. This means that almost half of active SDF officers were mobilized.

14 Jieitaihō [Self Defense Forces Act], Law no 165 of 1954, art 83.

15 Ibid art 94.

16 Keisatsukan shokumu shikkohō [Police Officer Job Execution Act], Law no 136 of 1968, art 4.

owned property, buildings, ships, and cars in the course of rescue operations.[17] Moreover, SDF officers acting in teams deployed for emergency rescue missions are authorized to undertake emergency measures akin to those permitted for municipal heads under the Basic Act on Disaster Countermeasures.[18] SDF officers are thus authorized to cordon off disaster areas, prohibit entry, compel dispersal,[19] make use of private property or buildings,[20] remove barriers to rescue operations,[21] and order local residents to engage in rescue missions[22] if municipal heads or authorized persons are not present. When police officers are not present and automobiles or other physical barriers are blocking the passage of emergency SDF vehicles, SDF officers can also order owners or operators to remove them[23] and can even remove them unilaterally if such orders are refused or if the owners or operators are unavailable to receive such orders.[24] Given these emergency powers, there was no question as to the legality of SDF rescue activities following this disaster.[25]

2.2.3 Provision of shelter, food, and medical help

Those fortunate enough to survive the disaster suffered tremendous hardship in the aftermath. Most lost family and friends in addition to their homes. They bore eyewitness to the tsunami sweeping away all that they held dear. Municipal governments set up emergency shelters, mostly in civic halls and public schools. At one time, more than 450,000 residents had to be evacuated. Most evacuees were forced to live in these emergency shelters for days, weeks, or even months in some cases.[26]

All lifeline infrastructures had been destroyed. Electricity, LP gas, and even tap water were all offline.[27] Evacuees spent several nights in darkness without light or heat except in rare cases where kerosene heaters were undamaged

17 Ibid art 6.
18 Self Defense Forces Act (n 14) art 94–3(1).
19 Saigai taisaku kihonhō [Basic Act on Disaster Countermeasures], Law no 223 of 1961, art 63(3).
20 Ibid art 64(1), applied by art 64(8).
21 Ibid art 64(2), applied by art 64(8). The removed items must be stored. Ibid art 64(1), applied by art 64(8). It is the responsibility of the head of the team of SDF officers to store these items. Ibid art 64(9).
22 Ibid art 65(1), applied by art 65(3).
23 Ibid art 76–3(1), applied by art 76–3(3).
24 Ibid art 76–3(2), applied by art 76–3(3). When SDF officers take such measures, they must notify the local police chief. Ibid art 76–3(6).
25 There were some confusion, however, among the SDF officers, police officers, and firefighters as to the rescue operation. See n 158.
26 Many non-evacuees also suffered extreme hardship because of the earthquake. *See* Elmer Luke & David Karashima (eds), *March Was Made of Yarn: Reflections on the Japanese Earthquake, Tsunami, and Nuclear Meltdown* (Vintage Books 2012); Lucy Birmingham & David McNeill, *Strong in the Rain: Surviving Japan's Earthquake, Tsunami, and Fukushima Nuclear Disaster* (Palgrave 2012); John F. Morris, "Recovery in Tohoku," in *Natural Disaster and Nuclear Crisis in Japan: Response and Recovery after Japan's 3/11* (Jeff Kingston, ed. Routledge 2012) 33.
27 Cabinet Office, Infratō no higai/hukkyu joukyo [Damage and Recovery] (Cabinet Office 14 July 2011) www.cao.go.jp/shien/2-shien/1-infra.html accessed 12 January 2018.

and kerosene was available. Telephone lines had been destroyed and cellular phone reception was unavailable.[28] Evacuees had little access to information on the extent of damage and whether help was on the way. Similarly, infrastructure damage also restricted the flow of information from seriously affected areas to the rest of the country. Generally, the public knew little of the extent of the damage during the night. They realized the devastation only the next morning through live television coverage.

With public transportation systems and roads destroyed,[29] many evacuees were left isolated. It took days before food and emergency supplies were delivered to them. In many cases, even when emergency supplies were delivered to municipal headquarters, they could not be delivered to individual shelters because of critical gasoline shortages or the absence of navigable roadways.[30] Nonetheless, SDF officers attempted to transport necessary goods together with American military forces stationed in Japan under Operation Tomodachi (friendship).[31] Many foreign countries sent emergency rescue teams to Japan. Doctors and nurses were sent into affected areas to treat survivors. Some foreign doctors were also sent in.

2.2.4 Red tape

However, some media outlets pointed out how Japanese red tape was hindering immediate and effective help from foreign rescue teams. For instance, *Time* reported as follows:

> One major bottleneck has been Japan's fondness for red tape. "In special times, you have to do things in a special way," says Kensuke Kobayashi, an IBM employee in Tokyo who has tried to organize relief efforts to Tohoku from the Japanese capital. "But in Japan, there is a legal wall that stops everything." Japanese shipping company NYK offered to provide a container ship for helicopters to land on when ferrying in relief supplies to coastal areas. But the government rejected the offer because the NYK shipmates lacked the proper licenses to help with such work. After some wrangling, volunteer foreign doctors were told that because they didn't have Japanese medical licenses, they could conduct only the "minimum necessary medical procedures" in the disaster zone.
>
> Some medicine donations from overseas haven't reached the many elderly suffering in the earthquake's aftermath because Japanese regulatory agencies

28 Ibid.

29 Ibid.

30 Cabinet Office, Higashinihon daishinsai niokeru saigai oukyu taisaku no omona kadai [Major Tasks for the Emergency Responses during the Great East Japan Earthquake Disaster] (Cabinet Office July 2012) www.bousai.go.jp/jishin/syuto/taisaku_wg/5/pdf/3.pdf accessed 12 January 2018.

31 For the significance and implications of this operation, see Richard J. Samuels, "3.11," in *Disaster and Change in Japan* (Cornell 2013) 19–23: Gerald L. Curtis, "Tohoku Diary: Reportage on the Tohoku Disaster," in Kingston (n 26) 15, 17–18; Chris Ames & Yuiko Koguchi-Ames, Friends in Need: "'Operation Tomodachi' and the Politics of US Military Disaster Relief in Japan," in *Kingston* (n 26) 207.

> have not yet given the drugs approval. Local logistics companies have complained—off the record, for fear of angering the bureaucrats whom they depend on for future licensing—of days-long waits for permission from the central government to deliver donated goods. Only when their trucks get the magic pass can they start moving toward Tohoku. Until then, the boxes of relief goods, some of which were donated just hours after the earthquake and tsunami hit, sit in Tokyo warehouses.[32]

There are reasons to suggest the concerns raised in this article are warranted.

According to the Physicians Act,[33] persons without a proper medical license cannot provide medical services to patients. Technically, therefore, foreign doctors without Japanese medical licenses could not provide medical services in Japan. Anyone violating this prohibition could be punished.[34] There is no statutory exception for times of emergency. This issue was raised in the aftermath of the Hanshin Awaji Earthquake and the Ministry of Health, Labor and Welfare (MHLW) issued notification to municipal governments informing that foreign medical services would be acceptable as part of emergency measures, even without a specific statutory exception. In the aftermath of the Tohoku Earthquake, the MHLW similarly issued a notification permitting acceptance of foreign medical services offered as an emergency measure.[35] However, this notification came several days after the earthquake. Bureaucratic lethargy in the MHLW likely frustrated immediate rescue efforts that might have been undertaken by foreign rescue teams and doctors in the critical first days.[36]

Moreover, under the Pharmaceutical Affairs Act, all drugs must be approved by the MHLW.[37] There is no ban on importing unapproved drugs for personal use, but distribution of unapproved drugs may violate the statute.[38] When foreign rescue teams brought pharmaceuticals not approved by the Japanese government

32 Hannah Beech, "Is Japan's Bureaucracy Strangling Humanitarian Aid?" (*Time* 22 March 2011) www.time.com/time/world/article/0,8599,2060773,00.html accessed 12 January 2018.

33 Ishihō [Physicians Act], Law no 201 of 1948, art 2 & art 17.

34 Ibid art 31(1)(i).

35 Ministry of Health, Labor and Welfare, Gaikoku no ishimenkyo wo yusurumono no iryoukoui no toriatsukai ni tsuite [On Treatment of Medical Service by Foreign Doctors] (MHLW 14 March 2011) www.mhlw.go.jp/stf/houdou/2r98520000015nly-img/2r985200000166pg.pdf accessed 12 January 2018.

36 A team of doctors was sent from Israel and its members were permitted to offer medical services together with Japanese doctors. It was reported that this was the first official exceptional treatment by a team of foreign doctors that had been sent by a foreign government. "Israel ga iryou butai haken: Ggaikoku kara hatsu, Minamisanriku de chiryo [Israel Sends a Team of Doctors: First from Foreign Country and Start Treatment in Minamisanriku]" (*Asahi Shimbun* 26 March 2011) www.asahi.com/special/10005/TKY201103260448.html accessed 12 January 2018.

37 Yakujihō [Pharmaceutical Affairs Act], Law no 145 of 1960, art 56. The title of the Act was thereafter renamed as Iryohin, iyakuhintō no hinshitsu, yukosei oyobi anzensei no kakuhotō ni kansuru hōritsu [Act on Securing the Quality, Efficacy and Safety of Drugs and Medical Equipment], Law no 145 of 1960, in 2014.

38 Ibid art 84(xix).

or such drugs were sent from overseas, government officials were reticent about officially permitting use of these medications.[39]

Even without a specific exception permitting medical attention administered by those who have medical knowledge and skills but nonetheless lack a Japanese medical license, allowing such services in a time of emergency and for the purposes of saving lives is more than justified. Permitting the use of unapproved drugs in a time of emergency would also be justified if these drugs were widely approved throughout the world and proven to be safe and effective. However, it might be preferable to insert statutory exceptions for emergency situations that permit foreign doctors to provide medical services upon approval or that allow the use of unapproved drugs during such times.[40]

The same kinds of emergency exceptions must be introduced into all sorts of regulation in order to facilitate immediate rescue and assistance. Unfortunately, however, as we already saw, there is no constitutional or statutory grant of power to the prime minister or to the government to make sweeping exceptions to all sorts of regulation during times of massive natural disaster. As a result, in this crisis, each Ministry was forced to examine the possibility for introducing exceptions individually and then notifying their local office or local governments separately.[41] This is a critical defect of the Japanese legal system.

39 The MHLW issued several memos allowing provision of prescription drugs right after the Tohoku Earthquake without prescription, but it never issued a memo allowing foreign doctors to provide unapproved drugs to patients. Ministry of Health, Labor and Welfare, Saigai hasseiji ni kouseiroushou ga hasshutsushita iyakuhintō no toriatsukai nikakawaru jimurenraku [Memos Issued by the MHLW during the Time of Disaster] (MHLW) www.mhlw.go.jp/bunya/iyakuhin/yakubuturanyou/dl/iryo_tekisei_guide2017_24.pdf accessed 12 January 2018. However, the MHLW issued a request to the customs office urging allowance of foreign emergency crews bringing unapproved medical drugs with them. Ministry of Health, Labor and Welfare, Kinkyu enjobutai ga keikousuru iyakuhintō no tsūkan no saino toriatsukai ni tsuite [On Treatment of Medical Supplies during Customs Proceedings Brought in by Emergency Rescue Teams] (MHLW 14 March 2011) www.mhlw.go.jp/stf/houdou/2r98520000014tr1-img/2r98520000015fjx.pdf accessed 12 January 2018.

40 One volunteer was later arrested for providing medical services without a medical license. He did not have any requisite knowledge or skills for treating patients but presented a fake certificate and pretended to be a doctor. "Hisaichide katsudo, jishou ishi no 42sai otoko taiho, iryoukoui no utagai [A 42 Years-old Man Was Arrested for Providing Medical Service Without License]" (*Nihonkeizai Shimbun* 19 August 2011) www.nikkei.com/article/DGXNASFK19003_Z10C11A8000000/ accessed 12 January 2018. This episode shows the need for some kind of regulation even during a time of emergency.

41 Various measures to suspend regulation and make exceptions to regulation have been adopted by many agencies for the victims of disaster. Cabinet Office, Higashinihon daishinsai ni kanrenshita kakuhushou no kiseikanwatō no joukyou [Current Situation of Deregulation in Response to the Great East Japan Earthquake Disaster] (Cabinet Office 18 April 2011) www.cao.go.jp/sasshin/kiseiseido/publication/230419/item230419.pdf accessed 12 January 2018. See n 114. There was also a problem deriving from the difficulty of matching the local needs and offers. See Hiroyuki Banzai, "Higashinihon daishinsai niokeru kaigai shien ukeire no mondaiten [Problems in Accepting the International Support during the Great East Japan Earthquake Disaster]" (2011) 4 *Waseda Shakai Anzen Seisaku Kenkyu Kiyo* 67; Yutaka Katayama, "Higashinihon daishinsai no kokusai kynkyu shien ukeire to gaimushou [International Emergency Assistance during the Great East Japan Earthquake and the Ministry of Foreign Affairs]" (2013) *Journal of International Cooperation Studies* 45.

2.3 Aftermath of the earthquake and tsunami

After rescue missions had been completed, government officials collected the remains of the deceased.[42] A vast number of corpses remained inside the temporary morgue for surviving family members to identify the dead. However, questions were then raised as to how to bury or cremate the bodies of the departed.

Moreover, the tsunami left huge amounts of debris including the debris of destroyed houses on the property of other landowners. Furthermore, many personal properties of the residents had been swept away and ended up on the private property of others. The tsunami also caused huge numbers of automobiles to be damaged and left behind. Similarly, a vast quantity of home electrical devices were damaged. Questions were raised as to how the government could dispose of all of this.

In its attempt to respond to these legal questions, the Japanese government had to resolve them as quickly as possible and without any preparation. How had the Japanese government responded to them?

2.3.1 No riots and no serious public disturbance

It was indeed amazing that all the surviving victims of this massive earthquake and tsunami—who were of course shocked and terrified—remained calm and relatively patient. Most of the evacuees remained in the emergency shelters and waited for food, water, and other assistance. During the initial days, damage to infrastructure, critical shortages of gas, and lack of coordination had prevented the effective and smooth distribution of help to all residents who needed it. Isolated from the rest of the country, though, they must have felt helpless and desperate, but there was no rioting or any serious disturbance of the peace.[43]

As a result of the peace and calm that was maintained, there was no need to introduce a curfew or any other restrictions on civil rights in the aftermath of the Tohoku Earthquake. If there had been such riots or disturbances of the peace in the disaster-stricken areas, the Japanese government would have faced an extremely difficult question because there is no provision in the Basic Act on Disaster Countermeasures or any other statutes such as the Police Act that authorizes the prime minister or the central government to introduce any

42 SDF officers were assigned to collect the remains of the deceased. Although it is doubtful that the collection of civilian corpses is included in the job descriptions of SDF officers, they were likely the only personnel available for the job. "Maisou, Jieitai danomi: Saigaihaken dehatsu, tsujoushien e eikyo kenen [No One Was There to Ask for Burial but for the Self Defense Forces : First Time during the Disaster Rescue Mission and Some Concerns on the Possible Impacts on Regular Rescue Activities]" (*Asahi Shimbun* 4 April 2011) www.asahi.com/special/10005/TKY201104030233.html accessed 12 January 2018.

43 "Japan Disaster: We Are All Terrified: There Is No Road Map and We Have No Idea Where We Go from Here' (*London Evening Standard* 14 March 2011) www.standard.co.uk/news/japan-disaster-we-are-all-terrified-there-is-no-road-map-and-we-have-no-idea-where-we-go-from-here-6577261.html accessed 12 January 2018.

restriction on civil rights in times of emergency. The Japanese government did not have to face this issue this time.[44]

2.3.2 Burial of the deceased

More than 15,000 people were killed as a direct result of the earthquake and tsunami. The huge number of corpses were collected and transferred to the temporary morgue for identification. Some were identified by surviving family members or by friends but many remained unidentified. It was mandatory that bodies identified by family members be cremated. However, many cremation facilities were destroyed and thus surviving families faced extreme difficulty finding such facilities that remained operational. Bodies that had yet to be identified piled up in temporary morgues. After a week the bodies began to decompose. There was an urgent necessity to bury them in the ground.

According to the Act concerning Graveyard and Burial, burial or cremation requires a permit from a municipal government head.[45] Burial outside of a graveyard is prohibited as is cremation outside of a proper cremation facility.[46] Municipal government heads grant permits for such activities after receiving notification of death[47] and it is these officials that must issue permits for burial or cremation.[48] When there is no next of kin or other suitable party available to request such permission, the municipal government takes responsibility for burial or cremation.[49]

Burial was common in Japan at one time but cremation has gradually become the norm. Nowadays, although burial is technically legal, owing to a shortage of graveyards it is seldom permitted in practice.[50] One result of the tsunami disaster, however, was that many cremation facilities were destroyed and there were too many dead bodies to cremate. Furthermore, the municipal government apparatus

44 After the Kanto Earthquake, mass panic set in. Disaster victims had no access to radio communication and became reliant on rumors as the only available source of information. Fearing the truth of rumors that Korean immigrants were responsible for a number of post-disaster murders, earthquake survivors lashed out, killing thousands of resident Koreans. Soo-Kyung Yi, "Kantou daishinsai chokugo no chousenjin gyakusatsu to nikkan houdo [A Study of Reporting in Korea and Japan on The Great Kanto Earthquake and the Massacre of Koreans]" (2004) 10 *Bulletin of the Faculty of International Studies, Yamaguchi Prefectural University* 1. In light of this experience, the Japanese government may have to consider the possibility of some kind of restriction on civil rights and civil liberties during emergencies, such as curfew.

45 Bochi, maisoutō ni kansuru hōritsu [Act concerning Graveyard and Burial], Law no 48 of 1948, art 5(1).

46 Ibid art 4.

47 Ibid art 5(2).

48 Ibid art 8.

49 Ibid art 9(1).

50 Some local governments authorized governors to designate areas where burial was to be prohibited by local ordinance. For instance, the Tokyo Metropolitan Government authorized the governor to designate areas where burial was prohibited. Bochitō no kōzō secchi kanri no kijuntō ni kansuru jourei [Ordinance concerning Standards for Structure, Establishment and Management of the Graveyard], Tokyo Metropolitan Government Ordinance no 125 of 1984, art 14. However, many municipalities banned such practices via internal guidelines.

had been virtually obliterated in many areas and thus local governments were not functioning properly. They were unable to check with the family registry to confirm the death of the victims to issue a permit for burial or cremation.[51] Thus, the MHLW issued a notification to municipal governments allowing burial and cremation with special permission. This special permission could be issued without official corroboration with family registry records and permitted burial or cremation without permission based on a medical death certificate.[52] This special exception was not based on statute, though this same exception was granted after the Hanshin Awaji Earthquake. Moreover, although many municipalities practically prohibited burial, some municipalities were forced to allow burial as an exception or by changing their policies.[53]

These exceptional measures were practically unavoidable and entirely reasonable.[54] Nevertheless, exceptional treatment granted internally based on administrative discretion raises questions as to its appropriateness particularly because the administrative agency was exercising discretion without any statutory authority. Exceptions to permitting requirements for burial and cremation along with procedures for emergency burial should have been provided for by statute and/or local ordinance rather than being dependent on administrative discretion.[55]

2.3.3 Disposal of debris

After the earthquake and tsunami, local governments and residents faced another difficult task: disposing of the debris left behind by the earthquake and tsunami.

51 Japan has a family registration system. Every Japanese citizen upon birth needs to be registered on the family registry and the municipal government checks the family registry with the death certificate, removes the registration from the registry (adds the description of removal to the registry) and issues a permit for burial or cremation. Kosekihō [Family Registration Act], Law no 224 of 1947.

52 Ministry of Health, Labor and Welfare, Heisei 23 nen Tohoku chihō taiheiyōoki jishin no hassei wo uketa itai hozon, itai hansou, kasō taisei no kakuhotō ni tsuite [On Securing the Proper Preservation of Corpses, Transportation of Corpses, and Cremation after the 2011 Tohoku Region Earthquake off the Pacific Coast] (MHLW March 2011) www.mhlw.go.jp/stf/houdou/2r98520000014tr1-img/2r985200000156ji.pdf accessed 12 January 2018; Ministry of Health, Labor, and Welfare, Heisei 23 nen Tohoku chihō taiheiyōoki jishin no hassei wo uketa bochi, maisōtō nikansuru hōritsu ni motoduku maikasou kyoka no tokureisochi ni tsuite [On Special Measures with Respect to Burial and Cremation Permission under the Act concerning Graveyards and Burial after the 2011 off the Pacific Coast of Tohoku Earthquake] (HHLW 14 March 2011) www.mhlw.go.jp/stf/houdou/2r98520000014tr1-img/2r985200000156hy.pdf accessed 12 January 2018.

53 "Giseisha, shudan bochide dosoumo—Tohoku enganbu no shichoson [Burial of the Victims of the Disaster in Coastal Municipalities of Tohoku]" (*Wall Street Journal* 22 March 2011) http://jp.wsj.com/public/page/0_0_WJPP_7000-206460.html accessed 12 January 2018.

54 However, many people were simply disappointed because they could not cremate the bodies of their loved ones. Moreover, the number of caskets available was simply insufficient and many bodies had to be buried in body bags. Many residents later dug up the buried bodies and cremated them when it became possible. Akihiko Umehara, Mineyoshi Numada, & Kumiro Meguro, "Kouritsuteki katsu izokushinri nimo hairyoshita kyodaisaigaiji no itaishori gyoumu no process no teian [Analysis of Dead Body Processing during the 2011 Great East Japan Earthquake]" (2014) 66:4 *Seisan Kenkyu* 393.

55 Later this exception was explicitly inserted into the statute. Basic Act on Disaster Countermeasures (n 19) art 86–4; Chapter 6 n 45.

Many volunteers entered the affected areas to facilitate cleanup, but they needed clear guidelines about how to dispose of the debris.

In usual circumstances, homes and buildings destroyed by earthquakes remain the property of the owners. It is the owner's responsibility to dispose of debris and, if necessary, to remove destroyed homes and buildings if they are unsafe. It is the owner's responsibility to pay all costs necessary to dispose of the debris. However, debris disposal and damaged building removal are quite expensive and, after the Hanshin Awaji Earthquake, the central government decided to facilitate the removal and destruction of damaged property almost exclusively through the use of tax dollars. The central government explained the use of public funding for these purposes as an exceptional case. After the Tohoku Earthquake, however, the central government again decided to pay all costs incurred by municipal governments for removing destroyed houses and disposing of debris.[56]

Moreover, under the Act on Disposal and Clean-up of Waste, it is the responsibility of the municipal government to collect and dispose of "ordinary household waste" in contrast to "industrial waste."[57] Post-earthquake or tsunami debris may not technically be considered "waste," because it was generated by natural disaster. If it were waste, there was the question whether it was ordinary household waste or industrial waste. If it was ordinary household waste, then it is the responsibility of the municipal government to collect and dispose of it. However, since many municipal governments had suffered serious loss of or damage to waste burning facilities, not to mention many public employees, they were short-staffed and under-equipped. The central government thus decided to allow the prefectural governments to dispose of debris for the municipal governments. Ultimately, the central government felt it necessary to take over the job and decided to perform this task by itself.[58] Furthermore, the central government decided to dispose of all debris as "disaster waste" (*saigai haikibutsu*) regardless of whether it was household waste or industrial waste.[59] This was apparently a temporary solution applicable to debris produced by the Tohoku Earthquake and tsunami. The Diet needed to prepare for waste disposal caused by future massive natural disasters.[60]

2.3.4 *What should be done with debris left on private property?*

Moreover, there are legal questions about how to dispose of debris left on private property as well. The homes and buildings of many property owners had been swept

56 Higashinihon daishinsai niyori shoujita saigai haikibutsu no shori ni kansuru tokubetsu sochihō [Special Measures Act on Disposal of Disaster Waste Caused by the Great East Japan Earthquake Disaster], Law no 99 of 2011 (Disaster Waste Disposal Act), art 5.

57 Haikibutsuno shori oyobi seisou ni kansuru hōritsu [Act on Disposal and Clean-up of Waste], Law no 137 of 1970 (Waste Disposal Act), art 6–2(1).

58 Disaster Waste Disposal Act (n 56) art 4(1).

59 Ibid art 2. Ministry of Environment, Higashinihon daishinsai ni kakawaru saigai haikibutsu no shori shishin [Disposal Principles for Disaster Waste Caused by the Great East Japan Earthquake Disaster] (MOE 16 May 2011) www.env.go.jp/jishin/attach/haiki_masterplan.pdf accessed 12 January 2018.

60 Eventually this exception was later explicitly inserted into the statute. Basic Act on Disaster Countermeasures (n 19) art 86–5; Chapter 6 n. 46.

away and found on the property of others. The owners of these properties could not enter the property of others to retrieve their own displaced properties without the consent of the landowners, but in many cases they had difficulty even finding the whereabouts of their lost homes and/or the owners of the land.

On the other hand, the owners of the land upon which the property of others had surfaced now had to dispose of such debris. However, issues arose with respect to non-consensual removal of such debris: it was impossible to obtain such consent without knowing who the property belonged to. Even if the rightful owners of such property could be identified, they were most likely staying in an emergency shelter or had relocated, making discovery of their whereabouts almost impossible. Otherwise, landowners had the option of filing a suit asking the court to order the owner of the debris to secure its removal. However, such litigation can require a lot of time and money. Landowners had to make decisions about whether they could or even should dispose of such debris without going to the courts. Moreover, as for virtually any landowner, prompt removal was undoubtedly preferable. They thus had to dispose of the debris under risks that they might be sued by the real owners for destruction of property. Most debris was likely worthless so the landowner would not have had to pay any compensation for lost property anyway (indeed, the owners of the debris might have had an obligation to pay for its removal). However, there was a possibility that owners of debris would claim that such property had value as antiques or that, despite meager economic value, it had significant sentimental or personal value to them.

The central government with the Ministry of Environment (MOE) immediately established a study group to tackle the questions related to justifiable disposal of debris and issued a memorandum to municipal governments.[61] Basically, this memorandum allowed local government officials to enter private property and dispose of debris without requiring the consent of property owners, yet also obliged the municipal government to collect and store, if possible, valuables such as jewelry, or other items that might have value to residents such as photos, albums, or mortuary tablets. It permitted individual owners to remove debris in a similar fashion.

It would be preferable, of course, if valuables or personal items could be salvaged and kept for owners to collect them. Indeed no one should be allowed to steal the valuables of others even when they have landed on your property due to a tsunami. However, in an emergency situation of this nature, landowners should not be blamed for disposing of debris on their property, even if it belongs to another person. The exercise of rights is subject to restrictions for the sake of the public welfare[62] and no abuse of rights is permitted.[63] Therefore, even if debris belonging to another was disposed of without prior consent, courts should not

61 Ministry of Environment, Tohoku chihō taiheiyōoki jishin ni okeru sonkai kaokutō no tekkyotō ni kansuru shishin [Guidelines for Removal of Damaged Homes and Other Property after the off the Pacific Coast of Tohoku Earthquake] (MOE 26 March 2011) www.env.go.jp/jishin/sisin110326.pdf accessed 12 January 2018 (Removal Guideline).

62 Minpō [Code C.], art 1(1).

63 Ibid art 1(3).

hold the person disposing of the debris liable for damages. However, it might be more fitting and efficient to provide for these stipulations explicitly by statute.

2.3.5 Disposal of damaged automobiles, home electronics, and other items

The disposal of damaged automobiles presented somewhat different problems. The tsunami had swept away countless automobiles, thrusting many onto the property of others. In Japan, all automobiles must be registered.[64] It is therefore relatively easy to discover the identity of a vehicle owner, though tracking down such individuals is a more difficult task, especially in a time of emergency. Many vehicle owners had perished or gone missing and, even if they had survived, there was often no way of discerning their whereabouts in the fallout of the disaster.

In normal circumstances, there are established and mandatory procedures for disposing of automobiles for recycling. When an owner decides to dispose of an automobile, he or she must transfer said automobile to a registered disposal company, receive an official receipt for the transfer and apply for the disposal. Disposal costs are pre-paid by the automobile owner while disposal companies collect recyclables and sell them.[65] Upon disposal, the central government repays the tax paid by the owner at the time he or she renewed the vehicle's registration.

It was impossible to follow such procedures after the devastation wrought by the tsunami. However, there was no statutory provision permitting local government to dispose of automobiles damaged by the tsunami without following this procedure.[66] The guideline on disposal of damaged buildings and other properties published by the MOE thus instructed local governments to move such automobiles to temporary storage facilities, notify their owners and hand the automobiles over to their rightful owners, while allowing local governments to treat damaged automobiles as no longer in use.[67] The guidelines for disposal of damaged automobiles published by the MOE allowed municipal governments to dispose of damaged automobiles with the owners' consent.

64 Douro unsou sharyouhō [Road Transportation and Vehicle Act], Law no 185 of 1951, art 4.

65 Shiyōzumi jidousha no saishigenkatō ni kansuru hōritsu [Act on Resource Recycling of Automobiles No Longer in Use], Law no 87 of 2002.

66 These damaged automobiles might be considered "waste" as per the definition given in the Waste Disposal Act. Waste Disposal Act (n 57) art 2(1). If so, local governments could remove abandoned and damaged automobiles (ibid art 19–7 and art 19–8), if the registered owner ignored orders to remove such "waste" (ibid art 19–4, 19–5, 19–6). The Dourohō [Public Road Act], Law no 180 of 1952, also allows the governmental disposal of property left on public roads for lengthy periods (ibid art 44–2), and the Douro kōtsuhō [Road Traffic Act], Law no 105 of 1960, also allows for the removal and temporary storage, as well as sale and disposal of automobiles parked illegally (ibid art 51) or illegal property on public roads (ibid art 81). There were some doubts as to the local government's authority to dispose of automobiles left unattended. Some local governments enacted ordinances allowing local government to treat these unattended automobiles as abandoned and to dispose of such automobiles. In most jurisdictions in affected areas, however, there were no such local ordinances. There were thus questions as to whether local governments had the authority to dispose of these automobiles that had apparently been abandoned.

67 Removal Guidelines (n 61).

It also allowed municipal governments to publish notifications to owners urging that they come forward to claim their vehicles. If no one claimed ownership after a certain period following public notification, local governments could dispose of the automobiles as though they were no longer in use.[68]

Again, this procedure was not based on any statutory authorization. There were questions over whether local governments could constitutionally dispose of unclaimed automobiles because owners still had property rights over them and they had not been deprived of these property rights by a statute. As a result, local governments were somewhat reluctant to abide by this exceptional procedure. Some kind of statutory provision that allows municipal governments to dispose of abandoned automobiles if no one comes forward to claim them needs to be created by the legislature, even during times of emergency.

Indeed, even in September (roughly 6 months later), only 20% of the damaged automobiles had been handed over to disposal companies by municipal governments, despite estimates placing some 240,000 damaged automobiles in affected prefectures.[69] Local governments were not eager to dispose of damaged automobiles without owner consent. Eventually, however, the local governments managed to dispose of all damaged vehicles without legal challenges.

Disposal of home electronic devices presented a similar problem. According to the Specified Home Electric Devices Recycling Act, when disposing of home electric devices, consumers are obliged to turn them over to a person engaged in collection of such devices and to pay any necessary fees.[70] Therefore, consumers are not free to dispose of refrigerators, washers, dryers, air conditioners or television sets, but instead must hand them over to the retailers who sold them or to someone engaging in their collection for the purposes of returning them to their manufacturers. There were an immeasurable number of home electronic devices swept away or seriously damaged by the tsunami. Residents naturally wanted to dispose of them. The MOE thus issued a notification to municipal governments allowing them to dispose of home electronic devices as "disaster waste" together

68 Ministry of Environment, Tohoku chihō taiheiyōoki jishin ni yori hisaishita jidousha no shori ni tsuite [On Disposal of Automobiles Damaged by the off the Pacific Coast of Tohoku Earthquake] (MOE) www.env.go.jp/jishin/attach/jidosha_shori.pdf accessed 12 January 2018.

69 "Hisaisharyo, haishadekizu nozumi [Automobile Damaged by the Tsunami Simply Piling up]" (*Yomiuri Shimbun* 26 September 2011) www.yomiuri.co.jp/stream/?id=02003 accessed 12 January 2018. As of July 11, 2013, some 72,000 vehicles were transferred to the temporary storage site and 16,000 of them were transferred to the owners and 48,000 of them were transferred to the recycling operators. Ministry of Economy, Trade and Industry, Higashinihon daishinsai ni tomonatte shoujita hisai jidousha no shori jokyotō ni tsuite [On Disposal of Automobiles Damaged by the Great East Japan Earthquake Disaster] (METI 11 July 2013) www.meti.go.jp/committee/sankoushin/sangyougijutsu/haiki_recycle/car_wg/pdf/031_06_01.pdf accessed 12 January 2018. It took a while to dispose of all damaged automobiles. Ministry of Economy, Trade and Industry, Higashinihon daishinsai ni tomonatte shoujita hisaijidousha no shori jokyotō nitsuite [On Disposal of Automobiles Damaged by the Great East Japan Earthquake Disaster] (METI) www.meti.go.jp/committee/sankoushin/sangyougijutsu/haiki_recycle/car_wg/pdf/032_03_02.pdf accessed 12 January 2018 (reporting the end of all disposal).

70 Tokutei kateiyou kiki saishouhinkahō [Specified Home Electronic Devices Recycling Act], Law no 97 of 1998, art 6.

with other rubble.[71] However, once again, there was no statutory authority for this measure.

Fish stored in the refrigerators of the fishermen's association or fish processing companies raised another serious problem. Many storage facilities lost power because of the tsunami and all refrigerated fish began decomposing. Under normal circumstances, decomposed fish must be disposed of as industrial waste at the expense of the owner. The total volume of decomposed fish in Miyagi Prefecture alone, however, amounted to 60k ton and there were no temporary storage facilities to store them in before disposal. The MOE thus permitted the prefecture to allow the dumping of rotting fish into the sea as an exception[72] to the Act against Ocean Pollution and on Prevention of Ocean Disasters.[73] Whether this exception was indeed legal remains uncertain.

In all cases discussed above, there were no statutory provisions contemplating the exceptions made, with officials making ad hoc exceptions based on discretion. Needless to say, exceptions to statutory obligation undertaken via administrative discretion and absent explicit authorization are legally troubling. Such tinkering is perhaps even more troubling than statutory authorization of special powers in times of emergency. The Diet should have enacted emergency legislation authorizing government to make such exceptions during emergencies.

2.4 Recovering from the disaster

The Great East Japan Earthquake Disaster produced a tremendous number of evacuees and disaster victims. The Japanese government had to provide various types of assistance to them. It had to provide financial assistance as well as granting exceptional treatment. How to provide such exceptional treatment, however, raised very important legal questions.

2.4.1 Government assistance

Local governments provided shelter for evacuees. At one time, more than 450,000 residents had been evacuated.[74] Since most evacuees left their homes without

71 Ministry of Environment, Hisaishita kaden risaikuruhō taisho hinmoku no shori ni tsuite [On Disposal of Home Electronic Devices Damaged by the Earthquake] (MOE) www.env.go.jp/jishin/hisai_kaden_recycle.pdf accessed 12 January 2018.

72 Ministry of Environment, Kinkyu tekina kaiyō tounyu shobun ni kansuru kokuji [Notice on Emergency Disposal of Fish in the Ocean] (MOE 7 April 2011) www.env.go.jp/jishin/attach/an23_44a.pdf accessed 12 January 2018.

73 Kaiyō osentō oyobi kaijō saigai no boushi ni kansuru hōritsu [Act against Ocean Pollution and on Prevention of Ocean Disaster], Law no 136 of 1970 (Ocean Pollution Prevention Act). See also "Gyokou no suisanbutsu 6manton huhai; Miyagiken, umi eno touki mitomeru [60,000t of Decomposing Fish in Port Facilities: Miyagi Prefecture Permits Dumping into the Ocean]," (*Asahi Shimbun* 2 April 2011) www.asahi.com/special/10005/TKY201104010520.html accessed 12 January 2018.

74 Cabinet Office, Hinan seikatsushasu no suii [Changes in the Number of Evacuees] (Cabinet Office) www.cao.go.jp/shien/1-hisaisha/pdf/5-hikaku.pdf accessed 12 January 2018.

taking any money, the central government decided to loan temporary money to purchase everyday necessities.[75] Financial institutions allowed exceptional measures for withdrawing cash without bank cards, bank books, or personal seals.[76] During the initial weeks, the delivery of food and everyday necessities was encumbered by fuel shortages and lack of coordination. However, all sorts of assistance came to be offered gradually. Within two months, the number of evacuees residing in shelters declined to 115,000, representing a substantially reduced but still significant dependence on these shelters.[77]

Although affected municipalities had some difficulties accepting volunteers from other parts of Japan, eventually many people entered the Tohoku Region to assist disaster victims in removing debris and clearing roads.[78] Many Japanese firms allowed their employees to go to Tohoku as volunteers while continuing to pay their salaries.[79]

In order to secure passage of emergency traffic, major highways were closed to all except emergency vehicles under article 76, paragraph 1, of the Basic Act on Disaster Countermeasures.[80] Only vehicles with special permits were permitted to use these highways. In addition, preferential treatment for purchasing gas was given to these vehicles in affected areas.[81]

Frequent aftershocks terrified evacuees in shelters. However, aftershocks gradually subsided and the debris blocking major streets was removed. Some evacuees returned to their homes, which were damaged but could be repaired. Some evacuees moved from shelters to homes of relatives. Other evacuees who lost their homes or who had no places to go to were forced to stay at shelters.

For evacuees such as these, the local government must provide temporary accommodation. Some evacuees were thus moved from shelters to vacant hotel rooms or private apartments assigned by municipal governments. Some were granted temporary use of public apartments owned by the local government, or in some cases, another neighboring local government or by the central government. For others, the local government has a responsibility to provide

75 Cabinet, Responses to the Great East Japan Earthquake Disaster (kantei) www.kantei.go.jp/saigai/note.html#living-finance accessed 12 January 2018. Residents were obliged to eventually repay this money.

76 Ibid. In lieu of signatures, personal seals (name stamps) are commonly used in Japan for official purposes.

77 Cabinet Office (n 74).

78 Curtis (n 31) 18.

79 Ibid 19; Samuels (n 31) 18–19.

80 National Police Agency, Higashinihon daishinsai nitomonau kōtsukisei [Traffic Regulation as a Result of the Great East Japan Earthquake Disaster] (NPA September 2011) www.npa.go.jp/archive/keibi/biki/traffic/koutu_kisei/koutsukisei.pdf accessed 12 January 2018.

81 The critical shortage of gas was caused by the damage to the oil refinery that was providing gas to most of the Tohoku area and the blackout. Moreover, many gas stations were severely damaged, and since most of the roads were blocked by the huge amount of debris, it was not possible to deliver the gas to any remaining gas stations. Agency for Natural Resources and Energy, Higashinihon daishinsai niokeru nenryo kyokyu nitsuite [On the Fuel Supply during the Great East Japan Earthquake Disaster] (METI 15 November 2011) www.meti.go.jp/committee/kenkyukai/energy/sekiyu_gas_antei_wg/001_s01_00.pdf accessed 12 January 2018.

temporary housing. Local governments thus made devoted efforts to construct "temporary housing" (*kasetsu juutaku*) for evacuees remaining in shelters for extended periods.[82] Eventually, almost all of the more than 300,000 evacuees one week after the disaster were relocated to temporary accommodation and all shelters in the Iwate Prefecture and Miyagi Prefecture were closed by December 2011.[83]

2.4.2 *Exceptions granted according to pre-existing statutes*

A variety of exceptions were made for victims of this unprecedented disaster. Some of these exceptions were granted under a provision included in statutes in anticipation of such an emergency. For instance, the deadline for submission of income tax returns was 15 March but the National Tax Agency extended the deadline for people living in affected areas[84] under a provision included in the National Taxation Act, which gives the Agency discretion to extend this deadline in a time of emergency.[85]

Some exceptions were granted according to general statutes specifically designed for emergency situations. Government agencies thus extended the duration of licenses and privileges granted by them under the Rights of the Disaster Victims Protection Act.[86] This Act was passed after the Hanshin Awaji Earthquake and was intended to protect the rights and legal interests of victims of powerful earthquakes and other natural disasters. This Act is applicable when

82 Ministry of Land, Infrastructure, Transport and Tourism, Oukyu kasetsu jutaku chakkousu, kansei kosu no suii [Changes in the Number of Constructed Temporary Housings] (MLIT 11 March 2012) www.mlit.go.jp/common/000143900.pdf accessed 12 January 2018. Moving evacuees from the shelters is important because of all the inconveniences of living in the shelters for a long time and also because many shelters are school gyms or classrooms of the neighboring community and the neighboring community needed to use these facilities for the education of school children.

83 Fire and Disaster Management Agency, Hinan no jokyo [Evacuees] (FDMA) www.fdma.go.jp/concern/publication/higashinihondaishinsai_kirokushu/pdf/honbun/03-06.pdf accessed 12 January 2018, 182. The last shelter remained was located in Saitama prefecture for the evacuees for Futaba Town who were forced to evacuate because of the Fukushima nuclear accident and this was shut down on 27 December 2013. "Shinsai, saigo no hinansho heisa: Genpatsu hinan no Futaba cho 4 setai ga taisho [The Last Shelter Was Shut Down: Four Families from the Futaba Town Left the Shelter]" (*Asahi Shimbun* 28 December 2013) www.asahi.com/shinsai_fukkou/articles/TKY201312270431.html accessed 12 January 2018.

84 National Tax Agency, Tohoku chihō taiheiyōoki jishin niyori tadaina higai wo uketa chiiki ni okeru shinkoku, nouhutō no kigen no enchou no sochi nitsuite [On Extension Measure of Tax Return and Payment Deadlines in Areas Where Extensive Damage Was Caused by the off the Pacific Ocean of Tohoku Earthquake] (NTA 15 May 2011) www.nta.go.jp/sonota/sonota/osirase/data/h23/jishin/index.htm accessed 12 January 2018.

85 Kokuzei tsūsokuhō [National Taxation Act], Law no 66 of 1962, art 11. The Diet later passed a statute allowing exceptional treatment to be extended to disaster victims with respect to income tax. See n 108.

86 Tokutei hijōsaigai no higaisha no kenririeki no hozentō wo hakarutameno tokubetsusochini kansuru hōritsu [Act concerning Special Measures to Preserve Rights and Legal Interests of Victims of Specified Emergency Disaster], Law no 85 of 1996 (Rights of Disaster Victim Protection Act) art 3.

the cabinet designates a particular disaster as a "specified extraordinary disaster" (*tokutei hijo saigai*) when an "highly unlikely and extremely serious extraordinary disaster" (*ichijirushiku ijo katsu gekijin na hijo saigai*) has occurred and the government believes it is particularly necessary to take measures to preserve administrative rights and legal interests of victims of these disasters, among other individuals.[87] The cabinet order must specify the necessary measures to be adopted under the Act.[88] If adopted, the relevant administrative agency can extend limitation periods of rights and legal interests granted by administrative order and based on statute, if those rights or interests were due to expire after the date of the emergency disaster. The term of these legal rights and/or interests can be extended for up to six months as specified by cabinet order, if the agency believes that such extension is necessary to preserve the rights and legal interests of victims or to restore rights and legal interests already expired.[89] The central government can also give legal immunity for up to four months, as specified by cabinet order, to persons who had a legal obligation to perform a duty prior to a date that falls after a disaster occurs but who could not fulfill this obligation before the required date because of the disaster.[90] The Act also grants a special extension for temporary housing to victims of these disasters under the Construction Standards Act,[91] and a special exemption from obligations to keep the streets looking good for the purposes of permitting the construction of temporary housing.[92]

After the Tohoku Earthquake, the Cabinet issued a cabinet order[93] designating the disaster as a "specified extraordinary disaster" and decided to apply measures to extend expiration dates and grant certain immunities.[94] The National Police Agency (NPA) thereby extended the expiration dates of driver's licenses for drivers living in affected areas until 31 August 2011.[95]

87 Ibid art 2(1).
88 Ibid art 2(2).
89 Ibid art 3(1).
90 Ibid art 4(1).
91 Ibid art 8.
92 Ibid art 9. The Act also prohibited the filing of bankruptcy proceedings (for up to two years) initiated by a creditor against a company that could not repay a debt as a result of the disaster. Ibid art 5.
93 Heisei 23nen Tohoku chihō taiheiyōoki jishin niyoru saigai nitsuiteno tokutei hijousaigai oyobi korenitaishi tekiyousubeki sochi no shitei nikansuru seirei [Cabinet Order concerning Declaration of Specified Extraordinary Disaster and Designation of Measures to Be Adopted with Respect to Disasters Caused by the 2011 off the Pacific Coast of Tohoku Earthquake], Cabinet Order no 19 of 2011.
94 Ministry of Internal Affairs and Communication, Press Release, Tohoku chihō taiheiyōoki jishinn nioite tekiyousareru gyouseijouno kenririeki nikakawaru manryoubi no enchou nikansuru sochi [On Extension of Expiration Date of Rights and Legal Interests in Administrative Law Applicable to the off the Pacific Coast of Tohoku Earthquake] (MIC 18 March 2011) www.soumu.go.jp/menu_news/s-news/42625_1.html accessed 12 January 2018.
95 National Police Agency, Tohoku chihō taiheiyōoki jishin nitomonau untenmenkyoshou no yūkōkikantō no enchō no sochi nitsuite [On Extension of Expiration Date of Drivers' License with Respect to the off the Pacific Coast of Tohoku Earthquake] (NPA) www.npa.go.jp/archive/keibi/biki/traffic/extension.pdf accessed 12 January 2018.

2.4.3 Exceptions granted by skewed statutory reinterpretation

In some cases, however, exceptions are granted based on skewed reinterpretation of pre-existing statutory provisions. The treatment of missing persons is just one typical example.

Bodies of the dead are typically examined by doctors and certificates of death are issued to surviving family members. The family can then register the death with the municipal government, which issues a permit for burial or cremation. Missing persons whose remains have yet to be found are still classed as missing and thus are not treated as deceased. According to the Civil Code, a person missing for over seven years can be declared by the family court as "officially missing" based upon the application of interested parties.[96] If a person has gone to war, gone down with a sunken ship or was involved in a disaster that caused death, *and* is missing for one year after any of these events, he or she can similarly be declared "officially missing."[97] Then, that person can be regarded as dead.[98] Therefore, the surviving family of a missing person must wait for at least one year before registering his or her death. This means that the surviving family will not be entitled to receive a survivor's pension under the National Pension Act, survivor's compensation under the Workers Compensation Act, succeed to property ownership, or receive any life insurance payments until then.

The National Pension Act stipulates, however, that a person who was on board a sunken ship or a crashed airplane can be regarded as dead three months after the accident for the purposes of pension payments.[99] The MHLW believed that the surviving families of missing persons assumed dead in the Tohoku Earthquake should be granted similar exceptional treatment because they required immediate assistance.[100] However, in order to succeed to property or to receive life insurance payments, this exception would not be sufficient. The central government thus decided to allow an exception by invoking article 86 of the Family Registration Act,[101] which allowed municipal governments to accept registration of a death upon the submission of written documentation demonstrating the facts of the presumed death even before the passage of one year.[102]

96 Minpo [Civ. C.], art 30(1).

97 Ibid art 30(2).

98 Ibid art 31. If the missing person is ever found alive, the family court must cancel the declaration. Ibid art 32.

99 Kokumin nenkinhō [National Pension Act], Law no 141 of 1959, art 18–2.

100 Ministry of Health, Labor and Welfare, Director of Pension Administration, Higashinihon daishinsai niyoru saigai niyori yukuehumei tonatta mono nikakawaru izoku kouseinenkintō no seikyu ga atta baaino toriatsukai nitsuite [On Treatment of Pension Claims Brought by Families of Persons Missing as a Result of the Great East Japan Earthquake Disaster] (MHLW 7 June 2011) www.mhlw.go.jp/stf/houdou/2r9852000001erdk-att/2r9852000001esbd.pdf accessed 12 January 2018.

101 Kosekihō [Family Registration Act], Law no 224 of 1947, art 86.

102 Ministry of Justice, Higashinihon daishinsai niyoru yukuehumeisha nikakawaru shiboutodoke no toriatsukai nitsuite [On Treatment of Registration of Death for Missing Persons during the Great East Japan Earthquake Disaster] (7 June 2011), MHLW www.mhlw.go.jp/stf/houdou/2r9852000001fod6-att/2r9852000001fy66.pdf accessed 12 January 2018.

The use of this exception undoubtedly made sense, given the circumstances. What is questionable, however, is whether the Family Registration Act can or should be invoked to grant such exceptional treatment. Such (re)interpretation of the Family Registration Act was highly irregular and undoubtedly arose from the unusual circumstances of the time. As there was a legal requirement to treat missing persons as dead within one year, the Civil Code should have been amended to permit this.

2.4.4 Granting exceptions through enactment of special legislation

Since there were no statutory provisions for emergency despite the fact that they were necessary, some exceptional measures had to be adopted through enactment of special legislation. For instance, the Diet enacted special legislation to allow postponement of local elections scheduled for April 2011.[103] It was simply impossible for affected local governments to conduct elections in the wake of the earthquake and tsunami. The Diet also enacted a special statute permitting local elections scheduled for June to be postponed until September.[104] The Diet further passed a special act allowing persons who had lost passports along with their homes as a result of the Great East Japan Earthquake Disaster to apply for special passports without paying any additional fees and to extend their validity for as long as the original would have been valid.[105] The Diet also passed a special statute allowing the heirs of disaster victims to postpone decisions on succession until the end of November.[106] In normal circumstances, heirs must decide whether to refuse succession rights or to succeed in property ownership conditionally within three months after the death of an ascendant from which an

103 Heisei 23 nen Tohoku chihō taiheiyōoki jishin nitomonau chihō koukyoudantai no giin oyobi chou no senkyo kijitsutō no rinjitokurei nikansuru hōritsu [Act to Provide Temporary Special Treatment on Election Day for Assembly Members of Local Government and Heads of Local Government in Response to the 2011 off the Pacific Coast of Tohoku Earthquake], Law no 2 of 2011.

104 Heisei 23 nen Tohoku chihō taiheiyōoki jishin nitomonau chihōkoukyoudantai no giin oyobi chou no senkyo kijitsutō no rinjitokurei nikansuru hōritsu no ichibuwo kaiseisuru hōritsu [Act to Amend Parts of the Act to Provide Temporary Special Treatment on Election Day for the Assembly Members of the Local Government and Heads of Local Government in Response to the 2011 off the Pacific Coast of Tohoku Earthquake], Law No 55 of 2011. The Diet also passed another statute postponing the election of fishing district adjustment commissioners and farming commissioners. Higashinihon daishinsai nitomonau kaiku-gyogyo chousei iinkai oyobi nougyou iinkai no iin no senkyo no rinjitokurei nikansuru hōritsu [Act concerning Temporary Exception to the Election of Maritime District Fishing Adjustment Commission and Farming Commissioners in Light of the Great East Japan Earthquake Disaster], Law no 44 of 2011.

105 Higashinihon daishinsai no hisaisha nikakawaru ippan ryoken no hakkyu no tokurei nikansuru hōritsu [Act concerning Special Treatment of Victims of the Great East Japan Earthquake Disaster with Respect to Passport Issuance], Law No 64 of 2011.

106 Higashinihon daishinsai nitomonau souzoku no shounin matawa houki wo subeki kikan ni kakawaru minpō no tokurei nikansuru hōritsu [Act to Provide for Special Treatment of the Period in the Civil Code for Electing Acceptance or Refusal of Succession as a Result of the Great East Japan Earthquake Disaster], Law no 69, 2011. The Diet later added this exception in the Rights of the Disaster Victims Protection Act (n 86) art 6.

estate has been bequeathed. Otherwise, heirs will succeed in property ownership unconditionally, debt responsibilities included.[107] It was simply impossible for heirs to decide whether to refuse succession rights or to accept succession rights conditionally or unconditionally within three months in the aftermath of the earthquake and tsunami. The Diet similarly passed a statute allowing special treatment for disaster victims with respect to income tax,[108] another authorizing the central government to take over construction and restoration operations relating to public facilities damaged by the earthquake and tsunami,[109] another allowing local governments to prohibit construction of new houses in affected areas,[110] and another providing special support to affected municipal governments.[111] The Diet also enacted a statute authorizing the central and local governments to restore and desalinize farmland covered by tsunami seawater along with special funding for these purposes.[112] The Diet even introduced a statute authorizing the postponement of long-planned digitalization of terrestrial broadcasting signals in the affected prefectures.[113]

107 Minpō [C. Code], art 915(1).

108 Higashinihon daishinsai no hisaishatō nikakawaru kokuzei kankei hōritsu no rinjitokurei nikansuru hōritsu [Act concerning the Temporary Exceptional Treatment for Disaster Victims of the Great East Japan Earthquake Disaster with Respect to National Tax Statutes], Law no 29 of 2011. This statute granted extension of tax return deadlines and tax payment deadlines, immunity or reduction of income tax for victims of the disaster along with other exceptional treatments. The Diet also passed the Chihōzeihō no ichibu wo kaiseisuru hōritsu [Act to Amend Parts of the Local Tax Act], Law no 30 of 2011, to give local tax exemptions on property and homes affected by the tsunami, property acquisition tax exemptions when residents bought new property in exchange for destroyed property and tax deductions for loans when affected residents borrowed money to rebuild their homes.

109 Higashinihon daishinsai niyori higai wo uketa koukyou doboku shisetsu no saigaihukkyu jigyotō nikakawaru kōji no kunitō niyoru daikou nikansuru hōritsu [Act concerning Governmental Substitution with Respect to Disaster Restoration Construction of Public Facilities Damaged by the Great East Japan Earthquake Disaster], Law no 33 of 2011.

110 Higashinihon daishinsai niyori jindaina higaiwo uketa shigaichi niokeru kenchikuseigen no tokureitō nikansuru hōritsu [Act concerning Exceptional Construction Limitations in Urban Cities Seriously Damaged by the Great East Japan Earthquake Disaster], Law no 34 of 2011.

111 Higashinihon daishinsai ni taisho surutame no tokubetsu no zaiseienjo oyobi josei nikansuru hōritsu [Act concerning Special Financial Assistance and Support in order to Respond to the Great East Japan Earthquake Disaster], Law No 40 of 2011. The Diet also passed the Higashinihon daishinsai ni taisho surutō notameno heisei 23 nendobun-no chihō kouhuzei no sougaku no tokureitō nikansuru hōritsu [Act on Special Treatment of Total Amount of Local Distribution Aid in 2011 as a Countermeasure to the Great East Japan Earthquake Disaster], Law no 41 of 2011, to add additional distribution benefits to local government and the Higashinihon daishinsai nitomonau gappei shichouson nikakawaru chihōsai no tokurei nikansuru hōritsu [Act concerning the Special Treatment of Local Bonds Issued by Merged Cities and Towns in Light of the Great East Japan Earthquake Disaster], Law no 102 of 2011, to extend the period for merged cities and towns affected by the Tohoku Earthquake to issue local bonds.

112 Higashinihon daishinsai nitaisho surutameno tochikairyohō no tokurei nikansuru hōritsu [Act concerning Exceptions to the Land Improvement Act in order to Respond to the Great East Japan Earthquake Disaster], Law no 43 of 2011.

113 Higashinihon daishinsai nitomonau chijo digital hōsō nikakawaru denpahō no tokurei nikansuru hōritsu [Act concerning Exception to the Air Waves Act with Respect to Digital Broadcasting as a Result of the Great East Japan Earthquake Disaster], Law no 68 of 2011.

These statutes were passed by the Diet without any substantial objections. All of these exceptional measures were made for the sake of residents affected by the Tohoku Earthquake but are not designed to provide for future disaster victims who may require similar exceptions when another massive earthquake strikes in Japan.

2.4.5 Granting exceptions through administrative discretion

Further exceptional measures aimed at assisting victims of the earthquake and tsunami were brought in without statutory authorization. These measures were introduced without the aid of express statutory provision, statutory reinterpretation, or enactment of any special statute.

For instance, the police issued new driver's licenses without official certification of residence being issued by the municipal government even in cases where applicants resided in shelters.[114] The police also issued certificates of driver training, usually issued by driving schools, in cases where the relevant driving school had been destroyed by the tsunami.[115] When residents who had lost their automobiles in the disaster decided to buy new automobiles, the police adopted informal measures to issue mandatory parking space certificates.[116] The police also issued special parking permits for residents forced to seek shelter outside of their home prefecture.[117] In other cases, the central government allowed financial institutions to accept certain customer declarations as sufficient proof if they had lost their identification documents.[118] Further, loan companies were permitted to show flexibility with respect to maximum limits on loans taken out by residents victimized by the disaster.[119] The central government did not enforce food labeling obligations for food distributed in affected areas.[120] The central government also adopted flexible measures as to labeling requirements on bottled water to promote the timely production and speedy distribution of bottled water.[121] In addition, the central government allowed cellular network service providers to adopt informal measures with respect to customer identification.[122] The central government also granted immunity for customs tax to goods sent from overseas to disaster victims and adopted informal measures

114 Cabinet Office, Higashinihon daishinsai nikanrenshita kakuhushouno kiseikanwatō no joukyo [Current Situation of Deregulation in Response to the Great East Japan Earthquake Disaster] (Cabinet Office 12 December 2012) www.cao.go.jp/sasshin/kisei-seido/publication/241212/item241212.pdf accessed 12 January 2018.

115 Ibid.

116 Ibid. Note also that in Japan, proof of a dedicated parking space is basically a prerequisite for registration of vehicle ownership.

117 Ibid.

118 Ibid.

119 Ibid.

120 Ibid.

121 Ibid.

122 Ibid.

with respect to importation.[123] The Ministry of Foreign Affairs issued visas via informal measures to foreign students who left Japan following the disaster without obtaining re-entry permits.[124] The Ministry of Education, Culture, Sports, Science and Technology (MEXT) permitted a special academic calendar for schools within the affected areas and distributed free school textbooks to students who had lost their textbooks after moving to new schools.[125] Affected residents were permitted to see doctors even without a proper national health insurance certificate.[126] The central government also allowed pharmacists to dispense prescription drugs to patients unable to see a doctor to obtain prescriptions.[127] These are just some examples of situations where the central government adopted exceptional measures on behalf of affected residents and businesses in the affected areas.

These measures are necessitated because there is a huge number of administrative regulations on all aspects of the lives of residents in Japan and government officials, bureaucrats, generally adopt a highly bureaucratic and inflexible attitude toward their enforcement. They are generally unwilling to make exceptions unless there is an explicit authorization.

Of note is the fact that all of the above-mentioned measures were adopted through the exercise of administrative discretion. Administrative agencies simply refrained from enforcing certain statutory obligations in respect to disaster-affected persons or businesses. However, all of these exceptional treatments were, nonetheless, granted on a case by case basis following the earthquake and tsunami. The necessity of such exceptional treatments should have been well anticipated. Instead of coming up with a list of exceptional measures after the earthquake, the central government should have prepared a list of exceptional measures necessary in emergency situations and enacted legal authorization for swift application of these exceptional measures.

Moreover, all of these exceptional measures were decided on by individual governmental departments having authority to enforce such measures. Furthermore, these exceptional measures were indicated in instructions, memos, and notifications originating at departmental central offices and addressed to local offices, local branches, or local governments or municipalities. They simply instructed these local bodies to grant exceptional measures in dealing with disaster victims without addressing the contents of these instructions to the general public. For those with Internet access, understanding the availability of these exceptional measures would have involved little more than logging on to the relevant website, but for disaster victims forced into shelters, it was virtually impossible to secure Internet access. Whether more than a handful of disaster victims residing in shelters knew of some or all of these exceptional measures is doubtful.

123 Ibid.
124 Ibid.
125 Ibid.
126 Ibid.
127 Ibid.

2.5 Earthquake, tsunami, and failures of law and politics

Why did such devastating loss and damage have to happen? What was wrong with Japanese disaster law? Why did the Japanese government fail to prepare for the Tohoku Earthquake and provide adequate response to the disaster?

2.5.1 What went wrong?

First, the tragedies were all caused by the failure of the Japanese government to anticipate and prepare for an earthquake as powerful as the Tohoku Earthquake. The government also failed to consider the serious tsunami risks separately.[128] In retrospect, everyone knows that powerful earthquakes are possible off the shore of the Sanriku region. There is a substantial historical record indicating periodic powerful earthquakes in this region and the possibility of huge tsunamis;[129] which was why the Japanese government had prepared for powerful earthquakes and some of the towns had massive tsunami barriers to fend off tsunamis. But most did not anticipate such a massive earthquake as the Tohoku Earthquake with a magnitude of 9.0 on the Richter scale and very few researchers warned about the danger of such a powerful tsunami.[130] Thus, the government did not anticipate such a powerful tsunami with waves more than 17 meters high—strong enough to reach the rooftops of three-storied buildings.

Despite the Japanese government's failure to prepare for such a strong earthquake, it did adopt various preparatory measures against powerful earthquakes.[131] What happened to these preparatory measures? Why was the outcome so disastrous?

One of the reasons for the devastation could be attributed to the failure of the residents to try to evacuate or their failure to evacuate swiftly enough.[132] Some of the residents believed that the tsunami barriers were strong enough to fend off the tsunami and therefore erroneously believed there was no need to evacuate.

128 Federica Ranghieri & Mikio Ishiwatari, *Leaning from Megadisasters: Lessons from the Great East Japan Earthquake* (World Bank 2014) 30.

129 Ministry of Land, Infrastructure and Transport, Kokudo kotsu hakusho 2011 [Land, Infrastructure, and Transport Whitepaper 2011] (MLIT) www.mlit.go.jp/hakusyo/mlit/h22/hakusho/h23/html/k1223000.html accessed 12 January 2018.

130 It has now been revealed that the earthquake was a combination of triple mega earthquakes, the first offshore of the Miyagi Prefecture, the second further offshore, and the third closer to the shore of Ibaraki Prefecture, spanning about six minutes. The earthquake started offshore of the Sanriku region but its destruction ranged over 100,000 km^2—500 km long in the north–south direction and 200 km wide in the east–west direction. University of Tokyo, Earthquake Research Institute, 2011 nen3gatsu Tohoku chihō Taiheiyouoki jishin [The off the Pacific Coast of Tohoku Earthquake of March 2011] (University of Tokyo) www.eri.u-tokyo.ac.jp/TOPICS_OLD/outreach/eqvolc/201103_tohoku/eng/ accessed 12 January 2018.

131 Seismic upgrade proved to be effective again, although there are extensive nonstructural damages. Ranghieri & Ishiwatari (n 128) 38.

132 Masanobu Kanei & Toshitaka Katada, Higashinihon daishinsai no tsunami giseisha/tsunami hisaisha no hinankoudou nimiru 3.11 no kyoukun [Lesson of March 11 in Light of the Evacuation Behavior of Those Dead or Suffered as a result of Tsunami of the Great East Japan Earthquake Disaster] (Katada Lab) www.katada-lab.jp/doc/n240.pdf accessed 12 January 2018.

Some might attribute blame to the JMA and the television stations that reported the estimated height of the tsunami to be much lower than the actual wave (initial prediction was 3 meters high in some areas)[133] and also correctly reported that the first wave of the tsunami was only 20 centimeters in some places, giving a false sense of security for those who remained at home.[134] There is often a possibility that the second and third waves will be much more powerful, which in this case they were. Although the expected height of the tsunami wave was upgraded later, there was a question whether the residents were aware of this update due to blackouts.[135] Some residents might have also erroneously believed that they had sufficient time to evacuate and did not rush into evacuation.[136] However, the very powerful second wave came ashore in some places within 30 minutes of the earthquake, killing many who were attempting to evacuate. Everyone was instructed to evacuate on foot, but many tried to flee in their automobiles, causing serious traffic jams and a standstill, leading to many drivers and passengers being wiped out by the tsunami.[137] These losses could have been easily mitigated, if not outright prevented.

Some of the loss could be attributed to poor choices by those who were supposed to take the people to safer places. For instance, in the case of Okawa Elementary School, all the children were gathered in the schoolyard and waited for about an hour before being instructed to evacuate to nearby higher ground just before the tsunami instead of the mountain behind the school. As a result, 74 out of 108 children were killed by the tsunami.[138] Hiyori Kindergarten, even after

133 NHK, Dou hinan wo unagasuka: Kawaru ootsunami keihō [How to Encourage the Residents to Evacuate? Change in the Tsunami Warning System] (*NHK* 9 November 2011) www.nhk.or.jp/gendai/articles/3117/1.html accessed 12 January 2018. The initial warning was issued three minutes after the first tremor and was based on the estimate of the earthquake as 7.9 on the Richter scale. This was a practice adopted after the Okushiri Island Earthquake. *See* Chapter 1 n 249. The earthquake continued after the first tremor and a more powerful tremor was registered after the initial estimate. But the measurement system failed to indicate the precise tremor and it took almost 30 minutes to upgrade the warning and another 15 minutes to further upgrade the warning. Japan Meteorological Agency, Tsunami keihō kaizen nimuketa torikumi [Attempt to Upgrade the Tsunami Warning System] (JMA) www.jma.go.jp/jma/kishou/books/hakusho/2012/HN2012sp2.pdf accessed 12 January 2018.

134 Ibid.

135 Ibid. See also Ranghieri & Ishwatari (n 128) 10, 91, 101. Some municipalities failed to announce the upgraded tsunami information through their loud-speaker systems because of the blackout and because they allocated the emergency power according to priority, leaving the public announcement system without power.

136 Kanei & Katada (n 132).

137 "Hinan juutai, tsunami higaiwo kakudai: Unagasshitemo kuruma oriruhito shousuu [Evacuation by Car Expanded the Tsunami Casualties: Very Few Residents Got off even after Prompted]" (*Asahi Shimbun* 1 April 2011) www.asahi.com/special/10005/TKY201104010283.html accessed 12 January 2018; Ranghieri & Ishiwatari (n 128) 10.

138 Richard Lloyd Parry, *Ghosts of the Tsunami* (Jonathan Cape 2017); "Okawa shougakkou: Mikaimei no nazo—Tsunami toutatsu madeno kuuhaku no 50hun ni naniga attanoka [Okawa Elementary School: Unsettled Question—What Had Happened during the 50 Minutes before the Tsunami]" (*Huffington Post* 12 March 2014) www.huffingtonpost.jp/2014/03/11/okawa-elementary-school-blank-50-minutes_n_4944128.html accessed 12 January 12 2018. However, overall the evacuation of school children was very successful. Ranghieri & Ishiwatari (n 128) 78.

the tsunami warning had been issued, decided to bus some children back to their homes closer to the seashore instead of taking them to the higher mountain and five of them together with the bus were washed away by the tsunami.[139] These losses might also have been prevented, and also present a tough question on whether the school or kindergarten should be held liable for negligence.

2.5.2 Failures of law in the disaster preparation

It is important to note that not all of these problems were necessarily problems stemming from flaws in the legal scheme pertaining to natural disasters. All of this proves that what matters most is the actual implementation of the natural disaster countermeasures regardless of the legal system.

Nonetheless, it can without doubt be said that it was a failure of the law not to require the government to prepare for the most powerful possible earthquake. Indeed, the law is utterly silent on what kind of earthquake the government is required to prepare for. The disaster law was woefully inadequate for its failure to mandate the government to prepare for this kind of powerful earthquake and tsunami.

Second, past neglect over the earthquake and tsunami risk in the Tohoku Region is definitely one of the reasons for such devastating damage. The Japanese government had focused on a possible Tokai Earthquake as well as the next possible Kanto Earthquake. It had not paid much attention to the possibility of powerful earthquakes in other regions, including the Sanriku region, where there was sufficient data to indicate the possibility of a powerful earthquake and tsunami.

Third, the government's preparation for evacuation was extremely inadequate. The government did not anticipate the widespread blackout and communication failure after the earthquake and the difficulty of transmitting tsunami warnings through the public announcement system. It did not know the whereabout of persons who needed assistance to evacuate. The government did not provide a very effective and realistic evacuation procedure. The failure of the law to mandate an effective evacuation procedure definitely contributed to the seriousness of the tragedy.

Finally, disaster law in Japan had focused on disaster prevention and had failed to prepare for post-disaster rescue and recovery, especially for the treatment of resident victims and the necessity of providing assistance. It failed to prepare for effective rescue and assistance and failed to anticipate the huge number of casualties, the vast amount of debris and large number of damaged automobiles and home electrical devices. It did not anticipate such a huge number of evacuees and failed to anticipate the necessity of providing exceptional treatment for all these

139 "Tsunami de sougei bus no enji shibou, 4izoku ga teiso [Kindergarten Kids Died together with the Bus: Four Families Filed Suits] (*Asahi Shimbun* 10 August 2011) www.asahi.com/special/10005/TKY201108100225.html accessed 12 January 2018.

evacuees. These are just the tip of the iceberg regarding the failures of law to anticipate what needs to be done after the devastation.

2.5.3 Failures of law in the disaster response

It is possible the Japanese government did all it could do to rescue and assist victims of the disaster. The lessons learned after the Hanshin Awaji Earthquake surely paid off.

However, there were also some disturbing problems in the Japanese legal system in the responses from the Japanese and local governments. One problem stemmed from the serious damage to local governments, as well as the public officials themselves, who were supposed to provide help to disaster victims.[140] Some of the municipalities along the coastline lost city halls and other municipal buildings, as well as the lives of some of their mayors and a substantial number of public officials. Thus, the municipalities' ability to provide help was greatly diminished compared to what was anticipated. The Japanese government never anticipated such extensive loss and damage to municipal governments as a result of a natural disaster.[141] The law also did not provide any framework for how to respond when a municipal government—which was supposed to provide all of the relief—was itself paralyzed by the disaster.[142]

Also because of the telecommunications blackout, landline communication as well as cellphone communication was seriously disrupted.[143] As a result, it was difficult for the central government to measure the extent of the damage and for the local and municipal governments that were affected to report damages to the outside world. Moreover, because of the difficulty of communication, the emergency response was seriously hindered. The law did not prepare for such communication problems.

The government also did not anticipate such extensive damage. Since many municipalities lost cremation facilities and waste burning facilities, they were

140 Cabinet Office, Higashinihon daishinsai niokeru saigai oukyu taisaku no omona kadai [Problems in Emergency Response to Great East Japan Earthquake Disaster] (Cabinet Office July 2012) www.bousai.go.jp/jishin/syuto/taisaku_wg/5/pdf/3.pdf accessed 12 January 2018 2 (Emergency Response Problems). Otsuchi Town of Iwate Prefecture lost some 30 persons among 1,140 officials, including a mayor, and Rikuzentakata City lost 111 out of 443. See Chapter 4 nn 10–11. Municipal government is supposed to provide shelters for evacuees, distribute all the food, water, and other emergency goods to evacuees, check the family registry to issue permits for burial or cremation, check the degree of building damage and issue damage certificates, report to the prefectures, respond to mass media requests, and more. Japanese disaster law placed too much responsibility on the adversely affected municipal governments and did not anticipate the system for assistance from other local governments or central government.

141 Ranghieri & Ishiwatari (n 128) 149. There was also a failure to protect vital facilities for emergency operations against the tsunami. Ibid 55.

142 Anticipating the damages to the municipal government, the government should have prepared for much closer cooperation with non-profit organizations (NPOs) in the aftermath of the disaster. Ibid 125.

143 Emergency Response Problems (n 140).

unable to cremate the bodies of dead residents and burn waste. Furthermore, because of the extensive damage to medical facilities, there was significant difficulty in providing medical help to the survivors.[144] The government should have anticipated such damage and prepared for it in advance.

There were also problems in providing assistance to the disaster victims. Because of the serious damage to the transportation and highway systems, the government initially had extreme difficulty in providing the necessary food and goods for the survivors.[145] Even when food and goods were delivered to the local headquarters, it was not always possible to distribute it to individual survivors because many survivors stayed outside of established shelters and there was no way of knowing their exact number or where they were staying and what kinds of support were necessary.[146] Moreover, most of the roads were filled with debris and could not be used to deliver food and goods.[147] Furthermore, there was a critical shortage of gas to operate vehicles.[148] The government should have prepared for all these logistic problems.[149]

The government also did not have a system for checking who had survived, determining where they could be found, and discovering who was still missing. This produced chaos in the aftermath of the disaster. Moreover, there were significant discrepancies in the services provided by shelters and evacuation places.[150] Furthermore, there was no one who had expert knowledge or experience in running shelters.

2.5.4 The Tohoku Earthquake and much deeper failures of law

Unlike all of these failures, there are some much deeper failures of law: the failures inherent in the Japanese legal system that are not simply a mistake or error.

First, the government could also be blamed for its reluctance to restrict construction by law in areas where the it was well aware of tsunami vulnerabilities. Indeed, the best way to protect the residents would have been to ban house construction in vulnerable areas and move all the potentially affected residents to higher ground. But the Japanese government was reluctant to restrict property ownership. As a result, many residents remained in vulnerable places. As such, the government's unwillingness to introduce zoning and construction restrictions by law undoubtedly contributed to increased loss and damage.[151]

144 Ibid 5.
145 Ibid 7.
146 Ibid 9.
147 Ibid 8. Delivery of food and goods relied heavily upon trucks. The government should have prepared the possibility of other modes of transportation. Moreover, the government had not anticipated the emergency vehicle permission system and, therefore, had to prepare special permits only after the disaster, causing tremendous administrative burden. Ibid.
148 Ibid 10.
149 Ranghieri & Ishiwatari (n 128) 143.
150 Emergency Response Problems (n 140) 11.
151 Ranghieri & Ishiwatari (n 128) 111–12.

This unwillingness is a manifestation of the long-standing tradition of the Japanese government.

Second, the government did not have legal power to force residents to evacuate. The tsunami warning was issued and evacuation was recommended and instructed, but as we have seen, this was merely advisory. Evacuation was not mandatory. Surely, the municipal government heads have the power to designate certain areas as a "hazard zone" and legally prohibit entry or force persons to leave[152] but generally municipal heads were very reluctant to exercise this power, and the governor or prime minister does not have any legal power to force residents to evacuate. An evacuation recommendation or evacuation instruction is much more informal than an evacuation order. Perhaps the lack of statutory authority for the government to issue evacuation orders is a reflection of the fact that Japanese law as a whole is reluctant to use legal forces. The law provides for informal measures, even in statutes, and even when agencies and other delegated authorities are granted legal powers.[153] But the absence of mandatory evacuation orders and the preference for informal recommendation or instruction is a serious drawback of Japanese disaster law.

Another legal failure was the absence of concern for vulnerable minorities. There are questions in regard to whether persons with disabilities or health issues were adequately assisted during the evacuation.[154] Indeed, there was no system in place to provide evacuation assistance to the people who most needed it, nor was there even a system or method in place allowing the government to ascertain the names and whereabouts of the persons who needed it and allow non-profit organizations (NPOs) to help them evacuate.[155] Similarly, there was a question

152 See Chapter 1 n 177.

153 Frank Upham, *Law and Social Change in Postwar Japan* (Harvard 1987) 168; Ken Duck, "Now that the Fog Has Lifted: The Impact of Japan's Administrative Procedures Law on the Regulation of Industry and Market Governance" (1995) 19 *Fordham International Law Journal* 1686; Tom Ginsburg, "System Change?: A New Perspective on Japan's Administrative Procedure Law" (2002) 13 *ZJapanR* 56, 69. Professor John O. Haley argues that preference for informal control over legal control is the predominant characteristic of Japanese Law. John Owen Haley, *Authority without Power: Law and the Japanese Paradox* (Oxford 1991). For instance, the maximum working hours are provided for in the Roudou kijunhō [Labor Standard Act], Law no 49 of 1947, art 32 and its violation could lead to criminal punishment (ibid art 109(i)). Although the Labor Standard officers could act as police officers (ibid art 102), they usually sent notice of recommendation of correction when they found a violation and prompted voluntary correction. It is very interesting to note that the Oh-arai-machi of the Ibaraki Prefecture repeatedly announced "evacuation order" and "everyone is ordered to evacuate" through public speakers together with repeated loud sirens, and that there were no casualties from the tsunami. Hiroyuki Inoue, Oh-arai machi wa naze hinanseyo to yobikaketanoka [Why the Oh-arai-machi Called for Evacuation Order] (September 2011) *Hoso Kenkyu to Chousa* 32 www.nhk.or.jp/bunken/summary/research/report/2011_09/20110903.pdf accessed 26 February 2018.

154 Zenkoku shakai hukushi kyougikai [National Social Welfare Council], Saigaiji no shougaisha hinantō nikansuru kenkyu houkokusho [Report on the Evacuation of Persons with Disabilities during the Natural Disaster] (National Social Welfare Council April 2014) www.shakyo.or.jp/research/2014_pdf/20140530_jisedai.pdf accessed 17 January 2018.

155 This was a result of erroneous interpretation of the Gyosei kikan no hoyusuru kojinjouho no hogoni kansuru horitsu [Act on Protection of Personal Information Held by the Administrative Agency], Law no 58 of 2003 (Personal Information Act), which restricts collection and provision of personal information of the residents without consent.

whether the foreign residents who did not understand Japanese were able to evacuate and whether they could be properly assisted in the shelters.[156] The disaster law didn't mandate proper assistance toward these vulnerable people.

Moreover, apparently no serious attention was paid to the treatment of vulnerable minorities in the shelters. As a result, many women complained that they had no privacy, had difficulty in getting access to feminine goods, had difficulty caring for babies, and had no ability to participate in the management of the shelters.[157] There is also a question in regard to whether there was even a sufficient number of shelters that would have been able to accommodate persons with disabilities or health issues who would have needed assistance. The concern for women, minorities, or persons with disabilities in the shelters was clearly lacking.

Finally, the most disturbing flaw in the natural disaster response was the difficulty for various agencies to cooperate in the rescue operation and provision of help, especially between SDF officers, prefectural police officers, and municipal firefighters and rescue personnel.[158] Since all of these institutions are managed by three separate organizations and there was no one to coordinate their rescue operations, there was some confusion, such as two organizations searching the same area. Although close cooperation between various departments is essential at the time of a disaster, the law fails by the unwillingness of each department to ensure that such cooperation will be possible.[159] This is a clear manifestation of the strong departmentalism of Japanese bureaucrats, discussed below. It is also a serious failure of the law not to mandate much closer cooperation and to establish a system for much better coordination.

2.5.5 *The Tohoku Earthquake and failures of politics*

All of the failures that have been mentioned could be attributed to the political failure to prepare for this kind of powerful disaster, which in this case stemmed from the longstanding policy to prioritize economic development while sacrificing preparation against an unlikely massive natural disaster. To be sure, the

156 "Gaikokujin tachi no shinsai taiken [Evacuation of Foreigners]" (NHK) www9.nhk.or.jp/archives/311shogen/summary/evi/12/ accessed 17 January 2018.

157 Ranghieri & Ishiwatari (n 128) 18–19.

158 n 25. Emergency Response Problems (n 140) 4.

159 The absence of coordination is also apparent on the face of the statutes. For the purpose of responding to serious disaster, the disaster needs to be classified as "disaster," "extraordinary disaster," or "emergency disaster." See Chapter 1 nn 170–73. In order to allow the government to pay for municipal reconstruction work, the disaster must be designated as an "extreme serious disaster." See Chapter 1 n 199. In order to extend legal rights and privileges after a disaster, the disaster must be a "highly unlikely and extremely serious extraordinary disaster" to be designated as a "specified extraordinary disaster." See n 87. Moreover, in order to take over the police, the prime minister must declare "an emergency" (Chapter 1 n 206) and in order for the prime minister to order emergency measures when the Diet is in recess and there is no time to ask for an emergency session of the House of Councilors, the prime minister must declare a "disaster emergency declaration" (Chapter 1 n 200). The public has no clue as to how these different words are used to differentiate one particular disaster from others.

government had introduced all kinds of countermeasures against earthquakes and tsunamis—no other country in the world was better prepared against them. Nevertheless, all the preparations were based on the assumption of more likely and recurring powerful earthquakes and not on the assumption of a more unlikely but devastating super-powerful earthquake. The government placed economic development over any concern for a massive natural disaster, which was considered highly unlikely to happen. Apparently, this policy contributed to the great success of the Japanese economy post WWII.[160]

This position of the government, which emphasizes economic development over other concerns such as seismic safety, is the result of the predominance of the ruling party. The Liberal Democratic Party (LDP), formed in 1955, has pretty much formed the government ever since then[161] and has placed priority on economic development since the 1960s.[162] It is surely far more economical to prepare for the much more likely and weaker natural disasters rather than preparing for an unlikely yet massive one, leading to such serious casualties.[163] This political reasoning must provide an explanation for why all government countermeasures in response to the Tohoku Earthquake were so inadequate. The government did not anticipate such a seriously powerful earthquake, but rather believed such an earthquake to be extremely unlikely, ignoring the possibility of massive human casualties.

The government was eager to intensify the seismic resistance of the infrastructure and spent a huge amount of money improving it. This construction spending was a very lucrative source of money for many construction companies, the major supporter for the ruling LDP. Therefore, the government had an incentive to spend more money for public construction than to prepare for reduction of damages and better evacuation. Moreover, the government had relied upon the possibility of prediction. The assumption was that serious disaster could be avoided if the massive earthquake could be foreseen and predicted. This confidence in the ability to predict, and the faith in technology, led to the unfounded belief that ingenuity and technology could prevent disaster. A huge amount of taxpayers' money was spent on promoting earthquake prediction. It was also a very lucrative source of money for many businesses. Basically, all earthquake and tsunami countermeasures are designed to benefit businesses, and infrastructure seismic upgrade was always prioritized.

160 J.A.A. Stockwin, *Governing Japan: Divided Politics in a Resurgent Economy* (4th ed Blackwell 2008) 225; Bradley Richardson, *Japanese Democracy: Power, Coordination, and Performance* (Yale 1997) 200.

161 For a history of the JDP, see Masumi Ishikawa & Michisada Hirose, Jiminto: Chouki shihai no kouzou [LDP: The Structure of Long Dominance] (Iwanami 1989); Ellis S. Krauss & Robert J. Pekkanen, *The Rise and Fall of Japan's LDP: Political Party Organizations as Historical Institutions* (Cornell 2010). The LDP is certainly resilient. After losing the government to its rival Democratic Party of Japan (DPJ) in 2009, it came back to form the government in 2012 and would continue to dominate the government for the future.

162 Louis D. Hayes, *Introduction to Japanese Politics* (4th ed M.E. Sharpe 2005) 74.

163 Ranghieri & Ishiwatari (n 128) 233, 256 (limits of cost–benefit analysis employed by the Japanese government).

Furthermore, the government responses to the disaster were also marked by the reluctance to grant broad and flexible power to the prime minister, the political leader. Many varying governmental departments are tasked with preparation and enforcement of countermeasures against natural disaster, even in times of emergency. No departments wanted to surrender their own broad and flexible powers to the prime minister's cabinet. As a result, even in times of emergency, the decision to grant exceptions in each department comes down to each individual department head.[164]

This strong departmentalism or sectionalism is one of the leading characteristics of the Japanese government process.[165] Strong departmentalism is also a reason for the reluctance to establish a government agency that would hold primary responsibility for responding to massive natural disasters, such as the Federal Emergency Management Agency (FEMA) in the United States.[166] Indeed, since Japan is bombarded by so many natural disasters, it would make much sense to create such an agency and statutorily grant broad and flexible powers to it for the purpose of responding to massive natural disasters. Then the government would not have to establish new headquarters after each new disaster. Nevertheless, the Japanese government has been reluctant to establish such an agency, meaning the power to respond to natural disasters in times of emergency still falls to each of the departments, who then exercise the power they have been granted.

***

The Tohoku Earthquake and tsunami revealed that the legal system in Japan was unprepared for a massive disaster on this scale. The disaster law in Japan was not able to prevent such extensive damage from the massive natural disaster from happening and failed to provide adequate responses to such disaster. Some of the failures revealed much deeper flaws in the Japanese legal system that prevented the government from preparing for a natural disaster and responding to the disaster accordingly. Furthermore, there were political reasons for such failures. In this sense, the Tohoku Earthquake and tsunami revealed the miserable failures of law and politics in Japan.

164 Moreover, these exceptional treatments were granted by internal memo or instruction from the head of the department to local branches or local governments that enforce such regulations. See nn 114–27.

165 Hideki Kato, Political Reform of the Japanese System of Government (Tokyo Foundation 28 October 2008) www.tokyofoundation.org/en/articles/2008/political-reform-of-the-japanese-system-of-government-symposium-report-2 accessed 12 January 2018.

166 Federal Emergency Management Agency, About the Agency (FEMA) www.fema.gov/about-agency accessed 12 January 2018. See Chapter 6 n 144–48.

3 Nuclear meltdown in Fukushima

Another very grave development emerged in the aftermath of the Tohoku Earthquake: the nuclear meltdown at the Fukushima No 1 (Daiichi) Nuclear Power Plant operated by the Tokyo Electric Power Co. (TEPCO). Although power to the facility was knocked out, the Fukushima No 1 Nuclear Power Plant was able to withstand the impact of the earthquake. The power shortage was prevented by the initiation of back-up emergency power generators, which maintained the power supply. However, the ensuing extremely powerful tsunami inundated the plant and incapacitated the back-up power generators. This caused the plant to lose all power and, with that, the ability to cool the nuclear fuel rods. As a result, the fuel rods in the reactor cores and the fuel ponds overheated, causing the covering water to evaporate, which in turn meant that the fuel rods, being exposed and no longer cooled by water, began to melt down. This triggered hydrogen build-up that eventually led to hydrogen blasts that destroyed the facility and allowed radioactive materials to contaminate the environment outside the facility. Both TEPCO and the central government scrambled to contain this disaster.

This chapter examines the developments leading to the crisis at the Fukushima Nuclear Power Plant, the legal system as it relates to nuclear disaster, and the government response to this calamity. It examines the various legal questions presented by the nuclear disaster along with the lackluster government effort to address them. This examination will show that there were serious failures of law in the preparation for possible nuclear disaster, and that the response to nuclear disaster shows that there were serious failures of politics behind these failures of law.

3.1 Earthquake, tsunami, and the Fukushima Nuclear Power Plant

The Tohoku Earthquake and subsequent tsunami brought another serious disaster to Japan: nuclear meltdown in Fukushima. What happened in the Fukushima No 1 Nuclear Power Plant in the aftermath of the earthquake and tsunami? How did the tsunami bring about such a serious nuclear accident? The process of development of nuclear meltdown must be first examined.

3.1.1 Fukushima No 1 Nuclear Power Plant

TEPCO is a company that supplies electricity to the entire Kanto Region, including Tokyo. It was once a public corporation having a monopoly over the production and provision of electricity throughout the Kanto region. Owing to privatization and liberalization, TEPCO is now a private company producing electricity alongside other players, though TEPCO remains the main supplier of electricity to almost all Tokyo residents.[1]

TEPCO has several nuclear power plants, including the Fukushima No 1—its oldest.[2] It is located in the Futaba town and Ohkuma town in the Fukushima Prefecture near the Pacific Coast and contains six nuclear reactors. Reactors Unit 1 through Unit 4 are clustered together while Units 5 and 6 are somewhat separated from the others.

The Fukushima Prefecture occupies the south corner of the Tohoku Region and is located to the northeast of Tokyo. It is divided into three separate parts, the Japan side, the interior and the Pacific side. The prefectural capital, Fukushima City, is situated in the interior and is almost 60 km away from the Nuclear Power Plant. The population is 1.8 million, most of whom are living on the Pacific side. Agriculture, especially rice crop production, and fishing and fish processing are the two main industries in Fukushima but there are many electronics and high-tech companies on the Pacific side.

It looks as though all the nuclear reactors and vital facilities of the Fukushima Nuclear Power Plant withstood the impact of the massive earthquake.[3] Reactor Units 1 through 3 were in operation at the time of the earthquake. However, after the earthquake shook the plant at 2:46 pm on 11 March 2011 all reactors were automatically shut down (following a procedure known as a "scram").[4] They were no longer in a critical state. Unit 4 reactor was already shut down for maintenance and was not operating at the time of the earthquake, much the same as reactor Units 5 and 6. Even after nuclear reactors are shut down, however, the fuel rods inside the reactors must still be cooled. Spent fuel rods in reactors Unit 4, Unit 5, and Unit 6 had already been placed in fuel ponds as they would need cooling for a number of years.

1 For corporate information on TEPCO, *see* Tokyo Electric Power Company, Kaisha joho [Corporate Information] (TEPCO) www.tepco.co.jp/about/corporateinfo/index-j.html accessed 14 January 2018.

2 All reactors at the Fukushima No 1 Nuclear Power Plant were GE Boiling Water Reactors (BWR) of an early design from the 1960s supplied by GE, Toshiba and Hitachi with what is known as a Mark I containment. World Nuclear Association, Fukushima Accident (WNA October 2017) www.world-nuclear.org/info/Safety-and-Security/Safety-of-Plants/Fukushima-Accident/#.Um8AdpHaPUU accessed 14 January 2018 (WNA Report).

3 TEPCO, Fukushima daiichi genshiryoku hatsudensho wo osotta jishin oyobi tsunami no kibo to shinsui joukyou [Impact of Earthquake and Tsunami to Fukushima No 1 Nuclear Power Plant] (TEPCO) www.tepco.co.jp/nu/fukushima-np/outline/2_2-j.html accessed 14 January 2018. However, the Diet accident report concluded that it could not preclude the possibility that there was some major damage to the vital facilities. National Diet of Japan Fukushima Nuclear Accident Independent Investigation Commission, Final Report (Diet 5 July 2012) http://warp.da.ndl.go.jp/info:ndljp/pid/3856371/naiic.go.jp/pdf/naiic_honpen.pdf accessed 14 January 2018 (Diet Report) 27.

4 "Scram" is "a rapid emergency shutdown of a nuclear reactor." Merriam-Webster dictionary, scram (Merriam-Webster) www.merriam-webster.com/dictionary/scram accessed 14 January 2018. Indeed, eleven reactors at four nuclear power plants were operating at the time of the earthquake but all of them shut down automatically. WNA report (n 2).

3.1.2 Loss of all electricity at the power plant

Fukushima No 1 was equipped with several layers of safeguards to ensure the nuclear fuel rods could remain cooled and at safe temperatures. When the Tohoku Earthquake knocked down power lines and the power supply was cut off, back-up generators automatically began to supply electricity. Disastrously, however, the tsunami hit the plant starting at 3:27 pm, submerging and incapacitating the back-up power generators located in the basement of the plant. The plant subsequently lost all electricity at 3:42 pm.[5]

This was an extremely serious situation. The cooling system, which circulated cooling water to reactors and fuel ponds, was powered by the electricity. The nuclear power plant had thus lost the means to cool the fuel rods inside both the reactor cores and fuel ponds. Moreover, the entire plant lost all capacity for checking water levels inside the reactors and the cooling ponds. There was no way to ascertain the conditions of the reactor or fuel ponds, including whether the fuel rods remained covered by water.

In accordance with article 10 of the Nuclear Disaster Special Measures Act (*genshiryoku saigai tokusohō*), TEPCO notified the Nuclear and Industrial Safety Agency (*genshiryoku anzen/hoan in*) (NISA), an agency within the Ministry of Economy, Trade and Industry (METI) charged with regulating nuclear safety, at 3:42 pm when Masao Yoshida, the manager of the Fukushima Plant, confirmed all electricity was lost.[6] At 4:45 pm, when the central control center could no longer ascertain water levels in the reactors, TEPCO notified NISA again, this time in accordance with article 15 of the Nuclear Disaster Special Measures Act.[7] Believing this notification necessitated the declaration of a "nuclear emergency" (*genshiryoku kinkyu jitai*), Economy, Trade and Industry Minister Banri Kaieda reported the situation to Prime Minister Naoto Kan at 5:42 pm and requested such declaration.[8] Of note is the fact that it took nearly one hour for Kaieda to

5 TEPCO, Fukushima daiichi genshiryoku hatsudensho: Hisai chokugo no taiou joukyou ni tsuite [Fukushima No 1 Nuclear Power Plant: Initial Response Right After the Accident] (TEPCO) www.tepco.co.jp/cc/press/betu11_j/images/110618l.pdf accessed 14 January 2018 (TEPCO, Initial Response). A full account of the development leading to the meltdown can be found in Diet Report (n 3); Cabinet Office, Investigation Committee on the Accident at the Fukushima Nuclear Power Stations of Tokyo Electric Power Company, Final Report (Cabinet Office 23 July 2012) www.cas.go.jp/jp/seisaku/icanps/post-2.html accessed 14 January 2018 (Cabinet Report); TEPCO, Fukushima genshiryoku jiko chousa houkokusho [Fukushima Nuclear Power Plant Accident Report] (TEPCO 20 June 2012) www4.tepco.co.jp/cc/press/betu12_j/images/120620j0303.pdf accessed 13 February 2018; WNA report (n 2); David Lochbaum, Edwin Lyman, Susan Q. Stranahan and the Union of Concerned Scientists, *Fukushima: The Story of a Nuclear Disaster* (New Press 2014); Kenji E. Kushida, "Japan's Fukushima Nuclear Disaster: An Overview," in Edward D. Brandford & Scott D. Sagan (eds), *Learning from a Disaster: Improving Nuclear Safety and Security after Fukushima* (Stanford 2016) 10.

6 Genshiryoku saigai taisaku tokubetsusochihō [Special Measures Act on Nuclear Disaster Countermeasures], Law no 156 of 1999 (Nuclear Disaster Special Measures Act), art 10.

7 Ibid art 15. *See* TEPCO, Fukushima daiichi genshiryoku hatsudensho jiko no shodou taiou ni tsuite [Early Response to the Accident at the Fukushima No 1 Nuclear Power Plant] (TEPCO 22 December 2012) www.tepco.co.jp/cc/press/betu11_j/images/111222o.pdf.

inform Kan of this dire circumstance. Kan asked various technical and legal questions relating to this sequence of events and the prospective aftermath, but no one was able to provide answers to these questions. As a result, Kan suspended his decision on whether to declare a nuclear emergency and attended another non-emergent meeting. After that meeting, Kan eventually issued a nuclear emergency declaration at 7:03 pm.[9] It thus took more than 1.5 hours for Kan to decide to declare the disaster a nuclear emergency.[10] Chief Cabinet Secretary Yukio Edano organized a public press conference at 7:45 pm announcing the declaration of a nuclear emergency and the establishment of the Nuclear Disaster Response Headquarters (*genshiryoku saigai taisaku honbu*).[11]

However, an evacuation order was not immediately issued. Frustrated with the delay, at 8:50 pm, the governor of Fukushima instructed local residents within a 2 km radius of the Fukushima No 1 Nuclear Power Plant to evacuate.[12] Kan eventually issued an evacuation instruction at 9:23 pm, expanding the evacuation to include everyone within a 3 km radius of the plant while at the same time instructing all residents within a 10 km radius to remain inside their homes.[13]

3.1.3 Situation escalated

Even though all reactors had been shut down, the loss of electricity rendered the plant unable to cool the fuel rods inside the reactors. Yoshida made the first attempt at restoring electricity to the cooling system. Kan also tried to dispatch power trucks to supply electricity. However, all roads were severely damaged and trucks had extreme difficulty reaching the Fukushima plant. Even when these trucks finally arrived, they were useless because the voltage was incorrect, plug sockets were incompatible, and a longer cable was needed to connect the equipment.[14] While every effort was being made to restore power using these trucks, the radiation level inside the reactor building was gradually rising. Due to the power outage, central control was figuratively “in the dark” with respect to water levels inside the reactors. TEPCO workers were not sure whether the fuel rods were still immersed in cooling water. Moreover, it appears that

8 Nuclear Disaster Special Measures Act (n 6) art 15(1).
9 Ibid art 15(2).
10 Diet Report (n 3) 304–06.
11 Cabinet Report (n 5) 193–94.
12 Cabinet Office, Heisei 24nenban bosai hakusho [Disaster Prevention Whitepaper, 2012] (Cabinet Office), www.bousai.go.jp/kaigirep/hakusho/h24/bousai2012/html/honbun/1b_1h_2s_03_00.htm accessed 14 January 2018.
13 Ibid; Nuclear Disaster Special Measures Act (n 6) art 15(3).
14 Kenji E. Kushida, *Japan's Fukushima Nuclear Disaster: Narrative, Analysis, and Recommendations* (SSRN 1 November 2012) https://papers.ssrn.com/sol3/papers.cfm?abstract_id=2118876 accessed 14 January 2018 12–13.

the emergency cooling system was not functioning properly. The fuel rods had overheated, had evaporated the covering water, and, no longer being immersed in water, had become exposed. This exposure caused the rods to overheat and begin melting down. TEPCO admitted that the fuel rods "might be damaged" though they avoided (perhaps intentionally) the use of the expression "melting down."[15] In any event, the situation was graver than was made public. Unable to restore power, Yoshida decided to attempt to manually supply water to the reactors and fuel ponds.

Within hours, the Unit 1 reactor showed signs that extremely high pressure had built up within its reactor container, prompting TEPCO to notify NISA, in accordance with article 15 of the Nuclear Disaster Special Measures Act, at 12:49 am on 12 March. At this stage, TEPCO and plant workers attempted to activate the container vent in order to release the pressure and avert an explosion. The central government issued an order to activate the vent at 1:30 am on 12 March. Tragically, however, all back-up generators were now submerged under water brought in by the tsunami and the vent could not be operated mechanically. The only option was manual vent operation, but the prospects for this were ill fated as well. No workers were experienced with manual operation of the vent, so workers were forced to resort to the structural map of the plant just to ascertain the vent's location. Moreover, high levels of radiation near the vent were already registering. The workers needed to prepare for a quick operation. As a result, Yoshida was not able to activate the vent promptly.[16] Frustrated by the delay, Kan decided to visit the Fukushima plant himself on the morning of 12 March. En route to the plant, Kan asked Haruki Madarame, chairperson of the Nuclear Safety Commission (NSC), about the possibility of explosion. Madarame told Kan that there was no possibility of explosion.[17]

It took a while to actually open the vent but TEPCO eventually succeeded in doing so at 2:30 pm on 12 March.[18] However, by that time, the reactor

15 TEPCO was accused of intentionally attempting to hide the possibility of nuclear meltdown. TEPCO explained that "meltdown" is an ambiguous word and that it had no intention of hiding the fact that nuclear rods were damaged. TEPCO, Roshin no joukyou ni kansuru kouhyou ni tsuite [On Publication of the Status of the Nuclear Rods] (TEPCO) www.tepco.co.jp/nu/fukushima-np/interim/images/111202_16-j.pdf accessed 14 January 2018. TEPCO and the METI now speculate that the nuclear rods were exposed within 3 hours of the earthquake, started to melt down within 4 hours, and then melted down to bottom of the container, damaging the reactor pressure vessel, within 15 hours. Ministry of Economy, Trade and Industry, Fukushima daiichi genshiryoku hatsudensho 1–3gouki no roshin no joutai ni tsuite [On the Status of the Nuclear Rods in Unit 1 and Unit 3 Reactors at the Fukushima No 1 Nuclear Power Plant] (METI) www.meti.go.jp/earthquake/nuclear/backdrop/pdf/app-chap04-1.pdf accessed 14 January 2018. Most of the reactor core was believed to have melted down to the bottom of the reactor pressure vessel, sunk through and eroded the drywell concrete below, thus reducing the heat and enabling it to solidify. WNA report (n 2).

16 Kushida (n 14) 14.

17 Ibid 16.

18 Ibid 16–17. Some workers went on a "suicide mission" to carry out a manual vent where tremendously high radiation was detected and were exposed to a high dosage of radiation during this attempt; ibid.

had generated a large amount of hydrogen. This build-up led to a hydrogen blast from within the facility that literally blew the roof off of the building that housed the Unit 1 reactor at 3:36 pm.[19] Radiation density around the structure was measured at 1,015 μSv.[20] Radioactive contaminants escaped from the facility. Apparently, the nuclear rods were, in fact, melting down at this stage, perhaps even to the bottom of the container. Following the explosion, Kan was furious because of Madarame's failed assurances, and his distrust of experts and bureaucrats exacerbated.

Yoshida continued trying to pump water into the reactors and fuel ponds though it soon became apparent they would need to use seawater. Yoshida started pumping in seawater at 7:04 pm. However, when informed of the possibility that seawater might be used, Kan raised concern over whether such action could put the reactors back into a critical state. Kan asked Madarame about this possibility, and was told that the possibility was not zero. Kan and other government leaders thus started to reconsider this option. At 7:25 pm, TEPCO thus ordered Yoshida to stop pumping in seawater and to instead wait for a final decision in light of Kan's concern.[21] However, Yoshida so greatly feared that a scenario much worse would unfold if he stopped pumping in seawater that he ignored TEPCO's order and continued infusing seawater. Kan ultimately decided to proceed using seawater and, at 8:05 pm, Kaieda ordered TEPCO to continue. TEPCO ostensibly restarted at 8:20 pm.[22] Yoshida did not disclose his insubordination until May of 2011, with the result that TEPCO had believed the infusion of seawater had been halted for nearly one hour between 7:25 pm and 8:20 pm.[23]

Concurrently, the situation in the other reactors was gradually worsening. Though the emergency cooling system for the Unit 3 reactor appeared to be working at one point, the battery powering it stopped working shortly after. At 11:01 am on 14 March, a hydrogen blast destroyed the facility housing the Unit 3

19 Ibid 17.

20 Institute of Electrical and Electronics Engineers (IEEE), Spectrum, Timeline: The Japanese Nuclear Emergency (IEEE), http://spectrum.ieee.org/tech-talk/energy/nuclear/timeline-the-japanese-nuclear-emergency. For reference and comparison purposes, the International Commission on Radiological Protection's (ICRP) recommended individual dose limits for radiation are set at 100 μSv per year for radiation workers and 1 μSv per year for members of the general public. International Atomic Energy Agency (IAEA), Radiation in Everyday Life (IAEA) www.iaea.org/Publications/Factsheets/English/radlife.

21 "Yoshida chousho: Kaisui chunyu, meireiihan wo kakugo—Genpatsu jiko [Yoshida Memo: Continued Pumping of Seawater Ignoring the Order]" (*Nihonkeizai Shimbun* 11 September 2014) www.nikkei.com/article/DGXLASFS1000Y_Q4A910C1I00000/ accessed 14 January 2018.

22 "Fukushima daiichi no kaisui chuunyuu chuudan sezu: Touden shochou, honsha ni mudan [Pumping of Seawater Was Not Suspended at the Fukushima No 1 Nuclear Power Plant: Plant Manager Ignored Order from TEPCO Headquarters]" (*Asahi Shimbun* 27 May 2011) www.asahi.com/special/10005/TKY201105260339.html accessed 14 January 2018.

23 Diet Report (n 3) 311–13.

reactor, leaving only the skeleton of the structure and releasing a large volume of smoke.[24] The Unit 2 reactor also lost the capacity for cooling, and registered extremely high pressures within the reactor container. A loud noise erupted from its pressure suppression chamber on 15 March, followed by a sudden decline in interior pressure, indicating a possible rupture of the suppression chamber. White smoke was also detected.[25] At the Unit 4 reactor facility, although all fuel rods were already stored in the fuel pond, with the loss of electricity, this facility also lost cooling capacity which led to an explosion blowing off the roof and most of the containment facility's walls on 15 March.[26] Radiation levels at Fukushima No 1 power plant's main gate reached 11,930 μSv, marking the peak of recorded radiation release levels.

3.1.4 Efforts to contain the disaster

It was a tremendous undertaking to supply water to the nuclear reactors and fuel ponds. Unable to supply power to operate the cooling system, TEPCO thus decided to supply water manually. However, TEPCO did not have equipment on hand for supplying this water during the emergency. Moreover, after the hydrogen blast, debris contaminated by radioactive materials had been spread all over the plant. Radiation levels were too high for TEPCO employees to approach the reactors. Since all electricity had been cut off, it was hard to know how the reactors or fuel pond were functioning from the outside. It took tremendous effort, with foreign assistance, for TEPCO to infuse water in an attempt

24 Kushida (n 14) 20; TEPCO, 3gouki wa naze kakokujiko ni itattanoka [Why Did the Unit 3 Reactor Lead to the Serious Accident?] (TEPCO) www.tepco.co.jp/nu/fukushima-np/outline/2_7-j.html accessed 14 January 2018.

25 Kushida (n 14) 23; TEPCO, 2gouki wa naze kakokujiko ni ittatnoka [Why Did the Unit 2 Reactor Lead to Serious Accident?] (TEPCO) www.tepco.co.jp/nu/fukushima-np/outline/2_5-j.html accessed 14 January 2018. The Unit 2 reactor is believed to have emitted the most serious radiation because the TEPCO workers failed to carry out a vent and as a result radioactive materials spread to the outside without going through the water filter.

26 TEPCO, 4gouki no jiko no keika [Process Leading to the Accident of the Unit 4 Reactor] (TEPCO) www.tepco.co.jp/nu/fukushima-np/outline/2_10-j.html accessed 14 January 2018. The explosion in the Unit 4 reactor facility was of even more serious concern because, unlike the fuel rods in the Unit 1 to Unit 3 reactors that were protected by containment vessels, the fuel rods in the pond in the Unit 4 reactor facility were not well protected and were directly exposed to the outside atmosphere. Kushida (n 14) 23. In the end, the Fukushima nuclear accident emitted at least 168 times the amount of radioactive cesium 137 as did the Hiroshima atomic bomb; ibid 1. The accident was rated at level 7 on the International Nuclear Event Score (INES)—the maximum; ibid. See also Toshihiro Higuchi, "Radiation Protection by Numbers: Another 'Man-Made' Disaster," in Brandford & Sagan (n 5) 109. In contrast, Unit 5 reactor and Unit 6 reactor were already stopped for a regular checkup at the time of the earthquake. Although both lost electricity, emergency generators started working, and cooling of fuel rods commenced on 19 March, reaching a stable condition on 20 March. TEPCO, Fukushima daiichi genshiryoku hatudensho plant joukyotō no oshirase [News on Conditions at the Fukushima No 1 Nuclear Power Plant] (TEPCO 23 March 2011) www.tepco.co.jp/nu/f1-np/press_f1/2010/htmldata/bi1377-j.pdf accessed 14 January 2018.

to contain the situation. First, Self Defense Forces (SDF) helicopters tried to supply water from above the reactor on 17 March, with no significant impact on infusing water to the reactors.[27] Then, SDF officers started supplying water on 17 and 18 March from the ground but there was a limit to what they could accomplish. Therefore, the central government had no choice but to ask local firefighters to assist with infusing water into the reactors and fuel ponds from 19 March onwards.[28]

By 22 March, the direct power line to all reactors was connected which restored the power supply. On 24 March, the cooling pump became operational.[29] Gradually and slowly, TEPCO workers gained control of the situation. It took, however, more than six months to contain the disaster. It was only after December 2011 that all four reactors reached a cold shut down.[30]

Meanwhile, instructions issued to local residents on 11 March, which had initially ordered those within a 3 km radius of the plant to evacuate, and advised those within a 10 km radius to remain indoors, were eventually expanded so that those within a 20 km radius were instructed to evacuate, and those within a 30 km radius were advised to stay indoors.[31] These instructions were issued without careful coordination or without sufficient information provided to evacuees and therefore caused tremendous confusion and chaos. Moreover, the blasts seriously contaminated vegetables, water, and seafood, forcing the government to issue restrictions on the marketing and consumption of these products from the radioactively affected area, with the prime minister eventually having to ban the marketing and consumption of all of these products.[32]

These developments raised significant legal issues as to the power of the central (as well as the local) government to respond to a nuclear disaster, to impose evacuation, and to restrict the marketing, sale, and consumption of food sources contaminated by radioactivity. Furthermore, because of the critical shortage of electricity due to the catastrophe at the nuclear power plant, TEPCO had to implement rolling blackouts and the central government also faced the prospect of having to impose electricity consumption restrictions in order to avoid unexpected, large-scale blackouts.

27 Kushida (n 14) 25.

28 Ibid 25–26. Thereafter, many large concrete pump trucks were called in to supply water and water supply gradually became more efficient. ibid 26–27.

29 Ibid 27.

30 Nuclear Disaster Response Headquarters, Tokyo Denryoku Fukushima daiichi genshiryoku hatsudensho/jiko no shusoku nimuketa michisuji step 2 no kanryou houkokusho [Report on the Completion of Step 2 toward the Containment of the Accident of the TEPCO Fukushima No 1 Nuclear Power Plant] (METI 16 December 2011) www.meti.go.jp/earthquake/nuclear/pdf/111216a.pdf accessed 20 January 2018.

31 nn 117–19.

32 n 143.

This chapter examines how the legal system was prepared for all these legal questions raised during the Fukushima accident and how the Japanese government responded to them.[33]

3.2 Regulatory system for nuclear power plants

What was the regulatory system for nuclear power plants and their operation? How did the Japanese government attempt to ensure their safety? What was the plan for a serious accident that might occur in a nuclear power plant? To answer these questions, the regulatory system that existed prior to the Fukushima disaster must be examined next.

3.2.1 Basic Act on Atomic Energy

Japan is the only country in the world that has actually experienced nuclear warfare. On 6 August 1945, an atomic bomb was dropped on Hiroshima, instantly killing some 80,000 residents.[34] Some additional 16,600 residents died within four months because of the blast and radiation exposure.[35] On 9 August, the second atomic bomb was dropped on Nagasaki.[36] It is estimated that between 40,000 and 75,000 people died immediately following the atomic explosion, while the total deaths resulting from the bomb may have reached 80,000 by the end of 1945.[37] Many survivors and their children suffered from cancer and other

33 The nuclear reactors in the nearby Fukushima No 2 Nuclear Power Plant also lost power temporarily, stopped operations automatically, and emergency notification was sent. The evacuation of residents within a 3 km radius of the plant was instructed and the instruction was extended later to all residents within a 10 km radius of the plant. However, the power was restored and all cooling for the nuclear rods was also safely restored. There was no radiation leak. The evacuation instruction was later narrowed down to residents within an 8 km radius of the plant. Ministry of Economy, Trade and Industry, Tokyo denryoku kabushiki gaisha Fukushima daini genshiryoku hatsudensho no hinankuiki no minaoshi ni tsuite [On Reconsideration of the Evacuation Area around TEPCO's Fukushima No 2 Nuclear Power Plant] (METI 21 April 2011) www.meti.go.jp/earthquake/nuclear/shiji_2f.html accessed 14 January 2018. The nuclear emergency declaration was lifted on 26 December 2011 and the evacuation instruction was also lifted. Nuclear and Industry Safety Agency, News Release (26 December 2011), Tokyo denryoku kabushikigaisha Fukushima dai2 genshiryoku hatsudensho nikakawaru genshiryoku kinkyujitai kaijosengen nitsuite [Regarding Declaration on Cancelation of Nuclear Emergency Situation of Fukushima No 2 Nuclear Power Station, Tokyo Electric Power Co., Inc.] (NDL) www.dl.ndl.go.jp/view/download/digidepo_6011739_po_231226-4-1.pdf?contentNo=1&alternativeNo= accessed 14 January 2018.

34 Bombing of Hiroshima and Nagasaki, History (history.com) www.history.com/topics/world-war-ii/bombing-of-hiroshima-and-nagasaki accessed 14 January 2018.

35 Ibid*;* Bombings of Hiroshima and Nagasaki, 1045 (Atomic Heritage Foundation) www.atomicheritage.org/history/bombings-hiroshima-and-nagasaki-1945 accessed 14 January 2018. The City of Hiroshima estimates that 237,000 people ended up dying because of the bomb. Ibid.

36 Ibid.

37 Ibid.

health complications over the following decades.[38] There is no doubt that the Japanese people know about nuclear power's devastating effects.

Due to being an isolated island country and having a very limited amount of natural resources, Japan depended heavily on imports for its primary energy needs following the devastation of World War II. As it recovered from the war and started to rapidly develop its economy, Japan had to rely primarily on fossil fuel imports, particularly oil from the Middle East.[39] This area of the World is politically volatile and is often affected by regional conflicts. The 1973 oil crisis caused the price of oil to skyrocket, sending Japan into a panic over the fear that oil imports might stop.[40] Japan learned a very important lesson: it needed to diversify its energy sources and avoid relying too heavily upon the Middle East. This realization forced the government to place its primary focus on nuclear power.

Japan started the development of its nuclear power program in 1954. The Atomic Power Basic Act,[41] which detailed the fundamental policies concerning the use of nuclear power, was enacted in 1955. In the following year, the Atomic Energy Commission (*genshiryoku iinkai*) (AEC) was established.[42] The Ministry of Education, Culture, Sports, Science and Technology (MEXT) promotes nuclear technology and the METI promotes its industrial use.

The fundamental policies for using nuclear power established by the Atomic Power Basic Act, declare that the use of nuclear power is restricted for peaceful purposes and that the development and use of nuclear power should be conducted under the principle of autonomy and democratic administration, aspiring to ensure nuclear safety.[43] The AEC was established to enforce the government's nuclear policy systematically and to ensure the democratic oversight of nuclear administration.[44] The AEC's role is to prepare, review, and make decisions on anything related to the use of nuclear power.[45] The Atomic Power Basic Act requires any prospective developers who wish to construct nuclear reactors to follow government regulations under a separate statute.[46] It also mandates that

38 For cancer risks among atomic-bomb survivors, *see* Radiation Effects Research Foundation, "Solid Cancer Risks among Atomic-bomb survivors" (RERF) www.rerf.jp/radefx/late_e/cancrisk.html accessed 14 January 2018.

39 In 2014, Japan imported 99.7% of its oils from foreign countries and 80% of them came from the Middle East. Agency for Natural Resources and Energy, Energy hakusho 2016 [Whitepaper on Energy, 2016] (METI) www.enecho.meti.go.jp/about/whitepaper/2016html/2-1-3.html accessed 14 January 2018 # 3–1.

40 R.P. Sinha, "Japan and the Oil Crisis" (1974) 30:8 *World Today* 335.

41 Genshiryoku kihonhō [Atomic Power Basic Act], Law no 186 of 1955.

42 Atomic Energy Commission, Genshiryoku iinkai no yakuwari [Role of AEC] (AEC) www.aec.go.jp/jicst/NC/about/index.htm accessed 14 January 2018.

43 Atomic Power Basic Act (n 41) art 2.

44 Ibid art 4.

45 Ibid art 5. After the Nuclear Regulatory Authority (NRA) was established, matters on the safety measures of nuclear power plants were no longer within the jurisdiction of the AEC, but the NRA. ibid art 3–2 & art 5.

46 Ibid art 14.

prospective developers submit an operation plan and receive government approval before they begin operating.[47]

3.2.2 Nuclear Reactor Regulation Act

Of course, the government heavily regulates the use of nuclear power and the construction and operation of nuclear power plants. These regulations are meant to ensure nuclear power plants remain safe, and to prevent serious accidents that would cause grave damage to nearby citizens.[48]

The Nuclear Reactor Regulation Act[49] (*genshirotō kiseihō*) established the regulatory scheme for nuclear power plants. According to the Nuclear Reactor Regulation Act, a power company that wishes to establish a nuclear reactor to generate power (power-generating nuclear reactor) needs to obtain a government permit.[50] There has been a change on who has the power to grant this permit. Initially the prime minister had this power, but it was later vested with the Minister of Economy, Trade and Industry (regulatory power was actually enforced by the NISA, and the NSC was created from the AEC to supervise the safety issues). After the Fukushima disaster, the power to grant permits was given to the Nuclear Regulatory Authority (*genshiryoku kisei iinkai*) (NRA), an agency within the Ministry of Environment (MOE). Despite these changes, the overall regulatory system has not been altered much.

The government is prohibited from granting a permit unless the application satisfies the following four criteria:[51]

1 there is no danger that the proposed power-generating nuclear reactor would be used for anything other than peaceful purposes;
2 the applicant has the necessary technical capacity and financial basis to establish the power-generating nuclear reactor;
3 the applicant has the technical capacity necessary to implement countermeasures to prevent or contain any serious accidents and otherwise to operate the power-generating nuclear reactor properly; and

47 Ibid art 16.

48 The regulatory system before the Fukushima accident is summarized at Research Organization for Information Science and Technology, ATOMICA, Hatsudenyō genshiro no anzenkisei no gaiyō (ATOMICA) www.rist.or.jp/atomica/data/dat_detail.php?Title_No=11-02-01-01 accessed 14 January 2018, and the new regulatory system after the establishment of the NRA in 2012 is summarized at ibid, Genshirotō kiseihō no gaiyō (ATOMICA) www.rist.or.jp/atomica/data/dat_detail.php?Title_Key=10-07-01-05 accessed 14 January 2018.

49 Kakugenryou busshitsu, kakunenryou busshitsu oyobi genshiro no kisei nikansuru hōritsu [Act on Regulation on Nuclear Source Materials, Nuclear Fuel Materials and Nuclear Reactors], Law no 166 of 1957 (Nuclear Reactor Regulation Act).

50 Ibid art 43–3–5 (after 2012 amendment). Before the 2012 amendment, all nuclear reactors were treated the same but the 2012 amendment introduced a distinction between commercial power-generating nuclear reactor and others.

51 Ibid art 43–3–6 (after 2012 amendment). Before the 2012 amendment, these criteria were stipulated in article 24 of the Nuclear Reactor Regulation Act.

4 the location, structure, and equipment of the proposed power-generating nuclear reactor satisfies government standards . . . such as are sufficient to prevent disaster to be caused by nuclear fuel materials, anything contaminated by nuclear fuel materials, or the nuclear reactor itself.

If the power company wants to modify the fundamental design of the power-generating nuclear reactor, it needs to obtain a permit for the proposed modifications.[52] Also, before construction begins, the power company must obtain approval for its construction plan.[53] Moreover, the facility must pass an inspection after construction is complete and before operations start.[54] If the construction involves welding, the power company must inspect the welding before the start of its use, and the result of that inspection needs to be recorded and kept.[55] The government will also inspect the facility's organization, method, management of construction, and other factors to ensure safety of the welding.[56] Furthermore, the power company needs to submit an operation plan for the proposed nuclear reactor.[57] It must also implement measures to ensure the safe operation of the nuclear power plant, in addition to ensuring proper transport, storage, and disposal of nuclear fuel materials or anything contaminated by the nuclear fuel materials, even in the event of serious accident.[58] It also needs to establish a security protocol and submit it for approval before operation of the power-generating nuclear reactor can begin.[59, 60]

The government can revoke the permit or order the suspension of the operation of a nuclear power plant if there is a violation.[61] Moreover, if the government later determines that the location, structure, or equipment of the facility does not satisfy the fourth criterion of the requirements for a permit, the government may order the operator of the facility to cease operations, modify its operation protocols, repair or relocate the facility, adopt a different operation method for the facility, or adopt any other necessary measures for security.[62] The government may do the same when the technical standards mandated by the government are not met, or when the measures to ensure the safety of the nuclear reactor facility's operation, including the proper transport, storage, and disposal of nuclear

52 ibid art 43–3–9.
53 Ibid art 43–3–9.
54 Ibid art 43–3–11.
55 Ibid art 43–3–13(1)–(2).
56 Ibid art 43–3–13(3)–(4).
57 Ibid art 43–3–17.
58 Ibid art 43–3–22.
59 Ibid art 43–3–24(1).
60 Before the 2012 amendment, there was no obligation to retrofit the nuclear reactor after the permit had been granted. The 2012 amendment required the operator of the nuclear power plant to maintain the facility and ensure it complied with the current technical standards stipulated. Ibid art 43–3–14 (newly added by the 2012 amendment).
61 Ibid art 43–3–20(2).
62 Ibid art 43–3–23(1).

fuel materials or anything contaminated by the nuclear fuel materials are not sufficient.[63] As a result, the government and power companies have argued that nuclear power plants are safe because of these extensive regulations.

3.2.3 Nuclear Disaster Special Measures Act

Government response to nuclear accidents was stipulated in the Nuclear Disaster Special Measures Act.[64] Under the Act, it was the responsibility of the operator, normally a power company, to prevent nuclear disaster, to respond to such disaster by containing further damage, and to restore the facility.[65] The government, however, was responsible for adopting measures for responding to nuclear disaster, as stipulated in the Basic Act on Disaster Countermeasures.[66]

When a power company detected radiation levels above the prescribed maximum at an outer boundary of a nuclear power plant facility, or encountered any incident as delineated by the cabinet order, it had to notify the prime minister, NISA, and relevant governors and mayors.[67] This notification is generally referred to as an "article 10 notification."

When notified that extraordinarily high levels of radiation had been detected and that a nuclear emergency was believed to be in effect, the power company had to also notify NISA and the Economy, Trade and Industry Minister had to notify the prime minister.[68] This notification was generally referred to as an "article 15 notification." The prime minister was required to issue a declaration of "nuclear emergency," specifying the areas where emergency measures were to be adopted and the outline of these emergency measures.[69] Then, according to article 15, paragraph 3, the prime minister had to "instruct" governors and heads of municipal governments in the specified areas and provide recommendations or instructions relating to evacuation, remain-indoors advisories, or other instructions relating to implementation of nuclear emergency measures.[70]

Once a declaration was issued, the prime minister, with the support of cabinet, had to establish a Nuclear Disaster Response Headquarters (*genshiryoku saigai taisaku honbu*) inside the Cabinet Office.[71] The prime minister as a director of the Headquarters would oversee these headquarters,[72] supervise all emergency measures administered therein, and supervise all public officials engaged in "nuclear

63 Ibid.
64 Nuclear Disaster Special Measures Act (n 6).
65 Ibid art 3.
66 Ibid art 4. See Saigai taisaku kihonhō [Basic Act on Disaster Countermeasures], Law no 223 of 1961. See Chapter 1 (nn 158–99).
67 Nuclear Disaster Special Measures Act (n 6) art 10(1).
68 Ibid art 15(1).
69 Ibid art 15(2).
70 Ibid art 15(3).
71 Ibid art 16(1).
72 Ibid art 17(1).

emergency countermeasures" (*kinkyu jitai oukyu taisaku*).[73] According to article 20, paragraph 2, at the time of the accident, the prime minister, as a director of the Headquarters, could instruct the responsible minister to order necessary emergency measures and, according to article, paragraph 3, at the time of the accident, the prime minister as a director could issue a necessary instruction to the heads of relevant designated administrative agencies, heads of the local government or their government, designated public organizations as well as nuclear power companies, if it was necessary to carry out the emergency countermeasures properly and promptly. Since the 2012 amendment, both are combined together into article 20, paragraph 2.[74] Emergency countermeasures to be implemented included providing information on the disaster, recommending or instructing evacuation, collecting information such as that on radiation level measurements, providing assistance to victims, temporarily restoring facilities, maintaining social order by preventing crime or by regulating traffic, providing emergency transportation, providing food or medical supplies, dealing with radioactive contamination, and other measures aimed at containing the disaster.[75] As such, the central government followed this procedure in response to receiving notification from TEPCO.

3.2.4 Nuclear power plant subsidies and safety agreement

In order to build a nuclear power plant, it is of course politically essential to obtain the support of the local government. The government has passed various statutes that provide many grants to local governments who are willing to accept a nuclear power plant within their jurisdiction.[76] These grants are lucrative incentives for local governments and their residents to accept nuclear power plants. As a result, municipalities that host nuclear power plants are often equipped with luxurious public facilities such as gyms, public libraries, or music halls.[77]

On the other hand, the municipal or local government that accepts a nuclear power plant forces the power company to conclude a "nuclear safety agreement" (*genshiryoku anzen kyotei*). Basically, such agreement mandates the power company to measure the radiation level around the plant, notify the municipal

73 Ibid art 17(2).

74 Ibid art 20(2). After the establishment of the NRA, the prime minister is precluded from giving instruction on the safety matters of the nuclear power plant under the jurisdiction of the NRA. Ibid art 20(3). Chapter 6 n 289.

75 Ibid art 26(1).

76 Dengenkaihatsu sokushinzeihō [Act on Tax to Promote Development of Electricity Power], Law no 79 of 1974: Tokubetsu kaikei nikansuru hōritsu [Act on Special Finance Accounting], Law no 23 of 2007 (formerly Dengenkaihatsu sokushin taisaku tokubetsu kaikeihō [Act on Special Financial Accounting for Measures to Promote Development of Electricity Power], Law no 80 of 1974); Hatsudenyō shisetsu shūhenchiiki seibihō [Act on Development of Adjacent Areas of the Electricity Power Generation Facilities], Law no 78 of 1974.

77 Of course, the municipal government and local government can expect huge tax revenue, increased investment in nuclear power related business, and significant employment opportunities for local residents if it accepts the nuclear power plant.

and local government of any abnormality, and allow the municipal and local government to enter the plant for inspection and seek advance consent for any changes, including reactivation.[78] Although only the central government has a legal regulatory power over the nuclear power plant, this kind of nuclear safety agreement would allow municipal and local government to control the nuclear power plant.

3.2.5 Nuclear Damage Award Act

On top of the above mentioned assurances, in order to assure local residents that compensation would be provided for any kind of damage caused by nuclear accidents, the government passed the Nuclear Damage Award Act (*genshiryoku songai baishohō*).[79] Basically it mandates that power companies are to pay damages for any loss or injury related to nuclear accidents as "nuclear damages" (*genshiryoku songai*), regardless of fault, except when the loss or injury is caused by a "catastrophic natural disaster."[80] The Act also mandates the power company to prepare sufficient security for paying out damages by obtaining a nuclear damage insurance contract backed up by government indemnity or by submitting a security deposit.[81] It then expects the government to intervene in the event that the total liability of a power company for damage exceeds the limits of the indemnity or deposit or when the damage is caused by a "catastrophic natural disaster."[82]

This statute hedged the liability of the power company and prompted the power company to build and operate the nuclear power plant. It also guaranteed to the local residents that any damage would be covered either by the power company or by central government, making it easier for the local residents to accept the nuclear power plant.

3.3 Government efforts to stabilize the Fukushima Nuclear Power Plant

As the nuclear disaster was unfolding, the Japanese government had to scramble to contain it. How did the Japanese government respond? What kinds of legal questions were raised during the course of the containment effort? How were such legal questions answered? This section follows the government responses to see whether the containment effort was appropriate.

78 Hide Ara, "Genshiryoku hatsudensho no anzenkyotei [Safety Agreement of Nuclear Power Plant]," (1975) 580 *Juristo* 35; Tokaimura, Genshiryoku anzenkyotei [Nuclear Safety Agreement] (Tokaimura) www.vill.tokai.ibaraki.jp/as-tokai/05kyotei/anzenkyo.htm accessed 14 January 2018.

79 Genshiryoku songai no baishou ni kansuru hōrisu [Act on Damage Payment for Nuclear Damages], Law no. 147 of 1961 (Nuclear Damage Award Act).

80 Ibid art 3.

81 Ibid art 6 art 7.

82 Ibid art 16. See Chapter 5 n 50.

3.3.1 Government intervention

As is apparent from the text of the Nuclear Reactor Regulation Act, primary responsibility for responding to a nuclear disaster lies with the power company—TEPCO in this case.[83] In order to stabilize the disaster and cool the reactor and the spent nuclear fuel in the pool, however, the Japanese government actively intervened in TEPCO's operations. In so doing, the chain of command became unclear and chaotic. Information pertaining to the dangers and possible impacts were critically lacking, causing the central government to make several decisions based on insufficient information.

On 11 March, Kan established the Nuclear Disaster Response Headquarters in the basement of Cabinet House and held a meeting with all ministers of state and high-ranking officials of each department in the large fourth floor meeting room. Headquarters meetings were held, however, only ten times during the critical first week.[84] During this time, the prime minister was often found responding to the disaster together with small groups of people in his fifth floor office, collecting information, and issuing instructions.[85] Although the Headquarters is supposed to be the chief decision-making body, most decisions were made by the prime minister from his office.[86] Many decisions were made without sufficient supporting information. Furthermore, in many cases, information was not shared between the Prime Minister's Office and the Headquarters.[87]

The NSC was supposed to give technical advice to the prime minister with respect to the countermeasures against the nuclear power accident. However, its members were unable to gather immediately and its chairperson Madarame was called to Prime Minister Kan's office for the purpose of giving advice. As a result, the Commission did not function as a collegial body and the prime

83 At the time of the accident, however, TEPCO chairperson, Tsunehisa Katsumata, was in China and was not able to return to TEPCO head office until 12 March at 4:00 pm because all airplanes were suspended. TEPCO president, Masataka Shimizu, was in West Japan and was unable to return to TEPCO until 12 March at 9:00 am. Diet report (n 3) 253; TEPCO, Fukushima daiich genshiryoku hatsudensho jiko no shodou taiou nitsuite [Initial Response to Accident in the Fukushima No 1 Nuclear Power Plant] (TEPCO) www.tepco.co.jp/cc/press/betu11_j/images/111222o.pdf accessed 20 January 2018 8. As a result, the vice president took charge. The primary responsibility to respond to the accident lay with the plant manager, Yoshida.

84 Moreover, it was later revealed that records of the meeting were not kept. Upon receiving criticism, the central government decided to produce the minutes based upon recollection and publish them. Motoaki Hatake, "Gijiroku misakusei mondaino keii to genjou [Why the Records of the Meetings Were Not Created]," (2012) 333 *Rippo to Chousa* 160.

85 One of the reasons for the prime minister's move was an inability to use cellular phones in the basement where the emergency management center was located. Cabinet Office, Saigai hasseigo no soshikiteki taiou joukyo [Institutional Response Right After the Accident] (Cabinet Office) www.cas.go.jp/jp/seisaku/icanps/SaishyuHon03%280809%29.pdf accessed 14 January 2018 195–96. However, apparently, Headquarters consisted of such a large group of people and it was unsuited to making quick and immediate decisions.

86 Diet Report (n 3) 288.

87 Ibid 295.

minister acted upon Madarame's personal advice instead of the collective advice of the Commission.[88]

Moreover, after having informed by the TEPCO chairperson Katsumata that TEPCO wanted to withdraw all personnel from the plant, on 15 March, Kan stormed into TEPCO headquarters with anger, telling everyone never to think about abandoning the plant, and established the Integrated Response Headquarters (*taisaku tougo honbu*) within TEPCO headquarters, to be headed by himself.[89] Kaieda was charged with remaining in the new integrated headquarters as Kan's point of contact, while Kan returned to Cabinet House. This further exacerbated the already complicated chain of command.

Furthermore, the transmission of information was unnecessarily complicated. All notifications to the government were sent from TEPCO headquarters to the NISA, an agency under the umbrella of the METI. Information sent to the NISA was ultimately sent to Kaieda before being transmitted to Kan. As discussed above, it took some time for relevant and time-sensitive information to reach the prime minister. Moreover, all landline telecommunications were connected to the basement office and incoming information thus had to be hand delivered to Kan working from his fifth floor office.[90]

Kan and the Japanese government directly intervened in the on-site operations at the Fukushima power plant. Kan thus called on Yoshida for information.[91] Such direct contact with a power plant manager was apparently not anticipated. In light of the hesitation to use seawater, Ichiro Takekuro, a TEPCO representative stationed at Cabinet Office, directly instructed Yoshida to halt the pumping of seawater.[92] Such communications were just the tip of the iceberg. The chain of command was apparently broken in the chaos.

Some decisions made by the central government were definitely based on legal authority. For instance, Kaieda's order, as Economy, Industry and Trade

88 Ibid 296–97. Moreover, when a nuclear accident happened, it was supposed that the government officials of the relevant agencies would gather together at the off-site center located close to the nuclear power plant and this off-site center was supposed to take various countermeasures. But after the Tohoku Earthquake, not many people were able to gather together and the facility was useless because it lost power and the back-up generator did not work, losing all communication methods. Furthermore, the facility indicated the increase in the radiation level. As a result, the off-site center was utterly useless in the aftermath of the Fukushima Nuclear Power Plant accident. "Off-site center kinousezu [Off-site Center Did Not Function]" (*NHK* 6 June 2011) www3.nhk.or.jp/news/genpatsu-fukushima/20110606/2030_offsite.html accessed 14 January 2018.

89 Cabinet Office (n 85) 204. Katsumata later explained that he never meant to pull out all personnel from the plant but merely wanted to pull out non-essential personnel.

90 Kushida (n 14) 18–19.

91 "Kantei no shodou wa kajou kainyu: Fukushima genpatsu de kokkai jikochou [Initial Response of the Government Was Over-intrusive: Diet Accident Committee on Fukushima Nuclear Power Accident]" (*Nihonkeizai Shimbun* 9 June 2012) www.nikkei.com/article/DGXNASFS0901J_Z00C12A6MM8000/ accessed 14 January 2018. Moreover, the prime minister requested various information from Yoshida through Takekuro as to details of the operations. Diet report (n 3) 269.

92 Ibid 255, 267–71. TEPCO headquarters simply transmitted these requests to Yoshida without showing any interest in tempering or mitigating unreasonable requests.

Minister, that TEPCO activate the vent was issued based on the Nuclear Reactor Regulation Act.[93] However, other instructions that were issued might be based upon somewhat ambiguous legal grounds. Surely the prime minister, being in charge of the Nuclear Disaster Response Headquarters, has power to issue various instructions in a time of emergency under article 15, paragraph 3 of the Nuclear Disaster Special Measures Act. However, legally speaking, these instructions must be directed to prefectural governors and heads of the municipal government, instead of being issued directly to members of the public. TEPCO, as a power company, is surely a "designated public organization" and is subject to the power of Kan's instruction according to article 20, paragraph 2. Moreover, the power company is specifically listed as the persons who are subject to the prime minister's instruction as a director. However, unlike designated administrative agencies or local governments, whether the instruction against private companies could be binding or not is ambivalent even though they are designated as "public organizations." Moreover, some of the interventions are not official instruction: some of the interventions were suggestions transmitted by Takekuro and not through TEPCO headquarters. Even if the instructions that were issued did not technically carry any legal force, instructions coming from the prime minister's office do undoubtedly carry significant force and it would be hard for Yoshida to ignore them.

With respect to his visit to the Fukushima plant, whether Kan had any legal authority to enter and inquire about the problems personally remains dubious. Nonetheless, it would have been practically impossible for TEPCO and Yoshida to refuse his visit. Some criticized Kan's visit as a distraction to Yoshida's efforts to stabilize the plant. Others suggest Kan's visit might have even caused delay to the vent's activation, leading to further deterioration of the situation.

There is debate about whether the prime minister's intervention actually contributed to stabilization of the plant or whether his intervention hindered it, or at least added unnecessary confusion and chaos.[94] However, one thing that remains clear is that the legal authority for intervening in this nuclear disaster was unquestionably ambiguous.

3.3.2 Asking the local government for assistance

To cool down the nuclear rods in the reactors and the cooling pools, the central government needed all the help it could muster. It could, and surely did,

93 Nuclear Reactor Regulation Act (n 49) art 64(3).

94 'Yoshida chousho koukai: Touji no konran tsutaeru shougen namanamashiku [Yoshida Memo Disclosed: Vivid Testimonies as to Chaos] (*Mainichi Shimbun* 12 September 2014) http://mainichi.jp/articles/20140912/mog/00m/040/001000c accessed 14 January 2018 (reporting the added confusion by Kan's intervention).

order the deployment of the SDF to supply water from above the reactor by helicopter.[95] However, this was not effective. It is the municipal governments, not the central government, that manage fire departments[96] and, as such, fire engines are under their management. Thus, the central government had to request that the Tokyo metropolitan governor and other heads of municipal government lend fire engines for TEPCO's use and then ask for their cooperation in sending their firefighters and rescue personnel to assist with efforts to supply water to the nuclear reactors.[97]

Water is essential for cooling down nuclear rods in reactors and in cooling ponds. However, supplying this water in Fukushima was a difficult and dangerous job, since highly contaminated radioactive debris had been spread all over the facility and surrounding environment. Following the heroic efforts of these firefighters, the government did manage to supply water to the reactors and the cooling ponds. By using seawater for cooling, the government gave up all hope of being able to use these reactors for generating power in the future. Eventually, workers did manage to restore power and, along with it, the cooling system, without the need for further resort to seawater.

It could be argued that the Japanese government should have been more prepared to mobilize the SDF for an emergency of this nature. It is indeed surprising, if not unthinkable, that the central government had to request the cooperation of local governors and municipal government heads and the volunteer assistance of firefighters and rescue personnel for such a dangerous task.

3.3.3 Release of contaminated water into the sea

Some troubling legal questions also arose during the course of this crisis. It was TEPCO that confirmed that highly contaminated water was leaking into the sea.[98] Due to the facilities being seriously damaged because of hydrogen

95 Chief Cabinet Secretary, Press Release (kantei 17 March 2011) www.kantei.go.jp/jp/tyoukanpress/201103/17_a.html accessed 14 January 2018.

96 Shōbō soshikihō [Fire Department Organization Act], Law no 226 of 1947, art 6 & 7.

97 Chief Cabinet Secretary, Press Release (kantei 19 March 2011) www.kantei.go.jp/jp/tyoukanpress/201103/19_p.html accessed 14 January 2018. In the case of the nuclear power plant accident in Fukushima, the director of the National Fire and Disaster Management Agency requested cooperation from the governor of the Tokyo Metropolitan Government and the heads of other municipal governments and these officials accepted the requests. National Fire and Disaster Management Agency, Fukushima genshiryoku hatsudensho jiko (Higashinihon daishinsai) ni kanrensuru shoubou no taiou [Responses of the Fire Department in Connection with the Fukushima Nuclear Power Plant Accident (Great East Japan Earthquake Disaster)] (MCI) www.soumu.go.jp/main_content/000109177.pdf accessed 14 January 2018.

98 TEPCO, Press Release, Fukushima daiichi genshiryoku hatudensho 2gouki shusuikou hukinkara no houshasei busshitsu wo hukumu ekitai no umi eno ryuushutsu ni tsuite [On Leaks into the Ocean of Liquid Contaminated by Radioactive Materials Found in the Vicinity of the Water Intake of the Unit 2 Reactor at the Fukushima No. 1 Nuclear Power Plant] (TEPCO 5 April 2011) www.tepco.co.jp/cc/press/11040504-j.html accessed 14 January 2018.

blasts and fire, it was anticipated that the contaminated water used to cool the nuclear rods might be leaking into the sea. Moreover, a huge amount of water had been poured into each of the reactors and the cooling ponds with full knowledge that at least some would inevitably spill over and flow into the sea. The fact that this did indeed occur was a clear violation of the Nuclear Reactor Regulation Act.[99] It was incumbent on TEPCO to contain any leak of contaminated water.

This leak was accidental. However, when a significant amount of highly contaminated water was found inside the building that was preventing recovery work, TEPCO faced a difficult decision over how to remove it in order to continue work. Storage was undoubtedly needed for this highly contaminated water, but there simply was no storage facility suitable for this purpose. The central government thus decided to release the water from the reservoir that had contained waters with low-levels of contamination into the sea in order to make storage room for the highly contaminated water.[100] This move raised serious concern over possible effects on the environment, the fishing industry, and on nearby countries; afterwards both South Korea and China voiced outrage because they were not given prior notice of the release.

Some questioned whether this release violated the Ocean Pollution Prevention Act.[101] This statute prohibits ships, airplanes, and facilities on the water from discharging oil, poisonous materials, or waste into the water. The government operated under the assumption that the Ocean Pollution Prevention Act did not apply to the discharge of contaminated water into the ocean from a facility on land. As such, the discharge thus does not violate the Ocean Pollution Prevention Act.

There are also other questions relating to international law. Was the release of contaminated water a violation of the Convention on the Law of the Sea?[102] Or was it a violation of the Convention on the Prevention of Marine Pollution by Dumping of Wastes and Other Matter?[103] Some argued that the release was a violation of these international conventions. There was no provision in the Convention on the Law of the Sea as to the release of contaminated water from

99 Nuclear Reactor Regulation Act (n 49) art 43-3-22, which mandates that the operator of a nuclear power plant must take necessary measures to ensure the safety of the nuclear reactor facility, operation of the nuclear reactor, and the delivery, storage and disposition of radioactively contaminated materials.

100 Chief Cabinet Secretary, Press Release (kantei 6 April 2011) www.kantei.go.jp/jp/tyoukanpress/201104/6_a.html accessed 14 January 2018.

101 Kaiyō osentō oyobi kaijō saigai no boushi ni kansuru hōritsu [Act against Ocean Pollution and on Prevention of Ocean Disaster], Law no 136 of 1970 (Ocean Pollution Prevention Act).

102 United Nations, Convention on the Law of the Sea www.un.org/depts/los/convention_agreements/texts/unclos/unclos_e.pdf accessed 14 January 2018.

103 United Nations, Convention on the Prevention of Marine Pollution by Dumping of Wastes and Other Matter (IMO) www.imo.org/en/OurWork/Environment/LCLP/Documents/LC1972.pdf accessed 14 January 2018.

a facility on land as a result of a nuclear power plant accident. It is thus hard to say that the release was a violation of any specific provision of the Convention on the Law of the Sea.[104] The Convention on the Prevention of Marine Pollution by Dumping of Wastes and Other Matter is concerned with the dumping of waste from vessels or aircraft and does not cover the release of contaminated water from a facility on land.[105] The release would therefore not violate this convention either.

However, the Convention on the Law of the Sea imposes a general obligation on ratified states to protect and preserve the ocean environment[106] and obliges these states to adopt the best available and feasible measures to prevent ocean pollution within their capacity.[107] Therefore, it could be argued that the release was a violation of this obligation. The Japanese government would likely argue that the release was necessary to allow storage of highly contaminated water in the plant and to prevent its flow into the sea and that the release was the best available and feasible measure. Whether the release constituted a violation of this convention would ultimately depend upon how persuasively this argument could be made.

3.3.4 Workplace safety

This incident also raised serious legal questions as to workplace safety. During the initial attempt to contain the accident, six TEPCO workers were exposed to an accumulated dose of more than 250 mSv (one was exposed to 670 mSv) while 167 TEPCO and other workers were exposed to more than 100 mSv.[108]

Workers had to work in an extremely dangerous environment using heavy equipment and radiation measuring devices to protect them from radiation exposure. There were and still are many places that workers cannot reach because of extremely high radiation levels. The length of time they could work in these conditions was also restricted. Initially, the central government set a limit on radiation exposure for workers in the nuclear power plant at 100 mSv per year

104 Kentarou Nishimoto, "Fukushima daiichi genshiryoku hatdsudensho ni okeru osensui no hōshutsu sochi wo meguru kokusaihō (International Law on the Release of Contaminated Water from the Fukushima No 1 Nuclear Power Plant)" (University of Tokyo 2 April 2011) http://pari.u-tokyo.ac.jp/archives/publication/PI11_01_nishimoto.html accessed 14 January 2018. See also Toshiya Ueki, "Higashinihon daishinsai to Fukushima genpatsu jiko wo meguru kokusaihōjou no mondaiten [International Law Questions Regarding the Great East Japan Earthquake Disaster and the Fukushima Nuclear Power Plant Accident]," (2011) 1427 *Juristo* 107.

105 Nishimoto (n 104).

106 Convention on the Law of the Sea (n 102) art 192.

107 Ibid art 194(1).

108 TEPCO, Higashinihon daishinsai ni okeru genshiryoku hatsudensho no eikyo to genzai no joukyo ni tsuite [On the Impact of the Nuclear Power Plant and Its Current Status in the Great East Japan Earthquake Disaster] (TEPCO) www.tepco.co.jp/nu/fukushima-np/outline/pdf/f12np-gaiyou_1.pdf accessed 14 January 2018. See n 18.

but raised this limit to 250 mSv per year for workers engaged in operations at the Fukushima power plant.[109] The central government believed that this change was unavoidably necessary to facilitate recovery work. Some workers had to work in contaminated water that seeped into their boots, exposing them to radiation beyond this limit.[110]

Moreover, it was revealed that some of the workers did not carry devices for measuring radiation with them when engaging in work throughout this crisis.[111] The Ministry of Health, Labor and Welfare (MHLW) warned TEPCO over these violations of occupational safety law.[112] Nevertheless, in 2012, it was reported that some employees of a TEPCO sub-contractor had been covering radiation measurement devices with lead covers in order to reduce radiation exposure readings.[113] The MHLW conducted an investigation in response to these revelations. It found various cases of improper radiation exposure management practices, such as the reporting of falsified measurement data, failure to carry measurement devices, or faulty management systems leading to employees not using measurement devices or setting the alarm levels too high.[114] These incidents indicate that TEPCO had difficulty actually monitoring staff exposure to radiation.

Furthermore, the MHLW acknowledges that certain ex-employees of TEPCO are untraceable because their whereabouts are either unknown or they had already left their former company.[115] This indicates that TEPCO had difficulty keeping track of all the workers that might have been exposed to radiation during the containment effort.

109 Ministry of Health, Labor, and Welfare, Director on Labor Standards, Heisei23nen Tohoku chihō Taiheiyouoki jishin ni kiinshite shoujita jitai ni taiou surutame no denrihoushasen shougai boushi kisoku no tokurei ni kansuru shourei no sekou nitsuite [On Enforcement of Special Treatment of Regulation to Prevent Radiation Damage for Works Necessary to Respond to Situations Caused by the 2011 off the Pacific Coast of Tohoku Earthquake] (MHLW 15 March 2011) www.mhlw.go.jp/stf/houdou/2r9852000001gkcc-att/2r9852000001gkf6.pdf accessed 14 January 2018.

110 Press Interview of Health, Labor and Welfare Minister Hosokawa (MHLW 31 May 2011) www.mhlw.go.jp/stf/kaiken/daijin/2r9852000001e6tm.html.

111 Ibid.

112 Ibid.

113 "Fukushima genpatsu: Senryoukei ni namariban, hibaku sukunaku yosoou? [Fukushima Nuclear Power Plant: Lead Cover on Radiation Detection Equipment to Reduce Exposure Readings?]" (*Nihonkeizai Shimbun* 21 July 2012) www.nikkei.com/article/DGXNASDG21011_R20C12A7CR0000/ accessed 14 January 2018.

114 Ministry of Health, Labor and Welfare, Tokyo denryoku Fukushima daiichi genshiryoku hatsudensho no senryou kanri no jittai chousa kekka [Results of the Investigation of Radiation Measurement Management at TEPCO's Fukushima No 1 Nuclear Power Plant] (MHLW 30 October 2012) www.mhlw.go.jp/stf/houdou/2r9852000002n0ig.html accessed 14 January 2018.

115 Ministry of Health, Labor and Welfare, Tokyo densryoku Fukushima daiichi genshiryoku hatsudensho kinkyu sagyo jujisha no choukiteki kenkou kanri no jisshi joukyou nitsuite [On Long-term Health Management of the Emergency Workers at the Fukushima No 1 Nuclear Power Plant of the TEPCO] (MHLW) www.mhlw.go.jp/stf/houdou/0000014777.html accessed 14 January 2018 (out of 19,346 emergency workers at the plant, 472 workers are untraceable).

TEPCO was and still is responsible for monitoring individual radiation exposure of all workers engaged in containment and recovery work inside the plant, with those with radiation exposure above the limits, as discussed above, no longer eligible to work. There are doubts about the sufficiency of TEPCO's monitoring efforts where worker safety is concerned because most of its work was and still is being carried out by individuals sometimes several layers removed from direct employment by TEPCO. To illustrate this, many workers were and still are workers of sub-contractors, sub-sub-contractors, sub-sub-sub-contractors, sub-sub-sub-sub-contractors, or even sub-sub-sub-sub-sub-contractors of TEPCO. It remains to be seen whether TEPCO can keep adequate employment records and provide compensation in the future to employees claiming sickness due to work-related radiation exposure.

3.4 Evacuation

In order to save the lives and safety of the local residents living close to the Fukushima Nuclear Power Plant, the Japanese government had to order residents to evacuate. What kinds of evacuation measures were adopted? What was the legal nature of such orders? Was evacuation carried out appropriately? This section explores the evacuation measures adopted by the government.

3.4.1 Evacuation instruction

On 11 March, the prime minister declared a "nuclear emergency" at the Fukushima Nuclear Power Plant according to article 15, paragraph 1 of the Nuclear Disaster Special Measures Act.[116] The prime minister then instructed everyone living within a 3 km radius to evacuate while those within a 10 km radius were instructed to remain indoors.[117] The following day, the prime minister expanded the evacuation order to include everyone living within 10 km of the plant.[118] With the hydrogen blast in the Unit 1 reactor building on 12 March, however, the prime minister further expanded the scope of evacuation to include anyone living within 20 km of the plant.[119] The 20 km range was thus called the "evacuation instruction zone" (*hinan shiji kuiki*). All residents within a 30 km radius of the plant were advised to stay indoors.[120] Evacuees had to seek shelter outside of their communities. Since these decisions were made without

116 Chief Cabinet Secretary, Press Release (kantei 11 March 2011) www.kantei.go.jp/jp/tyoukanpress/201103/11_p3.html accessed 15 January 2018.

117 Chief Cabinet Secretary, Press Release (kantei 11 March 2011) www.kantei.go.jp/jp/tyoukanpress/201103/11_p4.html accessed 15 January 2018.

118 Chief Cabinet Secretary, Press Release (kantei 12 March 2011) www.kantei.go.jp/jp/tyoukanpress/201103/12_a3.html accessed 15 January 2018.

119 Chief Cabinet Secretary, Press Release (kantei 12 March 2011) www.kantei.go.jp/jp/tyoukanpress/201103/12_p2.html accessed 15 January 2018.

120 Prime Minister's Message (kantei 15 March 2011) www.kantei.go.jp/jp/kan/statement/201103/15message.html accessed 15 January 2018.

much consultation with local government, these evacuation instructions caused tremendous confusion. Local residents were simply told to leave without knowing where to go.[121]

The precise nature of the evacuation order was likely difficult to understand for foreign observers. Technically, all these orders were "instructions" to heads of local government issued by the director of the Nuclear Disaster Response Headquarters under article 15, paragraph 3 of the Nuclear Disaster Special Measures Act.[122] They had the force of law against the heads of local government and administrative agencies, and those evacuated on these instructions were regarded as having been forced to evacuate by government order. They were thus entitled to compensation or damage awards afterward.

However, there is no statutory provision authorizing heads of a local government to force local residents to evacuate. Therefore, these instructions were not directed at local residents and were thus not legally binding upon them. Naturally, municipal governments strongly recommended evacuation but, for local residents that refused to evacuate, there was nothing that could be done to force them to leave. As a result, even after the evacuation instruction was issued, some people still refused to evacuate and instead remained within a 20 km radius of the plant.[123]

Moreover, residents within a 30 km radius of the plant faced extremely difficult choices. Many feared the possible effects of radiation exposure. Pregnant women and families with small children were especially worried about possible effects on babies and small children. Furthermore, because of the instruction to remain indoors, many merchants within the 30km range were not even able to open their stores. Transportation companies refused to transport goods and food to locations within the 30 km radius. As a result, these residents were faced with extreme difficulty getting access to food and other goods. Many thus opted for voluntary evacuation even though they had not been so instructed.

Eventually, on 25 March, the central government announced that it would actively encourage voluntary evacuation for those who still remained within a 30 km radius of the power plant.[124] This announcement was made based on the complaints of residents remaining inside the 30 km radius, though the

121 Fears of radiation exposure triggered the exodus of many of the people living outside of the evacuation instruction zone. The United States government recommended that any of its citizens living within an 80 km (50 mile) radius of the plant evacuate and many foreign countries followed suit. "Edano kanbouchoukan no kishakaiken [Press Interview of Cabinet Minister Edano]" (*Asahi Shimbun* 19 March 2011) www.asahi.com/special/10005/TKY201103180600.html accessed 15 January 2018. Tokyo was outside of this 80 km radius but many voluntarily evacuated further west to Osaka and Kyoto. Some even went abroad.

122 Nuclear Disaster Special Measures Act (n 6) art 15(3).

123 "Genpatsu shuhen, hinan shiji ken-nai ni nao 60nin [60 Residents Still Remained in the Evacuation Instruction Zone around the Nuclear Power Plant]' (*Asahi Shimbun* 28 March 2011) www.asahi.com/special/10005/TKY201103270256.html accessed 13 February 2018.

124 Chief Cabinet Secretary, Press Release (kantei 25 March 2011) www.kantei.go.jp/jp/tyoukanpress/201103/25_a.html accessed 15 January 2018.

government was reluctant to expand the scope of the evacuation instruction to include residents from the area where the instruction to remain indoors had been issued. This decision further exacerbated the ambiguity because the central government was actively encouraging voluntary evacuation without instructing evacuation.

The central government should have given a guarantee that the evacuees would be entitled to compensation or damage awards regardless of whether residents were forced to evacuate based on government instruction, whether they were practically forced to evacuate because of the remain indoors instruction, or whether they were encouraged to evacuate voluntarily. They were likely entitled to seek damages from TEPCO for loss and suffering. However, the ambiguous nature of the evacuation order created fear that compensation or damage awards might not be forthcoming, ultimately hampering effective evacuation.

More fundamentally, the central government must be granted legal authority to order the evacuation of local residents in the face of nuclear disaster. Under the Basic Act on Disaster Countermeasures, when a disaster occurs and heads of municipal government believe it particularly necessary to prevent danger to human life or person, they can declare a "hazard zone" and order evacuation or prohibit or restrict entry to all persons other than those engaging in disaster emergency operations.[125] Violators of this prohibition, restriction, or evacuation order can be punished by a fine of up to 100,000 JPY (900 USD) or even by confinement.[126] However, no "hazard zone" was declared, nor were any prohibition against entry or evacuation orders issued in municipalities surrounding the Fukushima Nuclear Power Plant. The governor of Fukushima Prefecture thus requested that the central government declare a "hazard zone" and adopt appropriate legal measures. Fukushima's governor was especially worried about vacant houses in the area in light of potential susceptibility to burglars or looters. The prime minister, being in charge of the Nuclear Disaster Response Headquarters, can definitely instruct heads of relevant municipal governments to declare a "hazard zone" and adopt appropriate legal measures.

On 22 April 2011, the government finally decided to designate the area within a 20 km radius of the Fukushima No 1 Nuclear Power Plant as a "hazard zone" and prohibit entry.[127] Therefore, after 22 April, it became possible to impose criminal punishment on residents that refused to evacuate as well as on those who entered the zone. Certainly, this decision had the impact of discouraging burglary or looting in the area and contributed to the security of vacant homes. However, the fact still remains that the central government has no legal power to order mandatory evacuation or to prohibit entry into a "hazard zone."

125 Basic Act on Disaster Countermeasures (n 66) art 63(1).

126 Ibid art 116(ii). See Chapter 1 n 177.

127 Chief Cabinet Secretary, Press Release (kantei 21 April 2011) www.kantei.go.jp/jp/tyoukanpress/201104/21_a.html accessed 15 January 2018. This instruction was issued based on the Nuclear Disaster Special Measures Act, art 20(3) at that time.

3.4.2 Expansion of the scope of evacuation instruction

Some towns north of the Fukushima No 1 Nuclear Power Plant that were outside of the 20 km radius, such as IItate Village, parts of Namie Town, and parts of Minami Souma City, reported high concentrations of radiation. The government thus decided on 22 April to instruct residents of areas beyond the 20 km radius where there was a risk of high radiation exposure to evacuate within one month ("planned evacuation zone" (*keikakuteki hinan kuiki*), and instructed residents within a 30 km radius, except where evacuation was already instructed, to prepare for emergency evacuation ("emergency evacuation preparation zone" (*kinkyuji hinan junbi kuiki*).[128] All residents of the "planned evacuation zone" were thus forced to evacuate. Voluntary evacuation for all those living in the "emergency evacuation preparation zone" was still strongly recommended, especially for pregnant women and small children.[129] Entry into these areas was not prohibited but residents needed to be prepared to evacuate immediately, if necessary.[130]

Furthermore, the government decided on 16 June to designate certain spots outside of the "hazard zone" (i.e., beyond a 20 km radius of the plant) and "planned evacuation zone" which presented the possibility of exposure to radiation dosage beyond 20 mSv/year as a "specified evacuation recommendation spot" (*tokutei hinan kanshou chiten*) where, as the designation suggests, evacuation was recommended, though still voluntary.[131] But practically speaking, it was mandatory, and the evacuees were treated as if they were legally forced to evacuate.

This ambiguous and piecemeal measure was necessitated because of the central government's failure to instruct residents in areas beyond the 20 km radius to evacuate despite the predicted spread of radiation right after the blast at the plant. The Ministry of Education, Culture, Sports, Science and Technology (MEXT) has a system known as the "System for Prediction of Environmental Emergency Dose Information" (SPEEDI),[132] which is designed to predict the spread of radiation by simulation, and its report was sent from the Nuclear Safety Technology Center to the MEXT headquarters as well as to its officials in the Cabinet House

128 Chief Cabinet Secretary, Press Release (kantei 22 April 2011) www.kantei.go.jp/jp/tyoukan press/201104/22_a.html accessed 15 January 2018; Fukushima Prefecture, Hinan kuiki no hensen ni tsuite [On Changes of Evacuation Zones] (Fukushima Prefecture) www.pref.fukushima.lg.jp/site/portal/cat01-more.html accessed 15 January 2018. This instruction was issued based on the Nuclear Disaster Special Measures Act, art 20(3).

129 Chief Cabinet Secretary (n 128).

130 Designation of "emergency evacuation preparation zone" was lifted on 30 September because the situation at the Fukushima plant was practically under control. Ministry of Economy, Trade and Industry (30 September 2011), Kinkyuu hinan junbikuiku no kaijo ni tsuite [On lifting the Emergency Evacuation Preparation Area] (METI) www.meti.go.jp/earthquake/nuclear/pdf/20110930015-2.pdf accessed 15 January 2018.

131 Chief Cabinet Secretary, Press Release (kantei 16 June 2011) www.kantei.go.jp/jp/tyoukan press/201106/16_p.html accessed 15 January 2018.

132 Fujitsu, System for Prediction of Environmental Emergency Dose Information Network System (Fujitsu) www.fujitsu.com/downloads/JP/archive/imgjp/jmag/vol59-5/paper05.pdf accessed 15 January 2018.

basement. The data showed a likelihood of high radiation exposure in some areas further than 20 km from the plant. However, its report was not revealed until May. The central government knew that some towns outside of the 20 km radius might be exposed to high levels of radiation because of the direction of the winds. Nevertheless, the central government failed to disclose this data and, likewise, failed to take any action with respect to residents living in these dangerous areas.[133] After this data was published, the central government was forced to take action on behalf of residents living in those areas,[134] though by that time they had already been exposed to radiation during the initial months.

The terms "instruction" and "recommendation" in relation to evacuations are very ambiguous. The difference between "hazard zone," "evacuation instruction zone," "planned evacuation zone," and "specified evacuation recommendation spot" are also very difficult to understand. Further, it is difficult to distinguish an instruction to evacuate from an instruction recommending evacuation. Equally unclear is the precise legal nature of an "instruction" recommending voluntary evacuation. It would appear that the government should have been allowed to exercise its legal authority to order evacuation much more clearly.[135]

The ambiguous nature of these instructions also made it hard to predict whether evacuees would be compensated or awarded damages for having to evacuate. As indicated below, the central government compelled TEPCO to pay damages to residents within a 20 km radius, which in other words is the evacuation instruction zone, the planned evacuation zone, and the specified evacuation recommendation spot for the evacuation.[136] However, other residents were left in a difficult predicament, especially those within a 30 km radius or those in an "emergency evacuation preparation zone" where an evacuation recommendation was followed by instruction to prepare for possible emergency evacuation

133 President online, SPEEDI jouhou wa naze koukai sarenakattanoka [Why SPEEDI Information Was Not Disclosed Immediately?] (*President* 8 February 2012), http://president.jp/articles/-/5568?page=2&dt=2050/12/31%2023:59&pskinset=asari, accessed 15 January 2018. Some questioned whether the government intentionally concealed this data in order to downplay the seriousness of the contamination.

134 Moreover, U.S. military aircraft measured the radiation within a 45 km radius of the plant on behalf of the U.S. Department of Energy from 17 to 19 March and provided the data to the METI and the MEXT several days later. Although the data showed high radiation exposure to the northwest of the plant, beyond a 20 km radius, this data was not used for evacuation. This fact was not revealed until 18 June 2011. "Beino houshasen jissokuzu, seihu ga houchi: Genpatsu jiko hinan ni ikasazu [Map of Radiation Exposure Provided by the U.S. Military Was Left Unused: Evacuation Order Issued Without It Being Considered]" (*Asahi Shimbun* 18 June 2011) www.asahi.com/special/10005/TKY201206170453.html accessed 15 January 2018.

135 There is similar ambiguity as to the authority of the government to dispose of animals and pets that were left behind. On 12 May 2011, the prime minister instructed the governor of Fukushima Prefecture to put all animals and pets to death that were owned within a 20 km radius from the nuclear power plant with the consent of the owner and by humane means. Cabinet Secretary, Press Release (kantei 12 May 2011) www.kantei.go.jp/jp/tyoukanpress/201105/12_p.html accessed 15 January 2018. Since the consent of the owner was required, the governor could not put animals to death without this consent.

136 *See* Chapter 5 n 74.

(except for pregnant women and children, to whom evacuation was strongly recommended). Those who evacuated from these areas voluntarily before 20 June were to be paid damages from TEPCO while those residents who evacuated after 20 June would wait for further decisions, except for pregnant women and children.[137] These evacuees would only be paid damages from TEPCO for psychological pains together with those who remained. TEPCO's liability to these residents was left to be determined in the future by the courts. The central government should have clarified whether compensation or damage awards for evacuation would be forthcoming before issuing evacuation instructions or recommendations.

3.5 Contaminated vegetables, water, fish, and soil

The nuclear meltdown in the Fukushima Nuclear Power Plant caused serious radiation contamination to spread to neighboring communities. The Japanese government had to restrict the marketing, consumption, and cultivation of agricultural products in these nearby communities. Radiation left a significant impact not only on agricultural products but also on the entire environment. How did the Japanese government respond to such widespread contamination?

3.5.1 Contaminated vegetables

Since radioactive material had leaked into the air, it was expected that agricultural products from neighboring localities would be contaminated. Food safety in Japan is regulated by the Food Safety Act,[138] but at this time there was no limit on permissible radiation levels in food products. Thus, on 17 March, the MHLW issued a memo to all governors and municipal government heads instructing them to treat any food with radiation levels exceeding permissible limits set by the NSC as prohibited food[139] under the Food Safety Act.[140] However, under the Food Safety Act, only items "which contain or are covered with toxic or harmful substances or are suspected to contain or be covered with such substances" could be prohibited. If particular products were found to contain high levels of radioactive materials they could definitely be prohibited under this statute. However, prohibiting all products from a particular prefecture simply because a sample registered high radiation contamination, regardless of whether all such products were found to be the same, is another matter, and is, perhaps, not so cut and dried.

137 Ibid.
138 Shokuhin eiseihō [Food Safety Act], Law no 233 of 1947.
139 Ministry of Health, Labor and Welfare, Drug and Food Administration, Food Safety Section Chief, Houshanou osen sareta shokuhin no toriatsukai nitsuite [On Treatment of Food Contaminated by Radioactive Materials] (MHLW 17 March 2011) www.mhlw.go.jp/stf/houdou/2r9852000001558e-img/2r9852000001559v.pdf accessed 15 January 2018.
140 Food Safety Act (n 138) art 6(ii).

On 19 March, the government found high levels of radiation in untreated milk[141] from Fukushima Prefecture and also in spinach from nearby Ibaraki Prefecture.[142] Soon, various vegetables from Fukushima and neighboring prefectures were showing high levels of radiation. On 21 March, the government prohibited the marketing of spinach and other vegetables from Fukushima, Ibaraki, Tochigi, and Gunma prefectures along with milk from Fukushima.[143] On 23 March, the prime minister issued an instruction against consuming spinach, cabbage, broccoli, cauliflower, and other vegetables produced in Fukushima Prefecture while also expanding the marketing ban to include parsley and untreated milk from Ibaraki.[144] Later, a marketing ban was also issued with respect to shiitake mushrooms, baby bamboo, tea leaves, plums, and aromatic citron produced in the affected areas.

It is important to note, however, that these measures were adopted under then article 20, paragraph 3, of the Nuclear Disaster Special Measures Act,[145] at that time, which authorized the prime minister, as the director of the Nuclear Disaster Response Headquarters, to give necessary instruction to the heads of local and municipal governments. The prime minister can issue an instruction to the extent necessary, if the prime minister believes it particularly necessary in order for the Headquarters to carry out temporary emergency measures in light of nuclear disaster, properly and immediately in the areas where such temporary emergency measures are to be implemented. Therefore, technically speaking, the so-called marketing ban was an instruction of the prime minister, as the director of the Nuclear Disaster Response Headquarters, addressed to

141 In other words, milk that has not been treated with heat or pasteurized for the purposes of killing germs.

142 "Nousanbutsu kara houshanou: Tabetemo heiki? [Radiation Was Detected from Agricultural Products: Is it Safe to Eat Them?]" (*Asahi Shimbun* 20 March 2011) www.asahi.com/special/10005/TKY201103200071.html accessed 15 January 2018; "Nousanbutsu no kiseichi kosu houshasei busshitsu kenshutsu, 5ken ni kakudai [Detection of Radioactive Materials Beyond the Limit from the Agricultural Products Is Extended to Five Prefectures]" (*Asahi Shimbun* 21 March 2011) www.asahi.com/special/10005/TKY201103200340.html accessed 15 January 2018.

143 Ministry of Health, Labor, and Welfare, Drug and Food Administration, Food Safety Section, Shokuhin no shukka seigen nitsuite [On Marketing Restriction of Foods] (MHLW 21 March 2011) www.mhlw.go.jp/stf/houdou/2r98520000015p8a.html accessed 15 January 2018.

144 Ministry of Health, Labor and Welfare, Drug and Food Administration, Food Safety Section, Shokuhin no sesshu seigen oyobi shukka seigen nitsuite [On Restriction on Consumption and Marketing of Certain Foods] (MHLW 23 March 2011) www.mhlw.go.jp/stf/houdou/2r98520000015wun.html accessed 15 January 2018. The government later decided to lift the ban on an individual basis if the results of the tests were within the legal limit for three consecutive weeks. Cabinet Secretary, Press Release (kantei 4 April 2011) www.kantei.go.jp/jp/tyoukanpress/201104/4_p.html accessed 15 January 2018. For a regulatory response to radioactive contamination of foods, *see* Gijis Berends & Megumi Kobayashi, "Food after Fukushima—Japan's Regulatory Response to the Radioactive Contamination of Its Food Chain" (2012) 67 *Food & Drug Law Journal* 51.

145 Nuclear Disaster Special Measures Act (n 6) art 20(3) (currently art 20(2)).

the governors of the relevant prefectures,[146] to request that relevant business operators refrain from marketing specified products. It was not an order directed toward farmers that prohibited them from marketing. Moreover, the governors did not have legal authority to prohibit such marketing nor to impose punishments on violators. Therefore, they were limited to simply requesting that the farmers, farmers' associations, distributors, and marketplaces refrain from marketing the designated products. Similarly, the so-called consumption ban was merely a set of instructions issued from the prime minister as the director of the Nuclear Disaster Response Headquarters to the governor of Fukushima Prefecture which requested that residents refrain from consuming the listed foods.[147]

Although such requests are likely to be honored by everyone,[148] the precise legal nature of the instruction is very difficult to ascertain. Doubt in regard to whether the government could use the Food Safety Act to prohibit the marketing of all vegetables from a certain area where only some of the vegetables showed high levels of contamination forced the government to resort to relying upon the Nuclear Disaster Special Measures Act. Reliance on the Nuclear Disaster Special Measures Act, however, thrust highly ambiguous concepts, such as "instructions" not to market or eat contaminated vegetables, to the fore.[149]

146 Director of the Nuclear Disaster Response Headquarters, Instruction (MHLW 21 March 2011) www.mhlw.go.jp/stf/houdou/2r98520000015p8a-img/2r98520000015p9r.pdf accessed 15 January 2018.

147 Director of the Nuclear Disaster Response Headquarters, Instruction (MHLW 23 March 2011) www.mhlw.go.jp/stf/houdou/2r98520000015wun-att/2r98520000015wzl.pdf accessed 15 January 2018.

148 Fukushima 30 Years Project, Shukka seigen hin ga ryutsu shiteita mondai [Restricted Products Found in the Market] (Fukushima 30 Years Project) https://fukushima-30year-project.org/?p=2877 accessed 15 January 2018. There is no way to punish violators because the instruction was merely an instruction to prefectural governors and is not an order enforceable against citizens.

149 Moreover, as a result, the government had to instruct the governors to stop marketing and consumption individually after finding out that products were highly contaminated. For example, the contamination of beef became a serious problem after a short while. Cattle were fed with hay consisting of dried rice plant, a common practice in Japan. The central government instructed all farmers not to leave rice plant outdoors to dry because of possible contamination. However, farmers were not adequately notified and thus sold this rice plant hay that had been dried outside to cattle farmers whose cattle became contaminated. It was shocking that beef showed such high concentrations of radiation even though cattle had not shown such high levels of contamination. Some of the contaminated beef was already sold and likely consumed before the central government realized there was contamination, thus causing a panic among consumers. Ministry of Agriculture, Fishery, and Forestry, Press Release (MAFF 2 August 2011) www.maff.go.jp/j/syouan/0720.html accessed 15 January 2018. The central government immediately instructed against marketing all beef derived from cattle in Fukushima. Director of the Nuclear Disaster Response Headquarters, Instruction to the Governor of Fukushima (MHLW 19 July 2011) www.mhlw.go.jp/stf/houdou/2r9852000001jhm9-att/2r9852000001jhs8.pdf accessed 15 January 2018.

Moreover, this ambiguity may have given rise to doubt as to the possibility of compensation or damage awards.[150] If vegetables or fish are contaminated, the government surely has a power to ban them, and the government has no obligation to pay any damages. However, if such vegetables or fish are not contaminated, but their marketing was banned due to the possibility of contamination or in order to dispel consumer concern, then there is a possibility that farmers may be able to seek compensation for public use. It was also not clear whether these farmers would be entitled to seek damages from TEPCO either because the government order may not be illegal.

Furthermore, if it was a legal order, the public would have been required to follow that order and farmers might be entitled to seek compensation or damage awards. On the other hand, if it was merely a request issued by the governor based upon the prime minister's "instruction," some doubt arises as to whether farmers could be compensated or awarded damages because, after all, the farmers were simply voluntarily refraining from marketing, following governmental request. The central government, as we will see, thus ensured that TEPCO pay damages to the farmers who were effectively banned from marketing their products.[151] Nonetheless, having a more specific statutory provision authorizing legal restrictions on the marketing and consumption of certain food products contaminated by radioactivity would undoubtedly provide much more legal certainty and be desirable when circumstances dictate such a necessity.

3.5.2 Contaminated drinking water, soil, and fish

Similar ambiguity existed with respect to restrictions on tap water. On 22 March 2011, the Tokyo Metropolitan Government detected 210 Bq/kg of radioactive iodine 131 at one of its water purification facilities, lower than the 300 Bq/kg limit set by the NSC but higher than 100 Bq/kg limit set under the Food Safety Act for drinking by infants. The Tokyo Metropolitan Government thus advised all Tokyo residents to refrain from using tap water to make milk for infants or from otherwise providing tap water to infants.[152] It was merely

150 If the product contains a high level of radiation contamination, the ban on marketing and consumption is legal as a restriction on private property for public welfare and the central government has no liability for damages. Nihonkoku kenpō [Constitution of Japan], art 29(2). However, if the product does not contain a high level of radiation contamination but is nonetheless banned from marketing or consumption in order to ensure public confidence, the ban could be considered an expropriation and just compensation might be required from the central government. Ibid art 29(3). It appears that the central government believes that the government has no obligation to pay damages or compensation and that all of this loss was caused by the nuclear accident and TEPCO should be liable for paying damages directly to all farmers.

151 *See* Chapter 5 n 71.

152 Tokyo Metropolitan Government, Water Bureau, Suidousui no houshanou sokutei kekka nitsuite [On the Results of Radiation Measurement of Tap Water] (Tokyo Metropolitan Government 23 March 2011) www.waterworks.metro.tokyo.jp/press/h22/press110323-01.html accessed 15 January 2018.

advisory and residents were assured that it was not unsafe to drink tap water if there was no alternative. Many residents panicked and rushed into convenience stores and supermarkets to buy as much bottled water as they could, giving rise to immediate bottled water shortages. The Tokyo Metropolitan Government had to ask the bottled water industry to increase their production and to provide extra to Tokyo residents as soon as possible.[153] The radiation levels returned to below-limit levels on 24 March, however, prompting the Tokyo Metropolitan government to announce that tap water was once again safe to drink and to provide to infants.[154] Nevertheless, responding to concerns that the system in place was confusing to the public, the Tokyo Metropolitan Government requested that the central government establish clearer standards for drinking water.[155]

Contamination of soil was another serious concern, perhaps on par with concerns relating to food, drinking water, and seawater. Some of the nearby cities showed extremely high levels of radiation contamination in soil.[156] This prompted Fukushima Prefecture to urge farmers to refrain from cultivating farmland and from sowing rice fields with new seeds in spring.[157] The central government later instructed the governor of Fukushima Prefecture to ensure farmers refrained from cultivating rice in the planned evacuation areas and

153 Tokyo Metropolitan Government, Higashinihon daishinsai niokeru Tokyoto no taiou to kyoukun [Responses of the Tokyo Metropolitan Government to the Great East Japan Earthquake Disaster and Lessons to Be Learned] (Tokyo Metropolitan Government September 2011) www.bousai.metro.tokyo.jp/_res/projects/default_project/_page_/001/000/341/230914taiouhonsatu.pdf accessed 15 January 2018 21.

154 Tokyo Metropolitan Government, Water Bureau, Suidousui no houshanou sokutei kekka nitsuite [On the Results of Radiation Measurement of Tap Water] (Tokyo Metropolitan Government 24 March 2011) www.waterworks.metro.tokyo.jp/press/h22/press110324-03.html accessed 15 January 2018.

155 "Suidousui no sesshu seigen kijun aimai: Jichitai gawa ni tomadoi [Consumption Standard for Tap Water is Confusing: Local Governments Complain]" (*Asahi Shimbun* 2 April 2011) www.asahi.com/special/10005/TKY201104010532.html accessed 15 January 2018; Tokyo Metropolitan Government (n 154) 21.

156 Furthermore, some newly built condominiums showed higher radiation exposure. It turned out that pebbles and sand used in their construction had been exposed to radiation during the construction phase and that there was no check on their use. "Nihonmatsu no shinchiku mansion de kousenryo: Namie de dodaino zairyou saishu [New Condominium in Nihonmatsu Showed High Radiation: Building Materials Collected from Namie]" (*Asahi Shimbun* 16 January 2012) www.asahi.com/special/10005/TKY201201150290.html accessed 15 January 2018. Nobody anticipated the possibility of radiation exposure through their use. The METI decided to introduce some standards for their use in construction. "Saiseki, jari ni houshasen shukka kijun wo secchi e: Keisanshou houshin [Setting a Marketing Radiation Standard for Sand and Pebbles: METI]" (*Asahi Shimbun* 7 February 2012) www.asahi.com/special/10005/TKY201202070153.html accessed 15 January 2018.

157 "Fukushimano zen-nouka ni sakutsuke no enki wo yousei: Genpatsu jikode [All Farmers Are Requested to Postpone Rice Crop and Vegetable Planting Due to the Nuclear Accident]" (*Asahi Shimbun* 26 March 2011) www.asahi.com/special/10005/TKY201103250532.html accessed 15 January 2018.

emergency evacuation preparation areas.[158] Rice cropping in other areas was not prohibited.[159] Similar to other powers mentioned above, the government should have the legal authority to restrict the planting and cultivation of new crops in disaster-affected areas.

Another issue related to contamination arose from contaminated water that had leaked from the nuclear power plant and spread to contaminate other water sources in the vicinity. Although ocean fishing beyond the 30km radius was permitted, some of the fish brought into fish markets in the area were highly contaminated. The government thus issued the same marketing restriction instructions on fish as it did in relation to contaminated vegetables, as discussed above.[160] This marketing restriction instruction was also issued in respect to some types of fish caught in nearby rivers. Once again, the same ambiguity surrounding such instructions presented a host of troublesome issues. There is a good reason to favor granting government authority to legally restrict fishing or marketing of fish in times of necessity.

3.5.3 Loss due to "bad reputation"

Radioactive contamination brought grave problems for farmers and fishermen in the Fukushima area. Even for agricultural products not subject to the prohibitions, many consumers were simply so afraid of the possibility of contamination that they refrained from buying products produced in the Fukushima area.[161] Since consumers were not buying this produce, most supermarkets and other vendors were reluctant to distribute them. Therefore, regardless of whether their products were subject to the marketing prohibition, all Tohoku farmers lost customers. The same can be said for those in the fishing industry. Despite no evidence of contamination in their fish, the catches from fishermen in these areas

158 Ministry of Agriculture, Forestry and Fisheries, Press Release (22 April 2011), Tokyo denryoku Fukushima daiichi genshiryoku hatsudensho no jiko nitomonau ine no sakutuke seigen kuiki no settei nitsuite [On the Scope of the Limitation of Rice Planting Due to Fukushima No 1 Nuclear Power Plant Accident Operated by the TEPCO] (MAFF 22 April 2011) www.maff.go.jp/j/press/seisan/sien/110422.html accessed 15 January 2018.

159 However, since the bags of new rice contaminated beyond the limit were found, the government introduced the inspection of all bags of rice to exclude the bags of rice beyond the limit. After 2015, no bags of rice beyond the limit have been found. Ministry of Agriculture, Forestry and Fisheries, Fukushimasanmai no zenbukuro kensa no kekka [Result of Inspection of All Bags of Rice] (MAFF) www.maff.go.jp/j/export/e_info/pdf/safety_170124_japanese_2.pdf accessed 15 January 2018.

160 Chief Cabinet Secretary, Press Release (kantei 20 April 2011) www.kantei.go.jp/jp/tyoukanpress/201104/20_a.html accessed 15 January 2018.

161 Some Japanese consumers were very selective of products, ascribing strong importance to their origins. However, after the nuclear accident, some supermarkets suddenly started to affix labels giving information on the origins of their products. Naturally, if the products were produced in Fukushima, consumers would hesitate to pick them up. Nevertheless, banning such labels in supermarkets was a difficult proposition.

were not accepted at fish markets. Farmers and fishermen in these areas therefore suffered considerable damage due to "bad reputation." Hotels and restaurants in the affected prefectures similarly suffered tremendous loss owing to the sudden decline in customers.

There is, of course, no statutory provision that explicitly prohibits consumers from refusing to buy agricultural products or fish because of unsubstantiated fears. All the central and local government could really do was to emphasize the safety of these products and encourage consumers to buy them. However, legal questions remained over whether TEPCO would be liable to compensate farmers and fishermen for loss and damage caused by the disaster which negatively affected the reputation of their products.

3.6 Rolling blackouts and limitations on electricity consumption

Lastly, the nuclear accident in the Fukushima Power Plant triggered a critical shortage of electricity. Faced with the possibility of an unexpected occurrence of a wide blackout, TEPCO and the Japanese government had to introduce rolling blackouts and then cut electricity consumption in the aftermath of the accident. How were these measures planned and carried out?

3.6.1 Rolling blackouts

Since TEPCO had lost its nuclear generators, the maximum amount of electricity it could generate fell far short of what was demanded by customers in areas where the company supplied power. If consumption levels remained constant, risk of a large-scale blackout due to a supply shortage loomed large. TEPCO thus decided to introduce rolling blackouts in order to reduce consumption, beginning on the morning of 14 March. Apparently, this decision was made in coordination with the government.[162]

TEPCO's electricity supply contract with its customers did include a clause that allowed TEPCO to suspend or restrict supply when necessary for compelling reasons such as extreme drought, accidents at its facilities, repairs, emergency disasters, or security maintenance.[163] TEPCO's decision to implement rolling blackouts was therefore not a breach of contract.

However, the decision to carry out rolling blackouts was made without careful preparation. Since it was difficult for rail companies to operate railroad service without power in some places, Japan Rail (JR) along with many private rail companies in Tokyo decided to cancel or seriously limit their services on the first day

162 Chief Cabinet Secretary, Press Release (kantei 14 March 2011) www.kantei.go.jp/jp/tyoukanpress/201103/14_a.html accessed 15 January 2018.

163 TEPCO, Denryoku kyokyu yakkan (Electricity Supply Agreement) (TEPCO) www4.tepco.co.jp/ep/company2/pdf/280101kyouku000-j.pdf accessed 15 January 2018 #40.

of the blackouts, causing tremendous commuter chaos. Although most hospitals were equipped with emergency generators, some patients living at home on life support were seriously affected by the rolling blackout.[164] Moreover, several traffic accidents occurred because traffic lights were offline and no police officers were assigned to control traffic at intersections. So far, no lawsuit has been filed against TEPCO or the central government seeking damages, nor has any compensation been paid to TEPCO's customers or any affected members of the general public.

3.6.2 Limitations on electricity consumption

TEPCO managed to secure sufficient electricity in April so it decided not to implement the rolling blackout in April. However, in anticipation of the hot summer, during which most people use air-conditioning all day and every day, the central government and TEPCO had to come up with a plan to increase electrical capacity while at the same time reducing demand. The central government decided to ask everyone within TEPCO's service area, including large companies and individual consumers alike, to cut down on electrical consumption by 15% during the summer.[165]

In order to enforce this policy, the government issued an electrical consumption limitation order on 1 June.[166] This order was issued under the authority of the Electricity Business Act,[167] which authorized the Economy, Trade and Industry Minister to issue a regulation limiting the consumption of electricity if such regulation is necessary to prevent adverse impacts on the national economy, the lives of citizens, or to prevent harm to the public interest arising from the possibility of electrical shortage. This regulation required large corporate consumers of electricity to cut down on their consumption.

Initially, it was expected that other power companies, including the neighboring Chubu Electric Power Company, could supply additional power to TEPCO.[168] On 6 May, however, Kan asked the Chubu Electric Power Company

164 "Keikakuteki teiden no chuiten : Keitai, netto hutsumo, shingou, iryoumo eikyou [Watch Out for Rolling Blackouts: Mobile Phones and Internet May Be Down and Signals and Medical Services Might Be Affected]" (*Nihonkeizai Shimbun* 14 March 2011) www.nikkei.com/article/DGXNASDG1305H_T10C11A3EA2001/ accessed 15 January 2018.

165 Chief Cabinet Secretary, Press Release (kantei 13 May 2011) www.kantei.go.jp/jp/tyoukanpress/201105/13_a.html accessed 15 January 2018.

166 Denryoku shiyou seigentō kisoku [Regulation on Limitation of Electrical Consumption], Ministry of Economy, Trade and Industry Regulation no 28, 2011.

167 Denki jigyohō [Electricity Business Act], Law no 170 of 1964, art 27.

168 However, due to difference in power frequency between the Chubu Electric Company and TEPCO, there was a serious limitation in the capacity to convert and transmit power from the Chubu Electric Company to TEPCO. "Denryoku, naze nishinihon kara higashinihon ni yuuzuu mutukasii noka [Electric Power: Why Is It Difficult to Transfer Power from the West Japan to East Japan]" (*Nihonkeizai Shimbun* 24 March 2011) https://style.nikkei.com/article/DGXBZO25485130T20C11A3AA1P00?channel=DF130120166126&style=1 accessed 15 January 2018.

to halt operations at the Hamaoka Nuclear Power Plant in Omaezaki, Shizuoka Prefecture, over fears of possible disaster if a similarly powerful earthquake and tsunami were to affect that power plant.[169] Of course, there was no legal authority for the prime minister to order the power company to halt operations at the nuclear power plant. However, the president of the Chubu Electric Power Company decided to accept the prime minister's request on 14 May. As a result, Chubu Electric Power suddenly faced the prospect of having difficulty supplying sufficient power to consumers in its own service area, let alone assisting TEPCO. This move gave rise to national hysteria in opposition to nuclear power plants. Many municipal heads that had allowed nuclear power plants in their municipalities began refusing permission to restart plants after they were stopped due to earthquakes or for periodic maintenance and inspection. Consequently, other electric power companies also faced tremendous difficulty securing sufficient electricity. As a result, the government was forced to mandate the restriction on power use for the summer.[170]

The prime minister denied any intention of asking other power companies to stop operations at other nuclear power plants. Although Kaieda indicated his plan to give the go-ahead to reactivation of other nuclear power plants,[171] Kan suddenly came to demand a new stress test before giving the green light to activation of each nuclear power plant. As a result, the central government had to come up with a new stress test that all nuclear power plants had to pass before restarting.[172] Nuclear reactors could resume operations if they satisfied the informal stress test but all reactors must satisfy the new formal standard adopted by the regulatory agency. Kan also expressed his personal view that Japan should rid itself of nuclear power plants altogether in the future.[173]

169 Prime Minister's Press Interview (kantei 6 May 2011) www.kantei.go.jp/jp/kan/statement/201105/06kaiken.html accessed 15 January 2018.

170 Agency for Natural Resources and Energy, Denkijigyohō dai27jou nimotoduku shiyouseigen nitsuite [On Restriction on Power Use under article 27 of the Electricity Business Act] (METI June 2011) www.meti.go.jp/earthquake/shiyoseigen/pdf/gaiyo110601-02.pdf accessed 15 January 2018.

171 "Kaieda keisansho, kensa shuryo no genpatsu saikadou ni iyoku [Economy, Trade and Industry Minister Kaieda Is Wishing to Reactivate the Nuclear Power Plants after Inspection]" (*Nihonkeizai Shimbun* 10 June 2011) www.nikkei.com/article/DGXNASFS1000K_Q1A610C1EB1000/ accessed 15 January 2018.

172 "Zengenpatsude sutoresu tesuto, anzenkakunin no uede saikadouhandan: Kiaeada keisanshou [After the Stress Test for All Nuclear Power Plants, Decision to Restart After Safety Is Secured: Economy, Trade and Industry Minister Kaieda]" (Reuters 6 July 2011) http://jp.reuters.com/article/topNews/idJPJAPAN-22063220110706 accessed 15 January 2018.

173 Press Conference of Prime Minister Naoto Kan (kantei 13 July 2011) www.kantei.go.jp/jp/kan/statement/201107/13kaiken.html accessed 15 January 2018. Initially, Kan's statements seemed to reflect the official views of the prime minister in his capacity representing the Cabinet. However, other Cabinet members soon came forward to affirm that they were merely Kan's personal statements and Kan was forced to concede that it was just his personal opinion. "Kanshushou datsu genpatsu wa kojintekina kangae [Prime Minister Kan Concedes that the Abandonment of Nuclear Power Was His Personal Idea]" (*News24* 15 July 2011) www.news24.jp/articles/2011/07/15/04186538.html accessed 15 January 2018.

It is most unusual for the prime minister to ask a particular private company to halt operations at a power plant despite the fact that the power plant was constructed with legal permits from the government, satisfied all legal standards, and was complying with all statutory regulations. The majority of Japanese people supported Kan's decision, but questions remain over the appropriateness of the prime minister asking a private company to act beyond what is required by law. Moreover, the source of authority for imposing the stress test before restarting operations is legally unclear, as is the prime minister's order to revamp the stress test.

Although the consumption restriction regulation was lifted on 9 September 2011,[174] both TEPCO and the central government had to face the possibility of electricity shortages again in the winter, when people would need electricity for warmth. Suddenly, it became extremely difficult to rely upon nuclear power plants any more. Although the consumption regulation was not legally reintroduced, the government still asked the public to cut down on electrical consumption.[175]

Owing to all of these developments, the central government must anticipate that shortages of electricity may continue long into the future. Finding strategies for securing sufficient electricity became the urgent agendas of both the Japanese government and TEPCO for the foreseeable future.

3.7 Nuclear meltdown and failures of law and politics

3.7.1 Nuclear meltdown and failures of law

Why does such a devastating nuclear accident have to happen? What was wrong with the regulatory system for the nuclear power plant? How come the law was not able to prevent the accident?

The most fundamental reason for the Fukushima nuclear accident is the failure to anticipate that such a powerful earthquake would affect the safety of the Fukushima Nuclear Power Plant.[176] For the government, the Tohoku Earthquake

174 Chief Cabinet Secretary, Press Release (kantei 30 August 2011) www.kantei.go.jp/jp/tyoukanpress/201108/30_a.html accessed 15 January 2018.

175 Takeshi Oshima & Atsushi Nabetani, "Denryoku jukyu taisaku no keii to energy seisaku minaoshi no kentō [History of Balancing Demand and Supply for Electricity and the Reconsideration of Energy Policy]," (2012) 329 *Rippo to Chousa* 148.

176 The Japanese government and TEPCO anticipated the maximum strength possible for an earthquake at magnitude 7.9 and that a tsunami was supposed to be fended off by the tsunami barrier with a height of 3.1 meters. TEPCO built seawater intake buildings at 4 meters above sea level and the main plant buildings at the top of a slope 10 meters about sea level so that they could escape any tsunami damage. Thereafter, more recent research indicated the possibility of much higher tsunamis and TEPCO increased the height of the seawall to 5.7 meters. The Tohoku Earthquake was an earthquake with a magnitude of 9.0 and caused a tsunami with a height of 14 to 15 meters. *See* James M. Acton & Mark Hibbs, "Why Fukushima Was Preventable" (*Carnegie Papers* March 2012) http://carnegieendowment.org/2012/03/06/why-fukushima-was-preventabale-pub-47361 accessed 15 January 2018 9–10; International Atomic Energy Agency, Fukushima Nuclear Accident (IAEA) www.iaea.org/newscenter/focus/fukushima 51; Gregory D. Wyss, "The Accident that Could Never Happen: Deluded by a Design Basis," in Brandford & Sagan (n 5) 29.

was surely "unprecedented" and "unexpected." The calls for the necessity of considering much more powerful earthquakes in light of the Jogan Earthquake and for much higher tsunamis had been rejected by the government as well as TEPCO in the past.[177]

Moreover, the required tsunami countermeasures are apparently totally insufficient.[178] The government did not specifically require specific tsunami countermeasures for the nuclear power plant, which is likely to be built on the coastline because nuclear power plants need water to release the heat generated by producing the power. TEPCO and the government were totally ignorant of the serious tsunami risk to the nuclear power plant.

Furthermore, the government and TEPCO failed to prepare for the total power loss.[179] This was a critical error since in the United States, the federal Nuclear Regulatory Commission (NRC) has required all power companies to prepare for possible total power loss at least since the 11 September terrorist attacks.[180] The Japanese government failed to require TEPCO to adopt the same kinds of preparatory measures and TEPCO failed to institute such measures.[181]

TEPCO was also totally unprepared for the nuclear emergency and the government was reluctant to force the nuclear power plant to be well prepared for a serious nuclear accident. The Fukushima Nuclear Power Plant workers were unprepared for the manual vent operation and there was no adequate water pump to pour water into the reactors in the plant.

Apparently, all this reveals the serious failures of law since the law did not require or mandate the preparation against this as a condition for a permit or a permit for operation of the nuclear power plant.

3.7.2 Nuclear meltdown and much deeper failures of law

These failures could be said to reflect much deeper failures of the law in Japan. First, all these problems could be attributable to the nuclear regulatory law for its

177 Central Disaster Prevention Conference, Tohoku chihō taiheiyōoki jishin wo kyoukuntoshita jishin tsunami taisaku ni kansuru senmonchousakai houkoku [Report of the Expert Committee on Countermeasures against Earthquake and Tsunami in light of the off the Pacific Coast of Tohoku Earthquake] (Cabinet Office 28 September 2011) www.bousai.go.jp/kaigirep/chousakai/tohokukyokun/pdf/houkoku.pdf accessed 15 January 2018 (very powerful earthquake of 869 was ignored because past analysis was focused on recurrent powerful earthquakes). *See also* Acton & Hibbs (n 176) 11–12.

178 Ibid 13, 26.

179 Ibid 19.

180 Nuclear Regulatory Commission, Report: A Comparison of U.S. and Japanese Regulatory Requirements in Effect at the Time of the Fukushima Accident (November 2013) (NRC) www.nrc.gov/docs/ML1332/ML13326A991.pdf accessed 15 January 2018 15.

181 Costas Synolakis & Utku Kânoğlu, "The Fukushima Accident Was Preventable" (2015) 373 *Philosophical Transactions of the Royal Society A* 20140379; Kaoru Naito, "Security Implications of the Fukushima Accident," in Brandford & Sagan (n 5) 58, 68; Yasuko Claremont, "Disaster in Japan: A Case Study," in Simon Butt, Hitoshi Nasu & Luke Nottage (eds), *Asia-Pacific Disaster Management: Comparative and Socio-Legal Perspectives* (Springer 2014) 79, 96.

failure to require an independent regulatory agency that regulates nuclear power. Indeed, the nuclear power regulatory system in Japan had entrusted the METI, a government department that had promoted nuclear power, with the task of ensuring the safety of nuclear power. As a result, the METI did not have an incentive to ensure the safety of the plant at the power companies' expense. It was captured by the regulated industry.[182] This was a critical flaw in the law on nuclear power.[183]

Moreover, although the Nuclear Reactor Regulation Act anticipated the declaration of nuclear emergency, it did not grant the prime minister sufficient power to respond to nuclear disasters. The primary responsibility to respond to nuclear disasters remains with the power company, and it was only the Economy, Trade and Industry Minister who could order the power company to correct or adopt measures to respond to the disaster. The prime minister, as the director of the headquarters, only has the power to issue instructions.

Similarly, the prime minister did not have any power to order local residents to evacuate, nor to ban the marketing of contaminated products or the cultivation of crops in contaminated areas. All the prime minister had was a power to issue instructions as the director of the headquarters. Instead of authorizing the government to issue legal orders, the law was anticipating that the government would simply rely upon informal measures requesting voluntary cooperation. This preference for informal measures rather than legal powers resulted in awkward requests for evacuation and a request for marketing restrictions instead of a legal order for evacuation and marketing restrictions.

Finally, the chain of command inside the government to respond to the nuclear accident was not well organized or well coordinated. It was utterly unclear who had the ultimate responsibility in facing the disaster. The decision-making process within the government in response to this kind of nuclear emergency was too complicated and was not well designed, leading to a chaotic response to the nuclear emergency.[184] The law failed to allow the prime minister to act alone and swiftly.

These problems are not just a matter of mistake or oversight. They are inherent in the legal system. Many people are aware of these drawbacks but no one has attempted to remedy them. They turned out to be quite disastrous in the wake of the Fukushima nuclear accident.

3.7.3 Nuclear meltdown and failures of politics

The failure to establish an independent regulatory agency and to require sufficient safety regulation was rooted in the desire to promote nuclear power.

182 Nobumasa Akiyama, "Political Leadership in Nuclear Emergency: Institutional and Structural Constraints," in Brandford & Sagan (n 5) 97.

183 Akira Nakamura & Masao Kikuchi, "What We Know, and What We Have Not yet Learned: Triple Disasters and the Fukushima Nuclear Fiasco in Japan" (2011) 71:6 *Public Administration Review* 893.

184 Akiyama (n 182) 80, 82.

This desire to promote nuclear power led to the policy of facilitating economic development first and foremost. It was believed that the construction of nuclear power plants was essential to promoting economic development.[185] This economic-development-first policy surely resulted in ignoring or neglecting many safety issues to be required.

Nuclear power was eagerly promoted by government bureaucrats, Liberal Democratic Party (LDP) politicians, and the power companies. Local government also wanted to accept the nuclear power plant due to lucrative government grants and all the benefits the nuclear power plant could bring to the local government.[186] There are all sorts of people who committed to the promotion of nuclear power—the so-called "nuclear village" (*genshiryoku mura*).[187] Because of the strong endorsement of the government and assurances made by leading nuclear experts, the public came to believe that nuclear power is totally controlled, that it is totally safe, and that there would be no serious nuclear accidents—the so-called "safety myth" of nuclear power.[188]

Against this background, it was difficult to discuss the possibility of serious nuclear disaster let alone the countermeasures that should be implemented if a serious nuclear disaster happened.[189] It is no wonder there was no well-established system that specified the chain of command, the necessary kinds of countermeasures, and who would hold ultimate responsibility for responding to a nuclear disaster. Moreover, even when the new safety measures were introduced, there was no back-checking obligation: new obligations were not retroactive, meaning the new safety measures did not apply to nuclear reactors that had already received permits.[190] Such a measure would have raised the suspicion that existing facilities, which do not comply with the new additional safety measures, were

185 Forum on Energy, Genshiryoku no shourai: Nihon [Future of Nuclear Energy: Japan] (Forum on Energy) http://forumonenergy.com/2016/06/24/原子力の将来-日本/?lang=ja > accessed 15 January 2018.

186 Takuji Hara, "Social Shaping of Nuclear Safety: Before and after the Disaster," in Richard Hindmarh (ed), *Nuclear Disaster at Fukushima Daiichi: Social, Political and Environmental Issues* (Routledge 2013) 25. As a result, nuclear reactors in Japan tend to be clustered in a particular nuclear power plant. Many claim this concentration of nuclear reactors was one of the reasons for the serious nuclear disaster in Fukushima. Kohta Juraku, "Social Structure and Nuclear Power Sitting Problems Revealed," in ibid 41.

187 Andrew DeWit, Tesunari Iida, & Masaru Kaneko, "Fukushima and the Political Economy of Power Policy in Japan," in Jeff Kingston (ed), *Natural Disaster and Nuclear Crisis in Japan: Response and Recovery after Japan's 3/11* (Routledge 2012) 156; Kushida (n 14) 39–40; Jeff Kingston, "Japan's Nuclear Village," 10: 37 *Asia-Pacific Journal* 1 (9 September 2012) http://apjjf.org/-Jeff-Kingston/3822/article.pdf accessed 15 January 2018; Hara (n 186) 22.

188 Acton & Hibbs (n 176) 2; Charles D. Ferguson & Mark Janson, "Regulating Japanese Nuclear Power in the Wake of the Fukushima Daiichi Accident" (Federation of American Scientists) http://blogs.fas.org/wp-content/uploads/2013/05/Regulating_Japanese_Nuclear_13May13.pdf accessed 13 February 2018; Norimitsu Onishi, "'Safety Myth' Left Japan Ripe for Nuclear Crisis" (*New York Times* 24 June 2011) www.nytimes.com/2011/06/25/world/asia/25myth.html?pagewanted=all accessed 13 February 2018.

189 Acton & Hibbs (n 176) 27–28.

190 Ibid 14.

not safe. The government and the power companies apparently did not want such suspicion. It is also no wonder the legal system failed to grant broad legal power to order evacuations or marketing bans. Since if there was going to be no serious accident, it would have been simply meaningless to envision the necessity of such measures.[191]

Also, nuclear power in Japan has been subject to several different government departments: with respect to general nuclear power policy, it was the responsibility of the AEC inside the Cabinet Office; with respect to promotion of nuclear power in general, it was the responsibility of the MEXT; with respect to the development and regulation of power companies and nuclear power plants, it was the METI; and with respect to providing advice on nuclear safety, it was the responsibility of the NSC, again inside the Cabinet Office. Typical of bureaucratic organizations, jurisdictional turf wars and difficulties with inter-agency cooperation must have prevented effective and coordinated regulation on nuclear power.

Moreover, Japanese prime ministers are chosen by the Diet, and the general public does not have the power to choose the national leader.[192] In the past, most prime ministers were chosen by the internal politics of the LDP. As a result, it was difficult to have a powerful leader as prime minister. Even since the Democratic Party of Japan (DPJ) took over the government in 2009, apparently no leader has ever been chosen based on the power of leadership. It is therefore no wonder Kan failed to effectively respond to the nuclear disaster. Many have criticized Kan's blunders.[193] The inability to choose a capable leader turned out to be disastrous in the wake of the Fukushima nuclear disaster.[194]

Furthermore, since Japanese society generally prefers a collective consensus-building decision-making process, it must come as no surprise that the law anticipated the establishment of the headquarters and allowed the prime minister as the director of the headquarters to coordinate various countermeasures. It turned out, however, the crisis in Fukushima demanded swift and definitive solutions. Due to the tsunami disabling the nuclear power plant's emergency power generation system, we now know that the nuclear meltdown started immediately after the nuclear power plant lost power. The clock was ticking and the government simply had no time to gather, discuss, and form a decision based on consensus.

191 It is thus no wonder that the municipal government and local residents were not well prepared for evacuation. Akiyama (n 183) 91; Federica Ranghieri & Mikio Ishiwatari (eds), *Learning from Megadisasters: Lessons from the Great East Japan Earthquake* (World Bank 2014) 103.

192 Nihonkoku kenpō [Constitution of Japan], art 67(1); Makitaka Masuyama & Benjamin Nyblade, "Japan: The Prime Minister and Japanese Diet," (2004) 10:2–3 *Journal of Legislative Studies* 250.

193 "Lessons in Leadership from Fukushima Nuclear Disaster" (University of Pennsylvania, Wharton 3 October 2013) http://knowledge.wharton.upenn.edu/article/lessons-leadership-fukushima-nuclear-disaster/ accessed 15 January 2018. But see Kenji E. Kushida, "The Fukushima Nuclear Disaster and the Democratic Party of Japan" (2014) 40:1 *Japanese Political Economy* 29.

194 "A Crisis of Leadership, Too: The Many-headed Catastrophe Points to Deeper-seated Problems in Governing Japan" (*Economist* 24 March 2011) www.economist.com/node/18441143 accessed 15 January 2018.

The Japanese political system simply may not be suited for this kind of urgent emergency situation.[195]

Finally, Kan, well-known for his distrust of government bureaucrats, attempted to grab power back from bureaucrats in the DPJ government and give it back to politicians. When the nuclear disaster struck, the relationship between DPJ politicians and government bureaucrats was already a strenuous one. Kan tried to allow politicians to play leading roles in the response to the crisis. It is doubtful that he made use of all the wisdom and power the bureaucrats could have provided in responding to the urgent situation in Fukushima and it is doubtful that politicians did a better job in their handling of the situation.[196]

These problems revealed the failure of politics in Japan.

***

The Fukushima Nuclear Power Plant disaster proved that the Japanese legal system was not well prepared for such a serious nuclear disaster. The law failed to anticipate a serious nuclear accident and failed to establish effective countermeasures against it. The government's attempt to contain the disaster was filled with ambiguities and extreme awkwardness, raising at the same time a lot of legal questions. These failures of law are also a reflection of deeper failures of Japanese law: reluctance to create an independent regulatory agency and reluctance to grant broad legal powers to the prime minister to respond to the disaster. They are further a reflection of the failure of politics: existence of the nuclear village and the safety myth, the priority granted to economic development, reluctance to allow the public to choose a political leader, the inability to choose a reliable leader and strong government departmentalism. The Fukushima nuclear disaster was not simply an accident but a manifestation of all these failures of law and politics.

195 Bruce Klingner, Fukushima Crisis Shows Weakness in Japanese Crisis Management (Heritage Foundation 12 October 2011) www.heritage.org/asia/commentary/fukushima-crisis-shows-weakness-japanese-crisis-management accessed 7 March 2018 ("as time passed, a more critical assessment arose of Japanese indecisiveness, poor coordination amongst national and local governments, and unwillingness to assume responsibility. These factors, combined with the Japanese requirement for consensus-building leadership, hindered effective government disaster response"); Seijiro Takeshita, "What Japanese Leaders Can Learn from the Fukushima Nuclear Crisis" (*CNN* 6 July 2012) www.cnn.com/2012/07/06/opinion/takeshita-fukushima-management/index.html accessed 15 January 2018.

196 Akiyama (n 182) 89; Norimitsu Onishi & Martin Fackler, "In Nuclear Crisis, Crippling Mistrust" (*New York Times* 12 June 2011) www.nytimes.com/2011/06/13/world/asia/13japan.html accessed 7 March 2018.

4 Reconstruction of the Tohoku Region

After rescue and recovery missions were complete, the focus of government operations shifted to reconstruction of the Tohoku Region. The Japanese government attempted to provide assistance to disaster victims and to support community-rebuilding efforts. The central government adopted the fundamental policy for reconstruction and established the Reconstruction Agency. The reconstruction special zones program and reconstruction grants program were introduced to facilitate reconstruction. Large sums of public money have been spent on reconstruction. However, whether these measures have been effective and sufficient remains a hotly debated topic. Indeed, many of the local affected residents are deeply frustrated and disappointed. Why do they feel such frustration and disappointment? Is there something wrong with the reconstruction measures adopted by the Japanese government? This chapter examines the reconstruction process with particular focus on the legal system and its role to see whether they are indeed appropriate. It will reveal that the reconstruction process is fraught with roadblocks and show how fundamental problems of the Japanese legal system are manifesting in serious failures of law.

4.1 Assisting the disaster victims

The Tohoku Earthquake and ensuing tsunami brought a tremendous number of casualties and damage to the people in the Tohoku Region. Those who were lucky enough to survive suffered serious loss, damage, and inconvenience. The local and central government scrambled to provide various forms of assistance to those disaster victims.

4.1.1 Casualties and damage

A tremendous number of people suffered devastating losses because of the tsunami. As we already saw, as of 1 September 2017, 18,561 residents were left dead or missing.[1] Most survivors lost family members, relatives, and friends.

1 Reconstruction Agency, Hukko no genjo to kanren shoseido [Current State of Reconstruction and Related Systems] (Reconstruction Agency 6 November 2017) www.reconstruction.go.jp/topics/main-cat1/sub-cat1-1/20171106_torikumitoshoseido.pdf accessed 30 December 2017 2; 15,984 persons were found dead and 2,577 persons are still missing. If we add the number of persons who died due to earthquake related reasons after the disaster (3,591 persons), the total number of casualties reached to 22,152. Ibid.

Many lost their homes. Indeed, 121,776 houses were totally destroyed and 280,326 were half-destroyed.[2] Damage from the tsunami affected 561 square kilometers of land.[3] That is roughly equal to half of the city of New York. In the six affected prefectures, more than 23,000 hectares of farmland were wiped away or submerged in seawater.[4]

In some areas, entire communities were almost completely wiped out. For instance, in Rikuzentakata, Iwate Prefecture, the center of the city was totally wiped out, resulting in 1,757 deaths and missing out of a total population of some 24,246.[5] Ninety nine percent of all households were affected,[6] with more than 10,000 residents, almost half of the total population, having to be evacuated.[7] The town of Otsuchi lost almost 1,230 people out of a total population of some 15,000.[8]

Many municipal governments lost substantial numbers of public officials together with their local political leaders. Rikuzentakata lost its four storey city hall[9] together with 111 city officials out of 443, roughly one third of all city officials.[10] Otsuchi town also lost its town hall together with some 40 town officials out of 140, almost one third of all its officials, including a mayor and all high-ranking town officials.[11]

2 Ibid.

3 Cabinet Office, Heisei23nenban bosai hakusho [2011 Disaster Prevention Whitepaper] (Cabinet Office) www.bousai.go.jp/kaigirep/hakusho/h23/bousai2011/html/honbun/1b_1h_1s_2.htm accessed 30 December 2017.

4 Ibid; Ministry of Agriculture, Forestry, and Fisheries, Tsunami niyori ryuushutsu ya kansuitō no higai wo uketa nouchi no suitei menseki [Estimated Damage to Farmland Washed Away or Submerged in Sea-Water by the Tsunami] (MAFF 29 March 2011) www.maff.go.jp/j/press/nousin/sekkei/pdf/110329-02.pdf accessed 30 December 2017. This is roughly 2.6% of all farmland in these six prefectures. Ibid.

5 Rikuzentakata City, Jishin/tsunami no gaiyo, higaijoukyo [Loss and Damages from the Earthquake and Tsunami] (Rikuzentakata City) www.city.rikuzentakata.iwate.jp/shinsai/oshirase/hazard1.pdf accessed 30 December 2017 11.

6 Ibid 12.

7 JSCE, 2011 Great East Japan Earthquake (JSCE) http://committees.jsce.or.jp/2011quake/system/files/2011_2nd_0035.pdf accessed 30 December 2017 31.

8 Otsuchi Town, Higashinihon daishinsai jinteki hisai joukyo [Human Losses from Great East Japan Earthquake Disaster] (Otsuchi town 21 July 2017) www.town.otsuchi.iwate.jp/gyosei/docs/2012122100023/ accessed 30 December 2017; Ministry of Land, Infrastructure, Transport and Tourism, Otsuchichō chousa soukatsuhyo [Otsuchi town Summary] (MLIT) www.mlit.go.jp/common/000209534.pdf accessed 30 December 2017.

9 Rikuzentakata City (n 5) 13.

10 Rikuzentakata City, Rikuzentakatashi Higashinihon daishinsai kensho houkokusho [Review Report on Loss and Damage of the Rikuzentakata City during the Great East Japan Earthquake Disaster] (Rikuzentakata City July 2014) www.city.rikuzentakata.iwate.jp/kategorie/bousai-syoubou/shinsai/kshoukokusyo.pdf accessed 30 December 2017 110.

11 Shimada Keishi, "Iwateken Otsuchichō nimiru Higashinihon daishinsai no hukkoukadai [Reconstruction Agenda from the Great East Japan Earthquake Disaster in the Otuchi Town, Iwate Prefecture]" (2013) 421 *Jichisouken* 1, 3–4; Sachiko Seki, "Iwateken Otuchichō no shinsai hukkou no genjou to kadai [Present State of Reconstruction in the Otsuchi Town, Iwate Prefecture, and Its Agenda]" (2013) *Tōyō Daigaku PPP Kenkyu Center Kiyō* 148 www.toyo.ac.jp/file/pppc/bulletin3/10.pdf accessed 30 December 2017.

Direct losses resulting from the earthquake and tsunami were estimated at between 16 and 25 trillion JPY (145 billion USD to 227 billion USD).[12] If we include all the indirect losses, losses resulting from interruption of production due to supply-chain damage, decreases in consumer spending in affected areas after the disaster, declines in consumer spending in other areas due to self-restraint in solidarity with the affected areas,[13] among other factors, the total economic impact on Japanese society has been astronomical. We must also factor in substantial economic loss resulting from electricity shortages due to the nuclear power plant accident in Fukushima discussed previously. The disaster brought down the nominal GDP of Japan for 2011 by 1.4%.[14]

All of these economic impacts aside, the central government and local government first had to assist the surviving disaster victims.

4.1.2 Providing shelters and emergency assistance to victims

First, the government had to establish emergency shelters. As we already saw, at one point more than 450,000 local residents had to be evacuated to stay in shelters.[15] Most of these shelters were school gyms of public elementary schools or junior high schools. But other spaces in the city hall or civic centers were also used as shelters. Many stayed in cars parked in parking lots. Many others gathered in the houses of friends or relatives who had escaped the tragedy. After a while, many of the evacuees in the shelters returned home if their houses were left undamaged (or at least when they were livable in with some repairs and when they were told that they could return home safely) or moved out when they were able to find any of their relatives who were able to accept them.

12 Cabinet Office, Daishinsaigo no nihon keizai [Japanese Economy after the Great Disaster] (Cabinet Office) www5.cao.go.jp/j-j/wp/wp-je11/pdf/p01011_2.pdf accessed 30 December 2017 11.

13 Right after the disaster, people all over Japan were dominated by an overwhelming call for self-restraint. People cancelled festivals and celebrations, vacations and going-out, and enjoying entertainment. Anyone who violated this call for a self-restraint was criticized as "inconsiderate" or "imprudent." As a result, consumer spending during March 2011 dipped 8.2% below March of the previous year. Ministry of Economy, Trade and Industry, Sangyo katsudo bunseki (heisei23nenn4gatu-6gatsuki) [Analysis of Industrial Activities (April to June 2011)] (METI) www.meti.go.jp/statistics/toppage/report/bunseki/pdf/h23/h4a1109j2.pdf accessed 20 January 2018.

14 Cabinet Office, 2011 kakuhou: Sankou shiryo [2011 Data: Appendix] (Cabinet Office) www.esri.cao.go.jp/jp/sna/data/data_list/kakuhou/files/h23/sankou/pdf/point1.pdf accessed 30 December 2017.

15 Cabinet Office, Higashinihon daishinsai no hinansho seikatsushasu no suii nitsuite [On Trend of Evacuees after the Great East Japan Earthquake Disaster] (Cabinet Office) www.bousai.go.jp/taisaku/hinanjo/h24_kentoukai/1/pdf/8.pdf accessed 30 December 2017. There were 2,344 shelters established after the Tohoku Earthquake. Fire and Disaster Management Agency, Higashinihon daishinsai kirokushu [Records of Great East Japan Earthquake Disaster] (FDMA) www.fdma.go.jp/concern/publication/higashinihondaishinsai_kirokushu/pdf/honbun/03-06.pdf accessed 30 December 2017 182. See also Federica Ranghieri & Mikio Ishiwatari (eds), *Learning from Magadisasters: Lesson from the Great East Japan Earthquake* (World Bank 2014) 269.

For the many who lost their homes to the tsunami, however, there was nowhere to go and they had to stay in shelters for weeks or even for months after the earthquake.[16] Most likely no one had expected that so many evacuees would have to stay in shelters for such a long time. Life in shelters was hard and there were many restrictions. Although the management of these shelters was initially highly unorganized and unsophisticated, gradually it came to be much more organized.[17] While staying in shelters, many returned to their homes to get rid of debris and repair their damaged houses during the day before coming back to the shelters for the night.

Since most of the utilities, such as water, electricity, natural gas, and LP gas, as well as the telecommunication service were disrupted, those staying in shelters or homes faced extreme difficulty in surviving. They had to rely upon the delivery of food and goods from unaffected areas. All residents who stayed home or stayed in friends' houses had to come to shelters to receive food and water. Although the delivery was slow and unorganized at first, gradually a lot of food and goods came to be delivered thanks to donations from the general public and from many companies. Gradually, water, electricity, natural gas and LP gas came to be provided and various public services began to be offered again.[18]

4.1.3 Providing temporary places to stay

For those victims who lost homes and had no place to go, local governments provided temporary places to stay (transitional shelters) for them.[19] First, the local government found spaces for building "temporary housing," (***kasetsu jutaku***) contracted with construction companies, and rushed to build temporary housing on these spaces.[20] Building a sufficient amount of temporary housing for such a huge number of evacuees was not an easy task. First of all, it was difficult to decide how much housing was needed. Second, it was difficult to find suitable places to build temporary housing because many of the evacuees wanted to stay close to their original communities. Third, there were not sufficient stocks of materials to build enough temporary housing. But after several months the

16 Three months after the disaster, roughly 90,000 residents were still staying at temporary shelters. Cabinet Office (n 15).

17 Ranghieri & Ishiwatari (n 15) 155.

18 As a result of the earthquake and tsunami, a total of 4.6 million households lost power but 80% of households recovered power within three days and 94% recovered power within eight days. Ministry of Economy, Trade and Industry, 3gatsu11niti no jishin niyori Tohoku denryoku de hasseishita kouiki teiden no gaiyou [Summary of Wide-range Blackout as a result of the March 11 Earthquake] (Cabinet Office 10 September 2011) www.bousai.go.jp/kaigirep/chousakai/tohokukyokun/9/pdf/sub2.pdf 4. But some residents had to wait until 18 June to receive power. Ibid.

19 Ranghieri & Ishiwatari (n 15) 193.

20 As of January 2014, some 44,000 temporary housings were built to accept some 98,000 residents. Reconstruction Agency, Hukko no genjo [Current Status of Reconstruction] (Reconstruction Agency 10 March 2015) www.reconstruction.go.jp/topics/main-cat1/sub-cat1-1/20150310_genjyo.pdf accessed 30 December 2017 4.

local government managed to secure a sufficient amount of temporary housing. Many evacuees eventually left the shelters and moved into this temporary housing. The structure of the temporary housing was small and families had to endure all manner of inconveniences during their stay in them. However, they were still far better off than they were in the shelters, mostly school gyms, lying on the floor with nothing but blankets, and with no separate washrooms or showers.

Second, some disaster victims were assigned vacant rooms in assisted public apartments but in other communities.[21] Normally, eligibility for use of such public apartments is restricted to local residents. However, most local governments outside of the affected areas adopted temporary measures to accept evacuees. Most public housing is comprised of public apartments that are far better than the temporary housing built by affected local governments. However, many people had to move to other areas, often far away from their home cities, in order to accept these public apartments. The central government also had public apartments for public employees that the government decided to make available to evacuees if they were vacant. Moreover, local governments were permitted to rent private apartments to evacuees as a form of temporary residence.[22]

As of January 2015, still over 230,000 people were evacuees and roughly 210,000 people were staying in temporary accommodation.[23] As of September 2017, still roughly 80,000 residents are evacuees in affected prefectures including Fukushima prefecture.[24] They are awaiting the construction of permanent public housing for disaster victims, called "reconstruction housing," to be explained below.

4.1.4 Financial assistance for disaster victims

For survivors who had lost family members to the earthquake or tsunami, the "disaster condolence benefit" (*saigai chouikin*) was available under the Disaster Condolence Benefit Act.[25] The Diet amended the Act after the Tohoku Earthquake to include siblings of the deceased as persons eligible to receive the disaster condolence benefit and retroactively applied this provision of the Act to victims of the Tohoku Earthquake.[26]

21 As of January 2014, some 8,800 public apartments were made available for some 23,000 residents. Ibid.

22 As of January 2014, some 51,000 private apartments were made available for some 125,000 residents. Ibid.

23 Ibid.

24 Reconstruction Agency, Hukkou no genjou to kadai [Current Status and Agenda of Reconstruction] (Reconstruction Agency 6 November 2017) www.reconstruction.go.jp/topics/main-cat1/sub-cat1-1/20171106_genjoutokadai.pdf accessed 30 December 2017 3.

25 Saigai chōikin no shikyu ni kansuru hōritsu [Act concerning Payment of the Disaster Condolence Benefit], Law no 82 of 1973 (Disaster Condolence Benefit Act).

26 Saigain choikin no shikyu nikansuru hōritsu no ichibu wo kaiseisuru hōritsu [Act to Amend Parts of the Disaster Consolation Benefit Act], Law no 86 of 2011. The central government paid a total of 60.7 billion JPY (550 million USD) in disaster condolence benefits to families who lost their family members. Reconstruction Agency (n 1) 8.

For all residents who had lost their homes, government support designated as the "disaster victim life rebuilding support benefit" under the Disaster Victim Life Rebuilding Support Act[27] was available. As we already saw, this Act was brought in after the Hanshin Awaji Earthquake because many people were forced to endure double loans to build new homes. Eligible spending under this benefit had previously been seriously limited, but recipients were now permitted to use it for the purpose of rebuilding their homes.[28] Moreover, other kinds of benefits were also available as was financial aid donated from all around the world.[29] This was also distributed to disaster victims. Furthermore, the Diet enacted a statute prohibiting the seizure of the disaster condolence benefit, the disaster victim life support benefit, as well as all other assistance money, donation money, or support money extended to disaster victims.[30]

For those who had lost family members, insurance companies decided to pay life insurance payments despite exception clauses allowing them to refuse or reduce the payment in cases where insured persons had died because of natural disaster.[31] Moreover, in order to speed up the processing of payments, these

27 Hisaisha seikatsu saiken shienhō [Disaster Victim Life Rebuilding Support Act], Law no 66 of 1998.

28 *See* Chapter 1 n 101. Believing that 3 million JPY (27,000 USD) would be insufficient, however, disaster victims were calling for an increase in the amount of support. Sendai Municipal Assembly, Higashinihon daishinsai karano hukkyu/hukko nikakawaru kinkyu youbou [Emergency Request with respect to Restoration and Revival from the Great East Japan Earthquake Disaster] (Sendai City 30 May 2011) www.gikai.city.sendai.jp/saigai/image/youbousyo230530.pdf accessed 30 December 2017. The central government paid a total of 340 billion JPY (3 billion USD) in disaster victim life rebuilding support benefits. Reconstruction Agency (n 24) 8. The government amended the statute to raise the contribution of central government to the benefits from 50% to 80% with respect to the Great East Japan Earthquake Disaster. Higashinihon daishinsai ni taisho surutameno tokuebtsuno zaisei enjo oyobi josei nikansuru hōritsu [Act on Special Financial Aids and Subsidies in order to Respond to the Great East Japan Earthquake Disaster], Law no 40 of 2011 (Special Financial Aids Act), art 5–2.

29 Donations reached 381 billion JPY (3.5 billion USD). Reconstruction Agency (n 24) 8. Initially, these donations were not promptly distributed because of the bureaucratic attitude of those who were in charge. They decided to distribute the money depending upon the extent of damages suffered and they thus demanded a certificate of damage from the local government to receive the donation. It was surely not unreasonable to distribute more money to those who suffered more serious damage. But the local governments were not properly functioning in the initial months and local government officials were unable to check the degree of damage individually and issue certificates of damage promptly. As a result, very few victims were able to receive donations during the initial months. Eventually, however, all of the donated money was distributed among disaster victims. Ibid.

30 Saigai chouikin no shikyutō ni kansuru hōritsu oyobi hisaisha seikatsu saikenshienhō no ichibu wo kaiseisuru hōrtisu [Act to Amend Parts of the Disaster Condolence Benefit Act and the Disaster Victim Life Rebuilding Support Act], Law no 100 of 2011; Higashinihon daishinsai kanren gienkin ni kakawaru sashiosae kinshitō ni kansuru hōritsu [Act concerning Prohibition of Seizure of Support Money for Victims of Great East Japan Earthquake Disaster], Law no 103 of 2011. As a result of this ban, loan companies were prohibited from seizing various sources of assistance money even when disaster victims had defaulted on repaying outstanding loans.

31 Nihon seimeihoken kyokai [Life Insurance Association of Japan], Higashinihon daishinsai niokeru seimeihoken gyoukai no torikumi to kongo no kadai to taiou [Response of the Life Insurance Companies to the Great East Japan Earthquake Disaster and Future Agenda] (Nihon seimeihoken kyoukai 16 March 2012) www.seiho.or.jp/data/billboard/disaster01/info02/pdf/20120316.pdf accessed 30 December 2017. As of March 2012, life insurance companies made life insurance payouts to 19,969 claimants, totaling some 152 billion JPY (roughly 1.4 billion USD). Ibid.

companies adopted informal procedures for confirming death. For those who carried earthquake insurance on their homes, insurance companies decided to pay entire insurance payouts.[32] For survivors who had lost jobs because of the earthquake and tsunami, the central government also decided to extend periods for receiving unemployment benefits.[33]

However, for those who were merely carrying fire insurance on their houses, damage to their homes resulting from earthquake or tsunami, even damage caused by earthquake or tsunami related fire, was not covered.[34] Most automobile owners who lost automobiles because of the tsunami were not covered by auto insurance because damage caused by earthquake or tsunami was excluded unless a special earthquake liability clause had been added to auto insurance policies; few had opted for this clause.[35]

Moreover, many farmers lost their farmland or at least needed land improvement after the tsunami. They were unable to obtain any income from their products. Furthermore, since all ports, fish markets, and most companies related to fish storage and production were seriously damaged, many people lost their jobs and were left with no viable prospects for subsequent employment. As a result, many disaster victims were saddled with significant financial burdens.

In order to start a new life, and especially to rebuild a house, there is a further hurdle. Many disaster victims had loans outstanding on their lost homes. They thus faced the prospect of paying existing loans while, at the same time, borrowing more from a financial institution, and being forced to pay "double loans." The central government was concerned over this probability and decided to introduce measures for alleviating financial burdens on disaster victims. Cabinet ministers decided to introduce a moratorium on repayment of government loans, to refinance loans at a lower rate of interest, to promote public housing for disaster

32 As of 2 April 2012, insurance companies made insurance payouts to 771,403 claimants for earthquake insurance, totaling 1.2 trillion JPY (roughly 11.1 billion USD). Nihon songaihoken kyokai [SONPO], Higashinihon daishin nitaisuru songaihokengyoukai no taiou [Response of Damage Insurance Industry to the Great East Japan Earthquake Disaster] (SONPO) www.sonpo.or.jp/news/2011quake/pdf/taiou.pdf 211, 212.

33 Ministry of Health, Labor and Welfare decided to extend the period for receiving unemployment benefits to workers who lost jobs and could not find jobs in the affected prefectures under the Koyō hokenhō [Employment Benefit Act], Law no 116 of 1974, art 15. Special Financial Aids Act (n 28), art 82; Ministry of Health, Labor and Welfare, Higashnihon daishinsai ni tomonau koyō hoken shitsugyo kyuhu no kyuhu nissū no enchō [Extension of Period to Pay Unemployment Benefits to Survivors of the Great East Japan Earthquake Disaster] (MHLW 2 May 2011) www.mhlw.go.jp/bunya/koyou/dl/koyouhoken08.pdf accessed 30 December 2017 (extending additional 60 days to basic 60 days payment).

34 One may be tempted to challenge this exclusion clause, though the Japanese courts, including the Supreme Court of Japan, rejected all such challenges after the Hanshin Awaji Earthquake. Saikō Saibansho [Sup. Ct.], 3rd petty bench, 9 December 2003, 57 *Saikō saibansho hanreishu minji [Minshu]* 1887 (holding that the customer signed off on the exclusion clause and the failure of the insurance company to provide sufficient information on this clause was not illegal).

35 AXA Direct, Jishin demo sharyohoken wa tsukaerunoka [Is the Damage Caused by Earthquake Covered by the Auto Insurance?] (AXA insurance) www.axa-direct.co.jp/auto/coverages/for_earthquakes.html accessed 30 December 2017.

victims, and to facilitate "private renegotiation" (*shiteki seiri*) with financial institutions.[36] Financial institutions published guidelines for renegotiation between debtors and financial institutions.[37] Disaster victims could thus renegotiate with financial institutions to reduce outstanding loan amounts or reduce interest rates instead of filing for bankruptcy. Financial institutions that granted reductions in loan amounts could use those reductions as losses for tax purposes.[38] This private renegotiation procedure was beneficial for disaster victims because substantial monies would still be left for them while they would also not be blacklisted as delinquent debtors. Furthermore, financial institutions were able to receive at least some portion of the loans from disaster victim debtors.

For disaster victims wishing to rebuild their homes, special low-interest loans, called "disaster reconstruction housing loans" (*saigai hukkou juutaku yushi*), were made possible through the Japan Housing Finance Agency.[39] Individuals wanting to build a new home or purchase a home often make use of this independent administrative agency. The Agency extended special low-interest loans to disaster victims wishing to build or purchase homes.

4.1.5 Financial assistance for business operators

For business operators facing financial difficulty in keeping their businesses afloat, the "Great East Japan Earthquake Disaster reconstruction special loan" (*Higashinihon daishinsai hukkou tokubetsu kashitsuke*) became available from Japan Finance Corporation (*Nihon seisaku kinyu kouko*).[40] The Small and Medium Enterprise Agency of the Ministry of Economy, Trade and Industry (METI)

36 Decision of the Relevant Ministers, Nijū saimu mondai eno taiou houshin [Principles for Responding to the Double Loan Issue] (Cabinet Office 17 June 2011) www.cas.go.jp/jp/siryou/pdf/20110617taiouhousin.pdf accessed 30 December 2017.

37 Zenkoku ginko kyokai [Japan Bankers Association], Kojin saimusha no shitekiseiri ni kansuru guideline [Guidelines for Private Renegotiation for Individual Debtors] (JBA) www.zenginkyo.or.jp/news/entryitems/news230735.pdf accessed 30 December 2017.

38 In order to support financial institutions, which would undoubtedly suffer from the reduction of debts under this procedure, the government decided to relax requirements for financial institutions to receive financial assistance. Higashinihon daishinsai ni taishoshite kin-yukikantō no keieikiban no jūjitsu wo hakaru tameno kin-yukinō no kyouka no tameno tokubetsu sochi ni kansuru hōritsu oyobi kin-yu kikantō no soshiki saihensei no sokushin ni kansuru tokubetsu sochihō no ichibu wo kaiseisuru hōritsu [Act to Amend Parts of the Act concerning Special Measures to Strengthen Financial Functions in order to Improve the Financial Foundation of Financial Institutions and the Special Measures Act concerning Advancement of Reorganization of Financial Institutions in order to Respond to the Great East Japan Earthquake Disaster], Law no 80 of 2011.

39 Japan Housing Finance Agency (JHF), Higashinihon daishinsai niyori higaiwo ukeraretakata nitaisuru saigai hukkou jutaku yushi oyobi hensaihouho no henkou no seidokakujuutō nitsuite [On the Availability of Disaster Reconstruction Housing Loan and Changes to Payment Method for the Victims of the Great East Japan Earthquake Disaster] (JHF) www.jhf.go.jp/shinsai/hensai110502.html accessed 30 December 2017.

40 Japan Finance Corporation, Higashinihon daishinsai hukkou tokubetsu kashidashi [Great East Japan Earthquake Disaster Reconstruction Special Loans] (JFC) www.jfc.go.jp/n/finance/search/shinsaikashitsuke.html accessed 30 December 2017. Japan Finance Corporation is a public organization owned by the government to provide financial support for business corporations.

established an Industrial Rehabilitation Organization (*Sangyo hukkou kikō*) in each affected prefecture to help small and medium size business corporations.[41]

The Diet also enacted the Act on Great East Japan Earthquake Disaster Affected Business Operators Reconstruction Support Organization, Inc.[42] to assist these business operators. The Great East Japan Earthquake Disaster Affected Business Operators Reconstruction Support Organization, Inc. (*Higashinihon daishinsai jigyousha saisei shien kikō*), newly created to provide assistance to business corporations suffering from the Tohoku Earthquake, purchases loans taken out by affected business operators from financial institutions, provides necessary loans, provides security for new loans taken out from financial institutions by business operators, and makes investments in business operators.

4.2 Rebuilding communities

Second, the central government and local government had to assist the local residents in rebuilding their local communities. Public roads, river banks, bridges, tsunami barriers, public schools, public hospitals, city and town halls and other public facilities had to be rebuilt. Local residents had to be allowed to return to their homes if they were deemed safe and permitted to rebuild their houses. However, merely restoring the community as it existed before the disaster was apparently insufficient. Most people agreed that total reconstruction or revival was necessary instead of mere restoration. Especially, in light of the demonstrated vulnerability of these regions to powerful tsunamis, the local and central government had to make sure that the newly rebuilt communities were safe even when the next powerful tsunami struck.

4.2.1 Reconstruction and revival

The central government had already designated areas hit by the earthquake and tsunami under the Extremely Serious Disaster Act[43] as those affected by an "extremely serious disaster."[44] According to provisions of the Act, the central government would bear up to 90% of all costs necessary to rebuild public roads or

41 Small and Medium Enterprise Agency, Iwate sangyou hukkou kikouno setsuritsu ni tsuite [On Establishment of Iwate Industrial Rehabilitation Organization] (METI 11 November 2011) www.chusho.meti.go.jp/kinyu/2011/111111Iwatefukkou.htm accessed 30 December 2017.

42 Kabushikikaisha higashinihon daishinsai jigyousha saisei shien kikōhō [Act on the Great East Japan Earthquake Disaster Affected Business Operators Reconstruction Support Organization, Inc.], Law no 113 of 2011.

43 Gekijin saigai ni taishosuru tame no tokubetsu no zaisei enjotō ni kansuru hōritsu [Act concerning Special Financial Assistance in order to Cope with Extremely Serious Disaster], Law no 150 of 1962 (Extremely Serious Disaster Act).

44 Higashinihon daishinsai ni tsuiteno gekijin saigai oyobi koreni tekiyousubeki sochi no shitei ni kansuru seirei [Cabinet Order concerning Designation of the Great East Japan Earthquake Disaster as an Extreme Serious Disaster and Specification of Measures to Be Applied], Cabinet Order no 18 of 2011.

public facilities. In the case of recovery costs following the Tohoku Earthquake, the central government decided to subsidize almost everything to rebuild public facilities.[45] For this reason, the central government put itself in the position of taking responsibility for reconstructing all infrastructure as well as public facilities. However, in light of the magnitude of devastation, the central government had a responsibility to accomplish more than merely rebuilding infrastructure and public facilities.

The central government has taken responsibility for assisting disaster-affected people in rebuilding their lives. This process requires that the central government assist municipal and prefectural governments in rebuilding communities. This is quite a difficult task because these areas have proven to be vulnerable to tsunami and all safeguards adopted to defend against tsunami failed in the wake of the Tohoku Earthquake. The central government cannot simply rebuild the same communities according to the previous template. It must rebuild the communities with fortified safeguards to defend against another powerful tsunami in the future. However, the Tohoku Earthquake revealed that there is a limit to the defensive capacity of tsunami barriers and that future planning must incorporate damage reduction strategies when the next powerful tsunami hits this region in the future.

Indeed, some of the areas sunk below sea level following the Tohoku Earthquake.[46] Since it is well known that these areas are especially vulnerable to tsunami, there was serious concern about whether rebuilding homes and communities in these areas was a worthwhile endeavor. Some argued that residents would be better off moving to higher ground. Therefore, many local governments decided to encourage or facilitate the relocation of residents or prohibit reconstruction of new buildings in dangerous areas. Otherwise, the local government needed to enforce a redevelopment plan to raise the elevation of the ground and rebuild the community on the newly redeveloped land with more effective tsunami barriers.

Reconstruction of Tohoku is further complicated by a number of factors predating the disasters. Many of the municipalities affected are small fishing towns. With the gradual decline of the fishing industry, many fishermen had left

45 For a list of recovery and reconstruction works to be subsidized by the central government and the proportion of the burden of the local government, see Reconstruction Agency, Heisei 28nendo iko no hukkou jigyou nikakaru jichitaihutan no taishoujigyou oyobi suijun nitsuite [On the Reconstruction Works Which Require the Local Government's Responsibility and Its Proportion of the Expense after 2016] (Reconstruction Agency 3 June 2015) www.reconstruction.go.jp/topics/main-cat8/sub-cat8-3/20150603_1_zititaifutan.pdf accessed 30 December 2017. The government covered 95% of all local government's burden by "disaster reconstruction special tax redistribution grant" (*shinsai hukkou tokubetsu kouhuzei kouhukin*) in addition to central government's grant. Ibid.

46 As a result of the earthquake, the area in the Sendai Plain below sea level increased to 16km^2, 5.3 times larger than before the earthquake. Ministry of Land, Infrastructure, Transport and Tourism, Kokudokoutsu hakusho 2011 [Land, Infrastructure and Transport Whitepaper 2011] (MLIT) www.mlit.go.jp/hakusyo/mlit/h22/hakusho/h23/html/k1112000.html accessed 30 December 2017.

these towns and young workers had chosen to leave the towns owing to better job prospects in other urban centers. As a result, it was mostly seniors that were living in the towns that were concomitantly affected by rapid population decline.[47] In this sense, many communities affected by the tsunami were already struggling for survival. Merely rebuilding the facilities and communities with no hope for future growth would thus be a meaningless gesture. The central government had to find ways to promote development and growth in soon to be reconstructed communities.

4.2.2 Preparing for the reconstruction

Most municipal governments issued temporary bans on rebuilding new homes in affected areas under the Construction Standards Act[48] while continuing discussions on rebuilding plans. The Diet also passed a statute authorizing the extension of the ban until 11 September 2011.[49] Local governments had the option of further extending this temporary ban for another 2 months.[50] Violators could face fines of up to 1 million JPY (9,000 USD).[51] The temporary ban expired on 10 November 2011 and local governments were forced to institute permanent measures or give up on enforcing the restriction.

Some municipal governments decided to designate certain affected areas as "disaster hazard zones"(*saigai kiken kuiki*) under the Construction Standards Act. This prohibited any new buildings and prompted relocation.[52] This designation existed even before the Tohoku Earthquake but was not often used; however, this was the best choice for affected local governments. A "disaster hazard zone" must be designated by local ordinance and basically bans all construction within the area. The municipal government is supposed to purchase land included in this area. The municipal government will thus urge that all those who formerly lived in such areas accept group relocation.[53]

47 In this sense, a significantly larger portion of the disaster victims were seniors. Cabinet Office, Heisei25nenban kourei shakai hakusho [2013 Senior Whitepaper] (Cabinet Office) www8.cao.go.jp/kourei/whitepaper/w-2013/zenbun/s1_2_6_07.html accessed 30 December 2017 (among 15,681 identified victims in Iwate, Miyagi and Fukushima prefectures 10,360 were seniors over the age of 60, 66.1% of all victims).

48 Kenchiku kijunhō [Construction Standards Act], Law no 201 of 1950, art 84 (1) & (2).

49 Higashinihon daishinsai ni yori jindaina higai wo uketa shigaichi ni okeru kenchiku seigen no tokurei ni kansuru hōritsu [Act concerning Special Treatment of Construction Limitations in Urban Cities Seriously Affected by the Great East Japan Earthquake Disaster], Law no 34 of 2011, art 1(1) & (2).

50 Ibid art 1(3).

51 Ibid art 2(1).

52 Construction Standards Act (n 48) art 39.

53 For instance, a dozen cities and towns in the Miyagi Prefecture decided to designate certain areas along the coastline as "disaster hazard zones" to recommend families formerly residing in these areas for group relocation. Miyagi Prefecture, Saigai kiken kuiki [Disaster Hazard Zone] (Miyagi Prefecture) www.pref.miyagi.jp/soshiki/kentaku/saigaikikenkuiki.html accessed 30 December 2017.

Other areas could be designated as "urban disaster recovery promotion areas" (*hisai shigaichi hukko suishin chiiki*) under the Special Measures Act to Promote Reconstruction of Urban Cities Affected by Disaster, which would allow the construction of new buildings by landowners to serve as their own homes or be used for business purposes but would restrict construction for other purposes.[54] This Special Measures Act was enacted to allow flexible redevelopment for disaster victims. When a substantial number of buildings are destroyed by large-scale fire or earthquake, the affected urban area can be designated as an "urban disaster recovery promotion area."[55] Subsequently, municipalities are obliged to adopt such urban planning and to employ development strategies and other measures to accomplish recovery.[56] The Act provides for special procedures with respect to redevelopment in affected areas.[57] Municipalities wishing to rebuild communities in places where they were formerly located prior to the disaster might use this procedure.[58] In order to avoid further tsunami damage, local government must raise the elevation of communities by landfill and establish stronger and higher dykes and tsunami barriers. Local governments situated close to fishing ports, with many residents preferring to remain close to the port, adopted this option.

In order to implement the redevelopment plan, local governments must obtain agreement among affected communities. Owing to conflicting interests among concerned parties, agreement is sometimes quite difficult. Redevelopment plans following the Tohoku Earthquake also faced another difficulty; it was simply impossible to find some property owners. Although all land ownership is registered with government, heirs to land must change registration when they succeed to land ownership. However, after the Tohoku Earthquake, with so many people classified as missing, many heirs could not even begin succession proceedings. In some cases, entire families were killed or missing and nobody remained that could make a claim or commence succession procedures after the death of property owners. As a result, some properties were left without legal owners. Even when all the heirs were found, disagreement among heirs might prevent prompt succession. Any relocation program or redevelopment project would not be completed until the succession procedure was completed. Some thus argued for the enactment of special statutes allowing for the management of

54 Hisai shigaichi hukkou tokubetsu sochihō [Special Measures Act to Promote Reconstruction of Urban Areas Affected by the Disaster], Law no 14 of 1995.

55 Ibid art 5.

56 Ibid art 6.

57 Ibid art 10–art 20. Redevelopment areas are subject to construction restriction. Ibid art 29, 33, 58–2. For construction restrictions in areas vulnerable to tsunami, see n 64.

58 "Miyagi, hisaichi no kensetsu seigen shuuryou: 2wari no chiiki ga taishougai [Construction Ban Ends in Affected Areas in Miyagi: 20% of Affected Areas Remain Restricted]" (*Asahi Shimbun* 11 November 2011) www.asahi.com/special/10005/TKY201111090664.html accessed 30 December 2017; Kamaishi City, Hisaichiiki niokeru kakushu kenchiku kisei nitsuite [On Construction Restrictions in Disaster Areas] (5 April 2012 Kamaishi City) www.city.kamaishi.iwate.jp/fukko_joho/fukko_machidukuri/fukko_seibikeikaku/detail/__icsFiles/afieldfile/2015/03/24/20120725-092427.pdf accessed 30 December 2017.

such land by municipal governments.[59] However, in the absence of such special statutes, local governments had to verify all registrations individually in order to ascertain rightful ownership. If the legal owner died or was classified as missing, the local government had to wait for succession procedures to be completed.

Moreover, urban redevelopment is a long process that usually requires more than five years, sometimes over 20 years (reconstruction in the Tohoku areas would require a much longer period since it needs elevation of the ground). Consensus among landowners is essential and redevelopment requires each landowner to exchange their previous land for newly developed land. In most cases, owners must accept smaller plots of land on the premise that the newly developed land has a higher economic value than their former property. Since many owners do not want to surrender their previous properties, the consensus requirement proves to be considerably onerous. In order to implement urban redevelopment and to build new homes in the same places with additional landfill to raise property elevation, this arduous goal must be accomplished relatively quickly and within a few years. Since some residents have serious and valid concerns about their future safety, this redevelopment procedure may prove controversial.

4.2.3 Revamping tsunami preparation policy

Following this disaster, it became clear that the government needed a new tsunami preparation policy integrated into community rebuilding to enable these communities to avoid similar disasters in the future.

The Diet passed the Act concerning the Building of Community to Prevent Tsunami Disaster (Tsunami Disaster Prevention Act)[60] in December 2011. The Act mandated that the Land, Infrastructure, Transport and Tourism Minister publish a fundamental plan for prevention of tsunami disasters.[61] This Act further mandated that local governors publish a list of areas likely to be submerged under seawater in the event of a powerful tsunami.[62] It also directed governors and heads of municipal governments to construct and manage barriers.[63]

59 The Ministry of Land, Infrastructure, Transport and Tourism came up with various suggestions for coping with this issue. In addition to facilitating succession procedures by viewing missing owners as dead, the ministry suggested a system of having the family court appoint a property manager when none was designated by the owner and treating the inheritance estate as a separate legal person and having the family court appoint a manager of that inheritance property when no one claimed inheritance. Also, using the power of eminent domain to acquire the property was mentioned as one possible measure. Ministry of Land, Infrastructure, Transport and Tourism, Genko seido niokeru shoyuusha humei tochi eno taiou nitsuite [On Possible Responses to Property Whose Owners Are Uncertain] (MLIT) www.mlit.go.jp/common/001201303.pdf accessed 30 December 2017.

60 Tsunami bousai chiiki dukuri ni kansuru hōritsu [Act concerning Building Communities to Prevent Tsunami Disaster], Law no 123 of 2011 (Tsunami Disaster Prevention Act).

61 Ibid art 3.

62 Ibid art 6–art 8.

63 Ibid art 18.

The Act then authorized governors to designate certain areas as "tsunami disaster hazard zones" (*tsunami saigai keikai kuiki*) (yellow zones), which require special emergency evacuation plans, and categorize certain areas within these zones as "special tsunami disaster hazard zones" (*tsunami saigai tokubetsu keikai kuiki*), which require construction/development restrictions in order to protect the life and safety of residents (orange zones and red zones).[64] We must wait and see whether this power will actually be used to restrict construction in areas especially vulnerable to tsunami disaster.

Affected local governments have used this new framework together with the traditional "disaster hazard zone" recognized under the Construction Standards Act. However, since both designations pertain to legal restrictions on the construction of homes, they both face formidable obstacles where implementation is concerned.[65]

4.2.4 Group relocation program

The central government already has a group relocation (*bosai shudan iten*) program in place to facilitate the relocation of communities as a whole when they are hit by disaster and have been designated as disaster hazard zones under the Group Relocation Facilitation Act.[66] In order to make use of this program, a municipal government must come up with a relocation plan and apply to the Land, Infrastructure, Transport and Tourism Minister for its approval.[67] Only residents of areas affected by disaster or areas designated as "disaster hazard zone" under the Construction Standards Act can apply to this program.[68] Furthermore, the area must be designated as a "group relocation promotion zone" (*iten sokushin kuiki*).[69] Approval is granted only when facilitation of group relocation is found necessary to protect the life, person, and property of residents against disaster.[70] At least ten families must relocate together and, if there are more than 20 families wishing to move, at least half of the families must decide to relocate together. Basically, the local governments purchase the land from

64 Ibid art 53 & art 72. The Diet also passed the Tsunami taisakuno suishin ni kansuru hōritsu [Act concerning Promotion of Tsunami Countermeasures], Law no 77 of 2011 to promote detection of tsunami, prediction of damage, and implementation of countermeasures.

65 It was reported that only four prefectures have designated a "tsunami disaster hazard zone." Ministry of Land, Infrastructure, Transport and Tourism, Tsunami shinsui soutei no settei nitsuite [On Designation of Tsunami Flooding Areas] (27 June 2017 MLIT) www.mlit.go.jp/river/shinngikai_blog/shaseishin/kasenbunkakai/bunkakai/dai54kai/siryou2-1.pdf accessed 30 December 2017.

66 Bousai no tameno shudan-iten sokushin jigyou ni kakawaru kuni no zaiseijō no tokubetsu sochitō ni kansuru hōritsu [Act concerning Financial Measures of the Government to Facilitate the Group Relocation Program in order to Prevent Disasters], Law no 132 of 1972 (Group Relocation Facilitation Act).

67 Ibid art 3.

68 Ibid art 1.

69 Ibid art 2.

70 Ibid.

the applicants, decide on a site for relocation, build new homes and provide them to the applicants. If applicants need to take out new loans to relocate, local governments pay the interest on those new loans. Three-fourths of all costs for relocation will be covered by the central government. However, in general, the municipal government must assume one-fourth of relocation costs.[71]

After the Tohoku Earthquake, the central government decided to use the reconstruction grant and disaster reconstruction special tax distribution grant to cover all expenses for group relocation and therefore residents and local governments were relieved of responsibility for these expenses.[72] Moreover, requirements were relaxed to allow five families to relocate together and to exempt the requirement that at least half of the families in the community must relocate.[73] For disaster victims whose houses were completely or half destroyed, the disaster victim life rebuilding support benefit was available and additional loans were also available from the Japan Housing Authority at a special low-interest rate.[74] Moreover, when disaster victims sold their property for relocation, special tax breaks were granted.[75] However, in order to use this program, local residents must approve of the relocation decision.[76] Needless to say, it takes time for local residents to reach agreement on group relocation.

4.3 Reconstruction plan and reconstruction organization

Third, the central government needed to establish the fundamental policies for reconstruction and appoint some organizations to lead the reconstruction works. But how to frame these fundamental policies and how to appoint a government organization to lead the reconstruction works turned out to be quite controversial. As a result, it took some time to come up with the fundamental policies and the government organization to start the reconstruction works. Why were these such controversial issues? What were the main challenges?

4.3.1 Disputes over the agency tasked with reconstruction

In order to carry out reconstruction, the fundamental reconstruction policies or plan had to be established and some kinds of reconstruction organizations needed to be created.

71 Ibid art 7.

72 Ministry of Land, Infrastructure, Transport and Tourism, Higashinihon daishinsai no hisaichi de okonawareru bousai shudan iten sokushin jigyou [Disaster Prevention Group Relocation Program for Areas Adversely Affected by the Great East Japan Earthquake Disaster] (MLIT) www.mlit.go.jp/crd/chisei/boushuu/pamphlet23.pdf accessed 30 December 2017.

73 Ibid.

74 Ibid.

75 Ibid.

76 Group Relocation Facilitation Act (n 66) art 4 (necessity of respecting the opinions of residents and ensuring every family in the group relocation area relocated together). Reconstruction Agency anticipates that some 19,000 new houses need to be built by using this group relocation program. Reconstruction Agency (n 24) 2.

With respect to fundamental reconstruction policies and plan, Prime Minister Kan decided to establish national policies and plans instead of delegating them to local governments. But instead of declaring them by himself, he decided to entrust the experts to formulate them for him. This was a quite different attitude from that which was adopted after the Hanshin Awaji Earthquake, because in the aftermath of the Hanshin Awaji Earthquake on 17 January 1995, the central government created the government organization just one month after the earthquake, and adopted the policy of respecting the reconstruction plans of the local governments impacted by the earthquake. Hyogo Prefecture, which suffered the most serious damage, thus announced its reconstruction plan a half year later.[77]

In light of the wide-ranging damage and national impact, the decision to formulate and declare a national policy and plan could be understandable. But Kan's decision to delegate the authority to formulate the fundamental policy and plan to experts ended up taking significant time, bringing substantial delay to the start of the reconstruction.

With respect to government organizations leading the reconstruction, there was much debate after the Hanshin Awaji Earthquake as to what type of organization would be best suited for achieving rebuilding goals. It was argued that a special rebuilding agency should be established as was done after the Kanto Earthquake. When the Kanto Earthquake destroyed Tokyo, the central government immediately declared a plan for rebuilding Tokyo and established the Tokyo Rebuilding Organization (*Teito fukko-in*), headed by the prime minister. After the Hanshin Awaji Earthquake, however, the central government decided to establish the Hanshin Awaji Earthquake Disaster Reconstruction Headquarters,[78] headed by the prime minister and consisting of state ministers. The central government thus refused to establish a separate and independent agency.

After the Tohoku Earthquake, there was similar debate. The Democratic Party of Japan (DPJ) government was reluctant to establish an independent agency for reconstruction and preferred to follow the model of the Hanshin Awaji Earthquake while the opposition Liberal Democratic Party (LDP) preferred the establishment of an independent agency following the model of the Kanto Earthquake. As a result, the bill submitted by the DPJ government did not pass smoothly. The DPJ government ultimately decided to concede to the opposition in order to get reconstruction under way as smoothly and quickly as possible. According to the Great East Japan Earthquake Disaster Reconstruction Basic Act (*Higashinihon daishinsai hukkou kihonhō*),[79] therefore, the central government ultimately decided to follow the model of the Kanto Earthquake.

77 Hyogo Prefecture, Hanshin Awaji shinsai hukkou keikaku [Hanshin Awaji Earthquake Disaster Reconstruction Plan] (July 1995) (Hyogo Prefecture) http://web.pref.hyogo.lg.jp/wd33/wd33_000000043.html accessed 30 December 2017.

78 Hanshin Awaji daishinsai fukkou no kihon houshin oyobi soshiki ni kansuru hōritsu [Act concerning Basic Policy and Organization for Reconstruction after the Hanshin Awaji Earthquake Disaster], Law no 12 of 1995 (expired on 24 February 2000).

79 Higashinihon daishinsai hukkou kihonhō [Great East Japan Earthquake Disaster Reconstruction Basic Act], Law no 76 of 2011.

4.3.2 Reconstruction plan

This Act declared fundamental ideals for the reconstruction of affected communities[80] and established the Great East Japan Earthquake Disaster Reconstruction Headquarters (*Higashinihon daishinsai hukkou taisaku honbu*)[81] headed by the prime minister[82] and also established the Great East Japan Earthquake Disaster Reconstruction Design Council (*Hiagashinihon daishinsai hukkou kousou kaigi*) (RDC), an advisory group, to come up with specific reconstruction plans.[83] This statute gave rise to the establishment of the Reconstruction Agency (*hukkou cho*), charged with developing, coordinating, and executing the rebuilding plan from within the Cabinet Office.[84]

The RDC submitted its report to Kan on 25 June 2011[85] and the government adopted a basic reconstruction plan, the Great East Japan Earthquake Disaster Reconstruction Basic Policy (*Higashinihon daishin karano hukko no kihon houshin*), on 29 July.[86]

4.3.3 Reconstruction agency and reconstruction

To fulfill the mandate in the Great East Japan Earthquake Disaster Reconstruction Basic Act, the Act to Establish the Reconstruction Agency was passed on 16 December 2011.[87] The Reconstruction Agency started its work on 10 February 2012.[88] The Act to Establish the Reconstruction Agency increased the number of Cabinet ministers by one, assigned that position to the Reconstruction Minister,[89] and established the Reconstruction Agency headed by the Prime Minister[90] beneath the Cabinet.[91] The Reconstruction Agency was granted the

80 Ibid art 2.
81 Ibid art 11.
82 Ibid art. 13(1).
83 Ibid art 18.
84 Ibid art 24.
85 Great East Japan Earthquake Disaster Reconstruction Design Council, Hukkou eno teigen—Hisai no nakano kibou—[Towards Reconstruction: "Hope beyond the Disasters"] (Cabinet Office 25 June 2011) www.cas.go.jp/jp/fukkou/pdf/fukkouhenoteigen.pdf accessed 30 December 2017. For a provisional translation, *see* www.cas.go.jp/jp/fukkou/english/pdf/report20110625.pdf accessed 30 December 2017.
86 Great East Japan Earthquake Disaster Response Headquarters, Higashinihon daishinsai karano hukkou no kihon houshin [Great East Japan Earthquake Disaster Reconstruction Basic Policy] (29 July 2011, as amended on 11 August 2011) (Reconstruction Agency) www.reconstruction.go.jp/topics/110811kaitei.pdf accessed 1 January 2018 5. For a provisional translation, see Reconstruction Agency www.reconstruction.go.jp/topics/basic_guidelines_reconstruction.pdf accessed 30 December 2017.
87 Hukkouchou secchihō [Act to Establish the Reconstruction Agency], Law no 125 of 2011 (Reconstruction Agency Act).
88 Reconstruction Agency, www.reconstruction.go.jp/index.html. The Reconstruction Agency is set to be abolished by 31 March 2021.
89 Reconstruction Agency Act (n 87) art 8; Naikakuhō [Cabinet Act], Law no 5 of 1947, art 2(2).
90 Reconstruction Agency Act (n 87) art 6.
91 Ibid art 2.

task of implementing Tohoku reconstruction as smoothly and as quickly as possible, in line with the fundamental reconstruction principles of the Great East Japan Earthquake Disaster Reconstruction Basic Act.[92] The power granted to the Reconstruction Agency includes the power to make plans, coordinate various reconstruction measures and to facilitate and coordinate assistance from the central government to affected local governments.[93] The Reconstruction Agency is specifically assigned the role of managing and supervising all governmental reconstruction measures, accepting all demands of affected local governments, applying for and allocating the reconstruction budget, enforcing the reconstruction special zone program, as examined below, and all other necessary measures related to reconstruction.[94] If necessary, the Reconstruction Minister can demand the production of information and explanation from relevant administrative agencies,[95] advise heads of relevant administrative agencies,[96] and demand reports on measures adopted based on such advice from heads of the relevant administrative agencies.[97] The reconstruction minister is at liberty to ask the prime minister to exercise supervisory powers over the relevant administrative agencies on the advised matters, if necessary.[98]

On the surface of the statute, therefore, the Reconstruction Agency is a very powerful agency. However, the Reconstruction Agency coordinates actions across various government departments. Virtually all final decisions must be made by the government department having regulatory power over specific program(s) in question. The Reconstruction Agency was not granted independent power to administer projects and determine budgets.[99]

Furthermore, most public officers working in the Reconstruction Agency have been seconded from other government departments. The Reconstruction Agency does have the power to appoint its own staff[100] but, apparently, most important decisions must be made by public officials seconded from other government departments. These officials are ostensibly set to return to their original agencies after serving in the Reconstruction Agency. There is doubt over whether such officials, dispatched from other government departments, actually have budget allocation powers with which to facilitate reconstruction.

92 Ibid art 3.
93 Ibid art 4(1).
94 Ibid art 4(2).
95 Ibid art 8(4).
96 Ibid art 8(5).
97 Ibid art 8(6).
98 Ibid art 8(7).
99 "Hukkoucho, yakuwari hatasazu, kengen, yosan toboshiku [Reconstruction Agency Has not Played an Expected Role: Too Few Powers and Too Few Budget]" (*Tokyo Shimbun* 11 March 2014) www.tokyo-np.co.jp/feature/tohokujisin/archive/threeyears/140311-10.html accessed 30 December 2017. *See* Richard J. Samuels, 3.11; *Disaster and Change in Japan* (Cornell 2013) 8–9.
100 Reconstruction Agency Act (n 87) art 19.

4.4 Reconstruction measures

What kinds of measures were adopted to facilitate the reconstruction of the Tohoku Region? In order to allow victims to find permanent places to live, the government erected "reconstruction housing." In order to accomplish reconstruction, in addition to various benefits and assistance, two reconstruction programs are worth mentioning: the reconstruction special zone program and the reconstruction grant. These two programs are primary measures adopted by the Japanese government to facilitate the reconstruction. The government also offered various other reconstruction measures. Moreover, in order to stimulate the economy and build a more vibrant and energetic Tohoku Region, the Japanese government vowed to create a "new Tohoku."

4.4.1 Reconstruction housing

Since many residents lost their homes due to the tsunami, the government needed to allow the victims to rebuild their houses and, as we already saw, the government provided various grants and special reconstruction loans with low interest. The government also promoted the group relocation program and redeveloping project.[101]

For those victims who lost housing and had no financial resources to rebuild their houses, the government is obliged to build to provide "reconstruction housing" (*hukkou jutaku*). This housing is built by the local government or acquired by the local government and is provided to victims of disaster for lower rental charges with the possibility of public assistance for those with lower income.[102] The government decided to loosen the qualifications to enter this reconstruction housing for the victims of the Great East Japan Earthquake Disaster.[103] Moreover, the residents would be able to purchase this housing after some time,[104] and the government also relaxed the qualifications for the victims of the Great East Japan Earthquake Disaster to make such purchases.[105] Indeed, the reconstruction housing is offered to evacuees at a discounted rent with evacuees

101 Ministry of Land, Infrastructure, Transport and Tourism, Higashinihon daishinsai no hisaichi niokeru sigaichi seibijigyo no unyo nitsuite (guidance) [On the Enforcement of Redevelopment in the Great East Japan Earthquake Disaster Affected Areas] (MLIT September 2013) www.mlit.go.jp/common/001014480.pdf accessed 30 December 2017.

102 Kouei jutakuhō [Public Housing Act], Law no 193 of 1951, art 1 & art 8. The official name of this reconstruction housing is "disaster public housing" (*saigai kouei jutaku*).

103 Soumusho, Hukko suishin keikaku niyoru kisei/tetsuduki nikansuru tokurei [Exceptional Treatment with respect to Regulation and Procedure by Reconstruction Facilitation Plan] (Cabinet Office) www.cao.go.jp/sasshin/kisei-seido/meeting/2011/wg1/111213/item7_2.pdf accessed 30 December 2017 (Exceptional Treatment).

104 Public Housing Act (n 102) art 44.

105 Exceptional Treatment (n 103). In contrast to the regular requirement requiring one fourth of the life span, the purchase would be possible after one sixth of the life span of the housing (five years for wooden housing).

having the option to purchase after five years. The government estimates that some 30,000 reconstruction homes are necessary for victims of the Great East Japan Earthquake Disaster.[106]

In order to promote these tasks, the government has adopted several acceleration measures and came to adopt further general countermeasures to overcome some of the hurdles lying in the way of building reconstruction housing.[107]

4.4.2 Path to the reconstruction special zone program

The Diet passed the Reconstruction Special Zone Act[108] to establish "reconstruction special zones" (*hukkou tokku*) in areas affected by the Great East Japan Earthquake Disaster in order to remove some regulatory red tape and also to facilitate reconstruction, give tax exemptions to corporations, and assist business development.

The idea of "special zones" came to be adopted in 2002 as part of the general deregulatory movement under the LDP Koizumi government. Prime minister Jun-ichiro Koizumi, a well-known advocate of deregulation and the privatization of government corporations, especially Japan's Postal Service Corporation, decided to introduce the special zone program to allow local governments to apply for special zone designation in order to exclude certain government regulation in those zones.[109] The underlying rationale for introducing the special zone program was to facilitate national deregulation by giving local governments incentives to promote business development by excluding certain government regulations in special zones. The "structural reform special zone" accepted under this Act is a zone designated voluntarily by local government with the aim of vitalizing said zone by promoting designated business activities within it.[110] The local government must make a specific plan according to the fundamental structural reform policy of the central government and seek certification from the prime minister.[111] The "special zones" are meant to be experimental in nature though their successful implementation will likely lead to deregulation being expanded.

In 2012, the General Special Zone Act[112] was enacted under the DPJ government. Unlike the structural reform special zone program, this Act created two types of special zones: "international strategic general special zones" and "local vitalization special zones."[113] The local government must first apply for designation of either of the two types of special zones and the designation needs to be approved by the prime minister.[114] Then the local government is permitted

106 Reconstruction Agency (n 24) 2.
107 Reconstruction Agency (n 1) 11.
108 Higashinihon daishinsai hukkou tokubetsu kuikihō [Great East Japan Earthquake Disaster Reconstruction Special Zone Act], Law no 122 of 2011 (Reconstruction Special Zone Act).
109 Kozou kaikaku tokubetu kuikihō [Structural Reform Special Zone Act], Law no 189 of 2002.
110 Ibid art 2(1).
111 Ibid art 4(1).
112 Sougo tokubetsu kuikihō [General Special Zone Act], Law no 81 of 2011.
113 Ibid art 2(1).
114 Ibid art 8, 31.

to promote specific business activities designated in those zones according to the plans approved.[115] In addition to excluding certain government regulation in those special zones, tax breaks and other sorts of financial support from the central government were introduced.[116] Special zones were not meant to provide an experimental opportunity for deregulation nor were they an attempt to introduce deregulation at the national level.

4.4.3 Reconstruction special zones

After the Tohoku Earthquake, the DPJ government initially did not have any intention of using the special zones to facilitate reconstruction. Reconstruction special zones were thus not originally included in the Great East Japan Earthquake Disaster Reconstruction Basic Act as first tabled. However, during the course of its enactment, the DPJ, the opposition LDP, and the Komei Party agreed to introduce the special zone program. As a result, article 10 of the Great East Japan Earthquake Disaster Reconstruction Basic Act, as enacted, provided for the introduction of the special zone program for reconstruction.[117] The Reconstruction Special Zone Act was enacted based upon this inclusion.[118]

Unlike previous special zones, reconstruction special zones are designated by the Reconstruction Special Zone Act itself to include municipalities where the Disaster Assistance Act was applied as a result of the Great East Japan Earthquake Disaster or is deemed to apply to "specified disaster zones" (*tokutei hisai kuiki*) as specified by cabinet order.[119] A total of 227 municipalities in the 11 affected prefectures are thus already designated ("designated local governments"). Designated local governments can adopt one of three reconstruction programs within reconstruction special zones.[120] In the first case, a designated local government can apply to the prime minister for certification of a "reconstruction promotion plan" (*hukkou suishin keikaku*).[121] Alternatively, affected local governments can consult with relevant organizations through a local reconstruction development consultation body, a consultation body headed by the governor or municipal government heads that also consists of relevant administrative agencies, interested parties, and designated experts, and then publish a "reconstruction development plan" (*hukkou seibi keikaku*) with the consent of relevant organizations, including the central government.[122] Finally, affected local

115 Ibid art 12, 35.

116 Ibid art 26, 28, 55, 56.

117 Great East Japan Earthquake Disaster Reconstruction Basic Act (n 79) art 10.

118 Reconstruction Special Zone Act (n 108). For a detailed analysis of this reconstruction special zone program, *see* Hiroshi Saito, "Hukkou tokku no shikumi to un-you/kaisei no kadai [The Reconstruction Special Zones System, Its Actual Administration and the Agenda for Its Future Amendment] (1)–(3)" (2012) 341 *Ritusumeikan Hougaku* 20, 342 *Ritsumeikan Hougaku* 840, 343 *Ritsumeikan Hougaku* 1471.

119 Reconstruction Special Zone Act (n 108) art 4(1).

120 Ibid art 2(2).

121 Ibid art 4.

122 Ibid art 46.

governments can submit a "reconstruction grant" business plan (*hukkou kouhukin jigyou keikaku*) to the prime minister with the aim of using the grant to promote business activities.[123] Noteworthy is the fact that, in all cases, the central government has the power to certify, consent to, and ultimately make decisions on reconstruction plans.

If the reconstruction promotion plan is certified, various regulations are excluded to promote the provision of public housing for disaster victims, business activities, and community redevelopment.[124] Various tax breaks, such as those given to corporations, and other financial benefits, such as reconstruction zone support interest benefits, then become available.[125] Where a reconstruction development plan receives central government consent and is then published, the Ministry of Land, Infrastructure, Transport and Tourism and the Ministry of Agriculture, Forestry and Fisheries extend special regulatory treatment for development such as urban redevelopment, farmland development, group relocation, installation of tsunami barriers, repairs to port facilities and housing, along with repairs to fish-product manufacturing facilities.[126] For instance, government permission or approval for each stage of a given development is no longer required once a plan is published with the consent of relevant government agencies.

4.4.4 Reconstruction grant

As pointed out above, the "reconstruction grant" (*hukkou kouhukin*) plays a major role in providing financial stimulus for the reconstruction. Local governments impacted by the Tohoku Earthquake and tsunami can formulate a plan, standing alone or together with other similarly affected local governments concerned with ensuring the smooth and prompt reconstruction of areas experiencing serious harm such as loss or damage to a substantial number of housing, public facilities, and other structures.[127] Application files could be submitted to one of the branches of the Reconstruction Agency but the decision rests with each department of the central government, Ministry of Education, Culture, Sports, Science and Technology (MEXT), Ministry of Health, Labor and Welfare, Ministry of Land, Infrastructure, Transport and Tourism, or Ministry of Environment.[128]

This grant is available to the local government to carry out group relocation programs, redevelopment programs, creation of reconstruction housing, repairs to public roads, or repairs to port facilities. It is also available to carry out

123 Ibid art 77.

124 Ibid art 14 to art 36. For instance, the qualifications to enter into reconstruction housing could be loosened up and the qualifications to purchase reconstruction housings by resident victims could also be loosened up. Ibid art 20 & art 21.

125 Ibid art 37 to art 42, art 44.

126 Ibid art 48 to art 56.

127 Ibid art 77, 78.

128 Reconstruction Agency, Hukkou kouhukin kikan jigyo [Major Projects Eligible for Reconstruction Grant] (Reconstruction Agency) www.reconstruction.go.jp/topics/120405gaiyou.pdf accessed 30 December 2017.

programs proposed by the local government to reconstruct communities such as promotion of fishing products produced in these communities or facilitating the tourist industry.[129]

4.4.5 Other reconstruction measures

The government continued to rebuild the sewage system, river banks, seawalls, ports, public roads, airport as well as public schools, public facilities, hospitals, and other infrastructure.[130] Accordingly, public officials were sent in order to support affected municipal governments.[131] In addition, the government prompted the creation of a database of retired public officials who could be hired by the affected municipalities, encouraged the affected municipalities to accept the workers of private companies while retaining their employment status, allowed affected municipalities to contract out to non-public officials as helpers, allowed the Reconstruction Agency to hire part-time employees to send to the affected municipalities, and attempted to reduce the workload of the affected municipalities by contracting out.[132] In order to supplant the recovery and reconstruction works by the municipal and local governments, the government promoted the participation of volunteers by providing information on available funding, promoting cooperation, and supporting new volunteers.[133]

In addition to various financial assistance to disaster victims mentioned above such as disaster condolence benefit or disaster life rebuilding assistance benefit, the government decided to spend an additional 22 billion JPY (20 million USD) in 2016 and another 20 billion JPY (18 million USD) in 2017 as a "general disaster victim support grant" (*hisaisha shien sougo kouhukin*) to support the disaster victims in light of the long continuance of evacuation or new life in the reconstruction housing.[134] This grant is used to support housing reconstruction or life rebuilding of the victims, assistance to evacuees, assistance in creating new communities, and providing support for seniors or children. Moreover, the government decided to provide "reconstruction benefits" (*hukko kyuhukin*) to residents who owned a destroyed house, purchased a new house, and resided in that house for a cost corresponding to the increase of the sales tax. Benefits were also deemed applicable to residents who owned a damaged house, ordered a repair on that house and resided in that repaired house, for a cost corresponding to the increase of the sales tax.[135]

129 Reconstruction Agency, Hukkou kouhukin [Reconstruction Grant] (Reconstruction Agency) www.reconstruction.go.jp/topics/main-cat1/sub-cat1-14/170703_kouhukin.pdf accessed 30 December 2017.

130 Reconstruction Agency (n 1) 9.

131 Ibid 29.

132 Ibid.

133 Ibid 30.

134 Ibid 7; Reconstruction Agency, Hisaishashien sougou kouhukin [General Disaster Victim Support Grant] (Reconstruction Agency 1 March 2017) www.reconstruction.go.jp/topics/main-cat2/20170301_kokoroboshuu.pdf accessed 30 December 2017.

135 Reconstruction Agency (n 1) 13.

In addition, aside from the assistance to business operators by the Industrial Rehabilitation Organizations and by the Great East Japan Earthquake Disaster Affected Business Operators Reconstruction Support Organization to buy out the debt,[136] the government also provided the Great East Japan Earthquake Disaster reconstruction special loan, which was designed to assist small and medium size business operators and provide emergency assurance for small and medium size companies.[137] Further, the government provided loans to farmers, foresters, and fishermen and offered them assurance.[138] Finally, each prefecture with the help of the central government provided a subsidy to a group of companies essential to reconstruction, and that contribute to the significant increase of employment or are a vital part of the national supply chain.[139]

The government has also tried to create jobs and offer employment opportunities to disaster victims.[140] It has also provided job training and intensified the placement service.

4.4.6 New Tohoku vision

As stated above, the reconstruction could not merely be a restoration of Tohoku as it existed before the earthquake. Many of the local governments in the Tohoku Region suffering in the aftermath of the Tohoku Earthquake and tsunami were areas already struggling to survive. In order to reconstruct the Tohoku Region, the central government thus proposed the construction of "new Tohoku" (*atarashii Tohoku*) as a "land of creation and possibility."[141]

This vision consists of five ideas; first, to build a safe society that safeguards the energetic and healthy development of children; second, to secure an energetic society filled with elderly people with an adoption of standards suited to them; third, to build a society with sustainable energy (autonomous and decentralized energy society); fourth, to build an advanced society with the introduction of a stern and highly resilient social foundation system; and fifth, to build a society efficiently using the local resources with high transmission capability.[142] In particular, the central government started the programs to accelerate some of the innovative projects started by business companies, universities, or NPOs; initiated a matching program to find suitable workers outside of the Tohoku Region and send them to work in the Tohoku Region; began a "Revive Japan Cup" contest to find a profitable business idea to attract broad investment; and set up a consortium for business companies, universities, and NPOs to broaden their personal networks.[143]

136 Ibid 24.
137 Ibid 23.
138 Ibid.
139 Ibid 17.
140 Ibid 32.
141 Reconstruction Agency, Atarashii Tohoku no souzou ni mukete [Toward Creation of New Tohoku] (Reconstruction Agency) www.reconstruction.go.jp/topics/main-cat7/sub-cat7-2/20140425_02_teigen_gaiyou.pdf accessed 30 December 2017.
142 Ibid.
143 Reconstruction Agency (n 1) 32–37.

4.5 Reconstruction in progress

To what extent has the reconstruction been carried out? Has the situation for the victims of disaster significantly improved? The reconstruction of the Tohoku Region is no easy task and the progress of the reconstruction is hardly satisfactory.

4.5.1 No compensation for damage

Since all the damage was triggered by the earthquake and tsunami, the victims were unable to recover from the damages in general. The victims and their families could only receive government benefits and insurance payment if they were subscribed to earthquake insurance or life insurance.

Some of the victims filed suits seeking damages. For instance, a surviving family of a deceased wife killed by the tsunami sought a damage award against the Japan Meteorological Agency (JMA) and the city of Rikuzentakata, insisting on their negligence. The Morioka District Court, however, dismissed the claim because it found that there was a limitation on the tsunami forecast technology and the JMA was not at fault. It also found that it was not unreasonable for the city of Rikuzentakata to allocate the backup power according to priority, even though this prevented residents from receiving upgrade tsunami information by public announcement system.[144]

In some cases, victims sought damages against the managers or supervisors for their failures to ensure swift and effective evacuation. The court did find the Hiyori Kindergarten liable for damages because of the failure to take care, a breach of contract duty, and a tort, and ordered the school to pay the total amount of 177,0000 JPY (16,000 USD).[145] Apparently, the court did not believe that it was impossible to anticipate the powerful tsunami.[146] Similarly, in a case involving the Okawa Elementary School tragedy, the Sendai District Court found that the school officials could have anticipated the massive tsunami coming and could have avoided the tragedy, holding them negligent, and ordered the Miyagi Prefecture and Ishinomaki City to pay the total amount of 1.4 billion JPY (12.7 million USD) to the surviving families.[147]

Similarly, in a case involving a driving school which failed to save the lives of its employees and students, the Sendai District Court found that the driving school had a responsibility to ensure the safety of its employees and students and held that the driving school was liable for damages when it sent the students back home by courtesy car resulting in the death of 25 students and failing to evacuate its employees from the school, causing the death of one employee.[148] The court

144 Morioka chihō saibansho [Morioka Dist Ct], 20 February 2015, 2268 *Hanrei Jihō* 91. The Sendai High Court upheld the judgment, Sendai kōtō saibansho [Sendai High Ct] 15 April 2016, TKC Database, and the Supreme Court dismissed the appeal. Saikō saibansho [Sup Ct] 26 April 2017, 2nd petty bench, TKC Database.

145 Sendai chihō saibansho [Sendai Dist Ct], 17 September 2013, 2204 *Hanrei Jihō* 57.

146 Both parties settled on appeal.

147 Sendai chihō saibansho [Sendai Dist Ct], 26 October 2016 (saibansho) www.courts.go.jp/app/files/hanrei_jp/266/086266_hanrei.pdf accessed 20 January 2018. Both parties appealed to the Sendai High Court.

148 Sendai chihō saibansho [Sendai Dist Ct], 13 January 2015, 2265 *Hanrei Jihō* 69.

found that there had been a call for evacuation and it was possible to predict that the tsunami was coming. It ordered the driving school to pay 1.9 billion JPY [17 million USD].[149]

However, in the case against the 77th Bank, which evacuated its employees onto the roof of the bank, which led to their death, the court believed that the bank building satisfied the standards for evacuation place and the bank could not have anticipated such an unprecedented powerful tsunami, denying the liability of the bank.[150] The Sendai High Court sustained this judgment[151] and the Supreme Court of Japan dismissed the appeal.[152] Similarly, in a case involving Municipal Higashi Nursery School, managed by the Yamamoto town of Miyagi Prefecture, three children were left in its school grounds for parents to pick up, which led to the children being swept away by the tsunami; the Sendai District Court found that the school was located 1.5 km deep inland and it would have been hard to anticipate that the tsunami would reach to it.[153] The Sendai High Court upheld this judgment[154] and the Supreme Court of Japan dismissed an appeal.[155]

Therefore, the likelihood of getting a damage award or compensation for the loss might be rather limited. Most of the victims were not able to receive any damage award or compensation.

4.5.2 Financial plight of disaster victims still dire

The financial situation of most disaster victims remains very dismal. Many residents whose homes were damaged or destroyed are permitted to rebuild them unless prohibited by group relocation or redevelopment plans. However, doing so requires sufficient financial resources.

Despite the introduction of the private renegotiation program, very few people have actually accessed it.[156] Perhaps the requirements for this program are too demanding. Or perhaps few people actually know that it exists. The number of people that have actually made use of this program is thus far below

149 Both parties settled upon appeal.
150 Sendai chihō saibansho [Sendai Dist Ct], 25 February 2014, 2217 *Hanrei Jihō* 74.
151 Sendai kōtō saibansho [Sendai High Ct], 22 April 2015, 2258 *Hanrei Jihō* 68.
152 Saikō saibansho [Sup Ct], 2nd petty bench, 17 February 2016, TKC Database.
153 Sendai chihō saibansho [Sendai Dist Ct], 24 March 2014, 2223 *Hanrei Jihō* 60.
154 Sendai kōtō saibansho [Sendai High Ct], 20 March 2015, 2256 *Hanrei Jihō* 30.
155 Saikō saibansho [Sup Ct], 2nd petty bench, 17 February 2016, TKC Database.
156 According to the Japan Federation of Bar Associations, the number of agreements reached before 16 August 2011 was only 483 although it was initially estimated that the number of applications would reach over 10,000. Japan Federation of Bar Association, Hisai loan genmen seido un-yo kaishi kara man2nen wo mukaete no kaichou seimei [Statement of the President for the Tow-Years Anniversary of the Disaster Loan Reduction System] (JFBA 22 August 2013) www.nichibenren.or.jp/activity/document/statement/year/2013/130822.html accessed 30 December 2017. As of November 2017, the number of renegotiation reached agreements in only 1359 cases. Reconstruction Agency (n 24) 13.

initial estimates. As a result, many residents have been forced to bear double loans for the sake of rebuilding their homes.[157] Or many residents simply gave up on the idea of rebuilding their houses.

As we saw, local governments built permanent public housing for disaster victims ("reconstruction housing") so that they could move from temporary housing. Construction of reconstruction housing has been very slow. Three affected prefectures have plans to build 30,000 reconstruction housing units for victims of the Tohoku Earthquake but as of August 2017, roughly 27,000 reconstruction housing units out of the anticipated 30,000 have been completed—90% of all planned reconstruction.[158] The government anticipates that all stages of reconstruction housing will be completed sometime after 2018. This means that some residents are still waiting for the completion of the reconstruction housing.

Difficulty in finding suitable sites for reconstruction housing is a primary reason for the shortfall but, at the same time, some who are still living in temporary housing have lost their desire to move out. As a result, the Ministry of Health, Labor and Welfare decided to extend the period for which local government can provide temporary housing by one year when the two-year limitation period was set to expire.[159] All residents staying in temporary housing were initially allowed to stay until the end of 2013. Nevertheless, it was impossible for all Tohoku Earthquake disaster evacuees staying in temporary housing to be able to move into reconstruction housing as scheduled. The government therefore further extended the period of stay in temporary housing for one more year after the one year without any limittion.[160]

However, even when the construction of the housing is completed, the government might face difficulty in filling the homes since many evacuees are not willing to apply for reconstruction housing and move into it. Since most of the reconstruction housing is high rise apartments, many senior evacuees might feel hesitant to enter. Further, even with government subsidies, to rent reconstruction housing the evacuee needs to pay the rent (moreover, there is a possibility that the government subsidy might be cut). Furthermore, many evacuees have spent

157 It is estimated that some 140,000 houses were rebuilt or are in the process of being rebuilt; Ibid 2.

158 Ibid 4. See also Reconstruction Agency, Kokyo infra no honkaku hukkyu/hukkou no shinchoku joukyou [Progress of Reconstruction Works on Public Infrastructure] (Reconstruction Agency 30 November 2017) www.reconstruction.go.jp/topics/main-cat1/sub-cat1-2/20171130_FukkoShihyo.pdf accessed 30 December 2017 4.

159 Ministry of Health, Labor and Welfare, Higashinihon daishinsai ni kakawaru oukyuu kasetsu juutaku no teikyou kikan no enchou ni tsuite [On Extension of the Permissible Period for Temporary Housing for Disaster Victims of the Great East Japan Earthquake Disaster] (MHLW 2 April 2013) www.mhlw.go.jp/stf/houdou/2r9852000002yvh8.html accessed 30 December 2017.

160 Ministry of Health, Labor and Welfare, Higashinihon daishinsai ni kakawaru oukyuu kasetsu juutaku no teikyou kikan no enchou ni tsuite [On Extension of the Permissible Period for Temporary Housing for Disaster Victims of the Great East Japan Earthquake Disaster] (MHLW 2 April 2014) www.mhlw.go.jp/stf/houdou/2r9852000002yvh8-att/2r9852000002yvkv.pdf accessed 30 December 2017.

more than five years in temporary housing and created a community of evacuees. Thus, moving into reconstruction housing means that they need to move into an unfamiliar environment, necessitating them to create new friends once again. This might provide additional uneasiness for senior evacuees. Therefore, the government needs to consider various measures to motivate these evacuees to move into reconstruction housing.[161]

4.5.3 Slow progress of reconstruction

Restoration of almost all lifeline amenities, such as LP gas, electricity, water, and telecommunications, was complete by June 2011, as were most temporary repairs to roads, bridges, river banks, and port facilities aside from those in certain coastline municipalities in Fukushima where entry is still restricted.[162] Moreover, 97 percent of hospitals that were forced to refuse admittance or that restricted admittance of patients following the earthquake are now open and accessible and 98% of public schools that were damaged and applied for renovation are now open with renovations complete.[163] However, even by November 2017, less than half of necessary seashore reconstruction, and less than half of road reconstruction, have been completed.[164] Moreover, although 2,274.7 km of railroad has been repaired and resumed operation out of a total of 2,350.9 km affected, still 76.2 km has not been restored.[165] In other words, the railway network in the Tohoku Region is still not fully repaired.

This means that most major infrastructure and public facilities have already been repaired. What remains is renovation of infrastructure in response to redevelopment and group relocation. However, completion of reconstruction in Tohoku is hardly in sight.

First, the disposal of all the debris was a serious headache for the government and took a long time to overcome. Even two years after the earthquake and tsunami, huge volumes of debris remained undisposed of.[166] Since many disposal facilities were destroyed in the affected communities, there were serious limitations to the amount of waste these communities could dispose of. Furthermore,

161 Editorial, “Higashinihon daishinsai saigaikoueijutaku kuushitsu: Risk kaihi e taisaku ga kyuumu [Vacant Reconstruction Housing Rooms: Urgent Need to Consider Countermeasures]” (*Kahoku News* 12 September 2017) www.kahoku.co.jp/editorial/20170912_01.html accessed 30 December 2017.

162 Reconstruction Agency (n 1) 9.

163 Reconstruction Agency (n 158) 4. The reconstruction to public infrastructures are thus relatively quick. Ranghieri & Ishiwatari (n 14) 171.

164 Reconstruction Agency (n 1) 4.

165 Ibid 14.

166 As of February 2012, only 5% of all disaster waste had been disposed of in the three affected prefectures. Reconstruction Agency, Engan shichouson no saigaihaikibutsu shori no shinchaku joukyo [Progress of Disposal of Disaster Waste in Coastline Cities and Towns] (Reconstruction Agency 20 February 2012) www.reconstruction.go.jp/topics/shinchoku120220.pdf accessed 30 December 2017.

other municipal governments are unwilling to accept such debris for disposal owing to disposal capacity limitations and environmental impact concerns.[167] Even though affected communities have rebuilt disposal facilities, their waste disposal capacity remains limited. The total amount of disaster waste was estimated at more than 18 million tons and tsunami debris was estimated at 9.5 million tons.[168] It thus took a tremendous effort by the central government to facilitate the disposal of all the waste and debris. By March 2017 the central government was finally able to dispose of all the waste and debris, aside from the nuclear contaminated materials inside Minami Souma City.[169] It took almost six years to dispose of the waste and debris brought by the Tohoku Earthquake and subsequent tsunami. The delay in removing and disposing of debris and waste caused a significant delay in the reconstruction.[170]

Second, the group relocation and redevelopment projects are very slow to progress. As of November 2017, 332 areas were approved by the minister for group relocation and construction was already underway in 331 of these areas but only 313 areas had been completed with residents beginning to move in.[171] Why is it so difficult to implement the group relocation program? It is simply too arduous to reach consensus on the relocation plan and get consent from residents for relocation. Moreover, finding a proper place to relocate to is a significant challenge because most affected communities are surrounded by steep mountains and hills and much of the flat land that could be used for relocation was already dedicated to temporary housing. Furthermore, the relocation program requires experienced coordination but there are simply not enough coordinators with experience adequate for such work in the affected communities.

Similarly, in 50 areas where implementation of the land redevelopment program is anticipated, an urban redevelopment plan has already been adopted, with construction already underway in all 50 areas, but still only 18 redevelopment projects have been completed.[172] Local residents are still waiting for their plans to progress and for construction to finish in many places.

Redevelopment projects similarly require experienced coordinators. Moreover, since basically all property owners need to agree, the municipal government

167 The prime minister had to request the cooperation of other prefectural governors for disposal of disaster waste. Prime Minister Noda's Press Interview (kantei 11 March 2012) www.kantei.go.jp/jp/noda/statement/201203/11kaiken.html accessed 30 December 2017. As of November 2012, the disposal rate was improved to 34%, but a considerable volume of undisposed disaster waste still remained. Reconstruction Agency, Higashinihon daishinsai karano hukkou joukyo [Progress of Reconstruction after the Great East Japan Earthquake Disaster] (Reconstruction Agency December 2012) www.reconstruction.go.jp/topics/20130104_higashinippondaishinsai_fukkoh.pdf accessed 30 December 2017.

168 Ibid 2.

169 Reconstruction Agency (n 24) 4; Reconstruction Agency (n 158) 1.

170 Ranghieri & Ishiwatari (n 15) 203. The government should have prepared for the disposal of such disaster waste.

171 Reconstruction Agency (n 158) 3.

172 Ibid.

had to wait for completion of succession and settlement of all ownerships. Furthermore, the attainment of consensus is too burdensome. In addition, the redevelopment requires filling and elevating grounds; sometimes several meters and sometimes more than 10 meters. Naturally, in order to move on, it is vital to wait for the filled grounds to settle.

Third, since most of the affected municipalities consisted of scattered small villages, an increasing number of municipalities wanted to build a "compact city." A compact city basically gathers all the residents to clusters of much smaller communities. Then, the local government can provide service much more efficiently and the residents can enjoy all the amenities and services much more conveniently.[173] If the city could build such a compact city much closer to the mountain-side, then the rebuilt city would be much safer.

However, proposals to rebuild the city as a compact city after the disaster encountered many difficulties, including the difficulty of reaching consensus among local residents: those who would have to leave the previous place of residence would feel discomfort and those who did not suffer any loss because they live on the mountain-side may be left behind.[174] Moreover, since many residents affected by the earthquake and tsunami are senior persons, they may also show hesitation about moving into city centers. Furthermore, in order for a city to gather residents, naturally it will be forced to build many high-rise condominiums. Many senior persons might feel uneasiness at living in such high-rise condominiums. Even if the city can gather residents and provide stores for them, there is no guarantee that these stores can compete with much bigger shopping malls built in the suburbs, which can provide goods at much cheaper prices, and could attract these local residents.[175]

4.5.4 Business and industry still sluggish

In addition to assistance to business operators by the Industrial Rehabilitation Organization and by the Great East Japan Earthquake Disaster Affected Business Operators Reconstruction Support Organization to buy out the debt,[176] the

173 Higashinihon daishinsai hukko shien network [Network for Reconstitution after the Great East Japan Earthquake Disaster] http://hp-network.jimdo.com/housing-planning-networkについて/コンパクトシティの推進/ accessed 30 December 2017.

174 "Compact city kousou uchidasu Yamamoto cho: Jumin goui keiseino mutsukashisa [Yamamoto Town Proposes to Build a Compact City: Difficulty of Creating Consensus]" (*The Page* 12 March 2015) http://thepage.jp/detail/20150312-00000004-wordleaf?page=1&utm_expid=90592221-29.uzRA2AXrScmfXlXFfeP6qg.0&utm_referrer=http%3A%2F%2Fthepage.jp%2Fdetail%2F20150312-00000004-wordleaf%3Fpage%3D3 accessed 30 December 2017.

175 Mitsui bussan senryaku kenkyusho [Mitsui Global Strategic Studies Institute], "Wagakuni niokeru compact city no kadai to tenbou: Aomorishi, Toyamashi no jireiyori [Agenda and Prospect of Building Compact City: Case Studies of Aomori City and Toyama City]" (Mitsui October 2012) www.mitsui.com/mgssi/ja/report/detail/__icsFiles/afieldfile/2016/10/20/121016i_kurihara.pdf accessed 30 December 2017.

176 The Industry Reconstruction Agency prepared for 500 billion JPY (4.5 billion USD) for government assistance to buy out debt and the Great East Japan Earthquake Disaster Affected Business Operators Reconstruction Support Organization was funded with 37 billion JPY (335 million USD). Reconstruction Agency (n 24) 24.

government also provided the Great East Japan Earthquake Disaster Reconstruction Special Loan, for 6.6 trillion JPY (600 billion USD) and provided emergency assistance for small and medium size companies for 13 trillion JPY (118 billion USD).[177] Further, the government provided a loan to farmers, foresters, and fishermen for 350 billion JPY (3.1 billion USD) and provided assistance to farmers, foresters, and fishermen for 120 billion JPY (1 billion USD)[178] Further, each prefecture with the help of the central government provided a subsidy to groups of companies for a total of 501 billion JPY (4.5 billion USD) to 698 groups of companies, consisting of 11,330 business operators.[179]

With respect to the "reconstruction special zone' program created by the Great East Japan Earthquake Disaster Reconstruction Special Zone Act of 2011, more than 230 areas adopted reconstruction promotion plans to receive special tax and regulatory treatment with approval[180] and more than 860 local districts have already published reconstruction development plans to confer special reconstruction development consideration.[181] Reconstruction grants were distributed to local governments 17 times for a total amount of 3.8 trillion JPY (34 billion USD).[182] These grants were used to facilitate urban redevelopment, group relocation, building reconstruction housing, and other purposes. Apparently, however, since the progress of relocation and redevelopment in the affected areas is so slow, the recovery of the economy and industry in the affected areas is also taking time.

Additionally, the government also decided to create a take-away type of reconstruction fund and the central government supported the fund by contributing to it with special tax distribution money.[183] The total amount of the fund is 224 billion JPY (2 billion USD) and the central government contributed 196 billion JPY (1.8 billion USD). This fund allows the affected local government and municipal government to spend funds flexibly.

The local government and the central government also supported businesses by building temporary marketplaces and factories in 644 places, allowing more than 2,500 companies and business operators to start businesses temporarily.[184] They further provided assistance to the establishment of shopping malls and reconstructed permanent facilities.[185] Also the affected prefectures budgeted some

177 Ibid 23.

178 Ibid.

179 Ibid 17.

180 Reconstruction Agency, Hukkou suishin keikaku no nintei joukyou [Lists of Approved Reconstruction Promotion Plans] (Reconstruction Agency 22 December 2017) www.reconstruction.go.jp/topics/main-cat1/sub-cat1-13/2017_PDF/20171222_keikakuichiran.pdf accessed 1 January 2018.

181 Reconstruction Agency, Hukkou seibi keikaku no kouhyou joukyou [List of Published Reconstruction Development Plan] (Reconstruction Agency 8 December 2017) www.reconstruction.go.jp/portal/sangyou_nariwai/20171208_seibikeikaku.pdf accessed 1 January 2018.

182 Reconstruction Agency (n 1) 73. The central government covered 3 trillion JPY (27 billion USD). Ibid.

183 Ibid 79–80.

184 Ibid 18. An increasing number of business operators have moved out and there are now 1,638 operators still operating in the temporary marketplaces. Ibid.

185 Ibid 19.

49 billion JPY (45 million USD) to support fishermen's associations to re-acquire fishing ships and fishing equipment, 106 billion JPY (96 million USD) to repair and rebuild fishing storage and processing facilities, and 92 billion JPY (84 million USD) to help fishermen introduce new technology or facilitate cooperation with other fishermen.[186]

The government claims that manufacturing in the Tohoku Region has returned to pre-disaster levels and total amount of retail sales of major department stores in Tohoku has surpassed pre-disaster levels.[187] Indeed, the mechanical/electrical production industry suffered devastating losses as a result of the earthquake and tsunami. However, due to quick supply chain repairs, production levels in affected prefectures have returned to pre-earthquake levels.[188] Nevertheless, the government also has to concede that the recovery of the retail and service industry is facing a decline in the number of operators as well as workers.[189] And the wholesale and retail industry is facing a decline in total sales amount.[190]

Major industry in the Tohoku Region used to be rice farming, fishing and fish processing, and tourism. Although a significant improvement can be found in some industries, the progress is still very slow and is not promising in these major industries.

Farmers were hit hard. In six affected prefectures, more than 21,480 hectares of farmland were submerged under seawater by the tsunami. After the tsunami, as of January 2016 some 5,900 hectares of farmland had been treated to remove debris and sea salt and are now ready for cultivation (almost 74% of all affected farmland).[191] Still, a substantial number of farmers do not intend to restart farming.[192]

Fishing and the production of fish products used to be one of the primary industries in the Tohoku Region. The earthquake and tsunami destroyed most ports along the coastline and wiped out most storage and production factories. The central government moved to repair and renovate public port facilities but

186 Ibid 21.

187 Tohoku keizai sangyoukyoku [Tohoku Bureau of Economy and Industry], Tohoku chiiki no sangyo hukkou no genjou to kongo no torikumi [Current Status of Industry Reconstruction in the Tohoku Region and the Future Agenda] (METI 3 March 2014) www.tohoku.meti.go.jp/somu/topics/pdf/140303_2.pdf accessed 1 January 2018.

188 "Higashinihon daishinsai de arawa, jidousha maker chokumenshita supply chain no wana [Great East Japan Earthquake Disaster Revealed a Drawback of Supply Chain for Automobile-makers]" (*Toyokeizai Online* 17 May 2011) http://toyokeizai.net/articles/-/6960 accessed 1 January 2018.

189 Reconstruction Agency, Sangyo hukkou no genjou to koremadeno torikumi [Recovery of Industry and the Past Recovery Attempt] (Reconstruction Agency 26 March 2015) www.reconstruction.go.jp/topics/main-cat1/sub-cat1-20/shiryou1-2.pdf accessed 1 January 2018 8.

190 Ibid 7.

191 Ministry of Agriculture, Forestry and Fisheries, Shokuryo, Nougyo, nouson hakusho (heisei27nendo) [Food, Agriculture and Farm Village Whitepaper 2015] (MAFF 2016) www.reconstruction.go.jp/portal/sangyou_nariwai/20171208_seibikeikaku.pdf accessed 1 January 2018) 212.

192 Ibid (number of farmers declined 22.5%). The central government is facilitating the merger of farmland to make it possible to create larger farms.

decided to concentrate its efforts on selected ports intended to function as hubs.[193] People in the fishing industry who had previously used other ports understandably had difficulty with this decision, though such a course of action was likely unavoidable. Of the 319 port facilities damaged by the tsunami, almost all of them have been repaired or renovated but only 276 ports have totally resumed operations.[194] The volume of the catch brought to market in the three affected prefectures has recovered only to 70% of pre-disaster levels.[195]

4.5.5 Is there something wrong with reconstruction measures?

The slow progress of the reconstruction raises a question as to whether the reconstruction measures adopted by the Japanese government are sufficient or whether something may be wrong with these measures.

First, there is simply not a sufficient number of public officials to promote the reconstruction works. Despite the government's efforts to send their officials or public officials of other unaffected local governments to assist in the affected communities[196] and to encourage part-time appointment of public officials by these affected municipalities,[197] staff shortage has been the most serious problem for the reconstruction. Moreover, the group relocation program as well as redevelopment program requires a huge number of experienced workers, something that cannot be quickly created. The shortage of on-hand officials, especially experienced officials, poses a very serious challenge to affected communities. The government should have anticipated such shortages and should have prepared a countermeasure in advance.

Second, the bureaucratic process in Japan requires complicated coordination and huge amounts of paperwork. Despite the acceleration and simplification effort of the government to speed up the process, it still takes a tremendous amount of work to apply, review, and enforce various reconstruction decisions. The government should have left many tasks for reconstruction to private parties such as non-profit organizations (NPOs) or community groups.

193 "Miyagiken, 60 no kyoten gyokou ni kinou shuyakuka: Yuusenteki ni hukkyu [Miyagi Prefecture Will Concentrate on 60 Fishing Ports to Consolidate Port Functions in order to Prioritize Reconstruction]" (*Asahi Shimbun* 9 December 2011) www.asahi.com/special/10005/TKY201112080584.html accessed 1 January 2018.

194 Reconstruction Agency (n 158) 5.

195 Fisheries Agency, Suisangyo hukkou e muketa genjo to kadai [Current Status and Agenda for the Resurrection of Fisheries] (MAFF March 2017) www.jfa.maff.go.jp/attach/pdf/index-12.pdf accessed 1 January 2018 1. Only 21% of them have returned to pre-disaster level of production and almost half of them have reported roughly 80% of pre-disaster sales. Ibid 18.

196 As of 1 April 2017, 1,782 public officials have been sent by other local governments to the affected municipal government. Reconstruction Agency (n 1) 29. Ibid.

197 The effected prefecture as well as other local government hired 1,670 term-limited workers and sent them to the affected municipal government. Ibid. In addition, the Reconstruction Agency hired 97 part-time employees to work in the affected municipal government, hired reconstruction supporters (444 in 2016). Ibid. Furthermore, the affected municipal government accepted 29 workers while employed by private companies. Ibid.

To make matters worse, one of the fundamental problems of these reconstruction measures is that there are so many different grants and subsidies, with different criteria and eligibility requirements offered by different departments of the government. As a result, the victims were forced to go through these complicated procedures to receive grants or subsidies. Because of the different criteria and eligibility, sometimes there are no available grants or subsidies. And the final decision usually rests in the different departments in the central government.

Third is the administrative urge to seek accuracy. Of course, the government does not want members of the public pretending to be disaster victims and trying to fraudulently access government support. That is the reason why the government, for instance, required a certificate of damage from the municipal government to claim grants for damaged houses.[198] However, because of this requirement, the municipal governments were forced to send their public officials to each of the damaged houses to verify the extent of the damage to the house of each claimant. Because many affected municipal governments lost substantial numbers of their public officials and there were so many other tasks that required immediate attention, the affected municipal governments were simply overwhelmed. Moreover, many affected municipal governments lost their municipal offices, so there were simply no systems working to issue such a certificate. It thus took weeks to certify and issue the certificates. Definitely, the bureaucratic urge to seek accuracy brought significant delay in the recovery and reconstruction works.

Fourth, reconstruction necessitates the coordination of various parties with different interests and opinions. In Japan, in such complicated circumstances, the consensus-building type of solution is generally preferred. As a result, it usually takes a lot of time to come up with the decision in such proceedings. Probably no one wants the government to rush into making a decision without proper consultation and consideration of various voices. But following the normal procedure in times of emergency would surely cause significant delays in making decisions and implementing these decisions.

4.5.6 Is the reconstruction budget adequate?

Tohoku's reconstruction undoubtedly requires a significant budget. The DPJ government decided to allocate a total amount of 19 trillion JPY (172 billion USD) for reconstruction during the first five years.[199] In order to carry out all intended programs, the government passed the Act concerning the Special Measures to Secure the Necessary Financial Resources to Cope with the Great East Japan Earthquake Disaster[200] on 2 May 2011, spent 15.1 trillion JPY (137 billion USD)

198 See Chapter 1 n 196. Before the 2013 amendment, the certificate of damage used to be issued as a matter of practice.

199 n 86.

200 Higashinihon daishinsai karano hukkou no tameno sesaku wo jisshi surutameni hituyouna zaigen no kakuho ni kansuru tokubetsu sochihō [Act concerning the Special Measures to Secure the Necessary Financial Resources to Cope with the Great East Japan Earthquake Disaster], Law no 117 of 2011.

from the contingency fund for recovery and reconstruction in 2011, and secured a 4.01 trillion JPY (roughly 36 billion USD) budget for 2012.[201] With Japan's general budget in 2012 set at roughly 92.4 trillion JPY (roughly 840 billion USD), the reconstruction budget occupied roughly 20% of the total general government budget.[202]

Needless to say, reconstruction costs represent a colossal capital outlay. The massive budget for reconstruction placed particular strain on government debt that was already reaching critical stages.[203] The government of Japan does not have sufficient tax revenue to sustain this kind of spending. The DPJ government thus made it clear that the funding necessary for reconstruction must be obtained by issuing a special reconstruction bond (*hukkousai*), separate from the general government bond.[204]

In order to stabilize the financial situation, the DPJ government approved a tax increase to provide the necessary funding for reconstruction.[205] The central government increased income tax over the next 25 years by 2.1%, imposing a "reconstruction special income tax" (*hukkou tokubetsu shotokuzei*) on the central government income tax.

4.5.7 Frustration of disaster victims

Many disaster victims have come to feel that reconstruction is taking too long. Progress is simply proceeding too slowly. It took almost 11 months after the earthquake and tsunami for the central government to adopt the basic reconstruction plan and start reconstruction operations. Prime Minister Kan failed to

201 Reconstruction Agency, Koremadeno hukkou kankei yosan nitsuite [On the Past Reconstruction Budget] (Reconstruction Agency) www.reconstruction.go.jp/topics/main-cat8/sub-cat8-3/20140813_yosan.pdf accessed 1 January 2018 1.

202 Ministry of Finance, 24nendo yosan no point [Some Highlights of the 2012 Budget] (MOF) www.mof.go.jp/budget/budger_workflow/budget/fy2012/seifuan24/yosan001.pdf accessed 1 January 2018.

203 Ranghieri & Ishiwatari (n 15) 283. The total amount of government debt in 2015 was 1,193 trillion JPY (10 trillion USD). Ministry of Finance, Heisei 27nendo kuni no zaimu shorui no point [Main Highlights of the Government Finance in 2015] (MOF March 2017) www.mof.go.jp/budget/report/public_finance_fact_sheet/fy2015/national/fy2015point3.pdf accessed 1 January 2018. The ratio of the government debt to national GDP in 2016 was 232.4%, the highest in the world. Ministry of Finance, Saimu zandaka no kokusai hikaku [International Comparison of the Government Debt] (MOF) www.mof.go.jp/tax_policy/summary/condition/007.htm accessed 1 January 2018.

204 Great East Japan Earthquake Disaster Reconstruction Basic Act (n 79) art 8.

205 Higashinihon daishinsai karano hukkou no tameno sesaku wo jisshi surutameni hituyouna zaigen no kakuho ni kansuru tokubetsu sochihō [Special Measures Act on Securing Necessary Funds to Implement the Revival Plan following the Great East Japan Earthquake Disaster], Law no 117 of 2011. The central government initially planned to raise the sales tax from 5% to 8% in order to secure the necessary funds for reconstruction. However, the central government ultimately decided not to raise the sales tax for the purpose of reconstruction. Nevertheless, Japan has a massive debt and has been pressured to maintain fiscal stability. Therefore, the DPJ government decided to raise the sales tax to 8% in order to secure a sound financial basis upon which to sustain social security benefits. Since the DPJ promised in 2009 that it would not raise sales taxes during its governance, this completely violated the DPJ election campaign promises. This move ultimately contributed to the defeat of the DPJ government in the December 2012 election.

articulate his vision of reconstruction right after the disaster and simply delegated the task to a group of advisors. It took several months for these advisers to come up with recommendations. The disagreement over the establishment of the Reconstruction Agency forced further delay to the passage of the Basic Act on Reconstruction from Great East Japan Earthquake Disaster. Relocation and redevelopment procedures take time. Still some of those impacted by the disasters are unable to enjoy the benefit of the relocation and redevelopment program so far. Some of the people affected are still waiting for the completion of the construction of disaster public housing.[206] In order to receive approval for reconstruction plans, local governments must apply to central government departments and convince bureaucrats therein that the plans satisfy all requirements and are worthy of approval. Many conditions are attached to reconstruction grants and these grants, even when granted, are unlikely to produce immediate effects. Even seven years after the disaster, it is safe to say that not much has changed.

The frustration of disaster victims is supported by the fact considerable sums of monies allocated to reconstruction remain untouched. The Board of Audits Japan, the constitutional organ charged with auditing government spending, found that a significant percentage of budgets allocated for reconstruction were not actually used in 2011.[207] Even though budgets were allocated for reconstruction, actual projects put into operation fell far short of available funding. If residents were seeing steady progress, this might not be an issue. However, this does not appear to be the case and so this state of affairs leads to unavoidable questions over why reconstruction funds have been left untouched.

4.5.8 Questionable boost under the LDP government

Frustration over the slow pace of post-disaster progress is likely one reason that the DPJ lost the general election in December 2012 to the LDP in a

206 Even if all victims could move into the reconstruction housing, difficult issues may still remain. Since all reconstruction housing is high-rise apartments, many senior residents who used to live in detached houses in rural areas surrounded by friends would have to adjust themselves to the new environments. The residents who move in are decided by lottery, so they would lose community connections. Since the rooms are in high-rise apartments, seniors might not be willing to take an elevator to go up or down. There may be no places for seniors to gather. Moreover, since the reconstruction housing is more likely to be built in areas where construction is easy and economical, there might not be any stores or shops nearby. Many seniors may thus face difficulty in adjusting to the new environment. There is a serious risk that seniors, isolated and left unattended, might die without anyone noticing, so-called "kodokushi." "Tetsuno tobira no nakano kodoku [Isolation inside the Steel Door]" (*NHK* 13 January 2015) www.nhk.or.jp/heart-net/tv/summary/2015-01/13.html accessed 1 January 1 2018; "Shinsai 6nen: Kodokushi, hisai3ken 243nin [Six Years after the Disaster: 243 Residents Died Isolated in Affected 3 Prefectures]" (*Kahoku Shimbun* 4 March 2017) www.kahoku.co.jp/tohokunews/201703/20170304_13042.html accessed 1 January 2018.

207 Board of Audits Japan, Higashinihon daishinsai karano hukkoutō ni taisuru jigyo no jisshi jokyoutō ni kansuru kaikei kensa no kekka ni tusite no houkokusho (Gaiyo) [Report on the Results of the Audit on Reconstruction Spending on the Great East Japan Earthquake Disaster] (Board of Audits Japan October 2012) www.jbaudit.go.jp/pr/kensa/result/24/pdf/241025_youshi_2.pdf accessed 1 January 2018.

landslide victory. The LDP promised the acceleration of reconstruction as a necessity before the election.[208]And after the victory, the LDP decided to accelerate the reconstruction.[209] The government also indicated its willingness to increase the total budget for reconstruction.[210] It was thus decided to ignore the 19 trillion JPY (172 billion USD) budget limitation for reconstruction, to increase it up to 25 trillion JPY (227 billion USD) and so an extra 4.9 trillion JPY (44.5 billion USD) was budgeted in 2013.[211] The government has continued to allocate substantial money for reconstruction.[212]

Could we see a substantial improvement under the LDP government? For sure, the infrastructure reconstruction is progressing gradually. Moreover, in order to speed up the provision of housing to the disaster victims, the government has adopted various acceleration measures to facilitate reconstruction housing, group relocation, and redevelopment.[213] Because of these acceleration measures, it became much easier to acquire property for building reconstruction housing, group relocation or redevelopment, much easier to revise development plans, much speedier to investigate buried heritage property, increase the number of persons sent to affected municipalities, allow contact with the same company for design and construction, or secure the joint ventures of construction companies.[214] But even six years after the LDP took over the government, there are still not much changes to the progress of reconstruction. Moreover, local residents were furious about the absence of strong commitment by the government leaders, including the Reconstruction Minister himself, toward more rapid reconstruction.[215] Furthermore, the decision of the Japanese government to host another Olympic Games in Tokyo in 2020 increased the construction works in Tokyo, diverting construction workers from Tohoku to Tokyo, thus rendering reconstruction work in Tohoku more sluggish because of the worker shortage. The uncertainty still remains as to what changes are forthcoming and how long it will take for disaster victims to return to "normal" life.

208 Jiyu minshutou [Liberal Democratic Party], J-File 2012 Sougou seisakushu [J-File 2012 Election Manifesto] (LDP) https://jimin.ncss.nifty.com/pdf/j_file2012.pdf accessed 1 January 2018.

209 Jiyu minshuto & Komeito [Liberal Democratic Party & Komei Party], Hukkyu kasokuka notameno kinkyu teigen [Urgent Proposal for Acceleration of Reconstruction] (LDP 6 March 2013) www.jimin.jp/policy/policy_topics/pdf/pdf089_1.pdf accessed 1 January 2018.

210 "Fukushima ni saisei soukyoku shinsetsu, Hukkou yosan 19 chouen waku teppai: Seihu ga hukkou suishin kaigi [Establishing the Reconstruction Headquarters in Fukushima and Removing the 19 Trillion Yen Cap on the Reconstruction Budget]" (*Asahi Shimbun* 10 January 2013) http://sankei.jp.msn.com/politics/news/130110/plc13011023320024-n1.htm.

211 Reconstruction Agency (n 201) 2.

212 For the purpose of reconstruction, the Japanese government budgeted 4.7 trillion JPY (44.5 billion USD) in 2015, 3.7 trillion JPY (33 billion USD) in 2016, and 2.7 trillion JPY (24 billion USD) in 2017 for reconstruction. Reconstruction Agency (n 1) 58.

213 Ibid 11.

214 Ibid 12.

215 Minister of Reconstruction Masahiro Imamura had to resign because of his remark that it was better that the Tohoku and not Tokyo were hit. 'Imamura fukkosho jihyou teishutsu: Tohoku deyokatta hatsugende inseki [Imamura Reconstruction Minister Submitted Resignation: Taking Responsibility for His Remark that It was Better to Hit Tohoku]' (*Asahi Shimbun* 26 April 2017) www.asahi.com/articles/ASK4V3C5NK4VUTFK005.html accessed 1 January 2018.

4.5.9 Is the "New Tohoku vision" realized?

Despite the commitment to create "New Tohoku," it is still unclear how the Tohoku Region could be revitalized to become an energetic and vibrant society for seniors as well as for children. The ideal of revitalizing the struggling society is surely beautiful and fascinating, but the programs to be adopted lack specificity, and how effective they would be to attract vital investment and new business is utterly unclear. The Reconstruction Agency has published a progress report for these programs[216] but it is not promising.[217]

Indeed, the total population of the three affected prefectures is constantly declining.[218] Moreover, younger generations of residents seem to be running away and the proportion of senior residents among the population is rapidly increasing.[219] It appears that there are currently sufficient numbers of job openings for reconstruction work[220] but reconstruction work will not last forever. Without a significant increase in more long-lasting good job prospects, it will be difficult to attract younger workers to come to Tohoku. In that sense, the revitalization of Tohoku is indeed a daunting task for the Japanese government.

4.6 Reconstruction of Tohoku and failures of law and politics

4.6.1 Reconstruction of Tohoku and failures of law

Apparently, the Japanese law was unprepared for providing assistance to such a huge number of evacuees who lost homes and all the communities that lost basic infrastructure. The extensive damage to the municipal government and loss of

216 Reconstruction Agency, Atarashii Tohoku kakushu sesaku no shinchaku joukyou [Progress Report of Various Measures to Accomplish "New Tohoku"] (Reconstruction Agency July 2014) www.reconstruction.go.jp/topics/main-cat1/sub-cat1-11/20140812_newtohoku_gaiyo.pdf accessed 1 January 2018. See Reconstruction Agency (n 1) 32–37.

217 Among the chief accomplishment so far is a grant to innovative business plans such as the creation of a playground for children of local residents, the creation of a program whereby children and seniors can eat together, and the introduction of a credit card payment system using mobile phones. Ibid 33. It may be questioned whether such programs would actually lead to revitalization of Tohoku.

218 Cabinet Office, Chiiki no keizai 2013 [Local Economy, 2013], Higashinihon daishinsai karano hukkou no joukyo [Current Status of Reconstruction after the Great East Japan Earthquake Disaster] (Cabinet Office) www5.cao.go.jp/j-j/cr/cr13/chr130103.html accessed 1 January 2018.

219 Ibid (proportion of senior residents in Iwate prefecture was 34.9%, higher than the national average of 26.8%).

220 Toshiyuki Tanaka, "Higashinihon daishinsai karano hukkou niokeru kongono houkousei [Direction of Reconstruction from the Great East Japan Earthquake]" (2014) 353 *Rippou To Chousa* 3, 8, www.sangiin.go.jp/japanese/annai/chousa/rippou_chousa/backnumber/2014pdf/20140602003.pdf accessed 1 January 2018. See also Cabinet Office, Chiiki no Keizai 2017 [Local Economy 2017] (Cabinet Office) www5.cao.go.jp/j-j/cr/cr17/chr17_03-01.html accessed 1 January 2018.

public officials prevented swift and effective reconstruction.[221] The government thus mandated to search for land spaces to build temporary housing and scrambled to urge the construction companies to build them in a hurry.[222] But the staff shortages significantly affected the speed of the temporary housing construction and offer. The government certainly allocated a huge amount of the national budget to assist local communities in reconstructing themselves. However, the lack of prior preparation has prevented swift and efficient reconstruction.

The law also failed to prepare for reconstruction measures in advance. As a result, the government was forced to establish an organization to come up with the reconstruction plan and establish a government agency to enforce that plan. Since the government didn't have any plan, the government was bombarded with all manner of criticism and the reconstruction was delayed.[223]

The government also didn't have any idea of what kinds of reconstruction measures would be necessitated. As a result, it was forced to enact new statutes to introduce various reconstruction measures. Basically, the government was obliged to come up with a new plan for the sake of all tsunami victims without smooth cooperation with other departments in the government and without effective coordination with affected municipal governments.

The relocation program and redevelopment program have not progressed quickly enough. In addition to the significant hurdles mentioned above,[224] there is also a serious legal question to be sorted out: since many died or were missing, it took many years to settle the land ownership and succession procedures. There was no system to quickly settle these issues or to allow the municipal government to go ahead with relocation or redevelopment. Failure to introduce some kind of legal system to prompt settlement of land ownership and facilitate group relocation and redevelopment brought significant delay to the reconstruction.[225] Construction of reconstruction housing has also been significantly delayed. Without some kind of statutory measures to facilitate the reconstruction, it is simply a daunting task for the government to follow through normal legal procedures.

221 It is noteworthy that the government came to use modern technology to offset these losses; for instance, video data capture from helicopters and other air surveillance data to check the degree of damage to issue certificates of damage without actual site visits. Ranghieri & Ishiwatari (n 15) 233.

222 Ibid 317.

223 The government also did not consider the necessity of allowing for the sensibilities of vulnerable people during the reconstruction. Ibid 161.

224 Takeshi Fukuda, "Bousai shudan iten sokushin jigyo no genjo to kadai [Current State and Agenda of the Disaster Prevention Group Relocation Facilitation Program]," 2014:12 *Reference* 131. For other difficulties, see Ranghieri & Ishiwatari (n 15) 10, 307.

225 Ministry of Land, Infrastructure and Traffic, Shoyuken no shozai no haaku ga mutsukashii tochi nikansuru sesaku [Measures Applied to Land Whose Owner Is Hard to Identify and Locate] (MLIT) www.mlit.go.jp/common/001098603.pdf accessed 1 January 2018. Apparently, however, the local government is unwilling to resort to the power of eminent domain.

The reconstruction of industry is still a long way off. The goal of "New Tohoku" sounds fascinating but not much specific achievement can be seen in developing new industry and increasing employment in Tohoku. "Reconstruction special zone" could be a very interesting idea to exclude various government regulation to promote innovative and vibrant development. But still many companies in the reconstructed areas depend heavily upon government grants and support. Something more drastic such as deregulation might be necessary to promote the economy after the disaster.

4.6.2 Reconstruction of Tohoku and deeper failures of law

All of this vividly shows that Japanese disaster law was not ready to face the task of reconstruction after such a massive natural disaster. The disaster law should have prepared for everything in advance.

But there are certain characteristics of Japanese law that might be hindering more effective and swift reconstruction in Tohoku. The first is the bureaucratic dominance of the legislative process and its spillover effect on the content of the legislation. In Japan, most of the bills passed by the Diet are submitted by the government as government bills. They are prepared by bureaucrats inside each government department with approval of the responsible minister of state and the Cabinet. Although bureaucrats need prior approval from the ruling party in order to make sure that the bill will be passed without problems, they have a strong impression of the text and structure of the bill. That is the reason why the language and terms used in these statutes are so unfriendly to the general public and why each department tends to preserve the final say on any project for reconstruction. The statutes are not for the public but for the bureaucrats to apply and, in many cases, it is only experienced bureaucrats who can fully understand the meaning and implication of the statute. This is also the reason why disaster law in Japan reveals a very strong imprint of bureaucratic thinking. The same could be said with respect to reconstruction measures adopted by the Diet in the aftermath of the Tohoku Earthquake.

Moreover, this led to a lack of coordination among various departments of the government. Basically, each department is tasked with coming up with reconstruction measures in light of the Great East Japan Earthquake Disaster Reconstruction Basic Act. Each department came up with the proposal within its jurisdiction using its budget and using its implementation mechanism. Although the ultimate bill to be submitted to the Cabinet needs inter-departmental agreement, there is a clear absence of better coordination. This is the reason why there are so many different grants and projects for the victims to choose from and each of the grants and projects has various limitations and conditions and there is no one to coordinate these grants and projects.

Furthermore, in Japan, the central government has very strong authority over the local government. Central government bureaucrats hate losing their power and control to the local government. That is the reason why the central government never allowed free reign to local government over the reconstruction measures. Rather than providing a lump sum grant to affected local governments free to decide what kind of reconstruction measures were necessary, the central government never gave up the final say on the reconstruction measures. This has led to extremely complicated administrative proceedings and time-consuming decision-making, leading to delays and the frustration of victims.

The local government is also still reluctant to rebuild the community with additional safeguards against tsunamis. Certainly, the local government is promoting group relocation and redevelopment by elevating grounds and building much higher tsunami barriers. But, clearly, the earthquake revealed that there are serious tsunami risks to coastal parts of the Tohoku Region. Now, the legislature has introduced a system to restrict building in the vulnerable areas. However, even after another tsunami countermeasure was introduced, local governments are still reluctant to implement the designation of the construction ban.[226] The government is still unwilling to restrict property rights even for the protection of life and safety of the residents.

In addition, the government had been reluctant to seek help from NPOs and non-public organizations. In order to reconstruct the affected areas, it is more beneficial to ask for the cooperation of NPOs and non-public organizations. After the Tohoku Earthquake, many NPOs and volunteers actively intervened to assist the disaster victims and clean up the debris. The government came to acknowledge the importance of cooperation with NPOs and other non-public organizations.[227] However, there are still significant hurdles for NPOs and non-public organizations to actively participate in the decision-making process of reconstruction.[228] Japanese disaster law is surely doing a poor job of promoting cooperation with NPOs and non-public organizations.

4.6.3 Reconstruction of Tohoku and failures of politics

The failures of politics exacerbated the failures of law. Kan could not come up with a reconstruction plan swiftly and left the formulation of a plan to an advisory

226 Even in the Shizuoka Prefecture, which is most likely to be affected by the next Tokai Earthquake, two towns are designated as tsunami hazard watch areas (yellow zone) but no city or town is designated as a tsunami hazard special watch area (orange zone and red zone). Shizuoka Prefecture, Tsunami saigai keikai kuiki oyobi tsunami saigai tokubetsu keikai kuiki no shitei [Designation of Tsunami Disaster Hazard Districts and Tsunami Disaster Social Hazard Districts] (Shizuoka Prefecture) www.pref.shizuoka.jp/kensetsu/ke-320/measures/tsunamisaigaikeikaikuiki.html accessed 1 January 2018.

227 Reconstruction Agency, Volunteers, NPO, koueki houjin tono renkei [Cooperation with Volunteers, NPOs and Public Interest Organizations] (Reconstruction Agency) www.reconstruction.go.jp/topics/main-cat4/sub-cat4-2/ accessed 21 February 2018.

228 Yuko Kawato, Robert Pekkanen, and Yutaka Tsujinaka, Civil Society and the Triple Disasters, in Jeff Kingston (ed), *Natural Disaster and Nuclear Crisis in Japan: Response and Recovery after Japan's 3/11* (Routledge 2012) 78, 92; Kouichi Nakao, Shinsai hukkou katei no community keisei nikakawaru gyousei/NPOtō/chiiki juumin no kyodou [Cooperation among the Government, NPO, and Local Residents in the Creation of Community in the Course of Disaster Reconstruction] (Zenrousai December 2016) 59 (pointing out the tendency of the government to look down NPOs and non-public organizations as assistant for implementation of government policy).

group, leading to significant delays in adopting the reconstruction plan. The ruling DPJ could not agree with the minority LDP on what kind of reconstruction organization was best for the Great East Japan Earthquake Disaster, bringing further delay in establishing the organization. Although the LDP was willing to cooperate with the DPJ government with respect to some of the emergency measures, the LDP came to adopt the stance of non-cooperation insisting on Kan's resignation and general election. As a result, the reconstruction measures were not easily enacted.

Moreover, even after the Reconstruction Agency was established and reconstruction measures were introduced, almost all final decisions on various measures were left to each department of the government. As a result, even when an application was filed in the office of the Reconstruction Agency, each file was transferred to each department for review and final decision, thus leading to complexity and long delay.

The government also failed to show the vision of a reconstructed Tohoku to victims of the earthquake and tsunami. The vision of "New Tohoku" surely sounds fascinating but it does not carry specific measures to realize it. The government simply failed to provide the promising future for Tohoku after reconstruction.

Furthermore, all the reconstruction works tend to focus on infrastructure rebuilding. In order to redevelop affected communities, the government is filling the affected areas with land to elevate the height of property to 5 to 7 meters, even 12 meters in some places. A huge number of trucks are employed to transfer land cut off from the mountains to fill the affected areas. Some of the local residents expressed concern whether the redeveloped communities could survive the next massive tsunami and questioned whether the huge amount of spending was worthwhile.[229] The government is also building much higher tsunami barriers (sea walls) to defend the communities. In some places, the tsunami barriers reached 14.5 meter high, totally blocking the view of the ocean from the community and totally separating the community from the ocean. Some of the residents have criticized the huge amount of spending to build such a mighty tsunami barrier as a waste of taxpayers' money.[230]

Unfortunately, all the measures introduced to reconstruct Tohoku have not stopped the significant increase in the ratio of elderly people in the Tohoku

229 "Soujigyouhi 5363okuen, hisaichi de susumu kasaage jigyou ni juumin human no koe [Land Elevation with the Total Budget of 536 billion JPY: Criticism from Some Local Residents]" (*Livedoor News* 16 March 2015) http://news.livedoor.com/article/detail/9892193/ accessed 13 February 2018.

230 "2700okuen no kyodai bouchoutei wa darenotame? [Who Will be Benefitted from the Construction of Tsunami Barriers with the Total Budget of 279 Billion JPY?]" (*WEDGEInfinity* 21 June 2012) http://wedge.ismedia.jp/articles/-/2004 accessed 13 February 2018; "Kyodai bouchoutei, hisaichi de hantai undo: Giron ni juumin huzai [Growing Opposition to Building Huge Tsunami Barriers: No Residents' Participation in the Building Decision]" (*Nihonkeizai Shimbun* 7 April 2014) www.nikkei.com/article/DGXNZO74004420Z00C14A7X93000/ accessed 13 February 2018.

Region and the declining population.[231] Moreover, many business companies are simply waiting for the completion of reconstruction before being able to start business activities.[232] As a result, there is a significant decrease in the number of workers required to work in the Tohoku Region.[233] Shortage of workers hinders swift economic recovery.[234] Economic recovery must wait for the redevelopment in the affected areas but the delay in economic development is hindering the redevelopment.[235]

***

Japan was unprepared for reconstruction after this massive disaster. As a result, the central government had no choice but to come up with a reconstruction plan and reconstruction measures to be implemented on the fly. Although the Basic Act on Reconstruction from Great East Japan Earthquake Disaster was enacted and although the Reconstruction Agency was established, enforcement of reconstruction statutes in Tohoku is sluggish leaving many residents frustrated by governmental failure to move more swiftly and efficiently. The attempt to reconstruct the Tohoku Region after the earthquake thus also reveals fundamental problems in Japan's legal system.

A poll indicated 53% of the residents affected felt that the reconstruction was delayed.[236] Even after six years, 47% of the general public still believes that the reconstruction has not progressed appropriately.[237] These frustrations vividly

231 n 218. See Kyoko Deguchi, Koureika to jinko gensho toiu hisaichi no kibishii jouken [Aging and Population Decline: Hard Reality of the Suffered Areas] (Grips) www.grips.ac.jp/cms/wp-content/uploads/2011/05/prof.deguchi.pdf accessed 1 January 2018; Mitsubishi Research Institute, Higashinihon daishinsai karano hukkou joukyou no haaku nikansuru chousa bunseki gyoumu [Research and Analysis on the Status of Reconstruction after the East Japan Earthquake Disaster] (Mitsubishi Research) www.reconstruction.go.jp/topics/main-cat1/sub-cat1-1/20150907_houkokushoH25.pdf accessed 1 January 2018 27–28, .

232 Shingo Nagamatsu, "Higashinihon daishinsai karano keizaihukkou no genjou to kadai [Status and Agenda of the Economic Recovery after the East Japan Great Earthquake Disaster]" (2014) 117 *Shobo Kagaku To Joho* 14, 17.

233 Ibid 15.

234 Ibid 17.

235 The government is trying to create jobs inside the affected municipalities. Ranghieri & Ishiwatari (n 15) 211. But most of the jobs created are related to reconstruction and there is a question whether all these created jobs could be sustainable after the end of reconstruction.

236 "Higashinihon daishinsai 5nen [Five Years Anniversary from the Great East Japan Earthquake Disaster]" (NHK) www.nhk.or.jp/d-navi/link/shinsai5/ accessed 1 January 2018.

237 "Higashinihon daishinsai hukkou susundeinai 47% [47% of People Says that the Reconstruction Is Not Progressing Appropriately]" (*Nihonkeizai Shimbun* 16 March 2017) www.nikkei.com/article/DGXMZO14103420V10C17A3000000/ accessed 1 January 2018. The local residents who suffered might be more frustrated. After five years, more than 70% of the victims in three affected prefectures replied that the reconstruction was delayed. "Hisaisha 7 wari chou hukkou osoi [More Than 70% of the Victims Replies that the Reconstruction Is Delayed]" (*Yomiuri Shimbun* 8 March 2016) www.yomiuri.co.jp/feature/TO000305/20160307-OYT1T50168.html accessed 1 January 2018.

manifest that something is wrong with the legal system on reconstruction. Even after seven years, many would agree that the reconstruction of Tohoku is still far off.[238]

The Okushiri Island, west of Hokkaido, was devastated in 1993 by a massive tsunami caused by a very powerful earthquake.[239] After the devastation, a huge amount of public money was spent to build an even mightier tsunami barrier and support was provided for disaster victims to rebuild their houses, but after 20 years, it turned out that the population is rapidly declining because there is no industry to sustain employment. Moreover, since the local municipality could not sustain all the cost to maintain newly built evacuation facilities, these facilities became useless.[240] This experience proves the difficulty of reconstructing a struggling society by spending huge amounts of public money. We can only hope that the reconstruction of Tohoku will not follow the same path.

238 "Higashinihon daishinsai kara 7nen: Hinan seikatsu imamo 7man 3sen nin [Seven Years after the Great East Japan Earthquake Disaster: Still 73,000 Residents Are Evacuees]" (*Asahi Shimbun* 11 March 2018) www.asahi.com/articles/ASL393FSLL39UTIL00Q.html accessed 11 March 2018.

239 *See* Chapter 1 nn 247–48.

240 Yutaka Okada, "Tsunami hisaikara 20 nen no Okushirichou no kukyou [Plight of Okushiri Town after 20 Years from the Tsunami Disaster]" (Mizuho Research Institute) www.mizuho-ri.co.jp/publication/research/pdf/research/r130901region.pdf accessed 1 January 2018; Mizuho sougo kenkyusho [Mizuho Research Institute], Kakono shinsaijino hukkou karaeta kyoukun [Lessons from the Reconstruction of Past Disasters] (1 June 2011) www.mizuho-ri.co.jp/publication/research/pdf/policy-insight/MSI110601.pdf accessed 1 January 2018.

5 Aftermath of the nuclear meltdown

In the aftermath of the nuclear accident at Fukushima No 1 Nuclear Power Plant, the central government and Tokyo Electric Power Co. (TEPCO) *bear responsibility for fully containing the radiation leaks and abandoning the nuclear power plant. TEPCO also bears responsibility for paying damages and compensation to those affected by this disaster. But in order to make sure that all the damages were compensated, the government needed some mechanism to support TEPCO. The onus for accelerating environmental decontamination and enabling evacuees to return to their homes and communities lies with the central government. Further, the central government must adopt measures to facilitate reconstruction in Fukushima. All of these endeavors have given rise to many novel legal questions. This chapter examines a number of the legal questions presented by the aftermath of the nuclear accident in Fukushima and how the Japanese government responded to them.*

5.1 Roadmap to containment and abandonment

First, TEPCO and the Japanese government had to come up with a plan to effectively contain the accident. Then, TEPCO and the Japanese government needed to adopt a plan to decommission and abandon the Fukushima Nuclear Power Plant. There were many hurdles to get past before they could achieve these goals.

5.1.1 Roadmap to containment

Almost six months after the accident, TEPCO managed to get control of the situation; at that point, all fuel rods in the reactor cores and those in the fuel ponds were (and still are) being cooled by circulating water and are constantly monitored. Radiation is no longer leaking from the plant into the air. All reactors reached cold shut down on 16 December 2011.[1]

TEPCO has now achieved the first two steps in the initial containment process: (1) reduce radiation leaks and (2) contain radiation leaks.[2] TEPCO and

1 Prime Minister Noda's Press Interview (kantei 16 December 2011) www.kantei.go.jp/jp/noda/statement/2011/1216kaiken.html accessed 1 January 2018.

2 Ministry of Economy, Trade and Industry, Tokyo denryoku Fukushima daiichi genshiryoku hatsudensho: Jiko no shusoku ni muketa michisuji step 2 kanryo houkokusho [TEPCO Fukushima No 1 Nuclear Power Plant Accident: Completion Report on the Second Step toward Containment] (METI 16 December 2011) www.meti.go.jp/earthquake/nuclear/pdf/111216a.pdf accessed 1 January 2018.

the Japanese government have already published a long-range roadmap to final decommissioning of the nuclear reactors.[3] During the next stage, TEPCO will begin the process of removing spent fuel rods from the cooling ponds, without compromising their stability. This process will be ongoing over a ten-year period. TEPCO will also conduct research and development on technology for removing fuel rods and nuclear debris from the reactors during this period. Then, after ten years, during the second stage, TEPCO will start the process of removing the fuel rods and nuclear debris from the reactors themselves. Once that process is completed, TEPCO will abandon the nuclear reactors at the Fukushima No 1 Nuclear Power Plant. Final abandonment will be realized after a period of between 30 and 40 years.[4]

The Nuclear Reactor Regulation Act allows some nuclear facilities to be classified as "specified nuclear facilities," (*tokutei genshiryoku shisetsu*) referring to facilities that need special security or protective measures.[5] This designation is possible only after emergency measures have been adopted because an earthquake, fire, or some other disaster has affected the nuclear fuel material, material contaminated by nuclear fuel material, or a nuclear reactor and when special measures are especially needed in light of the circumstances in order to prevent disaster with respect to nuclear fuel material, material contaminated by nuclear fuel material or a nuclear reactor, or to protect designated nuclear fuel material.[6] When a facility is so designated, the nuclear power company must submit an implementation plan relating to such special measures and attain the Nuclear Regulatory Authority (NRA)'s approval.[7] If these procedures are followed, certain Nuclear Reactor Regulation Act rules no longer apply as long as the special measures outlined above are being adequately adopted.[8]

The reactor facilities at Fukushima have already been classified by the NRA as "specified nuclear facilities," meaning that the necessary cabinet order pertaining to the facilities has already been enacted[9] and that the facilities are being managed

3 TEPCO, Tokyo denryoku (kabu) Fukushima daiichi genshiryoku hatsudensho 1–4gouki no haishi sochitō ni muketa chuchouki road map (an) [TEPCO Fukushima No 1 Nuclear Power Plant Unit 1 to Unit 4 Reactors: Long-range Roadmap for Final Abandonment (draft)] (TEPCO 26 September 2017) www.tepco.co.jp/nu/fukushima-np/roadmap/2017/images2/t170926_04-j.pdf accessed 1 January 2018.

4 As of May 2017, TEPCO finished pulling out spent nuclear rods from the cooling pool of reactor unit 4 and started an attempt to pull out nuclear rods and debris from the other three reactor units. TEPCO, Chuchouki roadmap no shinchaku jokyo (gaiyo) [Progress Report of the Medium and Long-Term Roadmap (Summary)] (TEPCO 27 May 2017) www.tepco.co.jp/nu/fukushima-np/roadmap/2017/images1/d170525_05-j.pdf accessed 1 January 2018.

5 Kakugenryo busshitsu, kakunenryo busshitsu oyobi genshiro no kisei ni kansuru hōritsu [Act concerning the Regulation on Nuclear Source Materials, Nuclear Fuel Materials and Nuclear Reactors], Law no 166 of 1957(Nuclear Reactor Regulation Act), art 64–2(1).

6 Ibid.

7 Ibid art 64–3. The NRA is a newly created regulatory agency after the Fukushima nuclear accident replacing the former NISA. *See* Chapter 6 n 195.

8 Nuclear Reactor Regulation Act (n 5) art 64–4.

9 Tokyo denryoku kabushikigaisha Fukushima daiich genshiryoku hatsudensho genshiro shisetsu ni tsuite no kakugenryo busshitsu, kakunenryou busshitsu oyobi genshiro no kisei ni kansuru hōritsu no tokurei ni kansuru seirei [Cabinet Order concerning Special Treatment of the Nuclear Reactor of the Fukushima No 1 Nuclear Power Plant of TEPCO for the Act concerning Regulation of Nuclear Source Materials, Nuclear Fuel Materials and Nuclear Reactors], Cabinet order 53 of 2013.

with instructions from NRA.[10] The NRA instructions mandate that TEPCO take necessary measures promptly and effectively in order to remove nuclear fuel from the reactors, reduce risks at the facilities and ensure the safety of the facilities and surrounding areas.[11]

5.1.2 Abandoning the Fukushima Nuclear Power Plant

TEPCO and the central government had already given up on the idea of reusing the Fukushima Nuclear Power Plant shortly after the crisis began. It was known that using seawater to cool down the fuel rods would render the reactors inoperable for the future. Moreover, and for a whole host of other reasons, it is doubtful that anyone would want the Fukushima plant back in operation again anyway. Therefore, TEPCO and the central government knew from early on in this crisis that they would eventually need to devise a plan for disposing of the facility, its nuclear reactors, and all of its fuel rods.

The nuclear reactor at the Fukushima plant is not the first nuclear reactor to be decommissioned in Japan.[12] However, it will be the first to be decommissioned because of a serious accident. TEPCO and the NRA must find a way to remove all contaminated debris, contaminated equipment and machinery, the fuel rods from the contaminated reactors, and to dispose of the contaminated reactor itself. With so much radioactive contamination surrounding the reactor and the facility, this undertaking will be a daunting challenge for both TEPCO and the Japanese government.

Moreover, even if sound technology is developed for disposing of all of this contaminated debris, equipment, nuclear fuel, and the reactors, the central government has to find a place for final disposal somewhere. In the past, the central government has had difficulty establishing final disposal sites for spent nuclear fuel. The central government must now find a final disposal site for all contaminated materials, including the reactors. Since, as will be explained in more detail below, the central government is already having plenty of difficulty finding

10 Nuclear Regulatory Authority, Tokyo denryoku Fukushima daiichi genshiryoku hatsudensho ni secchisareru genshiro shisetsu no tokutei genshiryoku shisetsu no shiteitō ni tsuite [On Designation of Reactor Facility at TEPCO's Fukushima No 1 Nuclear Power Plant as a Specified Nuclear Facility] (kantei 30 November 2012) www.kantei.go.jp/jp/singi/genshiryoku/dai27/siryou5.pdf accessed 1 January 2018.

11 Nuclear Regulatory Authority, Tokutei genshiryoku shisetsu eno shitei ni saishi Tokyo denryoku Fukushima daiichi genshiryoku hatsudensho ni taishite motomeru sochi wo kouzubeki jikou ni tsuite [On Matters to Be Considered in Taking Measures Requested for TEPCO's Fukushima No 1 Nuclear Power Plant Being Designated as a Specified Nuclear Facility] (TEPCO 7 November 2012) www.tepco.co.jp/cc/press/betu12_j/images/121107j0901.pdf accessed 1 January 2018.

12 The Tokai Nuclear Power Plant of the Japan Atomic Power Company was the first commercial nuclear power plant to become operational. It halted operations in 1998, becoming Japan's first nuclear power plant to be decommissioned. Its reactors are in the process of disposal. The spent nuclear fuel has already been removed and the company is now removing the heat exchanger. The decommissioning process is scheduled to be completed by 2020. Japan Atomic Power Company, Tokai hatsudensho no haishi sochi [Decommissioning of the Tokai Nuclear Power Plant] (JAPC) www.japc.co.jp/haishi/tokai_haishi.html accessed 1 January 2018.

interim storage sites, let alone the final disposal sites for nuclear waste outside of nuclear plants,[13] it will face even more problems finding final disposal sites for all the highly contaminated nuclear waste to be produced in the process of abandoning the nuclear reactors.

5.2 Disposal of contaminated waste

In addition to containment and abandonment of the Fukushima Nuclear Power Plant, the Japanese government had to come up with a plan to dispose of all the nuclear waste produced inside the Fukushima Nuclear Power Plant as well as all the products and other materials contaminated by radioactive materials outside. This necessity imposed on the Japanese government an unprecedented and extremely daunting burden.

5.2.1 Nuclear waste and its disposal

The Fukushima nuclear power plant accident created huge amounts of highly contaminated debris and also produced a tremendous amount of contaminated water inside the facility. Even if TEPCO does successfully clean the facility up, there will still be a huge amount of highly contaminated waste in need of disposal. In addition, workers have already gone through a voluminous amount of protective wear during restoration work. How to dispose of the debris, contaminated water, and used protective wear remains an important item on the central government's agenda.

Moreover, the blasts at the plant seriously contaminated the environment, the soil, and many homes in the surrounding areas. All of the contaminated homes and soil must be dealt with before residents can return. Decontamination of the surrounding environment will be tremendously painstaking work. Further, methods for disposing of contaminated waste and soil remain unsettled. Uncertainty also remains where disposal of contaminated vegetables and other products is concerned.

The legal system, as it relates to waste disposal, had not anticipated such a tremendous amount of waste contaminated by radioactivity outside of a nuclear power plant. There simply were no statutory provisions relating to such waste. Environmental protection regulations were premised upon the assumption that such large-scale radiation contamination due to a serious nuclear power plant accident just would not happen. The central government had to scramble to come up with plans to deal with this contaminated waste.

5.2.2 Disposal of contaminated waste from inside the Fukushima plant

It is the responsibility of TEPCO to dispose of all waste produced by the nuclear accident inside the Fukushima plant.

13 Yumiko Ono, "Nuclear Cleanup Faces 'NIMBY' Challenge" (*Wall Street Journal: Japan* 31 October 2011) http://blogs.wsj.com/japanrealtime/2011/10/31/nuclear-cleanup-faces-nimby-challenge/ accessed 1 January 2018.

The nuclear power plant uses nuclear fuel and spent nuclear fuel, after extracting the remaining uranium and plutonium by recycling, which is then solidified as "high level radioactive waste." Such "high level radioactive waste" collected from all nuclear power plants has now reached 18,000 tons; it is stored at the recycling facility at the Rokkashomura of Aomori Prefecture and is supposed to be transported to its final disposal site for long-time underground disposal.[14] Low level radioactive waste produced during the process of power production is left for each power company to dispose of. According to the Radioactive Waste Final Disposal Act of 2000,[15] it is the responsibility of the central government to provide the final disposal site (*saishu shobunjō*) for such high level radioactive waste but the government has had extreme difficulty in selecting a final disposal site. It has not yet selected any final disposal site.[16]

Suddenly, TEPCO and the government were faced with the difficult task of disposing of all waste produced as a result of the nuclear accident and there was no legal scheme for this disposal.

First, TEPCO faced the task of disposing of all nuclear waste produced in the nuclear power plant. Ever-increasing amounts of used and contaminated protective gear were particularly troublesome. Such gear was simply piling up inside the plant.[17] TEPCO ultimately decided to build burning facilities inside the plant and burn all of this used protective gear.[18] Highly contaminated ashes need to be collected and stored inside the plant for future final disposal.

Second, the issue of contaminated water inside the plant was also clamoring for a resolution. There are still voluminous amounts of highly contaminated water inside the reactor facilities. Moreover, ground water is pouring into the plant every day. TEPCO is now diverting this water into storage tanks. The number of tanks has now reached over 900 and the amount of stored contaminated water has reached 1 million tons.[19] TEPCO decided to remove radioactive materials

14 Agency for Natural Resources and Energy, Houshasei haikibutsu no tekisetsuna shobun no jitsugen nimukete [Toward the Adequate Disposal of Radioactive Waste] (METI 26 June 2017) www.enecho.meti.go.jp/category/electricity_and_gas/nuclear/rw/final_disposal/column01/ accessed 1 January 2018.

15 Tokutei houshasei haikibutsu no saishu shobun nikansuru hōritsu [Act on the Final Disposal of Specified Radioactive Waste], Law no 117 of 2000 (Radioactive Waste Final Disposal Act).

16 Agency for Natural Resources and Energy (n 14).

17 "Shiyouzumi bougohuku 4000 rippou meter yamadumi: Tokyo denryoku ga shashin koukai [Used Protective Clothes Piling up: TEPCO Disclosed Pictures]" (*Nihonkeizai Shimbun* 15 October 2011) www.nikkei.com/article/DGXNASDG1502K_V11C11A0CR8000/ accessed 1 January 2018.

18 "Osenbougohukunado touden ga shoukyaku e: Genpatsu shikichinaini shoukyakuro zousetzu [TEPCO Plans to Burn Contaminated Protective Gears: Increasing the Burning Facility inside the Plant]" (*Nihonkeizai Shimbun* 15 August 2012) www.nikkei.com/article/DGXNASDG15047_V10C12A8CR8000/ accessed 1 January 2018.

19 "Hyakuman ton ga 900ki: Toudo shasuiheki de umigawa touketsu [One Million ton of Contaminated Water is Now Stored in 900 Tanks: Freezing Wall Closed the Sea Side]" (*Fukushima Minyu* 10 March 2017) www.minyu-net.com/news/sinsai/serial/0600/08/FM20170310-155308.php accessed 12 December 2017.

from the water[20] and plans to release the treated water into the ocean. However, removing all radioactive materials from the water is a difficult proposition and it is probable that fishermen will strongly object to the release of this water into the ocean if there is any chance it is still contaminated. Thus, collection and disposal of this contaminated water is also a significant challenge for TEPCO.[21]

Moreover, there is a leakage problem from the tanks and TEPCO and the government have had to adopt countermeasures, such as building much higher banks and creating shields to avoid spillage into the water.[22] Nevertheless, as recently as February 2014, there was a leak of 100 tons of highly contaminated water from the tank over the bank.[23] This incident clearly showed the difficulty of containment.

Finally, it became integral for TEPCO to prevent underground water from running into the nuclear power plant. Underground water was running into the power plant at a rate of 400 tons a day. If the underground water was allowed to continue running into the power plant, TEPCO and the Japanese government would have to collect the water contaminated with radioactive materials inside the power plant and dispose of the contaminated water. TEPCO and the Japanese government thus decided to create bypass measures, sucking up the underground water before it ran into the power plant and releasing it into the sea.[24] Moreover, TEPCO and the Japanese government decided to install a wall underground in order to shield the power plant from underground running water.[25] Such a wall is expected to divert the direction of underground water to avoid the nuclear power plant.[26] The NRA has approved this measure and installed the wall but how effective this measure might be still remains unclear.[27]

20 Ministry of Economy, Trade and Industry, Hairo osensui taisaku portal site [Portal Site for Decommissioning and Countermeasures against Contaminated Water] (METI) www.meti.go.jp/earthquake/nuclear/hairo_osensui/ accessed 1 January 2018.

21 Ministry of Economy, Trade and Industry, Osensui shori taisaku iinkai [Committee on Treatment of Contaminated Water], Fukushima daiichi genpatsu no hairo/osensui taisaku nitsuite [On Decommissioning and Treatment of Contaminated Water of the Fukushuma No 1 Nuclear Power Plant] (METI 11 November 2016) www.meti.go.jp/earthquake/nuclear/osensuitaisaku/committtee/takakusyu/pdf/001_02_01.pdf accessed 1 January 2018.

22 Ibid.

23 "Fukushima daiichi genpatsu no tank kara100ton no kounoudo osensui more [100ton of Highly Contaminated Water Leaked from the Tank in the Fukushima No 1 Nuclear Power Plant]" (*Reuters* 20 February 2014) http://jp.reuters.com/article/topNews/idJPTYEA1J01W20140220 accessed 1 January 2018.

24 TEPCO, Chikasui bypass [Underground Water Bypass Measure] (TEPCO) www.tepco.co.jp/decommision/planaction/groundwater/index-j.html accessed 1 January 2018.

25 TEPCO, Toudo houshikiniyoru rikugawa shasuiheki [Shielding Wall on the Land Side by Freezing Technology] (TEPCO) www.tepco.co.jp/decommision/planaction/landwardwall/index-j.html accessed 1 January 2018.

26 The wall is created by freezing the ground to shield off the power plant facility from running ground water. Ibid.

27 "Fukushima daiichi genpatsu no toudoheki, shadan kouka miezu: Akinimo zennmen touketu [Freezing Shielding Walls Will Be Completed but Its Effect Still Questionable]" (*Nihonkeizai Shimbun* 22 August 2017) www.nikkei.com/article/DGXLASGG22H36_S7A820C1EA2000/ accessed 1 January 2018.

How to prevent underground water from running into the power plant to avoid further contamination will be the most difficult task for TEPCO and the Japanese government, especially in light of the prospect of holding the Olympics in Tokyo in 2020. Prime Minister Abe promised in his final presentation before the IOC's decision that the issue of contaminated water would be completely solved before the start of the Olympics.[28] Now the Japanese government made a promise to the world to contain the contaminated water and must prove to the world that Japan can accomplish this promise.

Other contaminated equipment or materials found in the nuclear reactors or scattered around the plant, contaminated with high levels of radioactive materials, could also pose a challenge. Since they are likely to be somewhat different from the solidified spent fuel residue after recycling, it is not clear whether they could be treated as regular "high level radioactive waste" to be disposed of in the final disposal site. In addition, it appears that the recovery, storage, and disposal method for them is not well established and the regulatory scheme for these highly radioactively contaminated materials is not clear.[29]

5.2.3 Disposal of contaminated waste outside of the Fukushima plant

With respect to disaster waste contaminated by radioactive materials outside of the power plant, the Ministry of Environment (MOE) decided to allow local governments to burn flammable waste caused by the earthquake and tsunami in Fukushima prefecture as disaster waste at burning facilities equipped with sufficient filters.[30] This policy applies to all disaster waste collected from Fukushima, including waste contaminated by radioactive materials. Remnant ashes are tested and if they contain less than 8,000 Bq/kg of radiation, the local government is permitted to bury them underground. However, if they test higher than 8,000 Bq/kg, the local government must store them temporarily. For inflammable materials, the local government can bury them underground if they show radiation levels of no more than 8,000 Bq/kg. When they exceed 8,000 Bq/kg, the local government must store them separately, temporarily.

The MOE also instructed local governments to bury the ashes of general waste contaminated by less than 8,000 Bq/kg and to temporarily store ashes

28 "Tokyo gorin saishu presentation: Shushou osensui wa seigyo [Prime Minister Gave a Final Presentation for the Tokyo Olympic: Promised to Control Contaminated Water]" (*Nihonkeizai Shimbun* 8 September 2013) www.nikkei.com/article/DGXNASDG0703R_X00C13A9MM8000/ accessed 1 January 2018.

29 Atomic Energy Society of Japan, Fukushima genshiryoku hatsudensho jiko niyori hasseisuru houshaseihaikibutsu no shori/shobun [Disposal of Radioactive Waste Produced by the Fukushima Nuclear Power Plant Accident] (AESJ 2013) www.aesj.or.jp/special/report/2013/s_haikibutsusyorisyobun20140331.pdf accessed 1 January 2018.

30 Ministry of Environment, Fukushimaken-nai no saigai haikibutsu no shori no houshin [Principle on Disposal of Disaster Waste in Fukushima Prefecture] (MOE 23 June 2011) www.env.go.jp/jishin/attach/fukushima_hoshin110623.pdf accessed 1 January 2018.

that do eclipse this limit.[31] Subsequently, the MOE decided to allow the burial of ashes containing between 8,000 Bq/kg and 100,000 Bq/kg in long-lasting secured containers.[32]

Burning waste that might be contaminated, however, triggered serious concerns from local residents and, thus, many municipal governments have had difficulty disposing of waste that might be contaminated through incineration. As a result, contaminated waste was simply piling up as it waited for disposal. The central government encouraged the cooperation of other municipal governments having sufficient capacity to accept and dispose of such disaster waste from affected areas.[33] However, local residents are concerned over the possible spread of radiation from air pollution after incineration and thus it is quite difficult to find municipalities willing to accept waste from Fukushima.[34] As a result, the central government had no choice but to dispose of all the wastes produced in areas highly contaminated by radioactive materials.[35]

Eventually, the Diet passed the Radioactive Materials Contaminated Waste Act[36] to clarify the responsibilities of the central government where disposal of waste contaminated by radioactive materials is concerned. It imposed the obligation on the central government to dispose of "waste from contaminated areas" (hazard zone and planned evacuation zone) (*osen haikibutsu taisaku chiiki nai no haikibutsu*) and "designated waste" (*shitei haikibutsu*), highly contaminated radioactive waste, including contaminated ashes, sewer mud, and dry hay showing radiation contamination beyond 8,000 Bq/kg outside of the contaminated area.

Disposal of "designated waste" needs to be conducted within each prefecture. But the location for burial of highly contaminated waste gave rise to a very serious issue. These radioactive wastes must be collected and placed at the temporary storage sites (*ichijiteki shuseki basho*). Then they must be incinerated

31 Ministry of the Environment, Ippan haikibutsu shoukyaku shisetsu ni okeru shoukyakyubai no sokutei oyobi toumen no toriatsukai nitsuite [On Measurement and Temporary Treatment of Ashes at General Waste Burning Facilities] (MOE 28 June 2011) www.env.go.jp/jishin/attach/memo20110628.pdf accessed 1 January 2018.

32 Ministry of Environment, 8,000Bq/kg wo koe 100,000Bq/kg ikano shoukyakubaitō no shobun houhō ni kansuru houshin ni tsuite [On the Principles Concerning the Disposal Method of Ashes Showing More Than 8,000 Bq/kg and No More Than 100,000 Bq/kg] (MOE) www.env.go.jp/jishin/attach/no110831001.pdf accessed 1 January 2018.

33 Ministry of the Environment, Saigai haikibutsu no kouikishori no suishin nitsuite [On Promotion of Disposal of Disaster Waste by Other Municipalities] (MOE 11 August 2011) www.env.go.jp/jishin/attach/memo20120111_shori.pdf accessed 1 January 2018.

34 "Higashinihon daishinsai to gareki shori [Great East Japan Earthquake Disaster and Rubble Disposal]" (Jiji) www.jiji.com/jc/v4?id=saigai-haikibutsu0001 accessed 1 January 2018.

35 Ministry of Environment, Kuni niyoru daiko shori [Substitution Disposal by the Central Government] (MOE) http://kouikishori.env.go.jp/archive/h23_shinsai/alternate_processing/ accessed 1 January 2018.

36 Heisei 23 nen 3 gatsu 11 nichi ni hasseishita Tohoku chihō taiheiyouoki jishin ni tomonau genshiryoku hatsudensho no jiko niyori houshutsusareta houshasen busshitsu ni yoru kankyo no osen eno taisho ni kansuru tokubetu sochihō [Special Measures Act concerning Countermeasures to Contamination of Environment by Radioactive Materials Emitted as a Result of the Nuclear Power Plant Accident Caused by the off the Pacific Coast of Tohoku Earthquake], Law no 110 of 2011 (Radioactive Materials Contaminated Waste Act).

or transferred to the interim storage sites (*chukan chozou shisetsu*) for years before finally being transferred to the final disposal sites. The government faced extreme difficulty in selecting them.

Fukushima's governor as well as town heads of Futaba town and Ohkuma town eventually agreed with the central government's plan to purchase land around the nuclear power plant and build interim storage facilities.[37] And the government finally managed to build the final disposal site for radioactive waste showing higher than 8,000 Bq/kg but less than 100,000 Bq/kg in Tomioka town in Fukushima prefecture, near the Fukushima nuclear plant, and started its operation in November 2017.[38]

Governmental failure to foresee and prepare for such an accident is the primary cause of this bumbling delay around the issue of contaminated waste. The central government simply should have had better systems in place, especially in light of its enthusiastic promotion of nuclear power.

5.3 Damage and compensation

Third, the serious nuclear accident at the Fukushima Nuclear Power Plant created the significant legal issue of who should be held responsible and what kinds of damages must be paid. What is the liability of TEPCO and the Japanese government?[39]

5.3.1 Tort liability of TEPCO and the government

It is the responsibility of a nuclear power company to pay all damages to all persons affected by a nuclear accident at one of its facilities under article 709 of the Civil Code.[40] Thus, TEPCO is liable for all damages.[41]

37 Ministry of Environment, Chukanchozou shisetsu nikakawaru koremadeno ugoki [Past History of Construction of Interim Storage Facility] (MOE) http://josen.env.go.jp/chukanchozou/action/ accessed 1 January 2018; Ministry of Environment, Osen dojo nadono chuukan chozou shisetsu nituite [On Interim Storage Facility for Contaminated Soil] (MOE) http://josen.env.go.jp/material/pdf/dojyou_cyuukan.pdf accessed 1 January 2018.

38 "Shitei haikibutsu no saishu shobunjo ga kadou [The First Final Disposal Site Started Operation for Specified Waste]" (*Mainichi Shimbun* 17 November 2017) https://mainichi.jp/articles/20171117/k00/00e/040/229000c accessed 1 January 2018 Radioactive waste showing more than 999,999 Kq/kg is still stored in the interim storage site to be completed near the plant. The final disposal of this highly contaminated radioactive waste is undecided.

39 Criminal liability of TEPCO as well as TEPCO executives is also at issue. Ex-chairperson Tsunehisa Katsumata and two other executives are being prosecuted by lawyers appointed by judges based on the resolutions of the Prosecution Review Committee to file charges. Justin McCurry, "Fukushima Nuclear Disaster: Former TEPCO Executives Go on Trial" (*The Guardian* 30 June 2017) www.theguardian.com/environment/2017/jun/30/fukushima-nuclear-crisis-tepco-criminal-trial-japan accessed 1 January 2018.

40 Minpō [C. Code], art 709.

41 It should be noted that all salaried workers who were unable to work because of the evacuation instruction or instruction to remain indoors were treated as unemployed and eligible to receive unemployment benefits from the government. Chief Cabinet Secretary, Press Release (kantei 20 April 2011) www.kantei.go.jp/jp/tyoukanpress/201104/20_p.html accessed 1 January 2018.

It is likely that TEPCO is liable for all damages caused to local evacuees, to companies that were forced to shut down because of the accident, and to farmers whose products were precluded from marketing because of radiation contamination or fears thereof. However, in order to receive a damage award, those who were harmed must prove that the accident was caused by the negligence of the power company. In this case, TEPCO might argue that the accident was caused by the unprecedented tsunami, which was beyond reasonable expectation, and that therefore TEPCO itself was not negligent. Indeed, the nuclear reactors withstood the impact of the earthquake but all of the troubles were caused by the tsunami, which washed away all the emergency power generators and fuel. There is some evidence, however, suggesting that the possibility of a tsunami of this magnitude was anticipated and that TEPCO had been urged to reconsider its safety standards but refused to do so.[42] Moreover, the Nuclear Regulatory Commission (NRC) of the United States came to require the nuclear power plant to prepare for the total loss of electricity and came to demand the security measures against total power loss after the September 11 attack in 2001; TEPCO should have been aware of this new requirement, but it failed to take any action.[43] If this evidence is accepted, the courts might find TEPCO negligent. Moreover, the courts have a tendency to require a much higher duty of care when it comes to facilities or organizations dealing with highly dangerous materials, such as chemical companies.[44] The courts might be willing to require a higher duty of care for a nuclear power company. Furthermore, even if the company had complied with all statutory requirements to ensure safety, the courts might still find TEPCO liable for negligence.

Under the Government Liability Act[45] the central government could also be held liable for its negligent failure to require stricter safety standards from TEPCO. In some cases in the past, the courts have questioned the appropriateness of government regulation and held the government liable for failure to regulate dangerous private activities.[46] The central government might insist that the safety

42 Ministry of Economy, Trade and Industry, Transcript of the 32nd Meeting of the Joint Working Group on Earth and Tsunami and Ground and Base of the Subcommittee on Earthquake Resistance and Structure of the Committee on Nuclear Safety and Security, Co-ordinated Resource Energy Investigation Committee (NDL 24 June 2009) http://warp.da.ndl.go.jp/info:ndljp/pid/1246938/www.nisa.meti.go.jp/shingikai/107/3/032/gijiroku32.pdf accessed 1 January 2018 16–17, 29–30.

43 U.S. Nuclear Regulatory Commission, NRC Regulation (10 CFR #50.63); Nuclear Regulatory Commission, Enhancement of NRC Station Blackout Requirements for Nuclear Power Plants (NRC 4 April 2012) http://warp.da.ndl.go.jp/info:ndljp/pid/1246938/www.nisa.meti.go.jp/shingikai/107/3/032/gijiroku32.pdf accessed 1 January 2018.

44 Niigata chihō saibansho [Niigata Dis Ct], 29 September 1971, 642 *Hanre ijihō* 96 (Niigata Minamata Case); Kumamoto chihō saibansho [Kumamoto Dist Ct], 20 March 1973, 696 *Hanrei jihō* 15 (Kumamoto Minamata Case).

45 Kokka baishohō [Government Liability Act], Law no 125 of 1947, art 1.

46 Saikō saibansho [Sup Ct], 3rd petty bench, 27 April 2004, 58:4 *Saikō saibansho minji hanreishu [Minshu]* 1032; Saikō saibansho [Sup Ct], 2nd petty bench, 15 October 2004, 58:7 *Saikō saibansho minji hanreishu [Minshu]* 1802.

standards it required for the construction and operation of the nuclear power plant were sufficiently strict for the purposes of avoiding any major catastrophe. However, given what happened, it seems readily apparent that safety standards relating to electricity loss following the tsunami were insufficient and that, therefore, the central government could indeed be held liable for negligence on this count. Moreover, the nuclear regulatory agency, Nuclear and Industrial Safety Agency (NISA), knew of the development of regulations in the United States demanding preparation for total power loss, but it failed to require the same kinds of measures for Japanese power companies.[47] In general, however, Japan's courts are reluctant to hold the central government liable and the potential for receiving damages from the central government for its failure to require stricter safety standards at nuclear plants might be limited.[48] It will be very interesting to learn how Japanese courts will respond to this issue in a growing number of tort actions against TEPCO as well as against the government.[49]

5.3.2 Liability under the Nuclear Damage Award Act

Amid their enthusiastic promotion of nuclear power, government officials apparently felt the need to enact a statute clarifying the liability of nuclear power plants. Therefore, as we already saw, the Diet enacted the Nuclear Damage Award Act[50] in 1961. According to this Act, brought in to clarify the liability of nuclear power

47 Toshihiro Okuyama, Beikoku genpatsu no zendengen soushitsutaisaku de hoan-in kentou was shitaga taiou niwa itarazu [U.S. Requirement for All Power Loss Situation: NISA Knew It but Failed to Respond] (*Asahi Journal* 1 February 2012) http://judiciary.asahi.com/articles/2012013100008.html accessed 1 January 2018. If the standards required by the statutes are not sufficiently demanding, then it is the responsibility of the Diet for its failure to put sufficiently demanding requirements in place. Saikō saibansho [Sup Ct], grand bench, 14 September 2005, 59:7 *Saikō saibansho minji hanreishu [Minshu]* 2087. The public could seek damage against the government for the intentional or negligent failure of the Diet to introduce sufficient regulation but in general the courts are reluctant to hold the government liable for the failure of the legislature. *But see* Kumamoto chihō saibansho [Kumamoto Dist Ct], 11 May 2001, 1748 *Hanrei Jihō* 30 (holding the government liable for the failure of the Diet to repeal the mandatory confinement of leprosy patients even after it was discovered that leprosy is a curable disease and effective drugs to treat them were found).

48 As explained below, the government practically forced TEPCO to shoulder all the liability for damages caused by the accident; n 66. This move might be viewed as an attempt to prevent the discussion on the possible liability of the government. For the issue of government liability, see Joel Rheuben, "Government Liability for Regulatory Failure in the Fukushima Disaster: A Common Law Comparison" (2014) 23 *Pacific Rim Law & Policy Journal* 113; Joel Rheuben, "Government Liability for Regulatory Failure in the Fukushima Disaster: An Australian Comparison," in Simon Butt, Nasu Hitoshi, & Luke Nottage (eds), *Asian-Pacific Disaster Management: Comparative and Socio-legal Perspectives* (Springer 2014) 101.

49 Ministry of Justice, Fukushima genshiryoku hatsudensho jiko nitomonau kokkabaishou seikyu soshou [Government Liability Actions Related to the Fukushima Nuclear Power Plant Accident] (MOJ) www.moj.go.jp/shoumu/shoumukouhou/shoumu01_00046.html accessed 1 January 2018. As we will see, the judgments of the courts are split.

50 Genshiryoku songai no baishou ni kansuru hōristu [Act on Damage Payment of Nuclear Damages], Law no 147 of 1961 (Nuclear Damage Award Act). See Chapter 3 n 79.

companies, protect potential victims, and promote the healthy development of the nuclear industry,[51] nuclear power plant operators are liable for "nuclear damage" (*genshiryoku songai*) except for that caused by a "catastrophic natural disaster or social disturbance" (*ichijirushiku kyodaina tensaichihen matawa shakaiteki douran*).[52] It must be noted, first, that the nuclear power companies are liable for damages regardless of who caused the damages.[53] Second, negligence is not required for the liability. When damages are caused by a "catastrophic natural disaster or social disturbance," it is the responsibility of the central government to take necessary measures to assist victims and prevent the expansion of damage.[54] Third, the liability of the nuclear power companies is unlimited.

However, in order to ease the liability of nuclear power plant operators, two additional mechanisms were introduced. First, a nuclear power plant cannot operate nuclear reactors without securing "measures against nuclear damage" (*genshiryoku songai baisho sochi*)[55] "Measures against nuclear damage" means the carriage of "nuclear damage liability insurance" and a "nuclear damage liability indemnity contract" or deposit, in the amount of 120 billion JPY (1.1 billion USD) per plant to cover damage liability.[56] In other words, the nuclear power company cannot operate a nuclear power plant unless it subscribes to nuclear damage liability insurance. Much like most other forms of insurance, nuclear damage liability insurance is an insurance contract whereby an insurer covers possible damage awards arising from a nuclear accident in exchange for receiving insurance premiums.[57] A nuclear damage liability indemnity contract is a contract with the central government whereby the central government covers damage liabilities that are not covered by nuclear damage liability insurance.[58] This measure is necessitated because the private nuclear damage liability contract does not cover any damage caused by the earthquake or eruption of volcanos. As a result, when the nuclear damage is caused by such natural disaster, it is the central government upon conclusion of the nuclear damage liability indemnity contract and

51 Nuclear Damage Award Act (n 50) art 1.
52 Ibid art 3(1). Therefore, it relieved the liability of other parties such as a manufacturing company or construction company.
53 Ibid art 4(1). However, when the damage was caused by the intentional conduct of the third party, the power company has a right to seek reimbursement from that third party. Ibid art 5(1).
54 Ibid art 17.
55 Ibid art 6.
56 Ibid art 7(1).
57 Ibid art 8. Basically, only liability insurance companies are permitted to issue liability insurance according to the Hokengyohō [Insurance Company Act], Law no 105 of 1995. Since the possible liability could be so astronomical, 20 Japanese liability insurance companies created the joint system called the Japan Nuclear Damage Insurance Pool (*Nihon genshiryoku hoken pool*) (currently 24 liability insurance companies licensed to operate in Japan are included in this system), and share possible liability. Besides, every country in the world has a similar pool and each pool has an indemnity contract to share the possible indemnity liability. Atomic Energy Commission, Wagakunino genshiryoku songai baisho seido no gaiyo [Summary of Nuclear Damage Award System] (AEC) www.aec.go.jp/jicst/NC/senmon/songai/siryo01/siryo1-6.pdf accessed 1 January 2018.
58 Nuclear Damage Award Act (n 50) art 10(1).

upon payment of the premium that will cover the liability.[59] The specific details of this nuclear damage liability indemnity contract are to be specified by a separate statute.[60] The power company can make a deposit instead of concluding the nuclear damage liability contract and the nuclear damage liability indemnity contract.[61] Second, the central government has a responsibility to assist the nuclear power plant operators when the amount of damages reaches beyond the limit. In other words, when nuclear damage liability exceeds the amount of the above "measures against nuclear damage" and when the central government believes it necessary for the purposes of realizing the objectives of the Act, the central government is supposed to provide assistance for the nuclear power company to pay damages to the victims.[62] The liability of the power companies is thus hedged. And when the damage was caused by a "catastrophic natural disaster," the central government is supposed to provide "assistance measures" to help the victims or to prevent extension of damages.[63]

In the case of the Fukushima No 1 Nuclear Power Plant, it appears that all damage was caused by the radiation leak after the plant lost the electricity needed to cool its fuel rods and thus, there is little doubt that the damage inflicted fits the characterization of "nuclear damage." TEPCO is liable for the resulting damage, regardless of its negligence, unless it can cast the disaster as being caused by a "catastrophic natural disaster or social disturbance."[64] Although TEPCO initially

59 Genshiryoku songaibaishou hoshō keiyaku ni kansuru hōritsu [Act concerning the Nuclear Damage Liability Indemnity Contract], Law no 148 of 1961 (Nuclear Damage Liability Indemnity Contract Act), art 3(i).

60 Nuclear Damage Award Act (n 50) art 10(2); Nuclear Damage Liability Indemnity Contract Act (n 59).

61 After the Fukushima nuclear accident, the Japan Nuclear Insurance Pool decided not to accept renewal of the nuclear damage liability insurance with TEPCO because it believed the insurance too risky for private insurance companies. Since TEPCO could not find any foreign liability insurance company to accepts its insurance, it was forced to make a deposit to continue working on the Fukushima nuclear power plant. "Toden, 1200 okuen kyoutaku e: Fukushima daiichi genpatsu no hoken [TEPCO Decided to Make Deposit: Insurance with respect to Fukushima No 1 Nuclear Power Plant]" (*Asahi Shimbun* 11 January 2012) www.asahi.com/special/10005/TKY201201100691.html accessed 1 January 2018.

62 Nuclear Damage Award Act (n 50) art 16. The government "is supposed to" provide assistance to the power company and it is the responsibility of the power company to pay all the damages. The responsibility of the government is obligatory but the textual language is a bit weaker than the provision that the government "should" or "must" provide assistance. This kind of expression is often used in statutes in Japan, imposing general obligation on the government.

63 Ibid art 17. The government will provide assistance directly to victims under this provision. It must be noted, however, that the Act avoided the use of the word of compensation and opted to use the word "assistance measures" to provide for the government assistance. And the government again "is supposed to" provide assistance to the victims.

64 Eri Osaka, "Corporate Liability, Government Liability, and the Fukushima Nuclear Disaster" (2012) 21 *Pacific Rim Law & Policy Journal* 433; Eric A. Feldman, "Fukushima: Catastrophe, Compensation, and Justice in Japan" (2013) 62 *De Paul Law Review* 335; Ken Kerner & Edward Tanzman, "Making Victims Whole: Compensation of Nuclear Incident Victims in Japan and the United States" (2014) 17 *New York University Journal of Legislation & Public Policy* 543; Julius Weitzdorfer, "Liability for Nuclear Damages under Japanese Law; Key Legal Problems Arising from the Fukushima Daiichi Nuclear Accident," in Butt, Nasu & Nottage (n 48) 119.

intimated that this accident was a result of "catastrophic natural disaster," it has been the position of the Japanese government that in this case, the damage was not caused by such an exceptional event and that TEPCO should be liable for damages.[65] Thus, the Japanese government practically forced TEPCO to pay all the damage awards to all the victims.[66] When it became clear that the amount of damage liability was likely to exceed the "measures against nuclear damage," however, the central government, as we will see, decided to assist TEPCO in paying damages.

5.3.3 First guideline and second guideline for damages

The Nuclear Damage Award Dispute Resolution Commission (*genshiryoku songai baisho hunsou shinsakai*), established in the Ministry of Education, Culture, Sports, Science and Technology (MEXT), must determine details of damage liability under the Nuclear Damage Award Act.[67] On 28 April 2011, the Commission issued the first guideline for damages in order to facilitate compensation to evacuees.[68] The first guideline set the standard for damages caused by government instruction, while leaving other damage issues for further discussion.[69] It thus allowed residents who were forced to evacuate or to remain indoors to receive a damage award for the cost of radiation testing, evacuation, medical expenses for injury or sickness resulting from the evacuation, psychological pain, lost business income or lost work income, and lost property interest due to evacuation.[70] It also allowed farmers and fishermen to receive compensation for lost income caused by the government instruction limiting the marketing of their products.[71]

65 "Touden no genpatsu jiko menseki, keiito shakai joukyoukara arienai: Kanbouchoukan [Chief Cabinet Secretary Comments that Immunity for TEPCO over Nuclear Accident Is Impossible in Light of History and Social Situation]" (*Reuters* 25 March 2011) http://jp.reuters.com/article/businessNews/idJPJAPAN-20261720110325 accessed 1 January 2018.

66 During the legislative discussion, the government explained that this "catastrophic natural disaster" means natural disaster truly unprecedented and substantially more powerful than the Kanto Earthquake, one almost "beyond imagination." Dai38kai kokkai, shuugiin, kagakugijutsu shinko taisaku tokubetsu iinkai no. 9 [38th Diet, House of Representatives, Ad Hoc Committee on Facilitation of Science, Hearing No. 9] (Diet 12 April 1961) http://kokkai.ndl.go.jp/SENTAKU/syugiin/038/0068/03804120068009.pdf accessed 1 January 2018 6. It is surely debatable whether the Tohoku Earthquake was such a "catastrophic natural disaster." Some criticized the Japanese government as depriving the opportunity for the judiciary to clarify the meaning of this phrase by practically forcing TEPCO to shoulder all the liability.

67 Nuclear Damage Award Act (n 50) art 18. *See generally* Tadashi Otsuka, "Fukushima daiichi genpatsu jiko niyoru songai baishou to baishou shienkikouhō [Damage Awards for the Fukushima No 1 Nuclear Power Plant Accident and the Act on Organization to Support Damage Liability]" (2011) 1433 *Juristo* 39.

68 Nuclear Damage Liability Conflict Resolution Commission, Tokyo denryoku (kabu) Fukushima daiichi, daini genshiryoku hatsudensho jiko niyoru genshiryoku songai no han-i no hanteitō ni kansuru daiichiji shishin [First Guideline concerning the Scope of Nuclear Damage Caused by TEPCO's No 1 Fukushima Nuclear Power Plant and No 2 Fukushima Nuclear Power Plant] (MEXT 28 April 2011) www.mext.go.jp/b_menu/shingi/chousa/kaihatu/016/houkoku/__icsFiles/afieldfile/2011/04/28/1305640_1.pdf accessed 1 January 2018.

69 Ibid.

70 Ibid.

71 Ibid.

The Japanese government requested that TEPCO pay damage awards as soon as possible to these victims in accordance with the Commission's guideline.[72] Damage awards for those who voluntarily evacuated and for farmers who suffered tremendous loss due to "bad reputation" or consumer skepticism were left for future discussion.

The second guideline[73] also mandated that TEPCO pay damages for expenses pertaining to evacuees returning home temporarily or permanently, evacuation-related psychological pain, loss suffered from the decision not to cultivate products because of the marketing ban, economic loss caused after lifting the marketing ban, and loss caused by "bad reputation." With respect to losses caused by "bad reputation," the second guideline basically allowed farmers and fishermen in Fukushima to receive damage awards for their losses but limited damage awards for others to situations where there was a causal relationship between their loss and the nuclear accident. It thus allowed hotels and restaurants located in Fukushima to receive damage awards but left the potential for damage awards being extended to other hotels and restaurants for future discussion.

5.3.4 Consolidated Interim Guideline

These two guidelines were incorporated into the Interim Guideline for damage awards published on 5 August 2011.[74] The Interim Guideline clarified the scope of damage awards for evacuees. It ordered TEPCO to pay damages to those who were forced to evacuate from the "hazard zone" within a 20 km radius

72 Ministry of Economy, Trade and Industry, Genshiryoku hatsudensho jiko keizaihigai taiou team [Team concerned with Economic Damage Resulting from the Nuclear Power Plant Accident], Decision of Relevant Cabinet Ministers (METI 12 May 2011) www.meti.go.jp/earthquake/nuclear/pdf/songaibaisho_110512_02.pdf accessed 1 January 2018. In order to ease difficulties for disaster victims, the government decided to pay temporary payment on behalf of TEPCO. Heisei 23 nen genshiryoku jiko niyoru higai ni kakawaru kinkyusochi ni kansuru hōritsu [Act concerning Emergency Measures on Damages Resulting from the Nuclear Accident in 2011], Law no 91 of 2011.

73 Nuclear Damage Liability Conflict Resolution Commission, Tokyo denryoku (kabu) Fukushima daiichi, daini genshiryoku hatsudensho jiko niyoru genshiryoku songai no han-i no hanteitō ni kansuru dainiji shishin [Second Guideline Concerning the Scope of Nuclear Damage Caused by TEPCO's No 1 Fukushima Nuclear Power Plant and No 2 Fukushima Nuclear Power Plant] (MEXT 31 May 2011) www.mext.go.jp/b_menu/shingi/chousa/kaihatu/016/houkoku/__icsFiles/afieldfile/2011/05/31/1306698_1_1.pdf accessed 1 January 2018. The supplement to the second guideline clarified the scope of psychological pain to be awarded. Nuclear Damage Liability Conflict Resolution Commission, Tokyo denryoku (kabu) Fukushima daiichi, daini genshiryoku hatsudensho jiko niyoru genshiryoku songai no han-i no hanteitō nikansuru dainiji shishin tsuiho [Supplement to the Second Guideline Concerning the Scope of Nuclear Damage Caused by TEPCO's No 1 Fukushima Nuclear Power Plant and No 2 Fukushima Nuclear Power Plant] (MEXT 20 June 2011) www.mext.go.jp/b_menu/shingi/chousa/kaihatu/016/houkoku/__icsFiles/afieldfile/2011/06/20/1307518_1_3.pdf accessed 1 January 2018.

74 Nuclear Damage Liability Conflict Resolution Commission, Tokyo denryoku (kabu) Fukushima daiichi, daini genshiryoku hatsudensho jiko niyoru genshiryoku songai no han-i no hanteitō ni kansuru chukan shishin [Interim Guideline Concerning the Scope of Nuclear Damage Caused by TEPCO's No. 1 Fukushima Nuclear Power Plant and No. 2 Fukushima Nuclear Power Plant] (MEXT 5 August 2011) www.mext.go.jp/b_menu/shingi/chousa/kaihatu/016/houkoku/__icsFiles/afieldfile/2011/08/17/1309452_1_2.pdf accessed 1 January 2018 (Interim Guideline).

of the plant, the "planned evacuation zone" beyond the 20 km radius, and the "specified evacuation recommendation spot," along with some evacuees from an "emergency evacuation preparation zone." With respect to damages for psychological pain, the Interim Guideline mandated that TEPCO pay 100,000 JPY (900 USD) per month to evacuees of these areas for the first six months (120,000 JPY or 1,100 USD for evacuees who had to stay in school gyms) and then 50,000 JPY (450 USD) per month for the next six months. Those evacuated from the emergency evacuation preparation zone after 20 June were excluded from receiving this compensation except for children, pregnant mothers, persons with disabilities, and hospitalized patients. Moreover, the Interim Guideline made no mention of damages for those who had evacuated voluntarily from outside of these areas. Those who were forced to remain indoors were also granted damage awards (50,000 JPY or 450 USD per person) for their psychological pains.

Farmers and fishermen who suffered losses, workers who lost jobs, and factories and businesses forced to shut down because of the accident were also granted damage awards. Hotels and restaurants in Fukushima prefecture and in neighboring Ibaraki, Tochigi, and Gunma prefectures were also awarded damages for loss of income due to "bad reputation." Manufacturers and service providers in Fukushima received damage awards for their economic losses, as did business operators who suffered indirect loss due to the accident. Damage awards were also given to workers, Self Defense Forces (SDF) officers, firefighters, police officers, and other personnel who suffered sickness or death, if any, as a result of radiation exposure during work relating to the accident.

Subsequent to this Interim Guideline, the Commission published four supplements to the guideline. The first supplement on voluntary evacuees mandated that TEPCO pay voluntary evacuees and those who opted to remain in the affected areas an equal lump sum amount of 80,000 JPY (730 USD) per person because it believed that it would be unfair to compensate voluntary evacuees more handsomely in comparison with those that chose to remain.[75]

Moreover, in anticipation of the return of evacuees, the second supplement indicated damage awards for the psychological pain of evacuees depending upon how long they had been evacuated.[76] As will be examined below, the areas

75 Nuclear Damage Liability Conflict Resolution Commission, Tokyo denryoku (kabu) Fukushima daiichi, daini genshiryoku hatsudensho jiko niyoru genshiryoku songai no han-i no hanteitō ni kansuru chukan shishin tsuiho (jishutekihinanto nikakawaru songai nitusite) [Supplement to Interim Guideline Concerning the Scope of Nuclear Damage Caused by TEPCO's No 1 Fukushima Nuclear Power Plant and No 2 Fukushima Nuclear Power Plant (Concerning Damages for Voluntary Evacuees)] (MEXT 6 December 2011) www.mext.go.jp/b_menu/shingi/chousa/kaihatu/016/houkoku/__icsFiles/afieldfile/2012/01/18/1315180_1.pdf accessed 1 January 2018 (First supplement). Voluntary evacuees outside of 30 km radius were deeply upset.

76 Nuclear Damage Liability Conflict Resolution Commission, Tokyo denryoku (kabu) Fukushima daiichi, daini genshiryoku hatsudensho jiko niyoru genshiryoku songai no han-i no hanteitō ni kansuru chukan shishin dainiji tsuiho (seihu niyoru hinankuikitōno minoasitō ni kakawaru songai nitsuite) [Second Supplement to Interim Guideline Concerning the Scope of Nuclear Damage Caused by TEPCO's No 1 Fukushima Nuclear Power Plant and No 2 Fukushima Nuclear Power Plant (Concerning Damages over Reconsideration of the Evacuation Restriction)], (MEXT 16 March 2012) www.mext.go.jp/b_menu/shingi/chousa/kaihatu/016/houkoku/__icsFiles/afieldfile/2012/03/16/1318795.pdf accessed 1 January 2018 (Second supplement).

surrounding the Fukushima plant were divided into "evacuation instruction removal preparation zone" (*hinan shiji kaijo junbi kuiki*) "residence restriction zone" (*kyoju seigen kuiki*) and "no-return zone" ("difficult-to-return zone") (*kitaku konnan kuiki*).[77] Evacuees formerly living in "no-return zone" are entitled to receive a lump sum of 6 million JPY (roughly 55,000USD), while those from "residence restriction zone" are entitled to 100,000JPY per month (roughly 900USD), with the possibility of receiving 2.4 million JPY (roughly 22,000USD) for two years' compensation, in a lump sum. On the other hand, evacuees of the "evacuation instruction removal preparation zone" would receive 100,000 JPY (900 USD) per month until they were permitted to return to their homes.

The third supplement expanded damages for "bad reputation" of farmers and fishermen[78] and the fourth supplement elaborated on how long the compensation for evacuation would be mandated after the evacuation instruction is lifted and to what extent the additional cost for acquiring the replacement housing is covered.[79]

5.3.5 Payment procedure

Although TEPCO should be liable for all the damages that have a reasonable causal relationship with the nuclear accident, the guideline has adopted the policy of streamlining the damage payments by showing the standard damage amount.[80] This is understandable because the number of victims is staggering and reviewing all the claims on an individual basis and deciding upon the specific amount of damages based on their individual claims would be too time-consuming and complicated. It would be far better for TEPCO to pay a standard amount and for victims to receive damage awards as quickly as possible. On the other hand, since the victims are legally entitled to claim the amount of damages beyond the

77 n 165. "No-return zone" is technically "difficult-to-return zone" and there is no legal ban for the return but practically the government prohibits the return. All the gates to the residents are securely shielded off so that no one can enter.

78 Nuclear Damage Liability Conflict Resolution Commission, Tokyo denryoku (kabu) Fukushima daiichi, daini genshiryoku hatsudensho jiko niyoru genshiryoku songai no han-i no hanteitō nikansuru chukan shishin daisanji tsuiho (nourin gyogyou,shokuhin sangyo no huuhyohigai ni kansuru songai nitsuite) [Third Supplement to Interim Guideline Concerning the Scope of Nuclear Damage Caused by TEPCO's No 1 Fukushima Nuclear Power Plant and No 2 Fukushima Nuclear Power Plant (Concerning Damage to Farmers, Fishers and Food Processing Business Operators due to Bad Reputation)] (MEXT 30 January 2013) www.mext.go.jp/b_menu/shingi/chousa/kaihatu/016/houkoku/1330965.htm accessed 1 January 2018 (Third supplement).

79 Nuclear Damage Liability Conflict Resolution Commission, Tokyo denryoku (kabu) Fukushima daiichi, daini genshiryoku hatsudensho jiko niyoru genshiryoku songai no han-i no hanteitō nikansuru chukan shishin daiyoji tsuiho (Hinanshiji no choukikato nikakawaru songai nitsuite) [Fourth Supplement to Interim Guideline Concerning the Scope of Nuclear Damage Caused by TEPCO's No 1 Fukushima Nuclear Power Plant and No 2 Fukushima Nuclear Power Plant (Concerning Damage Resulting from the Long Evacuation)] (MEXT 26 December 2013, revised 28 January 2016, revised 31 January 2017) www.mext.go.jp/component/a_menu/science/detail/__icsFiles/afieldfile/2017/02/03/1329116_011_2.pdf accessed 1 January 2018 (Fourth supplement). This fourth supplement was revised thereafter twice.

80 Interim Guideline (n 74).

standard amount if they suffered such damages, the guideline allowed victims to claim the amount of damages beyond the standard amount with proof.[81] Nevertheless, TEPCO was inclined to stick to the standard amount and was reluctant to increase the damage awards according to specific circumstances.[82] As a result, in order to claim more than the standard amount based on the individual circumstances, the victims often needed to file an application for arbitration, to be discussed below.

Moreover, the explanation distributed by TEPCO on nuclear damage application was initially very long and detailed and it was hard for many local residents to understand the procedure. TEPCO also initially demanded huge numbers of papers to claim damages and the claim papers were very difficult to fill in.[83] Thereafter, TEPCO came to require less demanding paperwork for claiming damages. Moreover, with extension of evacuation, TEPCO came to allow victims to receive damage awards for an extended period instead of asking them to submit claims every three months.[84]

5.3.6 Damage payment

Not everyone was happy with these guidelines. The Interim Guideline left the issue of damage awards for evacuees from the "emergency evacuation preparation zone" after 20 June unaddressed (except for children, pregnant women, patients in need of care, and hospitalized patients). The same could be said for damage awards pertaining to those from outside the "evacuation instruction zone" who had nonetheless evacuated voluntarily. Some of the residents are provided with damage awards by the subsequent supplements but some are still not covered. TEPCO has adopted the position that it is willing to pay damages even when the applicants are not covered by these guidelines but the amount of award for these residents is not clear. Moreover, since the guidelines provide merely generalized procedures, many residents felt that their individual circumstances were not appropriately considered.

Based on these guidelines, by December 2017, TEPCO paid the total amount of 7.68 trillion JPY (64.3 billion USD), including 3 trillion JPY (27.3 billion USD)

81 Ibid.

82 The governor of Fukushima Prefecture as a director of Council for Nuclear Damage Award for Fukushima Prefecture sent an urgent request to TEPCO to individually review the damages and pay damage awards accordingly. Fukushimaken genshiryoku songai taisaku kyougikai [Council for Nuclear Damage Award for the Fukushima Prefecture], Genshiryoku songaibaisho no kanzenjisshi nikansuru kinkyu yobosho [Urgent Request for Full Implementation of Nuclear Damage Award] (Fukushima Prefecture 31 May 2017) www.pref.fukushima.lg.jp/uploaded/attachment/219040.pdf accessed 1 January 2018.

83 TEPCO, Honbaisho niokeru seikyu shorui no kaizen oyobi baishoukijun no ichibu minaoshi nitsuite [On Improvement on Claim Papers for Damages and Reconsideration of Damage Standards] (TEPCO 24 November 2011) www.tepco.co.jp/comp/index2-j.html accessed 1 January 2018.

84 TEPCO, Press Release (TEPCO 17 September 2013) www.tepco.co.jp/cc/press/2013/1230627_5117.html accessed 1 January 2018.

to individual claimants, 4.16 trillion JPY (37.8 billion USD) to corporation claimants and 353 billion JPY (3.2 billion USD) to voluntary evacuees.[85]

5.3.7 Requests for arbitration

If damage award requests were denied from TEPCO or recipients were unhappy with award amounts suggested by TEPCO, they could resort to the Nuclear Damage Award Dispute Resolution Center (Arbitration Center) for arbitration.[86] The Arbitration Center is established under the Nuclear Damage Award Dispute Resolution Commission and is designed to provide informal, inexpensive, and speedy resolution to disputes on nuclear damage.

According to a MEXT press release, 5,659 applications were filed within the first 18 months of the Arbitration Center's opening with 1,770 applications ending in settlement.[87] That is, however, only one fourth of all applications and, given that the average period for review was eight months[88] there is reason to believe that the arbitration procedure was, perhaps, too bureaucratic, too inflexible, and too slow-moving.[89] The ability of the Arbitration Center seems to be lightly improved. By December 2017, 21,404 applications for arbitration were filed and 19,267 cases were disposed of, including complete settlement in 15,967 cases.[90] This means that in a significant number of cases (roughly a little over 80% of all applications), the arbitration procedure has worked.

Although the ADR procedure significantly contributed to the swift and informal resolution of disputes between TEPCO and resident victims, there have been some concerns and problems. One of the problems was the long delay in processing applications. Although it is supposed to entail a swift resolution of disputes,

85 TEPCO, Baishokin no oshiharai joukyou [Current Status of Damage Payment] (TEPCO) www.tepco.co.jp/fukushima_hq/compensation/results/index-j.html accessed 1 January 2018. Included is a payment of 153 billion JPY (1.53 billion USD) as a temporary payment. Ibid.

86 Nuclear Damage Award Dispute Resolution Center (MEXT) www.mext.go.jp/a_menu/genshi_baisho/jiko_baisho/detail/1329118.htm accessed 1 January 2018. *See also* Naoki Idei, "The Nuclear Damage Claim Dispute Resolution Center" (2012) 28 *Japan Commercial Arbitration Association Newsletter* 1; Naoki Idei, "Facing Mass Nuclear Damage Claims: Challenge of the Japanese Judicial System" (2013) 35 *University of Hawaii Law Review* 559.

87 "Genpatsu songai baisho: Touden ni seiiaru taio yosei—Monkasho [MEXT Requested Much Sincere Attitude to TEPCO: Nuclear Damage Award]" (*Denden Journal* 5 March 2013) www.denden-journal.com/new_society/2013/792.html accessed 1 January 2018.

88 Ibid; "Touden songai baisho, hutou taiou kaizenwo [Requesting the Better Handling of Nuclear Damage Award Claims]" (*NHK* 5 March 2013) www3.nhk.or.jp/news/genpatsu-fukushima/20130305/2030_baisho.html accessed 1 January 2018.

89 The Diet has passed a special statute extending the statute of limitations to all claims in which application has been filed for arbitration; n 105. And the Diet eventually extended the statute of limitation for tort claim arising from the Fukushima nuclear accident altogether; n 110.

90 Nuclear Damage Award Dispute Resolution Center, Heisei28nen niokeru joukyou nitsuite [On the Status of the Centre in 2016] (MEXT) www.mext.go.jp/component/a_menu/science/detail/__icsFiles/afieldfile/2017/09/22/1374251_01_1.pdf accessed 1 January 2018 12.

it turned out that many cases needed more than six months to process.[91] There are several background reasons for this delay. One is the absence of sufficient staff members and another is the careful start-up in the beginning.[92] But gradually, the number of staff came to be substantially improved,[93] the procedure was simplified,[94] and the period leading to the arbitration proposal became a bit shorter.[95] Another reason is the reluctance of TEPCO to cooperate with the arbitration procedure. It was reported that TEPCO demanded in some cases unnecessarily detailed explanation and evidence for damages, acted very slowly to respond to the procedure request, or failed to acknowledge the claim insisting on the absence of reference in the Interim Guideline.[96] The Arbitration Center published some of these problematic activities of TEPCO and also came to award extra delay compensation to victims.[97] However, it is doubtful whether such problematic attitudes of TEPCO have been totally reformed.

The most serious problem is the increasing number of cases in which TEPCO refuses to accept the decision of the Arbitration Center. TEPCO generally adopted the policy of respecting the settlement proposal of the Arbitration Center and reached settlement with arbitration applicants. Yet, in some cases, TEPCO came to refuse the acceptance of the settlement proposals. For instance, when Namie town applied for arbitration for its 150,000 local residents asking for an increase in the amount of damages for psychological pain due to prolonged evacuation, the Arbitration Center put forth a settlement proposal to increase the amount of damage awarded for psychological pain for those residents

91 Ibid 14; Masao Takase, "Genpatsu ADR no toutatsuten to kadai [Remaining Issues for Alternative Dispute Resolution after the Fukushima Nuclear Accident]" (2015) 27:3 *Fukushima Daigaku Gyosei Shakai Ronshu* 1.

92 Ibid.

93 There are three coordinating committee members, 278 arbitration members, 184 investigators, and 151 administrative staff, a total of 619 staff, working as of 2017. Genshiryokusongaibaishou hunsoukaiketu Center [Nuclear Damage Award Dispute Resolution Center], Genshiryoku songaibaisho hunsoukaiketsu center katsudo jikkyo houkokusho [Nuclear Damage Award Dispute Resolution Centre Activity Report (MEXT March 2017) www.mext.go.jp/component/a_menu/science/detail/__icsFiles/afieldfile/2017/09/22/1374251_01_1.pdf accessed 1 January 2018. Most of the arbitration members and investigators are lawyers.

94 For example, the Center allowed the application by a group. As a result, the number of applications significantly increased. Ibid at 5.

95 Ibid 14. The Arbitration Center also published internal guidelines for their resolution, supplementing the Interim Guideline and providing some ideas on how items not listed in the Interim Guideline should be handled in the arbitration procedure and some of the arbitration contracts concluded between residents and TEPCO for providing some ideas for victims on how some issues were solved by the Arbitration Center. Genshuryoku songaibaisho hunsoukaiketsu center [Nuclear Damage Award Conflict Resolution Center], Soukatsu kijun nitsuite [On Guidelines], (MEXT) www.mext.go.jp/a_menu/genshi_baisho/jiko_baisho/detail/1329129.htm accessed 1 January 2018.

96 Genshiryoku songaibaisho hunsokaiketsu center [Nuclear Damage Award Dispute Resolution Center], Tokyo denryoku kabushiki geisha no taiou ni mondaino aru jirei no kouhyou nit suite [On Publication of Cases Where the Questionable Responses by TEPCO Were Found] (TEPCO) www.mext.go.jp/a_menu/genshi_baisho/jiko_baisho/detail/1329350.htm accessed 1 January 2018.

97 Ibid.

of 50,000 JPY (450 USD) in addition to 100,000 JPY (900 USD) articulated in the Interim Guideline. TEPCO refused to accept this proposal, however, insisting that this would lead to unfairness against all other evacuees who accepted the damage award and would undermine the basic framework established by the Interim Guideline.[98] The Arbitration Center thus had to issue a statement calling for TEPCO to honor the settlement proposal.[99]

In response, the Japan Federation of Bar Association proposed to make the decision of the Arbitration Center binding upon TEPCO.[100] This proposal will make the Arbitration Center much like the administrative tribunal. Although it would not be permissible to deprive TEPCO of the right to file objection and challenge the decision of the tribunal, this would surely be beneficial for local residents because it will be TEPCO rather than the victims that need to go to the courts and prove that the decision was illegal. On the other hand, if it is an adjudicatory tribunal, it will have to abide by the formal adjudicative procedure, making the process much more formal, burdensome, and time-consuming.

5.3.8 Lawsuits

If applicants were unhappy with arbitration or if they preferred a judicial resolution, they had to file suits in court. It is still too early to assess how many local residents will file suits seeking damages from TEPCO and the government. In March 2013, several lawsuits had already been filed against TEPCO and the government in Tokyo and Fukushima by local residents who were forced to evacuate as a result of the nuclear accident.[101] Apparently, these plaintiffs were frustrated by long delays in the arbitration procedure and the accompanying paperwork, inflexibility in refusals to take individual circumstances into consideration, and generally low compensation awards. Numbers of plaintiffs and similar lawsuits of

98 "Wakaian kyohi no touden wo hihan: Hunsoukaiketsu senter, Baisho zougaku meguri [Conflict Resolution Criticizes TEPCO for Its Refusal to Accept Settlement Proposal to Increase the Damage Award]" (*Nihonkeizai Shimbun* 20 December 2015) www.nikkei.com/article/DGXLZO95362790Q5A221C1000000/ accessed 1 January 2018.

99 Ibid; Nuclear Damage Dispute Resolution Center, Coordinating Committee, Tokyo denryoku no wakaian eno taiou nitaisuru soukatsuiinkai shoken [Statement of the Coordinating Committee on TEPCO's Response to Settlement Proposal] (MEXT 4 August 2014) www.mext.go.jp/component/a_menu/science/detail/__icsFiles/afieldfile/2016/04/27/1329124_001_1.pdf accessed 1 January 2018.

100 Nihon bengoshi rengoukai [Japan Federation of Bar Associations], Fukushima daiichi genshiryoku hatsudensho jikohigaisha nitaisuru higaikaihuku to houtekishienwo motomeru ikensho [Opinion Calling for Restoration of Damages to the Victims of the Fukushima Nuclear Power Plant Accident and Their Legal Aid] (JFBA 19 March 2015) www.nichibenren.or.jp/library/ja/opinion/report/data/2015/opinion_150319_3.pdf accessed 1 January 2018. Professor Takase supports this proposal. Takase (n 91).

101 "Genpatsu hinansha no shuudan sosho: Genkokujumin 1.2man nin cho [Joint Litigation of Nuclear Accident Evacuees: The Number of Plaintiff Now Reaches over 12,000]" (*Nihonkeizai Shimbun* 18 March 2017) www.nikkei.com/article/DGXLASDG17HGI_X10C17A3EA3000/ accessed 1 January 2018.

evacuees significantly increased over the years.[102] The farmers and fishermen who suffered serious losses might also bring lawsuits.[103] Moreover, and sadly, some local residents actually died amid the chaos of evacuation. Family members surviving such persons might also move to seek damages.[104]

The Diet passed the Act on Special Treatment of Nuclear Damage Awards Dispute Arising from the Great East Japan Earthquake Disaster That Are Using the Arbitration Mediation Procedure of the Nuclear Damage Award Conflict Resolution Commission in order to Suspend the Application of the Statute of Limitations,[105] suspending the statute of limitations as it relates to nuclear damage award disputes in which arbitration has been filed for. Normally, the statute of limitations for tort claims excludes suits seeking damages that are brought more than three years after a victim has learned of the damages and the person responsible or 20 years after the tort.[106] However, the arbitration process is very slow, giving rise to the possibility that the statute of limitations will preclude damage actions from being brought in court if damage arbitration takes longer than the limitation period. The Japanese government believed that suspension of the statute of limitations was necessary to encourage wider use of the arbitration procedure. Now, when local residents file a suit within one month of arbitration, the suit is regarded as having been filed at the time the application for arbitration was filed.[107]

102 The total number of plaintiffs reached over 12,000. Ibid.

103 One family surviving a farmer who committed suicide because he lost his business as a result of the nuclear accident reached a settlement through ADR procedure. "Genpatsu baisho, jisatsude hatsuno wakai: Touden to Fukushima no nougyoudansei [First Nuclear Damage Settlement for A Person Who Committed Suicide: TEPCO and Fukushima Male Farmer]," (*Nihonkeizai Shimbun* 3 June 2013) www.nikkei.com/article/DGXNASDG03041_T00C13A6CR8000/ accessed 1 January 2018. The surviving family of a woman who had evacuated because of the accident and committed suicide due to depression was awarded 49 million JPY (445,000 USD) by the court. "Genpatsu de jisatsu, Touden ni 4900man en baishoumeirei—Fukushima chisai [Fukushima District Court Ordered TEPCO to Pay 49 million JPY for Evacuee Who Committed Suicide]" (*Nihonkeizai Shimbun* 26 August 2014) www.nikkei.com/article/DGXLASFK26H0O_W4A820C1000000/ accessed 1 January 2018.

104 Families of the patients who had been hospitalized in Futaba hospitals and died after being forced to evacuate were also awarded damages by the courts. "Tokyo denryokuni 3100man en baisho meirei, Fukushima ken no Hutaba byouin, hinannno kanja shiboude [TEPCO Was Ordered to Pay 31 Million JPY for Patients Who Were Forced to Evacuate from the Futaba Hospital]" (*Huffington Post* 27 April 2016) www.huffingtonpost.jp/2016/04/27/compensation-fukushima-daiichi-nuclear-power-plant_n_9783670.html accessed 1 January 2018. Families of the other Futaba Hospital patients reached settlements with TEPCO. "Hinan kanja shibou, Touden to wakai, Futaba byouin sosho [Families of the Futaba Hospital Patients Who Died after Evacuation Reached Settlements with TEPCO]" (*Nihonkeizai Shimbun* 19 November 2016) www.nikkei.com/article/DGXLASDG19H0X_Z11C16A1000000/ accessed 1 January 2018.

105 Higashinihon daishinsai nikakawaru genshiryoku songaibaishou hunsou ni tsuite no genshiryoku songaibaishou hunsou shinsakai niyoru wakai chuukai tetuduki no riyou ni kakawaru jikou no chuudan no tokurei ni kansuru hōritsu [Act on Special Treatment of Nuclear Damage Awards Dispute Arising from the Great East Japan Earthquake Disaster That Are Using the Arbitration Mediation Procedure of the Nuclear Damage Award Dispute Resolution Commission in order to Suspend the Applicability of the Statute of Limitations], Law no 32 of 2013 (Nuclear Damage ADR Time Limitation Suspension Act).

106 Minpō [Civil C.], art 724.

107 Nuclear Damage ADR Time Limitation Suspension Act (n 105) art 2.

However, the exception to the limitation period provided for in this statute is only applicable for disputes in which application for arbitration has been filed. All local residents who have not filed arbitration claims would still be precluded from suing TEPCO at the point when three years have passed since the accident. Lawyers were thus advocating that the applicability of the statute of limitations be excluded altogether for all damage claims resulting from the Fukushima accident.[108] In response, a resolution was added in the House of Councilors enabling all disaster victims to seek redress, and to do so for a sufficient length of time.[109]

Eventually, the Diet passed the Act concerning the Measures to Accomplish the Prompt and Sufficient Damage Award for Nuclear Damages Caused as a Result of the Nuclear Power Plant Accident during the Great East Japan Earthquake Disaster and Special Treatment of the Statute of Limitations on the Nuclear Damages[110] to extend the statute of limitation for tort damage claims resulting from the Fukushima nuclear power plant accident to ten years from the regular three years after the plaintiff found the damage and assailant and also modified the preclusion of tort claim after 20 years to start from the time damage was caused and not from the time of tort.[111]

5.3.9 Splitting court judgments

Eventually, more than 12,000 residents joined the suit against TEPCO and the government seeking damage awards.[112] On 17 March 2017, the Maebashi District Court handed down the first judgment in these lawsuits and ordered TEPCO and the government to pay 38.5 million JPY (35,0000 USD) in total to 62 residents.[113] The court found that TEPCO could have anticipated a much higher tsunami and could have adopted countermeasures but failed out of economic consideration. The government was also held liable for its negligent failure to legally mandate TEPCO to adopt countermeasures. The plaintiffs are evacuees from the

108 Nihon bengoshi rengoukai [Japan Federation of Bar Associations], Tokyo denryoku Fukushima daiichi genshiryoku hatsudensho jiko niyoru songaibaishou seikyuken no shoumetsu jikō nitsuite tokubetsu no rippou sochi wo motomeru ikensho [Opinion Calling for a Special Legislative Measure with respect to Statute of Limitations on Damage Award Claims Resulting from the Fukushima No 1 Nuclear Power Plant Accident of TEPCO] (JFBA 18 April 2013) www.nichibenren.or.jp/library/ja/opinion/report/data/2013/opinion_130418.pdf accessed 1 January 2018.

109 Nuclear Damage ADR Time Limitation Suspension Act (n 105) appendix art 1.

110 Higashinihon daishinsai ni okeru genshiryoku hatsudensho no jiko niyori shoujita genshiryoku songai ni kakawaru souki katsu kakujitsuna baishou wo jitsugen surutame no sochi oyobi tougai genshiryoku songai ni kakawaru baishou seikyuken no shoumetsu jikōtō no tokurei ni kansuru hōritsu [Act concerning Measures to Accomplish the Prompt and Sufficient Damage Award for Nuclear Damages Caused as a Result of the Nuclear Power Plant Accident during the Great East Japan Earthquake Disaster and Special Treatment of the Statute of Limitations on the Nuclear Damages], Law no 97 of 2013.

111 Ibid art 3.

112 n 102.

113 Maebashi chihō saibansho [Maebashi Dist Ct] 17 March 2017, 2339 *Hanrei Jihō* 4.

evacuation instruction zone as well as voluntary evacuees who had already received some compensation according to guidelines but claimed that they were entitled to more. But the total number of plaintiffs was 137 and they were demanding 1.5 billion JPY (13 million USD) in total. Although the court admitted the liability of both TEPCO and the government, the amount awarded was far lower.

On the other hand, on 22 September 2017, the Chiba District Court held TEPCO liable and ordered it to pay 376 million JPY (3.42 million USD) to 42 residents including four residents who evacuated outside of the "evacuation instruction zone."[114] But the Chiba District Court denied the liability of the government. Even based on the predictability of the very powerful tsunami, it was determined that the government did not have to take countermeasures immediately and there was no guarantee that any countermeasures could have prevented the accident. It specifically thought that there was no guarantee that the installation of a waterproof emergency generator could have prevented the accident. The Chiba District Court thus concluded that the failure to require additional countermeasures was not grossly unreasonable to render it unlawful for the purpose of the Government Liability Act.

On 10 October 2017, however, the Fukushima District Court again held TEPCO liable and ordered them to pay 490 million JPY (4.45 million USD) to some 2,900 residents.[115] The Fukushima District Court also held that the government could have foreseen the possibility of the very powerful tsunami and the vulnerability of the emergency generator was a violation of the Nuclear Reactor Regulation Act, and the government should have exercised the regulatory power to correct that violation. The failure of the government to exercise its regulatory power was grossly unreasonable and the government should be liable for damages.

Therefore, all three courts agree that TEPCO was liable for damages but there is still no consensus on the liability of the government.

5.3.10 How long could the damage award continue after lifting the evacuation instruction?

After decontamination, an increasing number of residents were allowed to return within the evacuation instruction removal preparation zone. The government decided to lift the evacuation instruction in the "evacuation instruction removal preparation zone" and the "residence restriction zone" by March 2017, six years after the Fukushima accident.[116] The evacuees are now facing the very

114 Chiba chihō saibansho [Chiba Dist Ct] 22 September 2017, TKC Database.

115 Fukushima chihō saibansho [Fukushima Dist. Ct.] 10 October 2017, TKC Database.

116 Nuclear Disaster Response Headquarters, Genshiryoku saigai karano Fukushima hukkou no kasoku nimukete (kantei) [Toward Acceleration of Fukushima Reconstruction from Nuclear Disaster (Revised)] (METI 12 June 2015) www.meti.go.jp/earthquake/nuclear/kinkyu/pdf/2015/0612_02.pdf accessed 1 January 2018 (Revised Acceleration Plan). The government lifted the evacuation instruction in four nearby towns except for the "no-return zone." "Hinan shiji kaijo: 31 nitini Namie, Iitate, Kawamata [Evacuation Instruction Will Be Lifted on 31 March in Namie, Iitate, and Kawamata]" (*Mainichi Shimbun* 30 March 2017) https://mainichi.jp/articles/20170331/k00/00m/040/114000c accessed 1 January 2018.

difficult choice of whether to go back or stay with the evacuation instruction lifted.[117] A very big concern for evacuees is how long the damage award will continue after lifting the evacuation instruction. The Nuclear Damage Award Dispute Resolution Commission has already hinted that the monthly damage award for psychological pain will continue for one year after the lifting of the evacuation instruction.[118] This would force evacuees to return during one year after the lifting of the instruction.

In light of the prospect that some residents would not return even six years after the accident, the government was forced to clarify the prospect of payment of compensation from lifting the evacuation instruction. As a result, the fourth supplement to the Interim Guideline published on 26 December 2015, revised on 28 January 2016, and on 31 January 2017, decided to pay residents who used to live in the "no-return zone" and Ohkuma and Futaba residents living in the "residence restriction zone" and "evacuation instruction removal preparation zone" a lump sum of 10 million JPY (90,000 USD) deduced by the monthly amount of the future portion of 6 million JPY (54,000 USD) after March 2016 and to pay the rest of the evacuees 100,000 JPY (900 USD) per month as a damage payment for psychological pain.[119] The fourth supplement also clarified the duration residents could receive damage payment for evacuation costs to last after the lifting of evacuation instructions until their return or movement, but if the residents failed to return or move during a reasonable period of time, then the payment would cover only the reasonable period.[120] Furthermore, payment for psychological pain and evacuation costs does not cover the time period after the proper period from the lifting of the evacuation instruction and that proper period of time means basically one year.[121] As a result, the damage payment for psychological pain was to end by March 2018.

117 Fukushima Prefecture used to provide free housing support for voluntary evacuees outside of the "evacuation instruction zone." But it decided to terminate this service by March 2017. Fukushima Prefecture, Oukyu kasetsu juutaku (kasetsu/kariage) no kyuyokikan nitsuite [On the Period of Provision of Temporary Place to Stay] (Reconstruction Agency) www.reconstruction.go.jp/topics/main-cat2/sub-cat2-1/kyoutsuu02_11hinanmoto.pdf accessed 1 January 2018.

118 "Fukuahima no hinan shiji 17nen3gatsu madeni kaijo, seihuga houshin [The Government Plan to Cancel Evacuation Instruction by March 2017 for Fukushima Residents]" (*Nihonkeizai Shimbun* 13 June 2015) www.nikkei.com/article/DGXLASDG12H7Z_S5A610C1CR8000/ accessed 1 January 2018.

119 Fourth supplement (n 79) 4. As a result, the evacuees from the "no-return zone" and Ohkuma and Futaba residents who used to live in the "residence restriction zone" or the "evacuation instruction removal preparation zone" were practically granted 7.5 million JPY (6,800 USD) until May 2017. Thereafter, the lump sum of 7 million JPY (64,000 USD) is being paid for them as a compensation for "being forced to lose the familiar community" (*hurusato soushitsu*). For other evacuees, the compensation of 100,000 JPY (900 USD) is being paid per month up to 8.5 million JPY (77,000 USD) until March 2018. TEPCO proposed that the Fukushima Prefecture should provide funds for the Prefecture after April 2018 to assist the payment of temporary housings for evacuees rather than paying damage awards to individual evacuees. Touden, yachin baisho wo jisshitsu encho: Fukushima-ken no shin jigyou ni shikin [TEPCO Substantially Continue the Payment for Rent: Providing Funds for the New Project of the Fukushima Prefecture] (*Jiji* 17 January 2018) www.jiji.com/jc/article?k=2018011701069&g=eco accessed 8 March 2018; n 172.

120 Ibid.

121 Ibid 4–5.

Consequently, the evacuees were guaranteed to receive damage payments for psychological pain and for evacuation even after the lifting of the evacuation instruction. But it became clear that the damage payment would not last forever. Now, almost all evacuation instructions are lifted as of the end of March 2017, and there are still many evacuees left undecided whether to return or to remain. The deadline for compensation will have a significant impact on the fate of these evacuees.

Moreover, TEPCO also decided to terminate the across the board payment due to inability to work for evacuees as of the end of February 2015.[122] TEPCO also made clear that any damages to evacuees after their return for their inability to work or continue previous work would be compensated during the 12 months after the start of damages.[123] Also based on the revised government plan, TEPCO decided to extend two years of damage awards to business damages from March 2015 until February 2017 as a lump sum payment.[124] Thereafter, TEPCO would pay damages individually based upon individual proof.

5.4 Support for TEPCO

5.4.1 TEPCO's total amount of liability

The total damages to be paid are still uncertain. The central government estimated that total damage awards would reach 7.9 trillion JPY (71.8 billion USD).[125] The total amount of money needed for damage awards, decommissioning of the reactors, decontamination, and other matters would reach 21.5 trillion JPY (195 billion USD).[126]

It is apparent that TEPCO alone cannot cover all these burdens. If TEPCO were forced to pay all these burdens, it may go bankrupt and become unable to pay damages to all the victims and also be unable to supply power to all residents in the Kanto Region, including Tokyo. Some kind of support system for TEPCO became necessary.

5.4.2 New scheme to support TEPCO

The central government thus decided to establish a new scheme to assist TEPCO in paying out damage awards.[127] In order to implement this scheme,

122 TEPCO, Press Release (TEPCO 24 February 2014) www.tepco.co.jp/cc/press/2014/1234445_5851.html accessed 1 January 2018.

123 Ibid.

124 TEPCO, Press Release (TEPCO 17 June 2015) www.tepco.co.jp/cc/press/2015/1252626_6818.html accessed 1 January 2018.

125 "Fukushima hairo/baishohi 21.5chouen ni baizou: Keisashou ga kouhyou [TEPCO's Burden for Damage Award and Decommissioning Will Reach 21.5 Trillion JPY: The Ministry of Economy, Trade and Industry Says]" (*Nihonkeizai Shimbun* 9 December 2016) www.nikkei.com/article/DGXLASFS09H0H_Z01C16A2000000/ accessed 1 January 2018.

126 Ibid.

127 Ministry of Economy, Trade and Industry, Genshiryoku hatsudensho jiko keizaihigai taiou team [Team concerning Economic Damages Resulting from Nuclear Power Plant Accident], Decision of the Relevant Cabinet Ministers (METI 13 May 2011) www.meti.go.jp/earthquake/nuclear/pdf/songaibaisho_110513_01.pdf accessed 1 January 2018. *See* Hatsuru Morita, "Rescuing Victims and Rescuing TEPCO: A Legal and Political Analysis of the TEPCO Bailout" (2012) 34 *Zeitschrift für Japanisches Recht* [Journal of .Japanese Law] 23.

the Diet passed the Nuclear Damage Award Support Organization Act on 3 August 2011.[128]

The new scheme established a new fund under the umbrella of the "Nuclear Damage Award Support Organization" (*Genshiryoku songai baisho shien kikō*) with mandatory contributions from all nuclear power operators.[129] This fund can be used to assist nuclear power companies in paying damages in the event of an accident.[130] No upper limit was set on assistance from this new fund. The Organization has to make a special business plan for any power company that receives its support and the approval of the central government is also a prerequisite.[131] The central government would supervise the assisted nuclear power company to ensure that the management would abide by the approved special business plan[132] and, in turn, the company would carry an obligation to repay special contributions, according to its profits.[133] The central government will support the Organization by issuing a bond[134] or by securing appropriate obligations in the event the Organization borrows money from financial institutions or issues its own bond.[135] If such assistance carries the possibility of generating serious problems in Japanese society or the national economy (by interrupting the stable supply of electricity or by imposing too great a burden on consumers), the central government would step in.[136]

TEPCO's damage awards were to be based on this statute with the government providing support as necessary.[137] Since TEPCO had to rely upon non-nuclear power to generate electricity, its costs naturally increased. TEPCO thus wanted to increase the electricity fees it charged its customers. However, the proposed electricity charge hikes outraged the public because many believed that TEPCO was simply transferring costs associated with its failure to operate the nuclear power plant safely onto its consumers. The central government thus reduced the proposed rate hikes, while reluctantly approving an electricity charge hike for

128 Genshiryoku songai baishou shien kikōhō [Nuclear Damage Award Support Organization Act], Law no 94 of 2011. In 2014, the Nuclear Damage Award Support Organization was renamed to Nuclear Damage Award and Decommissioning Support Organization (Genshiryoku sonbai baisho/hairotō shien kikō) after the enactment of the Genshiryoku songai baisho shien kikohō no ichibuwo kaiseisuru hōritsu [Act to Amend Parts of the Nuclear Damage Award Support Organization Act], Law no 40 of 2014.

129 Genshiryoku songai baishou/hairotō shienkikohō [Nuclear Damage Award and Decommissioning Support Organization Act], Law no 94 of 2011, art 38.

130 Ibid art 41.

131 Ibid art 45.

132 Ibid art 47.

133 Ibid art 52.

134 Ibid art 48.

135 Ibid art 61.

136 Ibid art 68.

137 Each of the power companies that maintain the nuclear power plant needs to pay a general contribution based on the revenue in accordance with the capacity of the total nuclear power plants maintained. Agency for Natural Resource and Energy, Genshiryokujiko no baisho no sonae nikansuru hutan no arikata nitsuite [On the Allocation of Burden for the Preparation of the Nuclear Accident] (METI 29 November 2016) www.meti.go.jp/committee/sougouenergy/kihonseisaku/denryoku_system_kaikaku/zaimu/pdf/05_03_00.pdf accessed 1 January 2018.

corporations and individual households in order to sustain TEPCO's revenue.[138] How TEPCO will manage to pay out damage awards and the government's ultimate financial burden remain to be seen.[139] The central government has so far provided 4.9 trillion JPY (44.5 billion USD) to TEPCO for support.[140] The government has already provided the 9 trillion JPY (81 billion USD) government bond for support and TEPCO will be able to acquire sufficient funds by using the government bond.[141]

5.4.3 Best choice?

There remains a question of whether this was the best choice for the Japanese government. TEPCO could file for bankruptcy proceedings or a corporate rehabilitation application.[142] If TEPCO became bankrupt, the claims of the victims would not be given any priority and victims would not be able to recover any damages from TEPCO. Shareholders would be most significantly affected because the value of their shares would be wiped out. But the government could pay compensation directly to the victims and TEPCO could continue its operation to supply electricity to its customers. Under the approach adopted by the Japanese government, on the other hand, the government pays support to TEPCO and it is TEPCO that is then supposed to pay the damages. Shareholders are not penalized for their failure to check up on the company's activities. It appears that the Japanese government wanted to avoid paying compensation directly to the victims at any cost.

Moreover, while TEPCO was provided financial assistance from the Support Organization to pay out damage awards, the Support Organization itself is

138 TEPCO, Denkiryoukin no neage nitsuite [On Electricity Charge Hike] (TEPCO 11 May 2012), www.tepco.co.jp/cc/press/2012/1203333_1834.html accessed 1 January 2018; TEPCO, Denryokuryoukin no neage no ninka nitsuite [On Approval of Electricity Charge Hike] (TEPCO 25 July 2012) www.tepco.co.jp/cc/press/2012/1206853_1834.html accessed 1 January 2018.

139 The central government's plan was to acquire more than two thirds of all TEPCO stock, thereby practically nationalizing the company. "Touden, Jijitsujo kokuyuuka e: kanmin de 2chou-en shien [TEPCO Practically Nationalized: 2 Trillion JPY Support]" (*Asahi Shimbun* 21 December 2011) www.asahi.com/special/10005/TKY201112210209.html accessed 1 January 2018. TEPCO executives objected to the nationalization but in July 2012, the Nuclear Damage Award Support Organization provided TEPCO with 1 trillion JPY (90 billion USD) and acquired more than half of its voting shares, essentially nationalizing TEPCO. "Touden kokuyuukaga kanryou: Genbaikikou 1chouen shusshi [Nationalization of TEPCO Completed: Damage Support Organization Provided 1 Trillion Yen]" (*Nihonkeizai Shimbun* 31 July 2012) www.nikkei.com/article/DGXNASFS3100B_R30C12A7MM0000/ accessed 1 January 2018.

140 Board of Audit Japan, Tokyo denryoku kabusiki geisha ni kakawaru genshiryoku songai no baisho nikansuru kunino shientō no jisshi joukyou nikansuru kaikei kensa no kekka nitsuite [On the Result of Audit on the Government Support to TEPCO with respect to Payment of Nuclear Damages] (BAJ March 2015) http://report.jbaudit.go.jp/org/pdf/270323_zenbun_01.pdf accessed 1 January 2018 17.

141 Ibid.

142 Many indeed claim that the government should force TEPCO to file a bankruptcy application. "Toukyou denryoku wa bunkatsu/hatan shorisubekida [TEPCO Should File for Bankruptcy and Should Be Divided]" (*Toyokeizai* 9 December 2013) http://toyokeizai.net/articles/-/25810.

supported by the general burden shared by all nuclear power companies and special burden to be paid by the power company that received the financial assistance. The Board of Audit Japan calculated how long it would take to collect all the tax money the government provided to help TEPCO to pay damage awards and suggested that it would take up to 30 years to collect the full amount.[143] If the power company to receive the assistance were a much smaller company compared with TEPCO, it would have required still more years to collect, and thus some criticize that this system will not be usable in the future for other power companies.[144]

5.5 Allowing local residents to return

Fourth, with the progress of the containment effort, the Japanese government needed to prepare for a return of evacuees. Instead of the previous evacuation plan, it had to come up with a new plan to allow gradual return. However, before allowing the return, the government must make sure that the environment is sufficiently decontaminated for the evacuees to return home safely. Moreover, the government needs to make sure that local residents can live without fear.

5.5.1 Government assistance to evacuees

As of April 2017, some 52,000 residents were classified as evacuees to other cities in Fukushima and to other prefectures from Fukushima.[145] Among them, roughly 24,000 residents are evacuees from the "no-return zone."[146] Many evacuees had to spend years in temporary housing before they were allowed to return to their homes. Some will not even be allowed to return at all. Many are still wondering whether to return even when they are allowed to. Most evacuees were and are living in other municipalities in Fukushima Prefecture but some have been forced to live in other prefectures.[147] For many residents who evacuated as a group, temporary town offices have been established where they were evacuated to, to serve local residents living away from home.

143 Board of Audit Japan (n 140) 57, 186.

144 Junko Takeuchi, Genshiryoku songai baishou seido no kadai to kousatu [Agenda for Nuclear Damage Award System], International Environmental Economic Institute (IEEI) http://ieei.or.jp/wp-content/uploads/2014/03/edd12711d8863bbd6d675cc3c76b8010.pdf accessed 1 January 2018.

145 Reconstruction Agency, Fukushima hukkou kasokuka eno torikumi [Measures to accelerate the Reconstruction of Fukushima] (Reconstruction Agency December 2017) www.reconstruction.go.jp/portal/chiiki/hukkoukyoku/fukusima/material/20171227_torikumi-fukusima.pdf accessed 1 January 2018 3.

146 Ibid.

147 Roughly 20,000 residents are living in other communities in Fukushima, while roughly 35,000 residents are living outside of Fukushima. Ibid 2.

It was imperative for the central government to introduce various measures to assist evacuees.[148] As an example, the central government made sure that evacuees were able to receive government assistance regardless of where they decided to live or were relocated to.[149] Further, since local residents were told to evacuate with little time to collect personal belongings and because they were concerned about their homes, most were later allowed to return home temporarily under strict conditions.[150]

In 2012, the Diet passed the Fukushima Nuclear Accident Victim Support Act[151] to declare the government assistance policy for Fukushima evacuees. The objective of this Act is to promote various disaster life support policies to vindicate and support the life of disaster victims, thereby contributing to the dissipation of fear and achievement of a stable life for disaster victims in light of the facts of the accident. These include that:

> There have been widespread radioactive materials produced by the Fukushima nuclear power plant accident, and residents who are living or used to live in areas where radiation levels exceed the maximum limit, or who have been forced to evacuate because of the government instruction, or who are in similar situations, have concerns about their health. They suffer various burdens because of insufficient scientific evidence on the impact of radiation materials to human health, and there is a need to care especially for the children.[152]

Then the Act declares the fundamental disaster life support ideals as requiring that accurate information on the disaster and reconstruction needed to be provided. The Act states that the decision of the disaster victims to choose whether to reside within the support area, to move into another area, or to return to their previous residence, must be a free choice and should be supported properly. Utmost attempts must also be made to dissipate public fear about the impact of

148 The Diet passed the statute to allow municipal governments to handle administrative matters pertaining to evacuees in offices where these evacuees are located. Higashinihon daishinsai niokeru genshiryoku hatsudensho no jiko niyoru saigai ni taisho surutame no hinan jūmin ni kakawaru jimushori no tokurei oyobi jūsho itensha ni kakawaru sochi ni kansuru hōrtisu [Act concerning Special Treatment of Administrative Matters Relating to Evacuees and Those Who Changed Residence as a Result of the Nuclear Power Plant Accident following the Great East Japan Earthquake], Law no 98 of 2011.

149 Tokyo denryoku genshiryoku jiko niyori hisaishita kodomo wo hajimetosuru jumintō no seikatsu wo mamori sasaeru tameno hisaisha no seikatsu shientōni kansuru sesaku no suishin ni kansuru hōritsu [Act concerning Facilitation of Various Life Support Measures for Evacuees in order to Protect and Assist Residents including Children Who Suffered from the Disaster because of TEPCO's Nuclear Accident], Law no 48, 2012 (Fukushima Nuclear Accident Victim Support Act).

150 "Genpatsu 3km ken ni ichiji kitaku: Jikokara 5kagetuhan buri [Temporary Visit Started Even within 3 km Radius from the Nuclear Power Plant: Almost Five and a Half Months Passed]" (*Asahi Shimbun* 26 August 2011) www.asahi.com/special/10005/TKY201108260146.html accessed 1 January 2018.

151 Fukushima Nuclear Accident Victim Support Act (n 149).

152 Ibid art 1.

radiation on the disaster victims' health as soon as possible, and proper consideration needs to be provided to prevent any unreasonable discrimination against disaster victims. Furthermore, special consideration needs to be paid to children and pregnant women including the reduction of radiation exposure and full health management in light of the susceptibility of children and fetuses to radiation impact, and full enforcement of support so long as the necessity is required, due to the long-term impact of radiation on health.[153]

The central government is then obliged to establish comprehensive disaster life support measures and enforce them[154] and adopt the necessary legal and budgetary measures to enforce them.[155] It is also mandated to establish fundamental policies on the promotion of disaster life support measures based on the fundamental ideals declared.[156] It is further mandated to investigate the contamination of the environment[157] and to take necessary measures to enforce decontamination continuously and swiftly.[158] Finally, the government is obliged to provide support to victims living inside the "support areas," showing radiation less than the impermissible level but beyond the maximum level,[159] victims living outside of these support areas,[160] disaster victims who have returned to their previous residence,[161] and evacuees from the "evacuation instruction zone."[162]

On the other hand, Fukushima evacuees have faced various subtle discrimination. One survey reported that 62% of the Fukushima evacuees experienced or witnessed discrimination or harassment.[163] Some of the Fukushima evacuees have been called "contagious" or accused of receiving compensation without work. Some were refused by hotels for stays. However, there is no comprehensive statutory ban on private discrimination in Japan.[164]

153 Ibid art 2.
154 Ibid art 3.
155 Ibid art 4.
156 Ibid art 5.
157 Ibid art 6.
158 Ibid art 7.
159 Ibid art 8.
160 Ibid art 9.
161 Ibid art 10.
162 Ibid art 11.
163 "Genpatsujiko hinansakide ijimeya sabetsu aru 62%: Kyodou chousa [Joint Survey Revealed 62% of the Evacuees Faced or Witnessed Discrimination or Harassment]" (*Asahi Shimbun* 25 February 2017), www.asahi.com/articles/ASK2N7VK8K2NUGTB014.html accessed 1 January 2018.
164 The Ministry of Health, Labor and Welfare issued a notification to local government to make sure that hotels would not refuse Fukushima residents because hotels are banned from private discrimination. Ministry of Health, Labor and Welfare, Fukushima genshiryoku hatsudensho jiko niyoru hinansha nikansuru ryokangyousha eno shuchi nitsuite [On Notification to Hotels with respect to the Acceptance of Fukushima Evacuees due to Nuclear Accident] (MHLW 19 March 2011) www.mhlw.go.jp/stf/houdou/2r98520000019yl1-att/2r98520000019z11.pdf accessed 1 January 2018; Ryokangyohō [Hotel Business Act], Law no 138 of 1948, art 5. There have been some conflicts between evacuees and original residents of the host communities. Evacuees do not pay local tax to host communities while receiving services and they are receiving compensation from TEPCO without work. Federica Ranghieri & Mikio Ishiwatari (eds), *Learning from Mega Disasters: Lessons from the Great East Japan Earthquake* (World Bank 2014) 333.

5.5.2 Allowing local residents to return home

Upon containment of the nuclear accident, the central government moved to modify the evacuation plan and allow some local residents to return to their homes. Some communities close to the plant have been classified as no-go zones for the long term and residents will not be allowed to return ("no-return zone"). However, with respect to other areas, after removing radioactive materials from the environment, the government decided to allow residents to return home.[165] Areas with radiation contamination levels of less than 20 mSv/year, were classified as "evacuation instruction removal preparation zones," while areas measuring more than 20 mSv/year were classified as "residence restriction zones" to further promote decontamination. Areas with radiation contamination levels above 50 mSv/year were classified as "no-return zones" to preclude the return of residents for a long period of time.

After issuing the above new classifications, the central government moved to modify evacuation zones gradually. As a result, the volume of land designated as being within an evacuation instruction zone has gradually been narrowed down and converted into "residence restriction zone" and "evacuation instruction removal preparation zone." And finally, on 31 March 2017 and on 1 April 2017, as announced, the evacuation instruction in most of the nearby communities was lifted, leaving only "no-return zone" out of reach for local residents.[166]

However, throughout the duration of the evacuations, which have been going on for more than six years and counting, many evacuees have grown accustomed to living in different communities and might not be willing to go back. Moreover, even if decontamination is accomplished and radiation levels are reduced, many residents have serious concerns over possible health impacts related to living in their former communities and homes. Young families are especially concerned over possible health impacts on their small children. Furthermore, even if they are able to return, there are legitimate concerns over job prospects in many of these communities. In November 2011, 26.9% of the evacuees from the town of Futaba were already indicating that they would not return, though 73% expressed a wish

165 Nuclear Disaster Response Headquarters, Step 2 no kanryou wo uketa keikai kuiki oyobi hinanshiji kuiki no minaoshi ni kansuru kihonteki kangaekata oyobi kongo no kentou kadai nitsuite [Fundamental Perspective and Future Agenda for Reconsideration of Hazardous Areas and Evacuation Instruction Areas with the Completion of Step 2] (METI 26 December 2011) www.meti.go.jp/earthquake/nuclear/pdf/111226_01a.pdf accessed 1 January 2018.

166 Nuclear Disaster Countermeasure Headquarter, Namie cho/ Tomioka cho niokeru hinansijikuiki no kaijo nituite [On Lifting Evacuation Instruction in Namie Town and Tomioka Town] (METI 10 March 2017) www.meti.go.jp/earthquake/nuclear/kinkyu/hinanshiji/2017/pdf/0310_01a.pdf accessed 1 January 2018. The current status of each community can be found in Reconstruction Agency (n 1) 20. The "hazard zone" designation was lifted for the Tomioka, Namie, Naraha, Ohkuma as well as Futaba by 28 May 2013. Ministry of Economy, Trade and Industry, Koremadeno hinan shijitō nikansuru oshirase [Evacuation Instruction in the Past] (METI) www.meti.go.jp/earthquake/nuclear/hinan_history.html accessed 1 March 2018. There is no longer any "hazard zone."

that they would like to return.[167] With the lifting of the evacuation instruction in most of the evacuation instruction preparation zones and residence restriction zones in March 2017, it was estimated that fewer than 10% of the local residents would return.[168]

5.5.3 Difficult choices for evacuees

The central government and Fukushima prefecture are committed to encouraging evacuees to return. For instance, voluntary evacuees outside of the evacuation instruction zone were provided with free housing to stay outside of Fukushima but this benefit was terminated as of 31 March 2017.[169] Most of the more than 4,700 voluntary evacuees want to stay where they are living[170] but they might be forced to pay for the housing, or they could be evicted.[171]

Fukushima Prefecture also cast doubt on how long it could provide free temporary places to stay for evacuees from evacuation instruction zones after lifting the evacuation instruction.[172] With the end of the evacuation instruction in March 2017, and especially in light of the deadline for TEPCO's damage payment for psychological pain due to evacuation, it is now unclear how long the government subsidy to evacuees who were forced to evacuate because of the evacuation instruction could be provided after its lifting.

167 "Hurusato modoritai 73%, modoranai wa 26%: Futabagun jumin [Residents of Futaba County Indicate that 73% Want to Return, While 26% Do Not]" (*Fukushima Minpo* 9 November 2011) www.minpo.jp/pub/topics/jishin2011/2011/11/post_2370.html accessed 1 January 2018; 52.3% of evacuees under the age of 35 indicated they did not want to return.

168 "Hinanshiji kaijo: 31nichi ni Namie, Iitate, Kawamata, kikan wa 1wari miman [Evacuation Instruction Will Be Lifted in Namie, Iitate and Kawamata on 31 March: Fewer Than 10% of Previous Residents Will Return]" (*Mainich Shimbun* 30 March 2017) https://mainichi.jp/articles/20170331/k00/00m/040/114000c accessed 1 January 2018.

169 n 117.

170 "Genpatsu jiko no jishu hinansha, yaku 8wariga kengaiseikatsu keizoku [Roughly 80% of Voluntary Evacuees outside of Fukushima Want to Continue Living outside]" (*Nihonkeizai Shimbun* 25 April 2017) www.nikkei.com/article/DGXLZO15676060U7A420C1L01000/ accessed 1 January 2018.

171 Some of the other prefectures where evacuees are staying have come to adopt some kind of measures to alleviate the burden of evacuees even after Fukushima Prefecture terminated the free provision.

172 Fukushima Prefecture (n 169). The provision of free temporary housing ended by March 2017 in some communities and will end in some other communities in March 2018. It is unclear whether any kind of assistance could be provided by the central government or by Fukushima Prefecture after March 2018. For the evacuees from Futaba, Ohkuma, Tomioka, Namie, and other communities, the free provision of temporary housing has been extended to March 2019 and the Fukushima Prefecture will again decide whether to extend it further. Fukushima Prefecture, Higashinihon daishinsai nikakawaru oukyu kasetsu jutaku no kyouyo kikan no encho nitsuite [Extension of Provision of Temporary Housings with Respect to Victims of Great East Japan Earthquake Disaster (Fukushima Prefecture 28 August 2017) www.pref.fukushima.lg.jp/sec/11050b/kyouyo.html accessed 8 March 2018. It looks as though the Fukushima Prefecture will use the fund provided by TEPCO to assist with temporary housing for these evacuees who are allowed to stay after April 2018; n 119.

In light of the declaration in the Fukushima Nuclear Accident Victim Support Act, leaving the decision to return to previous residences up to each of the victims and to respect their decisions, any measure that practically forces them to return would be inconsistent with the fundamental ideals in the Act.

5.5.4 Decontamination

In order for local residents to return, the government had to decontaminate the environment and reduce radiation exposure levels. The Diet passed the Special Measures Act on Countermeasures against Environmental Contamination by Radioactive Materials[173] in August 2011, thereby establishing a framework for decontamination.[174] Understandably, there were several controversial issues in need of resolution in order to facilitate decontamination efforts.

The first issue centered on deciding what level of radiation exposure would be acceptable to permit local residents to return. The central government considered the international standard and decided to focus on areas where radiation exposure was less than 20 mSv/year. It then suggested that the maximum exposure of 1 mSv/year should be set as a long-term goal for decontamination in these areas.[175] However, local residents insisted on a much stricter maximum standard and the fundamental plan adopted under the Act mandated that the central government focus on environmental decontamination where radiation exposure exceeded 1 mSv/year. As a result, it came to be viewed by the residents that areas would not be safe unless the maximum exposure level was reduced to 1 mSv/year.

This maximum standard is very demanding and led to various roadblocks to local residents being able to return to their homes.[176] Indeed, the international

173 Heisei 23nen 3gatu 11nichi ni hassenshita Tohoku chihō Taiheiyōoki jishin ni tomonau genshiryoku hatsudensho no jiko ni yori houshutsusareta houshasei busshitsu ni yoru kankyo no osen eno taisho ni kansuru tokubetsu sochihō [Special Measures Act concerning Countermeasures against Environmental Contamination by Radioactive Materials Released by the Nuclear Power Plant Accident as a Result of the off the Pacific Coast of Tohoku Earthquake of March 11, 2011], Law no 110 of 2011 (Radioactive Materials Contamination Special Measures Act). The cost of decontamination is to be paid by the government and the government will seek reimbursement from TEPCO afterwards.

174 MOE published guidelines for decontamination. Ministry of Environment, Josenkankei guideline no kouhyou nitsuite [On Publication of Decontamination Guidelines] (MOE 14 December 2011) www.env.go.jp/press/press.php?serial=14582 accessed 1 January 2018.

175 Ministry of Environment, Heisei 23nen 3gatu 11nichini hassenshita Tohoku chihō taiheiyōoki jishin ni tomonau genshiryoku hatsudensho no jiko niyori houshutsusareta houshasei busshitsu niyoru kankyo no osen eno taisho nikansuru tokubetsu sochihō: Kihon houshin [Fundamental Policy according to the Special Measures Act concerning Countermeasures against Environmental Contamination by Radioactive Materials Released by the Nuclear Power Plant Accident as a result of the Tohoku Region off the Pacific Coast Earthquake of 11 March 2011] (MOE 11 November 2011) www.env.go.jp/press/file_view.php?serial=18581&hou_id=14431 accessed 1 January 2018.

176 "Josen nenkan 1mSv no jukubaku: zero risk no wana [The Curse of 1mSv/year: Zero Risk Trap]" (*WEDGE* 23 May 2012) wedge.ismedia.jp/articles/-/1907 accessed 1 January 2018.

standard, while indicating that 1 mSv/year is the ideal, recommends that "a reference level in the lower part of the 1–20 mSv/year band be used to guide optimisation of protection in the recovery phase in which many operations will continue to improve the situation."[177] It does not require that the exposure level be reduced to 1 mSv/year before residents can be permitted to return home. On the other hand, many residents maintained the fear that the 20mSv/year limit was too lenient. They were concerned that higher radiation levels might still have negative health impacts.

Second, determining who should be responsible for decontamination also proved controversial. The government designated some communities as "special decontamination areas" (*josen tokubetsu chiiki*) where the central government has a direct responsibility for decontamination while the rest were designated as "intensive contamination survey areas" (*osen joukyou juten chousa chiiki*) to promote decontamination by local governments ("decontamination implementation zone" (*josen jisshi kuiki*) for the municipalities to implement decontamination).[178] This made it so that radiation exposure levels determined whether the central or local government was responsible for decontamination operations in any given community and former "hazard zones" and "planned evacuation zones" were included in the "special decontamination area." However, many local residents wanted the central government to play a greater leadership role in decontamination in other areas as well.

Third, many business operators saw decontamination as very lucrative work for the present and future and jumped at this new business opportunity head first. However, some did not have any relevant expertise and were simply exploiting local residents wishing to have their homes tended to as soon as possible. In some cases, therefore, decontamination work was neither sufficient nor effective in reducing exposure levels to a safe standard.[179] As a result, the central government was forced to tighten its supervision of qualifications for engaging in decontamination work.[180] Further, many workers were engaging in such work without sufficient protection against radiation exposure,

177 International Commission on Radiological Protection (ICRP), One Year Anniversary of the North-eastern Japan Earthquake, Tsunami, and Fukushima Dai-ichi Nuclear Accident (ICRP 12 March 2012) www.icrp.org/docs/Fukushima%20One%20Year%20Anniversary%20Message.pdf accessed 1 January 2018.

178 Ministry of Environment, Josen nitsuiteno kiso chishiki [Basic Information on Decontamination] (MOE) http://josen.env.go.jp/about/index.html accessed 1 January 2018.

179 "Tenuki josen oukou: Kaishu shita tuchi kawani touki [Improper Decontamination Is Rampant: Some Are Dumping Contaminated Soils into River]" (*Asahi Shimbun* 4 January 2013) www.asahi.com/special/10005/TKY201301040001.html accessed 1 January 2018.

180 Higashinihon daishinsai ni yori shoujita houshasei busshitsu ni yori osensareta dojoutō wo josensuru tameno gyoumutō ni kakawaru denrihoushasen shougai boushi kisoku [Regulation to Prevent Radiation Exposure for Workers Engaging in the Decontamination of Soil Contaminated by Radioactive Materials Due to the Great East Japan Earthquake Disaster], Ministry of Health, Labor and Welfare Order no 152 of 2011, required decontamination work operators to provide their workers with special decontamination training.

a serious violation of occupational safety law. The central government simply had no choice but to respond to calls for more stringent occupational safety regulations.[181]

Fourth, even if the central government and local government is eventually able to decontaminate all houses, streets, and residential neighborhoods, there are still broad swaths of mountain and forest that are unlikely to be decontaminated. Fallen leaves and trees show high levels of radiation exposure. When rains fall, running water brings higher levels of radiation back into residential areas. Decontamination of all of the natural environment is simply impossible and, even if it is possible, it would be extremely costly. The government therefore had to give up hope of decontamination of these natural environments.

Furthermore, decontamination produces a tremendous amount of contaminated waste. As discussed above, the government has extreme difficulty selecting final disposal sites and even interim storage sites for these materials. Problems related to finding interim storage sites are, in turn, confounding the task of finding temporary storage places for contaminated waste. As a result, decontamination work has not progressed as expected.

As of June 2017, the government claimed that all of the "special decontamination areas" to be decontaminated by the central government had been cleaned except for the "no-return zone,"[182] and other municipalities are continuing their decontamination efforts in other areas.[183] How effective this decontamination effort has been, however, is not evident.

5.5.5 Safety of returning residents

Long-term effects of the radiation leak remain unknown. Some residents were already exposed to higher than normal levels of radiation before and even

181 For instance, the Ministry of Environment set the limits on accumulative radiation exposure for workers, mandated the operator to measure the radiation exposure of workers, to check the radiation level of the work area in advance, to make a decontamination plan in advance and enforce it, to keep the records of radiation exposure in certain circumstances, to designate a supervisor, to provide medical checks in certain circumstances, to check the radiation level of clothing and equipment after work, and to provide protective gear. The Ministry of Health, Labor and Welfare, however, found violations of labor standards law and occupational health law at roughly half of the decontamination operators. Ministry of Health, Labor, and Welfare, Josen gyoumutō wo jisshi shiteiru jigyousha ni taisuru kantoku shidou no joukyotō nitsuite [On Supervision of Business Operators Engaging in Decontamination] (MHLW 18 January 2015) www.mhlw.go.jp/stf/houdou/2r9852000002szf4.html accessed 1 January 2018.

182 Reconstruction Agency, Kuni chokkatsu josen no genjou nitsuite [On Current Status of Decontamination by the Central Government] (Reconstruction Agency June 2017) www.reconstruction.go.jp/topics/main-cat8/sub-cat8-3/review_h29/rs29/32_kannkyou_setumei.pdf accessed 1 January 2018.

183 Ibid 21.

during evacuation.[184] Typically, most people are exposed to between 1 mSv and 3 mSv of radiation exposure per year from the natural environment.[185] A routine chest X-ray casts 50 µSv and a stomach X-ray 0.6 mSv.[186] A CT scan of the chest emits 6.9 mSv.[187] Flying aboard a jetliner causes elevated radiation exposure (5 µSv on a short flight and 30 µSv on a long intercontinental flight across the equator or more at higher latitudes).[188] Exposure to radiation of more than 10 Sv at one time could be fatal.[189] Exposure to more than 100 mSv can have various health impacts, but for exposure of less than 100 mSv, it is harder to say.[190] Some argue that health impacts are not scientifically proven but others argue that any exposure to radiation is accompanied by increased health risk. For a normal person, the upper limit of exposure in excess of natural exposure is 1 mSv/year and for professionals in the nuclear power industry the limit is 50 mS/year.[191]

The government has been trying to decontaminate the environment and reduce radiation levels to 1 mSv/year.[192] However, even with radiation exposure levels limited to less than 1 mSv/year, many residents fear such exposure carries serious health risks, including increased cancer risks, especially for babies

184 The World Nuclear Association reported that no harmful health effects were found among 195,345 residents living in the vicinity of the plant who were screened by the end of May 2011 and that all 1,080 children tested for thyroid gland exposure showed results within safe limits. Also, government checks of some 1,700 evacuated residents showed that two-thirds received external exposure within the normal international limit of 1 mSv/year, 98% were below 5 mSv/year and ten residents were exposed to more than 10 mSv/year. World Nuclear Association, Fukushima: Radiation Exposure (WNA) www.world-nuclear.org/info/Safety-and-Security/Safety-of-Plants/Appendices/Fukushima--Radiation-Exposure/ accessed 1 January 2018. The World Health Organization also reported that any additional cancer risks from radiation were small—extremely small, for the most part—and chiefly limited to those living closest to the plant. "Meltdown: Despite the Fear, the Health Risks from the Fukushima Accident Are Minimal' (*Time* 1 March 2013) http://science.time.com/2013/03/01/meltdown-despite-the-fear-the-health-risks-from-the-fukushima-accident-are-minimal/#ixzz2PG4MHblM accessed 1 January 2018.

185 The average annual radiation exposure is 3.1 mSv/year. U.S. Nuclear Regulatory Commission (NRC), Fact Sheet on Biological Effects of Radiation, NRC www.nrc.gov/reading-rm/doc-collections/fact-sheets/bio-effects-radiation.html accessed 1 January 2018.

186 Japan National Tourism Organization, Japan Travel Updates after 3.11 Earthquake (JNTO) www.jnto.go.jp/eq/eng/04_recovery.htm#city accessed 1 January 2018.

187 Ibid.

188 World Nuclear Association, Nuclear Radiation and Health Effects (June 28, 2013), www.world-nuclear.org/info/inf05.html (WNA) www.world-nuclear.org/info/Safety-and-Security/Radiation-and-Health/Nuclear-Radiation-and-Health-Effects/#.Ud3YfxY-Jpk accessed 1 January 2018 (WNA Health Effect).

189 Ibid.

190 Ibid.

191 Ibid. For medical impacts of the Fukushima nuclear accident, see Helen Caldicott, *Crisis without End: The Medical and Ecological Consequences of the Fukushima Nuclear Catastrophe* (New Press 2014).

192 n 175.

and small children.[193] Fearing for such increased risks, many will never be able to return to their communities. Even for those that are allowed to return, they are likely to live in a state of constant health anxiety. Children may even be prohibited from playing outside or be told to cover their mouths to and from school or be forbidden from touching grass or running water. In short, they will not be able to enjoy the natural environment.

To ease the concerns of returning residents, the central government must, at the very least, commit to long-term health care for residents.[194] These residents need to be periodically tested for possible health risks and provided with treatment funded by the central government and TEPCO. Although Japan has a mandatory public health insurance system, a separate health care scheme might even be warranted, one designed especially for these local residents.

5.6 Reconstruction of Fukushima

Evacuations also had the effect of forcing many businesses to shut down. Due to radiation contamination and accompanying fears, many farmers, fishermen, and forest industry workers lost their livelihoods. The people in Fukushima need government assistance to create jobs and provide employment even after the evacuees' return.

5.6.1 Reconstruction plan

The nuclear power accident brought tremendous economic damage to all the residents and businesses in Fukushima. After the accident was controlled and when evacuated residents were allowed to return, the central government needed to start the reconstruction of Fukushima. In order to provide for various measures for reconstructing and reviving communities, creating new jobs in these

193 UN Report concluded that the increase in cancer risk is unlikely following Fukushima exposure. United Nations Scientific Committee on the Effects of Atomic Radiation (UNSCEAR), Increase in Cancer Unlikely following Fukushima Exposure—says UN Report (UNIS 2 April 2014) www.unis.unvienna.org/unis/en/pressrels/2014/unisous237.html accessed 1 January 2018. However, it noted a theoretical possibility that the risk of thyroid cancer among the group of children most exposed to radiation could increase and concluded that the situation needs to be followed closely and further assessed in the future.

194 The interim report of comprehensive health checks of Fukushima residents after five years indicated that during the first four months 62.1% of residents were exposed to less than 1mSv of radiation and 99.8% were exposed to less than 5mSv. It indicated a significantly elevated number of suspected thyroid cancer patients (113 residents out of 300,000 residents), but in light of the relatively lower level exposure to radiation, the relatively short period between the accident and finding of cancer, absence of any patient less than five years old at the time of accident, and absence of any disparity among different parts of the prefecture, it concluded that the increase is unlikely to be considered as a result of the accident. Fukushima ken kenmin kenko chousa kentou iinkai [Committee on Residents Health of the Fukushima Prefecture], Kenmin kenko chousa niokeru chukan torimatome [Interim Summary of the Residents' Health Check] (Fukushima Prefecture March 2016) www.pref.fukushima.lg.jp/uploaded/attachment/158522.pdf accessed 1 January 2018.

communities and protecting the health and safety of residents after they return, the Special Measures Act on Reconstruction and Revival of Fukushima (*Fukushima hukkou saisei tokusohō*)[195] was thus enacted on 30 March 2012. Following the enactment of this statute, the cabinet adopted the Fukushima Reconstruction and Revival Basic Policy on 13 July 2012.[196]

After the Liberal Democratic Party (LDP) took over the government it decided to establish the Fukushima Reconstruction General Office, allowing the top ranking bureaucrats, including the cabinet adviser, secretary general, as well as managing officer to stay in Fukushima as one of the head offices together with Tokyo Fukushima Reconstruction Management Headquarters, placed directly under the Reconstruction Minister.[197] The establishment of the Fukushima Reconstruction General Office was designed to consolidate various reconstruction measures of government agencies into one department and to allow the top bureaucrats to coordinate their work. On the other hand, the creation of the Tokyo Reconstruction Management Headquarters also made it possible for the Reconstruction Minister to directly command bureau chiefs of relevant government agencies.

The government adopted a plan called "Toward Acceleration of Fukushima Reconstruction from Nuclear Disaster" in December 2013.[198] It also consolidated various existing individual grants totaling 160 billion JPY [1.45 billion USD] in 2014.[199] Since then the government budgeted 100 billion JPY (0.9 billion USD) to 80 billion JPY (800 million USD) each year.[200] This grant has been used to provide support for evacuees who are forced to stay away for a long time and to provide support for evacuees who returned back. For instance, it was used to create public housing for evacuees and provide a hub for them, clean up the living environment, provide incentives to restart businesses or to provide support for families who returned by providing a playground for children.[201] It also created the Fukushima Reconstruction from Nuclear Disaster Grant in 2014 and allocated 100 billion JPY [0.9 billion USD] in 2014.[202]

195 Fukushima hukkou saisei tokubetsu sochihō [Special Measures Act on Reconstruction and Revival of Fukushima], Law no 25, 2012.

196 Fukushima hukko saisei kihon houshin [Fukushima Reconstruction and Revival Basic Policy] (Reconstruction Agency 13 July 2012) www.reconstruction.go.jp/topics/main-cat1/sub-cat1-4/20170630_honbun.pdf accessed 1 January 2018. It was revised on 30 June, 2017.

197 Reconstruction Agency (n 145) 8.

198 Nuclear Disaster Response Headquarters, Genshiryoku saigai karano Fukushima hukkou no kasoku nimukete [Toward Acceleration of Fukushima Reconstruction from the Nuclear Disaster] (METI 20 December 2013) www.meti.go.jp/earthquake/nuclear/pdf/131220_hontai.pdf accessed 1 January 2018.

199 Ibid; Reconstruction Agency, Fukushima saisei kasokuka kouhukin [Fukushima Revival Acceleration Grant] (Reconstruction Agency) www.reconstruction.go.jp/topics/main-cat1/sub-cat1-17/20140331_fukushima_pr.pdf accessed 1 January 2018.

200 Reconstruction Agency (n 145) 9.

201 Reconstruction Agency (n 199).

202 Reconstruction Agency, Genshiryoku saigai karano Fukushima hukkou kouhukin [Fukushima Reconstruction from Nuclear Disaster Grant] (Reconstruction Agency) www.reconstruction.go.jp/topics/main-cat1/sub-cat1-4/20150324_1fukushimafukkoukoufukingaiyou.pdf accessed 1 January 2018.

To further accelerate the reconstruction of Fukushima, the government in 2015 adopted the revised acceleration plan and announced its plan to end the evacuation instruction by March 2017.[203] The Cabinet then adopted the Fundamental Guideline for Acceleration of Fukushima Reconstruction from Nuclear Disaster in December 2016.[204] With respect to concrete reconstruction measures, the government set up an expert council on the future vision of the affected 12 municipalities in Fukushima and received its report in July 2015.[205] It set the roadmap to accomplishing reconstruction, outlining the necessity of revitalization of industry, improvement of lifeline support, education of the next generation of leaders, infrastructure improvement, and promotion of cultural activities including tourism and sports.[206]

5.6.2 Various reconstruction measures

Agriculture had been an important industry in Fukushima. The central government seems to understand the need to promote Fukushima's agricultural products because consumers have tended to avoid them even after the marketing ban was lifted. Many consumers are so concerned about the safety of Fukushima's agricultural products that they have tended to avoid them even after the government declared them to be safe.[207] The central government has thus promoted Fukushima products and also introduced more rigorous testing to assure consumers of product safety, provided accurate information on the safety of Fukushima products, encouraged the expansion of the market for Fukushima products, prompted foreign governments to loosen trade restrictions on Fukushima products, and promoted tourists to visit Fukushima areas domestically and internationally.[208]

203 Genshiryoku saigai karano Fukushima hukkou no kasoku nimukete (kaitei) [Toward Acceleration of Fukushima Reconstruction from the Nuclear Disaster (revised)], Cabinet decision (METI 12 June 2015) www.meti.go.jp/earthquake/nuclear/kinkyu/pdf/2015/0612_02.pdf accessed 1 January 2018.

204 Genshiryokusaigai karano Fukushima hukkou no kasoku notameno kihon shishin [Fundamental Guideline for Acceleration of Fukushima reconstruction from Nuclear Disaster], Cabinet decision (METI 20 December 2016) www.meti.go.jp/earthquake/nuclear/kinkyu/pdf/2016/1220_01.pdf accessed 1 January 2018.

205 Fukushima 12 shichoson no shouraizou nikansuru yuushikisha kentoukai [Expert Council on the Future Vision of the Affected 12 Municipalities in Fukushima], Teigen [Proposal] (Reconstruction Agency 30 July 2015) www.reconstruction.go.jp/topics/main-cat1/sub-cat1-4/20150730_syoraizo_teigen.pdf accessed 1 January 2018.

206 Reconstruction Agency, Fukushima 12 shichouson shouraizou jitsugen roadmap 2020 kaiteiban (gaiyo) [The Future Vision of Fukushima's 12 Cities, Towns and Villages 2020 (revised)(summary)] (Reconstruction Agency 3 June 2017) www.reconstruction.go.jp/topics/main-cat1/sub-cat1-4/f12fup/20170603_02_siryou1.pdf accessed 1 January 2018.

207 "Anzen nanoni urenai: Fukushima huhyohigai wa ima [No One Buys Food Produced in Fukushima despite Their Safety: The Damage Due to Bad Reputation]" (*NHK* 24 May 2017) www.nhk.or.jp/gendai/articles/3979/ accessed 1 January 2018.

208 Reconstruction Agency, Hukko no torikumi to kanren shoseido [Progress of Reconstruction and Related Systems] (Reconstruction Agency 6 November 2017) www.reconstruction.go.jp/topics/main-cat1/sub-cat1-1/20171106_torikumitoshoseido.pdf > accessed 1 January 2018 51. For the impact of the Fukushima nuclear accident on the agriculture, *see* Tomoko M. Nakanishi & Keitaro Tanoi (eds), *Agricultural Implications of the Fukushima Nuclear Accident* (Springer 2013).

On the other hand, TEPCO had been the biggest employer in neighboring communities before the accident.[209] Now, these jobs are gone and residents will not be able to find similar jobs in the future since the Fukushima plant is to be abandoned. The central government admits the need to distribute all work related to abandoning the reactors, decontamination, and reconstruction to local residents[210] while at the same time encouraging other companies to come to Fukushima.

Indeed, the government has implemented various kinds of grants to promote the return of the residents. It has also built medical facilities for the residents and attempted to dispel the "bad reputation."[211] The government also announced the "Fukushima Innovation Coast" project in Fukushima coastline cities, attempting to entice technology companies related to decommissioning of the nuclear power plant and robotic technology to establish research facilities or labs.[212] The government also set up a joint organization together with Fukushima Prefecture and private companies to visit each of the companies that suffered loss and damage because of the nuclear accident, and to provide support.[213] In particular, the government provides financial support for three years to companies that hire nuclear disaster victims[214] and also provides grants to promote companies to build new facilities in Fukushima.[215]

Regardless, it will be quite some time before Fukushima businesses, including the prefecture's agriculture, fishery, and forestry industries, regain their pre-disaster status, let alone prosper more vibrantly than before.

5.6.3 Frustration of local residents

Six years after the accident, many residents are still under evacuation.[216] The population of residents in the evacuation zones will likely become only one

209 In eight nearby towns and villages in Futaba county close to the Fukushima nuclear power plant, roughly 10,000 residents were employed by TEPCO and its related companies out of 35,000 and GDP from the electricity and gas industry occupied roughly 70% of all GDP of these communities. Reconstruction Agency, Genshiryoku hatsudensho no jiko niyoru hinan chiiki ni kakawaru kikan shien oyobi chiiki saisei no tame no sangyo shinko/koyo sokushin plan [Promotion Plan for Industry and Employment for the Support of Evacuees' Return and Local Revival in Evacuation Areas as a result of the Nuclear Power Plant Accident] (Reconstruction Agency 4 September 2012) www.reconstruction.go.jp/topics/20120904_sangyoukoyouplan.pdf accessed 1 January 2018.

210 Reconstruction Agency, Genshiryoku hatsudensho no jikoniyoru hinan chiiki no genshiryoku hisaisha/jichitai nitaisuru kuni no torikumi houshin [Basic Policy of the Government toward Evacuating Victims of Nuclear Disaster due to Nuclear Power Plant Accident] (Reconstruction Agency 4 September 2012) www.reconstruction.go.jp/topics/20120904_gdhonbun.pdf accessed 1 January 2018 6.

211 Reconstruction Agency (n 208) 40.

212 Ibid 45.

213 Ibid 46.

214 Reconstruction Agency (n 145) 19.

215 Ibid 21.

216 "Shinsai/genpatsujiko kara 6nen: Data demiru Fukushima no hukkou [Six Years after the Earthquake and Nuclear Accident: The Progress of Reconstruction Based on Data]" (NHK) www.nhk.or.jp/d-navi/link/2017fukushima/ accessed 1 January 2018.

fourth of the previous population.[217] The number of children returning to public school in areas where the evacuation instruction was lifted in March 2017 was only 4.8% of the number before the accident.[218] Most of the large factories established or expanded after the accident relied upon the government grant.[219] This means that most companies have difficulty surviving without a government grant. The amount of fish caught in Fukushima offshore is merely 8% of the pre-accident level.[220] Only 23% of farmland in Fukushima has been able to resume production.[221] The number of tourists to Fukushima has not returned to the pre-accident level.[222]

Evacuees are naturally frustrated over the slow pace of recovery and face considerable uncertainty over their futures. Many complain that they remain completely in the dark over when they might be able to return and resume their lives as before.

The LDP government appears willing to facilitate Fukushima reconstruction as evidenced by its move to establish a robust Reconstruction Agency branch office in Fukushima.[223] In order to do this, both the central government as well as Fukushima prefecture are relatively committed to emphasizing the safety of Fukushima products and the safety of the environment in Fukushima. They are very concerned that the unsubstantiated fear about the safety of Fukushima products and the environment in Fukushima is producing an unfounded bad reputation against Fukushima products and residents.[224] When a famous comic writer wrote that there was a possibility of nose bleeding in Fukushima that could be a result of radiation exposure, the Environmental Minister as well as the Fukushima prefecture strongly condemned the comic as creating an unsubstantiated bad rumor.[225] It appears that the government is not tolerating any publicly expressed concerns over the safety of Fukushima products or life in Fukushima. As a result, it is difficult to locate similar fears or concerns among most major media outlets. But this kind of suppression will never reassure the local residents nor the public as to the safety of Fukushima products and life in Fukushima.

217 Ibid.
218 Ibid.
219 Ibid.
220 Ibid.
221 Reconstruction Agency (n 145) 27.
222 Ibid 30.
223 n 197.
224 Reconstruction Agency, Huhyo higai husshoku nikansuru torikumi [Responses to Wipe Out the Bad Reputation] (Reconstruction Agency) www.reconstruction.go.jp/topics/post_183.html accessed 1 January 2018.
225 "Oishinbo no hanaji byousha ni sanpi: Ishihara kankyusho to zen-Futaba chouchou ga tair-itsu [Description of Nose Bleeding in Oishinbo: The Splitting Opinion between the Ishihara Environment Minister and Former Town Head of the Futaba Town]" (*Huffington Post* 10 May 2014) www.huffingtonpost.jp/2014/05/10/oishinbo_n_5300120.html accessed 1 January 2018; Fukushima Prefecture, Shukan Big Comic Spirits Oishinbo nikansuru honken no taiou nit-suite [On Our Response to the Oishinbo Carried on the Weekly Big Comic Spirits] (Fukushima Prefecture 12 May 2014) www.pref.fukushima.lg.jp/sec/01010d/20140512.html accessed 1 January 2018.

It is questionable whether the initiatives of the LDP government actually did make any tangible differences. However, given that final containment is projected to take anywhere from 30 to 40 years or more, and communities in the vicinity of the Fukushima plant will likely be affected by high levels of contamination for many decades, residents of Fukushima are likely to endure much inconvenience and hardship for the foreseeable future.

5.7 Aftermath of the Fukushima accident and failures of law and politics

5.7.1 Aftermath of Fukushima and failures of law

In retrospect, the failure to prepare for the aftermath of the serious nuclear accident was a critical error. The law had not anticipated the fallout of a serious nuclear accident. The law didn't forecast the huge amount of nuclear waste inside and outside of the nuclear power plant. There was thus no provision for the method of disposal, nor the process of selecting the interim storage sites, let alone final disposal sites. There was also no provision for the radiation limits of the waste to be disposed of. There was, furthermore, no preparation for decontamination of the environment. The law was not prepared to handle the evacuation for such an extended time let alone the measures for allowing them to return. There was also no preparation for the decommissioning of the damaged nuclear power plant.

The law also did not anticipate such a huge amount of damage awards nor provide a specific mechanism to evaluate and pay for the damage. The law further did not anticipate the difficulty on the part of the power company to sustain itself while paying all the damages and while spending so much money on repairing the damaged nuclear reactors and preparing for decommissioning.

Finally, the law did not anticipate the measures that would become necessary to reconstruct the community after a serious nuclear accident. Because of the extensive environmental contamination, the local residents would not be able to return for a long period even if they were allowed to. The contaminated environment needed to be decontaminated. The government needed to make sure that the returning residents could live without fear and health concerns.

As a result, the Japanese government was forced to decide answers to all of these questions in an ad hoc fashion, one after the other when each issue came to the surface. Obviously, the government didn't have the luxury of thinking over the issue and trying to come up with a comprehensive plan.

Although the local residents were allowed to return to most of the evacuation zones, many residents are still worried about the health risks to themselves and their families. As a result, many former residents are reluctant to return. But the termination of compensation and subsidies would force them to return. Moreover, the returning residents still faced extreme difficulty finding work except for decontamination and decommissioning jobs.[226] Reconstruction of Fukushima is hardly

226 Ranghieri & Ishiwatari (n 164) 340.

likely to happen soon. Furthermore, returning residents must live in fear over the health effects of their environment.[227] All of this has been triggered by the failure of the law to ensure the safety of the nuclear power plant and to prepare for a possible serious nuclear accident.

5.7.2 Aftermath of Fukushima and deeper failures of law

All the difficulties in the aftermath of Fukushima could be related to deeper failures of law in Japan: the bureaucratic attitude toward law and its unwillingness to change the fundamental framework of post-disaster reconstruction established following the precedent. The legal system is premised upon the goal of allowing local residents to return and resurrect Fukushima. As a result, the government tried hard to decontaminate the environment and allow the evacuees to return. Moreover, it came to encourage (and practically force) the local residents to return by cutting the compensation and subsidies to evacuees.

This attitude is a reflection of the Japanese bureaucrats' tendency to stick to the precedent set by the pre-existing framework. It is also a reflection of a very conservative belief that it is best to follow the example already set and applied.

But the aftermath following the nuclear disaster is significantly different from the aftermath following the earthquake. The aftermath following the nuclear disaster requires disposal of the nuclear power plant as well as seriously contaminated nuclear waste. It also requires the decontamination of the environment. Still, many of the local residents who used to live close to the nuclear power plant will never be allowed to return and many would have to live constantly fearing for the health effects from remaining contamination even if they are allowed to return. There is no reason to follow the same past pattern in the aftermath of a serious nuclear accident.

227 Ibid 339. In 2017, the Special Measures Act on Reconstruction and Revival of Fukushima (n 195) was revised to allow the municipal government heads to apply for designation of the "specified reconstruction and revival base zone" (*tokutei hukkou saisei kyoten kuiki*) in the "no-return zone" and submit the "specified reconstruction and revival base zone reconstruction and revival plan" for approval by the prime minister. Then, with the support of the central government, the municipal government could concentrate their effort for decontamination and infrastructure improvement to make it possible to lift the evacuation instruction and allow local residents to return within 5 years. Ibid art 17–2; Reconstruction Agency, Tokutei hukkou saisei kyoten kuiki hukkou saisei keikaku [Specified Reconstruction and revival Base Zone Reconstruction and Revival Plan] (Reconstruction Agency) www.reconstruction.go.jp/topics/main-cat1/sub-cat1-4/saiseikyoten/20170913162153.html accessed 8 March 2018. Futaba town has already applied this designation and had its plan approved. Futaba town, Futabacho, tokutei hukkou saisei kyoten kuiki hukkou saisei keikaku no gaiyo [Summary of the Futaba Town Specified Reconstruction and Revival Base Zone Reconstruction and Revival Plan] (Futaba town) www.futaba-fukkou.jp/wp-content/uploads/2017/08/20170915gaiyou_futabafukkousaiseikeikaku.pdf accessed 8 March 2018. If the town can successfully accomplish its goal by reducing the level of radiation to 20 mSv/ per year, then the residents of Futaba town might be allowed to return by 2022. Ohkuma town and Namie town followed Futaba town. But this will raise a serious concern over whether the residents would return or whether they might be forced to return. Even if the radiation level is reduced below 20 mSv/per year, returning residents would be living under constant fear for their health.

In retrospect, it might be better to give up the idea of restoring the environment and shield off seriously contaminated zones for a long time, without forcing the evacuees to return.[228] Fukushima nuclear accident was a serious accident. No one can deny the disaster it caused. But what is important is how we are able to cope with it. It is a tragedy that some local residents will not be able to return. In light of all the difficulties, however, it might be better to leave the contaminated environment as it is and cordon off the contaminated areas from the public for a long time. Then the government could assist these evacuees to relocate. But this was not a viable option for the post-disaster law.

Moreover, just as the reconstruction measures in other Tohoku regions, the reconstruction in Fukushima is plagued by the same kind of bureaucratic mindset by those government officials charged with the reconstruction.[229] Moreover, the reconstruction in Fukushima requires coordinated effort among the Reconstruction Agency, the Ministry of Economy, Trade and Industry (METI), and the MOE. There is a question whether such coordination is in order. Furthermore, in implementing reconstruction measures, the central government plays a dominating role. Such reliance upon the central government might deprive the local touch with various reconstruction measures.

5.7.3 Aftermath of Fukushima and failures of politics

We can also find failures of politics behind the failures of law to anticipate all of these. As we already saw, the politics made it impossible to prepare since mere discussion of all these questions could lead to doubts about the safety of nuclear power plants. The nuclear policy in Japan is premised on the assumption that nuclear power plants are safe and there would be no serious nuclear accidents. It is no wonder that no one wanted to discuss them.

Although Kan declared his personal belief toward the abandonment of all nuclear power, the Democratic Party of Japan (DPJ) at that time was not able to support his belief. The DPJ is supported by the labor unions and the power company union was a very strong supporter of the DPJ. Apparently, many

228 Science Council of Japan, Higashinihon daishinsai karano hukkou seisaku no kaizen nitsuiteno teigen [Proposal for Improvement of Reconstruction Policy from the Great East Japan Earthquake Disaster] (Science Council of Japan 25 September 2016) www.scj.go.jp/ja/info/kohyo/pdf/kohyo-22-t200-1.pdf accessed 20 February 2018 (proposing the third option for the reconstruction in Fukushima). See also Masafumi Yokemoto, Accident Damage and Fukushima's Reconstruction Policy Confronting "Unequal Reconstruction" and the "Division" of Victims (2015) 66 *Keiei Kenkyu* 1 (proposing a reconstruction based on human dignity rather than the creative reconstruction proposed by the government).

229 This is apparent in the adoption of various different confusing definitions of emergency to be decided by different departments (Chapter 2 n 159) and also in the adoption of terms so unfriendly for the public, such as "evacuation instruction zone" (Chapter 3 n 120), "planned evacuation zone" and "emergency evacuation preparation zone" (Chapter 3 n 128), "specified evacuation recommendation spot" (Chapter 3 n 131), or "evacuation instruction removal preparation zone," "residence restriction zone," and "no-return zone" (or "difficult-to-return zone") (n 77). Only the experienced bureaucrats can understand them.

members of the DPJ feared the possible reaction from power company unions if the government decided to abandon all nuclear power.[230] Therefore, the DPJ government was able to adopt an ambivalent attitude toward nuclear power.

Moreover, when the LDP came back to power beginning in 2012, the LDP government apparently wanted to allow the reactivation of the nuclear reactors shut down. The government thus attempted all of the measures to facilitate the disposal of nuclear waste, facilitate the decontamination, and end the evacuation instruction. It was not a priority for the government to prepare a long-standing comprehensive plan for the returning residents for the future. It is, thus, again no wonder that the government did not hesitate to rush into adopting specific countermeasures for nuclear accident without a comprehensive plan.

Reconstruction of Fukushima raised the same kinds of issues as the reconstruction of the Tohoku Region. Although the Reconstruction Agency handles the reconstruction measures for Fukushima, basically it is each of the departments of the government that has power to apply for the budget and power to enforce specific measures. Although there is no longer an immediate crisis, the decommissioning of the Fukushima nuclear power plant will take a long time, with significant government as well as private efforts.

Seven years have passed since the accident, it appears that the prime minister and the cabinet have already lost their commitment to reconstruct Fukushima. Many of the Fukushima victims now believe that the reconstruction of Fukushima is not a priority on the agenda of the government. They have come to feel discarded and that the government no longer cares about the people of Fukushima.[231] For the LDP government, power companies and reactivation of the nuclear power plants might appear more important.[232]

***

230 "Datsu genpatsu wa komaru: Denryoku rouso, Minshu giin ni soshikitekina chinjo [Don't Abandon Nuclear Power: Power Company Unions Pressuring DPJ Members] (*Asahi Shimbun* 1 December 2011) www.asahi.com/special/10005/TKY201111300881.html accessed 19 February 2018.

231 "Genpatsu shuuhen sichoson: Masani shi no machi—Hachiro keisansho ga hatsugen [Municipalities around the Fukushima Nuclear Power Plant Are like the Town of Death: Economy, Trade and Industry Minister Hachiro Remarked]" (*Asahi Shimbun* 9 September 2011) www.asahi.com/special/10005/TKY201109090226.html accessed 19 February 2018; "Jishu hinan wa hon-nin no sekinin: Imamura hukkousho ga hatsugen [Voluntary Evacuees Evacuated on Their Own Responsibility: Reconstruction Minister Imamura Remarked]" (*Asahi Shimbun* 5 April 2017) www.asahi.com/articles/ASK452F4MK45UBQU003.html accessed 19 February 2018. These remarks of the responsible ministers outraged the evacuees.

232 In order to revitalize the economy of Fukushima, the central government and the Fukushima Prefecture have been actively promoting the "Fukushima Innovation Coast" project. n 212. For a progress of this project, see Fukushima Innovation Coast Project Promotion Subcommittee Office, Fukushima Innovation Coast kōsō no shinchaku nitsuite [Progress Status of the Fukushima Innovation Coast Project] (METI 27 November 2017) www.meti.go.jp/earthquake/nuclear/kinkyu/committee/innovation/bunkakai/pdf/171127_01g.pdf accessed 10 March 2018. Even if this project is successful, the benefit to the local residents will only be quite indirect.

The aftermath of the Fukushima nuclear accident brought the legal system's lack of preparedness for a disaster of this magnitude into clear focus. The disaster law in Japan had not been well prepared for the aftermath of a serious nuclear accident. As a result, the government was forced to solve many legal questions presented in the aftermath of the nuclear accident in an ad hoc fashion. Moreover, the certain characteristics of Japanese law further complicated these failures and prevented more adequate solutions. There are certain political reasons for these failures. In other words, these much deeper failures of law manifested the failure of politics in Japan.

6 Future of law and politics in Japan

Seven years have passed since the Tohoku Earthquake, tsunami, and nuclear meltdown. The triple disaster offered many lessons for Japan. How has the Japanese government learned from these lessons in relation to preparation for a future Kanto Earthquake, Tokai Earthquake, or the triple powerful earthquakes of the so-called Nankai Trough Megathrust Earthquakes which might take place in Tokai, Tohnakai, and Nankai? How have these lessons impacted nuclear energy policy in Japan? What lessons have the Japanese people learned from the failures of law and politics since the Tohoku Earthquake? This chapter will examine these questions and explore measures that should be put in place to prevent similar carnage following the next massive earthquake that will surely strike Japan in the future.

6.1 Preparing for future earthquakes and tsunamis

First, Japan needs to prepare for future powerful earthquakes. Everyone knows that another powerful earthquake in Tokai is likely to strike the central part of Japan. Everyone also knows that there is a strong likelihood that another powerful Kanto Earthquake will hit Tokyo. Some even suggest the likely possibility of a triple combination of very powerful earthquakes hitting Tokai, Tohnankai, and Nankai: the so-called Nankai Trough Megathrust Earthquake. Japan needs to learn lessons from the Tohoku Earthquake and revise its preparation against these kinds of future powerful earthquakes.

6.1.1 Shortcomings of previous disaster prevention plan

The Great East Japan Earthquake Disaster clearly underscored the importance of natural disaster preparedness. The demanding construction standards set by the Construction Standards Act once again prevented a significant amount of collateral damage to property and human life. Without such rigorous standards, an even greater number of homes and buildings might have collapsed and crushed those inside. The tsunami warning system also proved to save many lives once again. Without this tsunami warning system, it is quite probable that a significantly higher number of local residents would have perished in the tsunami.

Nonetheless, the Great East Japan Earthquake Disaster revealed serious problems in the existing earthquake and tsunami preparedness systems. Although the central government had established a national disaster prevention plan and mandated local governments to establish local disaster prevention plans based on the national one, the requirements of these disaster prevention plans were seriously deficient.

First, these plans did not anticipate an earthquake as massive as the Tohoku Earthquake. Moreover, it seems that these plans were premised upon the assumption that such a powerful earthquake simply would not strike. The same could be said for the tsunami. It is now unmistakably clear that earthquakes and tsunamis of similar magnitude may well indeed beset Japan in the future. As a result, the central, prefectural and municipal governments have been forced to reconsider their disaster prevention plans in light of the devastation wrought upon Tohoku. The government must recalculate what the estimated losses and damages could be from such powerful earthquake and tsunamis, and plan accordingly.

Second, the central and local governments must construct higher and stronger tsunami barriers, build stronger tsunami shelters on higher ground, and revise evacuation plans. Still, even if more formidable barriers are constructed, they may be insufficient for defending against powerful tsunamis. Rather than relying upon barriers, both the central and local governments must prohibit development in vulnerable areas and prepare for much more efficient evacuations. The government needs to think about how damages and losses could be reduced in addition to trying to prevent disaster.

Third, despite the tsunami warning system, many local residents did not evacuate to higher ground. They erroneously believed they would be safe without evacuating. Part of the problem lies in the unreliability of the tsunami prediction system. Even though tsunami alerts often sound to warn of an approaching tsunami, many end up being false alarms. Thus, local residents simply came to distrust the reliability of the warning system. Moreover, we have already seen that many residents did not feel the necessity of evacuation in light of the initial estimated height of the tsunami issued immediately after the initial shock and many were not informed of the subsequent updated and upgraded tsunami estimate because of the blackout and malfunction of the loud-speaker system.[1] The central government must definitely improve the reliability of tsunami prediction systems and public trust in them, and also reconsider how to issue tsunami warnings and deliver them during a power blackout.[2] However, the false sense

1 *See* Chapter 2 n 133.

2 The Japan Meteorological Agency (JMA) still believe that the initial warning needs to be issued within three minutes but revised the tsunami warning system to abandon descriptions of detailed estimated tsunami height, in order to prevent a false sense of safety. "Tsunami keihō ga kawarimashita [Tsunami Warning System Has Been Changed]" (NHK) www3.nhk.or.jp/news/0307newkeihou/ accessed 10 January 2018. Moreover, television announcers who read these warnings used to be instructed to remain calm and call for evacuation as calmly as possible but television stations are now encouraging their announcers to call for evacuation in more urgent tones of voice. Ibid.

of safety that came from overconfidence in the tsunami barriers and all the countermeasures adopted against the tsunami were also part of the problem. Many residents erroneously believed that they would be safe at home and thus did not attempt to evacuate. The central and local governments must find a way to educate the public of the importance of evacuation. Moreover, so far, the government had advised the public to evacuate on foot and not use motor vehicles. But this time, a huge number of evacuees attempted to evacuate by car. Not only is it simply unrealistic to expect residents to run on foot, this expectation is insufficient for disabled persons or seniors. The government needs to come up with a much more realistic evacuation plan.

Fourth, considerable government initiatives to date have focused on predicting earthquakes. The central government has put incredible emphasis on earthquake prediction and has even established an organization dedicated to predicting a future massive Tokai Earthquake. As a result, scientists are now able to gather tremendous volumes of data relating to tectonic plate movement, early signs of imminent earthquakes and estimated magnitudes. Accurate prediction will undoubtedly lead to more effective disaster prevention. However, the Tohoku Earthquake proved that accurate prediction is elusive, if not impossible. Consequently, it might be preferable to focus on how to minimize damage when earthquakes do strike rather than devoting such vast resources to earthquake prediction.[3]

Fifth, in addition to improving disaster preparedness, the central and local governments must also dedicate significantly more attention to post-disaster protocol. Government response to the Tohoku Earthquake was disorganized and chaotic. The central and local governments must prepare for immediate rescue, restoration, and recovery operations. Preparations for long-term post-disaster reconstruction with project planning and sequential task prioritization factored in are also advisable.

At the very least, the central and local governments have had reasons to reconsider disaster prevention plans as they relate to the future Kanto or Tokai earthquakes as well as the possibility of a simultaneous Nankai Trough Megathrust Earthquake.

6.1.2 Revising the Basic Act on Disaster Countermeasures: The 2012 Amendments

The Diet has amended the Basic Act on Disaster Countermeasures to reflect the lessons the government learned.

In 2012, the Diet passed an amendment to the Basic Act on Disaster Countermeasures[4] that intensified the cooperation between the central government,

3 "Nankai Trough jishin taisaku wa yochikara gensai e [Switch from Earthquake Prediction to Damage Reduction in order to Prepare for the Nankai Trough Mega Earthquake]" (*Nihonkeizai Shimbun* 29 May 2013) www.nikkei.com/article/DGXDZO55585640Z20C13A5EA1000/ accessed 1 January 2018.

4 Saigai taisaku kihonhō no ichibu wo kaiseisuru hōritsu [Act to Amend Parts of the Basic Act on Disaster Countermeasures], Law no 41 of 2012.

prefectures and municipal governments. It authorized the governor of the affected prefecture to request heads of affected municipalities to enforce disaster countermeasures or to instruct heads of other municipalities to lend assistance to affected municipalities.[5] It authorized the affected governors to request the prime minister to request governors of other prefectures to lend help to the heads of the affected municipal government and authorized the prime minister to ask the governors of other prefectures to lend help to them in response to the request[6] or even without such request if it is urgent.[7]

It also prepared for extended temporary stay at designated places other than shelters. Before the Great East Japan Earthquake Disaster, it was not anticipated that so many evacuees would have to stay in shelters for such a long time. The 2012 amendment authorized the heads of municipal governments to consult with the heads of other municipal governments and ask them to accept residents for temporary stay if they were unable to find a place to stay.[8] It further mandated the heads of other municipal governments to accept, if requested, temporary accommodation for residents unless there was a legitimate reason for refusal.[9] This agreement would allow evacuees to move out of shelters to places of temporary accommodation in other local governments. If necessary, the head of the affected municipal government can request a governor to consult with governors of other prefectures with respect to the acceptance of temporary accommodation.[10] The governor of the other government is mandated to comply with the request for consultation and the relevant municipal governments are mandated to accept unless there are legitimate reasons to refuse.[11] When the municipal governments are paralyzed, the governor of an affected prefecture is mandated to substitute the decision for the affected municipal government with respect to acceptance of temporary accommodation.[12] The governor, as well as the prime minister, is also mandated to give advice when requested by the affected governor or head of the affected municipal government.[13]

The 2012 amendment also authorized the governors of affected prefectures to request transportation of necessary goods needed to implement emergency countermeasures to the designated administrative agencies and authorized the heads of the affected municipalities to request the same to governors and also authorized the heads of relevant administrative agencies as well as governors to take necessary measures even without a request if it was urgent.[14] It also allowed

5 Saigai taisaku kihonhō [Basic Act on Disaster Countermeasures], Law no 223 of 1961, art 72(2).
6 Ibid art 74–2(2).
7 Ibid art 74–2(3).
8 Ibid art 86–8 (temporary stay).
9 Ibid art 86–8(3).
10 Ibid art 86–9(1).
11 Ibid art 86–9(2) & (5).
12 Ibid art 86–10(1).
13 Ibid art 86–12. The 2013 amendment further allowed the prime minister to substitute the action of governors. Ibid 86–13(1).
14 Ibid art 86–16(1).

governors or the heads of the designated administrative agencies to prepare for the transportation of emergency goods even before the requests were made.[15] Furthermore, they are authorized to request designated transportation companies to transport necessary goods, and, if they refuse, are allowed to instruct them to accept the request without legitimate reason.[16]

6.1.3 Revising the Basic Act on Disaster Countermeasures: The 2013 Amendments

Moreover, the 2013 amendment[17] declared the fundamental principles for disaster countermeasures for the first time,[18] and declared the minimization of damages and the accomplishment of prompt recovery as one of the fundamental principles.[19] Moreover, it mandated the government to assist victims in light of their age, gender, disability, or other particular circumstances, while at the same time respecting the autonomous responses made by the victims themselves.[20] It amended the responsibilities of the central government,[21] prefectures,[22] municipal governments,[23] and local residents,[24] adding the responsibility to cooperate with volunteers.[25]

The 2013 amendment further intensified the government response based on the "disaster emergency situation" declaration.[26] When this declaration was issued, the 2013 amendment mandates the government to adopt the fundamental policy to respond to the disaster emergency[27] and mandates the prime minister to instruct and supervise all government departments based on the fundamental policy.[28] Moreover, when the declaration was issued, various specific measures were now triggered automatically.[29] It also authorized the government to seek cooperation from the public.[30] It also allowed the central government to substitute the countermeasures to be carried out by the municipal governments or prefectures when the capability of the affected local governments was significantly

15 Ibid 86–16(2)
16 Ibid art 86–18(1) & (2).
17 Saigai taisaku kihonhōtō no ichibu wo kaiseisuru hōritsu [Act to Amend Parts of the Basic Act on Disaster Countermeasures and Others], Law no 54 of 2013.
18 Basic Act on Disaster Countermeasures (n 5) art 2–2.
19 Ibid art 2–2(i).
20 Ibid art 2–2(v).
21 Ibid art 3.
22 Ibid art 4.
23 Ibid art 5.
24 Ibid art 7.
25 Ibid art 5–3.
26 Ibid art 105.
27 Ibid art 108(1).
28 Ibid art 108(5).
29 Ibid art 108–4.
30 Ibid art 108–3. For instance, the prime minister can ask the public not to purchase important goods to sustain national life unnecessarily.

damaged by the disaster.[31] These amendments are designed to allow a much more active role for the central government.

On the other hand, the 2013 amendment mandated the heads of municipal governments to designate certain facilities as "designated emergency evacuation spots" as distinguished from regular "designated shelters" to allow residents to evacuate to these emergency evacuation spots according to the type of disaster.[32] This would prevent residents from evacuating to regular shelters such as school gyms at the time of tsunamis. It further authorized the heads of the municipal government to create a list of persons who needed special assistance during evacuation, such as elderly persons or the disabled, and provide such information upon consent to firefighters and other persons providing assistance,[33] such as police, other social welfare agencies, and even volunteer groups providing help with the evacuation.[34] It also mandated the central government or prefectural governors to respond to the request for advice with respect to evacuation.[35] Furthermore, it mandated the government to provide the necessary assistance to evacuees staying in shelters as well as evacuees staying elsewhere than in shelters.[36] Heads of the municipal governments were also authorized to create a list of affected victims and to collect personal information in order to manage all the assistance information.[37] It further mandated the heads of municipal governments to promptly issue official certificates of damage in order to promptly carry out various assistance measures.[38] These measures were designed to secure smooth evacuation and to provide assistance to affected residents. It further authorized the governors to request designated transportation companies to transport disaster victims if necessary for their protection,[39] and authorized the governors as well as heads of the local government to release information to survivors if requested.[40]

Moreover, the 2013 amendment encouraged local residents to strive to stock up on the necessary goods for emergencies,[41] and obliged business operators that supply materials or services that are necessary for emergency countermeasures or disaster relief to strive to continue their business activities in times of disaster.[42]

31 Ibid art 78–2.
32 Ibid art 49–4, art 49–7.
33 Ibid art 49–10, 49–11(3). Municipal heads are obliged to take care of evacuation of persons in need of assistance when evacuation is instructed. Ibid art 56(2).
34 Ibid art 49–11(1).
35 Ibid art 61–2. The amendment also obliges the prime minister to substitute the municipal heads for consultation of evacuees when the municipal government and prefectures are seriously affected. Ibid art 86–13.
36 Ibid art 86–6 & art 86–7.
37 Ibid art 90–3.
38 Ibid art 90–7.
39 Ibid art 86–14. If the transportation company does not comply with a request without legitimate reason, the governor can instruct them to comply. Ibid 86–14(2).
40 Ibid art 86–15(1).
41 Ibid art 7(3).
42 Ibid art 7(2).

Finally, the 2013 amendment gave textual authorization for some exceptional treatments for disaster victims. For instance, when a disaster is designated as a "specified extraordinary disaster" because it is a "highly unusual and extremely serious extraordinary disaster," fire regulation will be precluded for construction of shelter and temporary housing,[43] various requirements for hospitals will not be applicable to temporary medical facilities,[44] burial and cremation requirements will not be applicable to the handling of dead bodies caused by the disaster,[45] and exception will be granted to the treatment of waste disposal.[46]

Additional revisions were added in 2013 to other disaster laws together with revisions to the Basic Act on Disaster Countermeasures. For instance, those who lost family members as a result of a "specified extraordinary disaster," the usual period for deciding the acceptance or refusal of succession is extended.[47] The 2013 amendment further reorganized and substantially revised the Disaster Assistance Act.[48]

Furthermore, the Liberal Democratic Party (LDP) led Diet passed the National Resilience to Disaster Promotion Act[49] in 2013, mandating the central government to establish the National Resilience to Disaster Promotion Basic Plan in light of the basic principles declared in the Act.[50] It gave the prime minister the power to give recommendations to heads of relevant administrative agencies when necessary to implement the basic plan.[51] It also established the National Resilience to Disaster Promotion Headquarters inside the Cabinet.[52]

6.1.4 Enacting the Large-Scale Disaster Reconstruction Act

The Diet also enacted the Large-Scale Disaster Reconstruction Act[53] to prepare for the reconstruction after the large-scale disaster. Reconstruction from a large-scale disaster needs to be guided by the basic principle of the reconstruction of local life and the economy in the affected community and the smooth and swift promotion of building a safer environment against a future disaster,

43 Ibid art 86–2.
44 Ibid art 86–3.
45 Ibid art 86–4.
46 Ibid art 86–5.
47 Tokutei hijo saigai no hisaisha no kenririeki no hozentō wo hakaru tame no tokubetsu sochini kansuru hōritsu [Act concerning Special Measures to Preserve the Rights and Legal Interests of Victims of Specified Emergency Disasters], Law no 85 of 1996, art 6. *See* Chapter 2 n 106.
48 Saigai kyujohō [Disaster Assistance Act], Law no 118 of 1947.
49 Tsuyoku shinayakana kokumin seikatsu no jitsugen wo hakaru tameno bousai/mensaitō ni shisuru kokudo kyoujinka kihonhō [Basic Act on the National Resilience to Disaster Promotion for the Purpose of Contributing to the Prevention of Disaster/Reduction of Damages to Promote a Strong and Flexible National Life], Law no 95 of 2013 (National Resilience to Disaster Promotion Basic Act).
50 Ibid art 10(1). The basic plan needs to be approved by the cabinet meeting. Ibid art 10(3).
51 Ibid art 12.
52 Ibid art 15. The director of the Headquarters is the prime minister. Ibid art 19(1).
53 Daikibosaigai karano hukkou nikansuru hōritsu [Large-Scale Disaster Reconstruction Act], Law no 55 of 2013.

with the proper division of responsibility between the central government and local government while respecting the wishes of the local residents.[54] The designated large-scale disaster was defined as a "highly unusual and extremely serious extraordinary disaster" when the Emergency Disaster Response Headquarters was established in accordance with the Basic Act on Disaster Countermeasures.[55]

If it is necessary to promote the reconstruction from a designated large-scale disaster, the prime minister can establish ad hoc Reconstruction Headquarters inside the Cabinet office,[56] headed by the prime minister as a director.[57] The director can then manage the work of the headquarters and direct and supervise the officials.[58] The headquarters is tasked with the formulation of the basic policy of reconstruction, adjustment of various reconstruction measures by the heads of designated administrative agencies and the heads of local governments, promotion of implementation of measures based on the basic reconstruction policy, and others.[59] The basic reconstruction policy is supposed to provide for the significance and goal of reconstruction, basic policy on reconstruction measures, the current population and the prospect of future populations of affected communities, the basic policy on land use and other basic matters related to reconstruction, the proper division of responsibility between the central government and local government, and other matters necessary for reconstruction.[60]

The affected municipalities are authorized to establish the reconstruction plan in accordance with the reconstruction basic policy.[61] When the reconstruction plan is published, various permits and approvals under various statutes are deemed to be granted under certain conditions,[62] and there are special provisions on redevelopment projects,[63] land improvement projects,[64] group relocation projects,[65] and other projects.[66] And special measures are provided for the implementation of the reconstruction plan.[67] There are also various exceptional treatments with respect to urban planning.[68]

The Act also provides for the substitution of the disaster restoration work of the local government by the central government,[69] the request by governors to

54 Ibid art 3.
55 Ibid art 2(i).
56 Ibid art 4(1).
57 Ibid art 5(1).
58 Ibid art 5(2).
59 Ibid art 6(1).
60 Ibid art 8(2).
61 Ibid art 10(1).
62 Ibid 14.
63 Ibid art 15.
64 Ibid art 16.
65 Ibid art 17.
66 Ibid art 18–art 20.
67 Ibid art 28–art 38.
68 Ibid art 41–art 42.
69 Ibid art 43–art 52.

the heads of designated administrative agencies to dispatch their officials,[70] and the special financial arrangement to support the reconstruction.[71]

6.1.5 Revising the Basic Disaster Prevention Plan

Following these new developments, the Central Disaster Prevention Council revised the Basic Disaster Prevention Plan in January 2014 again, in addition to revision in response to the Hanshin Awaji Earthquake. With additional updates responding to lessons from the Kumamoto Earthquakes, described below, the Basic Disaster Prevention Plan now contains countermeasures to all sorts of disasters and special countermeasures against earthquake disasters as well as tsunami disasters.[72] The general countermeasures are divided into disaster prevention, emergency disaster countermeasures, and restoration and reconstruction measures, and provide details for each step.[73]

What is noteworthy in the disaster prevention against earthquakes and tsunamis is the mandate for the central government and local government to anticipate the strongest earthquake possible in light of all the possibilities and promote the necessary countermeasures against such earthquakes. Moreover, the anticipated disasters were divided into strong earthquakes and tsunamis, which are likely to happen, and the most powerful ones, which are unlikely to happen but could be possible. Furthermore, the revision intensified the countermeasures against tsunamis by using zoning regulations, establishing tsunami shelters, and improving tsunami warning systems. It also stressed the importance of the promotion of disaster prevention awareness among the public, especially facilitating the awareness for immediate evacuation after strong earthquake and distribution of tsunami hazard map.[74] The current Disaster Prevention Basic Plan declares in its basic principles that the total prevention of disaster is impossible and the fundamental principle of disaster prevention should be a reduction of damages and minimization of loss, especially the loss of human lives. Moreover, it stresses the necessity of improving the institutional and systematic aspects of disaster prevention together with improving the infrastructures. It also emphasizes the necessity of respecting the various needs of vulnerable people.

6.1.6 Preparing for a future Kanto Earthquake

In the wake of the Great East Japan Earthquake Disaster—an earthquake much stronger than previous disaster plans contemplated—the Tokyo Metropolitan

70 Ibid art 53.
71 Ibid art 57.
72 Central Disaster Prevention Council, Bousai kihon keikaku [Basic Disaster Prevention Plan] (Cabinet Office April 2017) www.bousai.go.jp/taisaku/keikaku/pdf/kihon_basic_plan170411.pdf accessed 30 January 2018. Before the 2013 amendment, the tsunami disaster countermeasures were parts of the earthquake countermeasures. But now they are separate and independent from earthquake disaster countermeasures.
73 Ibid.
74 Cabinet Office, Heisei24nenban bousai hakusho [Disaster Prevention Whitepaper 2012] (Cabinet Office) www.bousai.go.jp/kaigirep/hakusho/h24/bousai2012/html/honbun/4b_8s_01_34.htm accessed 31 January 2018. The nuclear disaster countermeasures were also intensified.

Government revised its disaster prevention plan to account for the possibility of a future Kanto Earthquake.[75] Now the Tokyo Metropolitan Government assumes the possibility of a future temblor on a par with the most powerful Kanto Earthquake in recorded history. Instead of the Tokyo Metropolitan Government's previous plan, based on an earthquake with an upper magnitude of 7.3, the 2012 revision contemplates the possibility of a magnitude 8.2 temblor, just like the one that struck the Kanto region in 1703. Concordantly, the new plan also revised damage estimates based on new data and the possibility of a massive tsunami that could be expected to follow such an earthquake.[76] The Tokyo Metropolitan Government also updated its disaster prevention plan in 2014 and estimated that the number of casualties in Tokyo alone might reach 9,641 and the possible number of people sustaining injury might reach 147,611, with 304,300 houses damaged and 3,385,485 evacuees.[77] The casualties and damage would be far much greater if those in the neighboring prefectures are added as well.

The central government's Central Disaster Prevention Council also published a final report on the estimated degree of casualties and damages that would result from a future Kanto Earthquake.[78] It is estimated that in the worst-case scenario the casualties would reach 16,000 to 23,000 and the number of those injured would reach 112,000 to 123,000, leaving 610,000 houses totally collapsed or burned down.[79]

It urges each government department to establish a business continuance plan that prioritizes essential business operations in phases corresponding to the progress of disaster response, recovery, and reconstruction.[80] It also points to the necessity of gathering and publishing information during an emergency, specifying what kind of information should be published and the chronological order it should be published in, depending on whether the information should be directed toward disaster victims, the public, market players, and foreign governments.[81] It also discusses the need to improve facilities and systems and to secure the necessary personnel in preparation for disaster. To this end, the proposal emphasizes ensuring that sufficient numbers of key personnel reside within walking distance of their workplaces, putting measures in place to facilitate job-sharing if necessary, making essential workplaces and facilities accessible in emergencies, and

75 Tokyo Metropolitan Government, Chiiki bousai keikaku (Shinsai hen) [Local Disaster Prevention Plan: Earthquake] (Tokyo Metropolitan Government revised 2014) www.bousai.metro.tokyo.jp/_res/projects/default_project/_page_/001/000/359/H26shinsai_honsatsu.pdf accessed 10 January 2018.

76 Ibid.

77 Ibid (scenario which would be caused by a 7.3 earthquake in the north end of Tokyo Bay).

78 Central Disaster Prevention Council, Shuto chokka jishin taisaku kentou working group [Working Group on Earthquakes Just below the Capital], Shuto chokka jishin no higaisoutei to taisaku nitsuite [On Damage Estimate and Countermeasures against an Earthquake Just below the Capital] (final report) (Cabinet Office December 2013) www.bousai.go.jp/jishin/syuto/taisaku_wg/pdf/syuto_wg_report.pdf accessed 10 January 2018 (Earthquake Just below the Capital report).

79 Ibid data 1 www.bousai.go.jp/jishin/syuto/taisaku_wg/pdf/syuto_wg_siryo01.pdf accessed 10 January 2018.

80 Earthquake Just Below the Capital report (n 78).

81 Ibid.

securing information systems, the electrical grid, and the availability of drinking water and food.[82]

The report also emphasizes the need to establish back-up systems and protocols.[83] If the Cabinet Office were to be seriously damaged and no longer capable of functioning as a central command office, the central government departments would need to have alternative facilities in place. Each department is required to provide for alternate facilities and communication systems that link to other departmental and governmental offices. Although no department has yet selected a site outside of Tokyo to serve as its alternate facilities, the report hints that an existing facility in Osaka could be considered for this purpose.

The report also emphasizes a need to prioritize the order of recovery operations, in addition to intended measures for restoring essential lifelines.[84] The central and local governments should also clarify, in advance, what assistance will be needed to assist essential service providers.[85]

In order to prepare for vast numbers of evacuees, the central and local governments must secure a sufficient number of shelters, publicize the locations and routes to evacuation sites, secure supplies of food and drinking water for shelters, prepare measures for transporting evacuees to safety, and prepare to provide temporary housing.[86] The central and local governments must also prepare for the likelihood that a large number of workers will be stranded and unable to return to their homes if a massive disaster were to strike.[87] With commuter transportation systems down, it is estimated that more than 5 million Tokyo-area workers would be unable to return to their homes. Ensuring sufficient shelter, food, and drinking water for these workers would be essential. The report thus urges Tokyo-based companies to ask their employees to refrain from returning home in times of emergency and for employers to keep a three-day supply of food and drinking water on hand for all employees.[88] Securing sufficient shelter for stranded commuters and providing them necessary information would be essential in the event that an earthquake devastated Tokyo.[89] The report also urges the central and local governments to contemplate whether and how they would provide assistance to stranded workers attempting to return home on foot.

In addition, the report urges the central and local governments to envision disaster recovery and reconstruction scenarios, institute quicker and more efficient recovery and reconstruction procedures, establish systems for assisting affected local governments, and prepare to dispose of disaster waste.[90]

82 Ibid.
83 Ibid.
84 Ibid.
85 Ibid.
86 Ibid.
87 Ibid.
88 Ibid.
89 Ibid.
90 Ibid.

The report is surely significant in showing that the central and local governments have definitely learned some valuable lessons from the Tohoku Earthquake. All levels of government now seem to grasp the importance of concretely planning ahead for rescue, recovery, and restoration operations.

In 2013, the Diet passed the Special Measures Act on Countermeasures against the Earthquake Just Below the Capital.[91] The Act authorized the prime minister to designate certain areas as an "Earthquake just below the Capital emergency countermeasures reinforcement zone" (*shuto chokka jishin kinkyu taisaku kuiki*) when there is a danger that a serious disaster is likely to happen and there is a necessity to adopt emergency countermeasures if a massive earthquake just below the national capital, Tokyo, occurs.[92] The government needs to adopt a basic plan for the promotion of emergency countermeasures to be implemented in these designated areas.[93] Based on this basic plan, the government needs to establish a plan concerning the preservation of essential government functions when such an earthquake strikes.[94] In order to implement the preservation of essential functions, the prime minister has to designate the districts which require this emergency improvement as "districts requiring improvement for preservation of essential government functions" (*shuto chusu kinou iji kiban seibitō chiku*).[95] Local governments inside these districts are authorized to make basic improvement plans and submit them to the prime minister for approval.[96] Various special treatments are granted to this improvement plan.[97] The Tokyo Metropolitan government and other prefectures included in the "Earthquake just below the Capital emergency countermeasures reinforcement zone" can also make a local emergency countermeasures implementation plan.[98] Affected local governments can make the emergency countermeasures operation promotion plan to implement emergency countermeasures and submit them to the prime minister for approval.[99] Various special treatments are granted for this promotion plan.[100] Subsequently, all the plans and countermeasures to be adopted against the Kanto Earthquake will be prepared under this Act.

6.1.7 Preparing for a future Tokai Earthquake

As we already saw, the Japanese government has prepared for the next Tokai Earthquake. The Special Measures Act on Large-Scale Earthquake Countermeasures

91 Shuto Chokka jishin taisaku tokubetsu sochihō [Special Measures Act on Countermeasures against the Earthquake Just Below the Capital], Law no 88 of 2013.
92 Ibid art 3(1).
93 Ibid art 4(1).
94 Ibid art 5(1).
95 Ibid art 7(1).
96 Ibid art 8.
97 Ibid art 16–art 20.
98 Ibid art 21(1).
99 Ibid art 24(1).
100 Ibid art 32–art 34.

was specifically enacted to prepare for a Tokai Earthquake. The areas where intensified countermeasures are necessary are designated as such, and a monitoring and prediction system was implemented. In May 2003, the Central Disaster Prevention Council adopted the "Tokai Earthquake Countermeasures Master Plan."[101]

Since the Japanese government has been focusing on predicting and preventing damages being caused by a future Tokai earthquake, it has not revised its disaster prevention plan since the Great East Japan Earthquake Disaster. Probably, the Japanese government believed that all the basic measures are already in place for a future Tokai Earthquake. It believes that the next Tokai Earthquake will cause 7,900 to 9,200 casualties, will destroy 230,000 to 26,000 houses, and trigger 37 trillion JPY [340 billion USD] in economic loss.[102]

However, the Shizuoka Prefecture, which is likely to be hit hardest when the next Tokai Earthquake will strike, revised its damage estimate in light of the Tohoku Earthquake.[103] Shizuoka Prefecture now estimates that there will be even more casualties because of the increased expected height of the tsunami. Shizuoka Prefecture published a new action plan based on this estimate.[104]

Shizuoka Prefecture also added another damage estimate for the Nankai Trough Megathrust Earthquake and prepared an action plan based on it as well. Now it estimates that the number of casualties might reach 5,000, the number of those injured might reach 10,400, and the number of houses totally collapsed or burned down might reach 27,000. Furthermore, if the Nankai Trough Mega Earthquake hits Shizuoka, the number of casualties might reach 69,000, the number of those injured might reach 81,000 and the number of houses collapsed or burned down might reach 231,000.[105] The local disaster plan divided its countermeasures into categories: preventive measures, emergency measures right after

101 Central Disaster Prevention Council, Tokai Jishin taisaku taiko [Tokai Earthquake Counter measures Master Plan] (Cabinet Office May 2003) www.bousai.go.jp/jishin/tokai/pdf/taikou.pdf accessed 10 January 2018.

102 Cabinet Office, Tokai jishin taisaku nitsuite [On Countermeasures against the Tokai Earthquake] (Cabinet Office) www.bousai.go.jp/jishin/tokai/pdf/gaiyou/gaiyou.pdf accessed 10 January 2018.

103 Shizuoka Prefecture, Shizuokaken dai4ji jishinhigai soutei (gaiyo) [4th Damage Estimate Result of the Earthquake] (27 June 2013) (Shizuoka Prefecture) www.pref.shizuoka.jp/bousai/4higaisoutei/documents/siuzokakendai4jijisinhigaisouteidai1jihoukokugaiyou.pdf accessed 10 January 2018. For an updated estimate, see Shizuoka Prefecture, Shizuokaken dai4ji jishingigai soutei (dai2jihoukoku) no souteikekka (gaiyo) [4th Damage Estimate result of the Earthquake (second report)] (Shizuoka Prefecture) www.pref.shizuoka.jp/bousai/4higaisoutei/documents/sizuokakendai4jijisinnhigaisouteidainijihoukokunosouteikekkagaiyou.pdf accessed 10 January 2018.

104 Shizuoka Prefecture, Jishin/tsunami taisaku action program 2013 (Shizuoka Prefecture November 2013) www.pref.shizuoka.jp/bousai/seisaku/documents/ap2013honbun.pdf accessed 10 January 2018.

105 Shizuokaken bousai kaigi [Shizuoka Local Disaster Prevention Council], Shizuokaken chiiki bousai keikaku: Jishin taisaku [Shizuoke Local Disaster Prevention Plan: Earthquake] (Shizuoka Prefecture updated June 2016) www.pref.shizuoka.jp/bousai/seisaku/documents/h28zishin.pdf accessed 10 January 2018.

the earthquake, and restoration and reconstruction measures, and provided for detailed countermeasures responding to each of these phases.[106]

6.1.8 Preparing for a possible future Nankai Trough Megathrust Earthquake

Even before the Tohoku Earthquake, the possibility of a Nankai Earthquake or Tohnankai Earthquake forced the Diet to pass the Special Measures Act concerning Promotion of Earthquake Disaster Prevention Countermeasures against Nankai and Tohnankai Earthquakes[107] in 2002. And the "Tohnankai and Nankai Earthquake Countermeasures Master Plan" was adopted by the Central Disaster Prevention Council in December 2003.[108]

After the Tohoku Earthquake, increased consensus on the likelihood of triple massive earthquakes consisting of Tokai, Tohnankai, and Nankai Earthquakes, a so-called Nankai Trough Megathrust Earthquake (*Nankai Trough jishin*), has drastically escalated potential damage projections. Now, in light of the prospect of a triple earthquake in the Nankai Trough, the estimated height of a potential tsunami has been elevated to more than ten meters high, with potential damage estimates increasing accordingly. Though casualty and damage estimates vary depending on the epicenter and magnitude of such a calamity, projections put the death toll at between 151,000 and 265,000 in the event of a Tokai region epicenter.[109] The central government also estimates that damage to lifelines (such as potable water, electricity, telecommunications, natural gas, etc.) and infrastructure (public roads, port facilities, and airports) would be extremely serious alongside other challenges relating to a projected 9.5 million evacuees and more than 6.6 million stranded workers.[110] This would necessitate over 32 million meals, 48 million liters (12 million gallons) of drinking water and 5.2 million blankets during the initial three days alone, never mind the fact that it would also generate up to 310 million tons (260 million m^3) of waste.[111] Property damage would likely

106 Ibid.

107 Tohnankai jishin/Nankai jishin ni kakawaru jishin bousai taisaku no suishin ni kansuru hōritsu [Special Measures Act concerning Earthquake Disaster Prevention Countermeasures against the Tohnankai Earthquake/Nankai Earthquake], Law no 92 of 2002. This Act was renamed in 2013. n 117.

108 Central Disaster Prevention Council, Tohnankai and Nankai jishin taisaku taiko [Tohnankai and Nankai Earthquake Countermeasures Master Plan] (Cabinet Office December 2003) www.bousai.go.jp/kaigirep/chuobou/9/pdf/haifu_2-1.pdf accessed 10 January 2018.

109 Central Disaster Prevention Council, Working Group Considering the Responses to the Nankai Trough Megathrust Earthquake, Nankai Trough kyodai jishin no higai soutei nitsuite [Estimated Casualties and Damage of the Nankai Trough Megathrust Earthquake] (Cabinet Office 29 August 2012) www.bousai.go.jp/jishin/nankai/taisaku/pdf/2_1.pdf accessed 10 January 2018.

110 Central Disaster Prevention Council, Working Group Considering the Responses to the Nankai Trough Megathrust Earthquake, Nankai Trough kyodai jishin no higai soutei nitsuite: Shisetsuto eno higai [Estimated Casualties and Damage of the Nankai Trough Megathrust Earthquake: Damages to Buildings] (Cabinet Office 8 March 2013) www.bousai.go.jp/jishin/nankai/taisaku_wg/pdf/20130318_shiryo2_3.pdf accessed 10 January 2018.

111 Ibid.

reach 169.5 trillion JPY (1.69 trillion USD), economic damage due to production delays would reach 44.7 trillion JPY (447 billion USD), and costs related to public transportation shutdowns would reach 6.1 trillion JPY (61 billion USD).[112]

In order to prepare for future earthquakes and tsunamis, the Working Group to Consider Responses to the Nankai Trough Megathrust Earthquake of the Central Disaster Prevention Council, published an interim report on measures for preparing for the Nankai Trough Megathrust Earthquake.[113] The report proposed preparing for tsunamis much higher than previously anticipated by fortifying barriers, promoting much more efficient evacuation plans, building stronger shelters, enforcing zoning requirements that reflect the possibility of massive tsunamis and promoting group relocation.[114] It also proposed preparing for earthquakes by establishing rescue and reconstruction plans.[115] The proposal also requires the government to make preparations for assisting affected local governments and disposing of disaster waste.[116]

The Diet passed the Nankai Trough Earthquake Special Measures Act[117] in 2013 and renamed the title of the 2002 Act the Special Measures Act concerning Promotion of Earthquake Disaster Countermeasures against the Nankai Trough Earthquake. It authorized the prime minister to designate certain areas as "Nankai Trough Earthquake disaster prevention countermeasures promotion area" (*Nankai Trough jishin bousai taisaku suishin chiiki*) when there is a danger that serious earthquake disaster is likely to happen and there is a necessity to promote earthquake disaster countermeasures if the Nankai Trough Earthquake strikes.[118] When these areas are so designated, the Central Disaster Prevention Council needs to establish the "Nankai Trough Earthquake disaster prevention countermeasures promotion basic plan" and promote its implementation.[119] Heads of the relevant administrative agencies are mandated to make a promotion plan concerning evacuation and safeguards against tsunamis in their

112 Central Disaster Prevention Council, Working Group Considering the Responses to the Nankai Trough Megathrust Earthquake, Nankai Trough kyodai jishin no higai soutei nitsuite: Keizaitekina higai [Estimated Casualties and Damage of the Nankai Trough Megathrust Earthquake: Economic Damages] (Cabinet Office 8 March 2013) www.bousai.go.jp/jishin/nankai/taisaku_wg/pdf/20130318_shiryo3.pdf accessed 10 January 2018.

113 Central Disaster Prevention Council, Nankai Trough kyodaijishin taisaku kento working group [Working Group Considering the Responses to the Nankai Trough Megathrust Earthquake], Nankai Trough kyodai jishin taisaku nitsuite [On Measures for Preparing for the Nankai Trough Megathrust Earthquake] (Cabinet Office May 2013) www.bousai.go.jp/jishin/nankai/taisaku_wg/pdf/20130528_honbun.pdf accessed 10 January 2018 (Working Group Report).

114 Ibid.

115 Ibid.

116 Ibid.

117 Tohnankai/Nankai jishin ni kakawaru jishin bousai taisaku no suishin ni kansuru tokubetsu sochihō no ichibu wo kaiseisuru hōritsu [Act to Amend Parts of Act concerning Earthquake Disaster Prevention Countermeasures against Tohnankai/Nankai Earthquakes](Nankai Trough Earthquake Special Measures Act), Law no 87 of 2013.

118 Ibid art 3(1).

119 Ibid art 4(1).

disaster prevention plans.[120] Public accommodation such as hospitals in the designated areas are also mandated to adopt countermeasure plans.[121] The prime minister is also authorized to designate areas where there is a likely risk of serious disaster and there is a special necessity to intensify tsunami countermeasures against the Nankai Trough Earthquake as "Nankai Trough Earthquake tsunami evacuation countermeasures special reinforcement area" (*Nankai Trough jishin tsunami hinan tokubetsu kyouka chiiki*).[122] Local governments included in this area are authorized to make a "tsunami disaster countermeasures emergency operation plan" regarding evacuation and group relocation.[123] Various special treatments are granted to such operations including group relocation operations.[124] And the Central Disaster Prevention Council adopted the fundamental promotion plan for disaster prevention against a Nankai Trough Megathrust Earthquake in March 2014.[125]

Furthermore, the Central Disaster Prevention Council adopted a fundamental plan for emergency response to the Nankai Trough Megathrust Earthquake in March, 2015, revised after the Kumamoto Earthquake in June 2017, which is examined below.[126] Especially noteworthy in this plan is a timeline of response from day one to day four of a disaster, which is divided into four parts: emergency rescue (rescue, emergency help and extinguishing fire), medical assistance, supply of emergency goods and lifelines (fuel, electricity, and gas). It also called on the central government to step in without waiting for requests from affected local governments and to coordinate between various government departments.[127] It anticipated that 16,000 police officers, 18,900 firefighters, and 110,000 SDF officers would be brought in for emergency rescue.[128] It also mandated the designation of emergency transportation routes and urged the government to establish a system of checking the availability of these routes right after the disaster, the immediate ban on the private use of these routes, and the designation of alternative routes if they are unavailable.[129] Furthermore, based upon the assumption that the residents could survive the first three days

120 Ibid art 5(1).

121 Ibid art 7(1).

122 Ibid art 10(1).

123 Ibid art 12(1).

124 Ibid art 15–art 17.

125 Central Disaster Prevention Council, Nankai Trough jishin bousaitaisaku suishin kihonkeikaku [Fundamental Plan for Promotion of Countermeasures against the Nankai Trough Earthquake] (Cabinet Office 28 March 2014) www.bousai.go.jp/jishin/nankai/pdf/nankaitrough_keikaku.pdf accessed 10 January 2018.

126 Central Disaster Prevention Council, Nankai Trough jishin niokeru gutaitekina oukyutaisakukatsudo nikansuru keikaku [Plan for Emergency Response to the Nankai Trough Megathrust Earthquake] (Cabinet Office March 2015, revised 23 June 2017), www.bousai.go.jp/jishin/nankai/pdf/nankai_oukyu_keikaku02.pdf.

127 Ibid.

128 Ibid.

129 Ibid.

of a disaster with their own personal preparation and municipal preparation, it anticipated the supply of emergency goods from day four, including 460,000m^3 of water, 72 million meals, and 5.7 million blankets, and mandated the preparation of securing and transporting them to emergency central hubs for further distribution for the first seven days without waiting for requests.[130]

6.1.9 Educating the public on preparing for earthquakes

Mere revision of disaster prevention plans will not be sufficient. After all, the existing tsunami warning system failed to save the lives of 18,561 people. Some had even run to emergency shelters but still perished because shelters were not built to withstand such powerful tsunamis. However, many victims simply stayed in their homes, believing that they were safe. The Central Disaster Prevention Council thus emphasized the need to raise public awareness on shelter whereabouts and evacuation routes along with the importance of swift evacuation and routine evacuation training. It also emphasized the importance of teaching children about disaster prevention.[131]

The citizenry should be aware of the fact that, in times of emergency, there may be no time for the local government to orchestrate evacuations. Decisions on evacuation may ultimately come down to matters of individual choice. Still, it is important ahead of time to give residents the information they need to make informed rational judgments on such matters. Additionally, preparations for the evacuation of seniors and persons with disabilities must be given apt consideration as part of any disaster plan.[132]

Moreover, evacuation plans must be realistic. As we already saw, after the Tohoku Earthquake, many evacuees attempted to drive to higher ground, causing tremendous traffic jams in which traffic was reduced to a standstill in some places. Many were swept away by the tsunami while attempting to evacuate in their cars. However, simply encouraging evacuation on foot might not be sufficient either. Finding a way to divert traffic so as to allow for more efficient and smooth evacuation by car is likely a necessary component of any disaster plan.[133]

6.1.10 Preventing information blackouts

Due to power outages, evacuees had no access to television news. Battery-operated radios were the only source of information for most evacuees. To facilitate

130 Ibid.

131 Central Disaster Prevention Council (n 72).

132 It is a significant improvement that as a result of the 2013 amendment, now the local government can collect personal information as to those in need of assistance for evacuation and hand over such information to those who will be supposed to provide assistance.

133 Central Disaster Prevention Council, Bousai taisaku suishin kaigi [Disaster Prevention Countermeasures Promotion Meeting], Jidousha de anzen katsu kakujitsu ni hinan dekiru housaku [How to Evacuate Safely and Effectively by Automobile] (Cabinet Office) www.bousai.go.jp/jishin/tsunami/hinan/5/pdf/3.pdf accessed 10 January 2018.

the flow of information about the safety of family members or other information vital to evacuees, the Ministry of Internal Affairs and Communications quickly moved to permit the establishment of several mini local radio stations in affected communities. The Ministry cut red tape and skipped regular licensing procedures, and instead granted temporary "disaster broadcasting station" (*rinji saigai housoukyoku*) licenses in affected municipalities in order to make these mini local stations possible.[134] The significance of the role played by these mini local radio stations should not be underestimated. This disaster showed that there is a definite need to prepare for large-scale power outages and to prevent information blackouts in times of emergency.[135]

Moreover, another grave problem revealed by the Great East Japan Earthquake Disaster was the vulnerability of Japan's telecommunications network. The earthquake and tsunami left many telecommunications facilities damaged, submerged, or swept away, with underground cables severed or damaged. Telephone poles were toppled and their cables damaged. Transmission towers and facilities for cellular phones were also seriously damaged. Moreover, power blackouts rendered many undamaged facilities virtually useless as their emergency generators soon ran out of fuel. After the disaster, more than 1.9 million landline telephones went offline and more than 29,000 transmission facilities for cell phones were destroyed.[136] As a result, almost everyone in affected communities lost all means of communication. It took more than a month to restore telecommunications in these areas.[137]

The Telecommunication Business Act requires telecommunication carriers to give priority to important telecommunications being used to provide assistance during times of emergency such as natural disasters, thereby mandating telecommunication carriers to secure the availability and reliability of the telecommunication infrastructure.[138] However, it appears that these requirements were insufficient. In the midst of massive natural disaster, it is perhaps impossible to prevent all damage to telecommunications infrastructure. However, providers should have prepared for the possibility of serious disaster. In the Tohoku area, mobile phones transmit wirelessly to transmission facilities but transmission cables connect transmission facilities with the main switchboard. When transmission facilities were destroyed or lost all power after emergency generators ran out of fuel, all mobile phones in

134 Ministry of Internal Affairs and Communications, Higashinihon daishinsai ni saisi kaisetsu sareta rinji saigai housoukyoku no joukyou [List of Temporary Disaster Broadcasting Stations Established in Response to the Great East Japan Earthquake Disaster] (MIC 27 June 2017) www.soumu.go.jp/main_content/000492069.pdf accessed 10 January 2018.

135 Ministry of Internal Affairs and Communications, Tohoku ni okeru rinji saigai housoukyoku no keiken to kongono torikumi [Experience of Temporary Disaster Broadcasting Stations in Tohoku and the Future Agenda] (29 August 2012), MIAC www.soumu.go.jp/soutsu/tohoku/hodo/h2407-09/0829a1001.html accessed 10 January 2018.

136 Ministry of Internal Affairs and Communications, Heisei 23nen johou tsushin hakusho [Information and Telecommunications Whitepaper 2011] (MIC) www.soumu.go.jp/johotsusintokei/whitepaper/ja/h23/pdf/n0010000.pdf accessed 10 January 2018.

137 Ibid. Most telecommunications were restored by the end of April 2011.

138 Denki tsushin jigyouhō [Telecommunication Business Act], Law no 86 of 1984, art 8.

those areas became useless. It is imperative for telecommunications companies to ensure that their transmission facilities can function during times of emergency and that they can connect with the main switchboard via multiple cables, satellite, or another means of wireless communication.[139]

The next Kanto Earthquake could very well knock out all communications in Tokyo if appropriate proactive measures are not put in place. It is essential for telecommunications companies to build back-up facilities elsewhere to ensure data backups and that access to vital data is not lost following a future Kanto Earthquake.[140] Such backup data centers are essential not only for financial institutions[141] but also for all the major companies that need data to restore their business activities after devastation in a massive earthquake. Since some local governments lost all data on their residents because of the tsunami, now the Ministry of Internal Affairs and Communications are facilitating the introduction of a cloud data center for all local governments, managing all the information on local residents.[142] The central government is also committed to preparing a back-up plan for their work should a massive earthquake destroy their workplaces, including the adoption of measures to make all the data available to their public workers without interruption.[143]

6.1.11 Japanese FEMA?

One possible reform in Japan would see the establishment of a permanent independent agency for emergency preparedness. As is well known, the United

139 Daikibosaigaito kinkyujitai niokeru tsushinkakuho no arikata nikansuru kentoukai [Study Group on Telecommunications in Times of Emergency such as Large Scale Disaster], Daikibo saigaitō kinkyujitai niokeru tsushinkakuho no arikata nitsuite [On the Telecommunications in Times of Emergency such as Large Scale Disaster] (MIC 27 December 2011) www.soumu.go.jp/main_content/000141084.pdf accessed 10 January 2018; Ministry of Internal Affairs and Communications, Jouhou tsushin gijutsu bunkakai [Subcommittee on Telecommunication Technology], Denki tsushin setsubi no anzen/ shinraisei taisaku ni kansuru jikou [Issues concerning Measures to Secure the Security and Reliability of Telecommunication Facilities] (MIC 17 February 2012) www.soumu.go.jp/main_content/000145731.pdf accessed 10 January 2018.

140 The Keidanren [Japan Business Federation], an association of major Japanese companies, also recommended this even before the Tohoku Earthquake. Kendairan [Japan Business Federation], Shuto chokka jishin ni ikani sonaeruka [How to Prepare for an Earthquake Just Below the Capital?] (Keidanren 14 October 2008) www.keidanren.or.jp/japanese/policy/2008/070/honbun.html accessed 10 January 2018.

141 Bank of Japan, Higashinihon daishinsai wo humaeta backup center no jikkousei kakuho [How to Secure the Effectiveness of Back-up Centers in Light of the Great East Japan Earthquake Disaster] (BOJ May 2012) www.boj.or.jp/announcements/release_2012/data/rel120530d2.pdf accessed 10 January 2018.

142 Ministry of Internal Affairs and Communications, Jichitai cloud portal site [Cloud Portal Site for Local Government] (MIC) www.soumu.go.jp/main_sosiki/jichi_gyousei/c-gyousei/lg-cloud/index.html accessed 10 January 2018.

143 Ministry of Land, Infrastructure, Transport and Tourism, Kokudo seisakukyoku [Land Policy Bureau], Tokyo-ken no chuusuu kinou no backup no kentou ni kakawaru haikeitō oyobi genjou [Background and Current Situation of Back-up of Essential Functions in the Tokyo Area] (MLIT 9 December 2011) www.mlit.go.jp/common/000185260.pdf accessed 10 January 2018.

States has the Federal Emergency Management Agency (FEMA). The FEMA was established in 1979 to take charge of natural hazard preparedness but also assumes responsibilities relating to civil defense.[144] Following the 9/11 attacks, the FEMA was reorganized and absorbed by the Department of Homeland Security (DHS) in 2003.[145] The FEMA regained its status as a stand-alone entity in 2006 though still under the umbrella of the DHS.[146] The agency is generally regarded as being responsible for supporting response to disasters that overwhelm the resources of local and state authorities or that spill over into several states.[147] The governor of an affected state must formally request that the president declare a "major disaster" or "emergency" to trigger federal disaster assistance and FEMA involvement.[148]

After the Tohoku Earthquake, some did propose the establishment of a Japanese-style FEMA.[149] Given Japan's susceptibility to natural disaster, establishing such an agency could be a prudent move indeed. However, making this agency a reality would be extremely difficult in Japan. We have already seen how extreme departmentalism is preventing quick and effective recovery and reconstruction. Each government department has a vested interest in safeguarding its regulatory and budgetary authority. Almost all bureaucrats would surely oppose the establishment of any independent agency that might chip away at their department's authority or budget. Bureaucrats in Japan, almost by definition, seek to preserve their own authority and budget. It is highly unlikely, therefore, that any proposal to establish an independent FEMA-like agency would succeed, especially if that agency were endowed with sweeping authority and an independent budget. If a proposal to establish such an agency is tabled, it is likely to be undermined, depriving the proposed agency of any substantive powers. After all, this is exactly what happened to the Reconstruction Agency after the Tohoku Earthquake.

144 Federal Emergency Management Agency (FEMA) www.fema.gov/about-agency accessed 10 January 2018.

145 Ibid.

146 Federal Emergency Management Agency (FEMA), About the Agency (FEMA) www.fema.gov/pdf/about/pub1.pdf accessed 10 January 2018.

147 James Lee Witt, "Federal Role Is Vital When the Need Is Great," (*New York Times* 30 October 2012) www.nytimes.com/roomfordebate/2012/10/30/do-we-really-need-fema/femas-role-is-vital-when-the-need-is-great accessed 10 January 2018.

148 Francis X. McCarthy, FEMA's Disaster Declaration Process: A Primer (Congressional Research Service 18 May 2011) www.fas.org/sgp/crs/homesec/RL34146.pdf accessed 10 January 2018. It must be noted, however, that there is very strong criticism against the FEMA, insisting that its establishment has not brought any significant changes to the disaster countermeasures. Andrew S. Mener, Disaster Response in the United States of America: An Analysis of the Bureaucratic and Political History of a Failing System (2007), http://repository.upenn.edu/curej/63. For a disaster legal system in the United States, see Daniel A. Farber, James Ming Chen, Robert R.M. Verchick & Lisa Grow Sun, *Disaster Law and Policy* (3rd ed. Kluwer 2015).

149 Indeed, Shinzo Abe, president of the LDP, now a prime minister, was among them. Shinzo Abe, Nihon saiki [Stand up Japan again], www.s-abe.or.jp/wp-content/themes/politicianA/img/seisaku2012.pdf accessed 10 January 2018. *See also* "Kinkyu jitai kanricho shinsetsu wo teigen: Jimin hukkou honbu [Creation of the Emergency Management Agency: LDP Reconstruction Headquarter Proposed]" (*Yomiuri Shimbun* 2 August 2014) www.yomiuri.co.jp/feature/TO000305/20140802-OYT1T50012.html accessed 10 January 2018.

6.1.12 Kumamoto Earthquakes

Japan faced another big challenge in 2016 with the Kumamoto Earthquakes (*Kumamoto jishin*). On 14 April 2016, a powerful earthquake hit the Kumamoto Prefecture, Kyushu, a southern part of Japan, with a magnitude of 6.5.[150] The government issued a warning to local residents to prepare for the aftershocks. But two days later, on 16 April, an even more powerful earthquake hit the same Kumamoto prefecture with a magnitude of 7.3.[151] The epicenter was slightly moved from the 14 April one but both were caused by the movement of active faults underneath. It is now generally believed that the 16 April earthquake is the main earthquake and 14 April earthquake was a precursor. The 16 April one was as powerful as the Hanshin Awaji Earthquake. Many powerful earthquakes followed nearby. These two earthquakes together with the many earthquakes that occurred nearby are generally called the Kumamoto Earthquakes of 2016. Fifty persons died because of the earthquakes.[152]

They were very unusual in that two very powerful earthquakes hit the same area so close in time.[153] Most of the buildings that collapsed were built before the 1981 construction standard revision. But some new buildings also collapsed. The construction standard was designed to make sure that each house could survive the strongest earthquake but it was not anticipated that two very powerful earthquakes would hit almost at the same time.[154] The earthquakes also knocked down many city government buildings that were supposed to provide help to survivors, as well as many shelters such as public school facilities that were supposed to accept evacuees.[155] Many of the municipal governments affected did not have a business continuity plan after the natural disaster.[156] Moreover, the earthquakes caused debris flow, landslides in many areas, and the destruction of many roads and bridges, preventing emergency traffic from coming in to municipalities.[157]

150 Hijo saigai taisaku honbu [Extreme Disaster Headquarter], Heisei 28nen (2016) Kumamotoken Kumamoto chihō wo shingen tosuru jishin nikakawaru higaijoukyoutō nituite [On Damages Resulting from Earthquakes in Kumamoto Region in Kumamoto Prefecture in 2016] (Cabinet Office 13 April 2016) www.bousai.go.jp/updates/h280414jishin/pdf/h280414jishin_39.pdf accessed 10 January 2018 (Kumamoto Earthquake Headquarters).

151 Ibid.

152 Ibid. An additional five persons died because of the subsequent heavy rain and an additional 196 persons died thereafter for earthquake related reasons.

153 When the JMA issued an aftershock warning to the residents after the 14 April earthquake, most of the residents assumed that the aftershocks would be less powerful than the 14 April one, an assumption that proved totally false because the 16 April one was more powerful.

154 National Diet Library, 'Heisei 28nen Kumamoto jishin eno taiou (shita) [Responses to Kumamoto Earthquakes of 2016 (part 11)]', (2016) 915 *Reference* 1, 5 (NDL(II)). As a result, some of the buildings that survived the first earthquake were not able to survive the second and more powerful one.

155 National Diet Library, Heisei 28nen Kumamoto jishin eno taiou (ue) [Responses to Kumamoto Earthquakes of 2016 (part I)], (2016) 914 *Reference* 1, 10, 12 (NDL(I)). The earthquakes revealed that many municipal government buildings as well as shelters have not received a seismic upgrade. Ibid 10, 12. Priority was not given to the seismic upgrade of city government buildings and many of the shelters survived the earthquakes but could not be used because ceiling or windows were destroyed. Ibid 12.

156 Ibid.

157 Kumamoto Earthquake Headquarters (n 150) 5.

As a result, even though emergency goods were delivered, they were not efficiently distributed.[158] These damages were apparently beyond the predictions made before the earthquakes. A total number of roughly 300,000 residents was forced to evacuate.[159] Also many residents stayed in their automobiles outside of the designated shelters because of their concern with the safety of the shelters and the continuing aftershocks.[160] The government had extreme difficulty tracking down these evacuees. Also there was an insufficient number of parking lots to accept all of them. Many evacuees also died of deep vein thrombosis, generally known as the economy class syndrome, while staying in their motor vehicles.[161] Furthermore, heavy rain fell from 20 to 21 June and caused additional landslides and flooding in this area, causing further loss and damages.[162] It was not anticipated that additional natural disasters unrelated to the earthquakes would hit the disaster areas soon thereafter.

However, aside from these problems, overall the government's response was quick and mostly effective. The Cabinet Countermeasure Office was established right after the 14 April earthquake and a half hour later the Emergency Disaster Response Headquarters was established.[163] The Prime Minister immediately issued instructions to evaluate the damage, to engage in countermeasures together with local governments, and to inform the public about the extent of the damage and the necessary evacuations.[164] The Disaster Assistance Act, Disaster Victim Life Rebuilding Support Act, and Serious Disaster Act were applied[165] and a "specified emergency disaster" was declared to provide exceptional treatment for victims.[166] The government sent emergency food and goods even without a request and decided to spend the reserve fund for assistance, recovery, and reconstruction.[167] Self Defense Forces (SDF) officers were sent upon request for emergency rescue together with police officers and firefighters.[168] The municipal government built 4,303 temporary housings for evacuees and allocated many vacant public apartments or hotel rooms to them.[169]

One month later, the government designated the disaster as an "emergency disaster," which allows the central government to require various recovery and reconstruction jobs to be performed by the local government under the Large-Scale Disaster Reconstruction Act.[170] Various financial assistance was provided by the central and local governments to the victims. Significant achievements can be

158 Ibid 11.
159 Ibid 4.
160 Ibid.
161 NDL (I) (n 155) 12.
162 Ibid 3–4.
163 Kumamoto Earthquake Headquarters (n 150) 23.
164 Ibid 27.
165 Ibid 28.
166 Ibid.
167 Ibid 28–29.
168 Ibid 44.
169 Ibid 29–30.
170 Ibid 28.

found six months later, although the government still needs to make much more serious reconstruction efforts.[171]

This does not mean that everything went as smoothly as was expected. With respect to disaster waste disposal, the Kumamoto prefecture had difficulty in facilitating its disposal.[172] Although it requires consent from an owner of a house to remove a totally destroyed or half destroyed house, the local government had some difficulty in finding the owners if houses were vacant.[173] Some of the houses contained asbestos and other harmful materials, and because of the destruction by the earthquakes, there was a risk that asbestos might be exposed.[174] There are some unanswered questions as well, such as the legality of allowing volunteers who delivered emergency goods to affected areas to bring waste with them on their way back, since it is only licensed waste disposal companies who are allowed to collect and transfer waste.[175] Moreover, the Ministry of Land, Infrastructure, Transport and Tourism reported that it took too much energy to collect information on the availability of connecting roads, since major routes classified as "emergency roads" were damaged and such damage prevented emergency vehicles and transporters of relief goods from using them. Also, many electricity poles were knocked down because of the liquefaction of the ground, which further prevented rescue and relief. Further, sufficient expert advice was not available for the central government to repair roads managed by the local government. Lastly, it took tremendous effort to individually review and issue special permits for emergency vehicles; there was no sufficient systematic coordination to prevent traffic jams, and some of the municipalities were left inaccessible because of the serious damage to emergency roads.[176]

171 NDL (II) (n 154) 1–14. Kumamoto Prefecture governor is now requesting the central government for long-term financial aid for reconstruction. Kumamoto Prefecture, Heisei28nen Kumamoto jishin karano hukyu/hukkou ni kakawaru youbou [Request with respect to the Reconstruction after the 2016 Kumamoto Earthquake] (Kumamoto Prefecture June 2017) www.pref.kumamoto.jp/common/UploadFileOutput.ashx?c_id=3&id=19916&sub_id=1&flid=107233 accessed 10 January 2018.

172 NDL(I) (n 155) at 13–14.

173 Ibid 14.

174 Ibid.

175 Ibid.

176 Ministry of Land, Infrastructure, Transport and Tourism, Kumamoto jishin wohumaeta kadai to ronten [Agenda and Issues for Discussion in Light of the Kumamoto Earthquake] (MLIT) www.mlit.go.jp/common/001135911.pdf accessed 10 January 2018. The MLIT thus urges the necessity of introducing a more efficient and effective method of collecting information on road availability (such as use of drones), to reconsider the construction standard for emergency roads, to introduce some kind of mechanism to prevent electricity poles from blocking major roads (such as removing all poles from emergency roads or placing a limit), to prepare for coordination between the central government and local government to allow the central government to repair roads managed by local government more smoothly, to introduce an automated permission system for emergency vehicles, to facilitate a coordinated effort to prevent traffic jams, and to make sure that the overall road network could be preserved. Ibid. The MLIT already decided to facilitate the seismic upgrade of emergency roads and facilitate countermeasures to prevent the collapse of overpasses and to allow much easier repair if damaged. Ministry of Land, Infrastructure, Transport and Tourism, Kinkyu yuso douro no taishinkyouka no kasokuka [Facilitation of Seismic Upgrade of Emergency Roads] (MLIT) www.mlit.go.jp/road/bosai/measures/index1.html#1-1 accessed 10 January 2018. It has also banned the establishment of new electricity poles alongside emergency roads. Ministry of Land, Infrastructure, Transport and Tourism, Mudenchuka suishin notameno aratana torikumi [New Measure to Promote the No Pole Policy] (MLIT) www.mlit.go.jp/road/road/traffic/chicyuka/chi_17.html accessed 10 January 2018.

These earthquakes showed that, despite the improvements and new countermeasures after the Great East Japan Earthquake Disaster, there might still be something left unprepared. They may thus necessitate further reform in disaster preparation, disaster response and reconstruction.[177]

6.1.13 Prediction is simply impossible

After the Tohoku Earthquake, an increasing number of scientists came to raise questions about Japan's earthquake countermeasure model based on the predictions of future powerful earthquakes.[178] As we already saw, Japan's earthquake countermeasures are premised upon the assumption that powerful earthquakes would recur in 100–150 years. The Special Measures Act on Large-Scale Earthquake Countermeasures was based on the possibility of prediction, authorizing the prime minister to issue an "emergency warning" and to adopt all preparation measures. The predictability of the earthquake is based on the assumption that there is the "preslip," a precursor to powerful earthquakes, and if this movement is caught quickly enough, then it is possible to predict an earthquake. However, many came to doubt whether such "preslip" necessarily occurs before the earthquake and whether the "preslip" can therefore be used as a precursor. In light of the possibility of the powerful earthquakes in the Nankai Trough area, the Central Disaster Prevention Council had set up an expert committee on predictability of the Nankai Trough Megathrust Earthquake. Its report was approved in May 2013, concluding that the prediction of earthquakes is "difficult' based on current scientific knowledge.[179] The Central Disaster Prevention Council continued its examination and the expert committee came to acknowledge that the date of the next Nankai Trough Megathrust Earthquake, just like the Tokai Earthquake, is "impossible" to predict within any acceptable degree of certainty.[180]

Although this report didn't call for abandonment or revision of the Large-scale Earthquake Countermeasures Act, it was a radical step toward a new paradigm for earthquake countermeasures in Japan. The Disaster Prevention Countermeasure Council of the Central Disaster Prevention Council adopted the new policy for

177 As we already saw, the Central Disaster Prevention Council revised its plan for emergency response to the Nankai Trough Megathrust Earthquake based on the experience of the Kumamoto Earthquake. n 126.

178 Robert J. Geller, "Japan Must Admit It Can't Predict Quakes" (2017) 545 *Nature* 289.

179 Nankai Torafu zoi no daikibojishin no yosokukanousei nikansuru chousabukai [Expert Committee on the Predictability of the Nankai Trough Megathrust Earthquake], Nankai Torafu zoi no daikibojishin no yosokukanousei nitstuite [On the Predictability of the Nankai Trough Megatrust Earthquake] Report (Cabinet Office May 2013) www.bousai.go.jp/jishin/nankai/yosoku/pdf/20130528yosoku_houkoku1.pdf accessed 10 January 2018.

180 Nankai Torafu zoi no daikibojishin no yosokukanousei nikansuru chousabukai [Expert Committee on the Predictability of the Nankai Trough Megathrust Earthquake], Nankai Torafu zoi no daikibojishin no yosokukanousei nitstuite [On the Predictability of the Nankai Trough Megathrust Earthquake] (Cabinet Office August 2017) www.bousai.go.jp/jishin/nankai/tyosabukai_wg/pdf/h290825honbun.pdf accessed 10 January 2018 12.

earthquake countermeasures based on this report in September 2017.[181] Even if the precise prediction of the earthquake is impossible, it was thought that the increased probability of the earthquake could be found through monitoring. The Japan Meteorological Agency (JMA) would thus issue statements on the occurrence of major changes, which could be a precursor to the earthquake, and then allow an expert committee to be established to issue a statement on the increased probability of the earthquake.[182] It is expected that the policy for earthquake countermeasures would be similarly revised to reflect this new paradigm.

6.2 Future of nuclear power

Japan needs a new nuclear policy and new regulatory scheme for nuclear powers. In order to avoid another serious nuclear disaster such as what happened in Fukushima, Japan must revise its safety standards and prepare for a possible nuclear emergency. Moreover, Japan needs to reconsider the power generation system and its entire energy policy.

The nuclear disaster in Fukushima totally shattered public faith in the safety of nuclear power. It became crystal clear that the safety of nuclear power was nothing more than a myth. No matter how hard scientists and nuclear physicists work to ensure nuclear safety, there is a limit to what they can do; accidents can and do happen and serious devastation can result. Simply put, inherent and potentially catastrophic risk necessarily accompanies nuclear power. This realization, now firmly entrenched in the national psyche, could significantly impact the future of nuclear power in Japan.

6.2.1 The future of nuclear power contested

As discussed previously, former Prime Minister Naoto Kan famously suggested that Japan should rid itself of nuclear power altogether.[183] Other leaders of the Democratic Party of Japan (DPJ) remained unconvinced over whether abandoning all nuclear power was a realistic choice for Japan. As a result, Kan's statement was immediately downgraded to a statement of his own personal opinion and not the official view adopted by the meeting of the Cabinet.[184] However, in the lead up to the 2012 election, the DPJ government decided to pursue the abolition of nuclear power in order to make this issue a central issue in the election.

181 Central Disaster Prevention Council, Nankai torafu zoi no jishin kansoku/hyouka ni motoduku bousai taiou no arikata nitsuite [On New Policy for Disaster Prevention Countermeasures Based on the Monitoring and Evaluation of the Earthquake in the Nankai Trough Area] (Cabinet Office September 2017) www.bousai.go.jp/kaigirep/chuobou/jikkoukaigi/10/pdf/shiryo2.pdf accessed 10 January 2018 15.

182 Ibid 34–36; Japan Meteorological Agency, Nankai Torafu jishin nitsuite [On the Nankai Trough Megathrust Earthquake] (JMA) www.data.jma.go.jp/svd/eqev/data/nteq/index.html accessed 10 January 2018.

183 *See* Chapter 3 n 173.

184 Ibid.

Moreover, during the 2012 election, other political parties such as the Socialist Party and the Japan Communist Party also supported the abolition of nuclear power. Furthermore, Ichiro Ozawa, a former DPJ leader and a chief contributor to the DPJ's election in 2009, left the DPJ and created a new political party calling for total abolition of nuclear power in Japan.[185] Many citizens supported these anti-nuclear stances.[186]

The LDP on the other hand took a more ambivalent stance toward nuclear power, arguing that the future of nuclear power should be carefully studied before any final decisions are made. The LDP appears to have sided with business associations' claim that total abolition of nuclear power is unrealistic and that Japan should continue using nuclear power.[187]

Deciding on whether to abolish nuclear power definitely poses a tough choice. Alternative energy sources, such as solar, wind or geothermal power are often viewed as unreliable and costly.[188] Critics contend that, unlike nuclear power, these energy sources do not offer a sufficient and consistent supply of energy. It was therefore natural for power companies to rely upon imported natural gas to cover energy shortages arising from nuclear power plant stoppages. However, imported natural gas is also costly and all of the power companies that had to shut down their nuclear power plants are now looking at significant losses because of rising natural gas import costs.[189] Japanese power companies want to increase electricity charges in order to reflect these increasing costs. Unsurprisingly, such price increases are unpopular among the general public and business circles are naturally opposed to any increase. Manufacturers fear that increased electricity charges will necessitate product price increases thus rendering Japanese products less competitive in international markets. Therefore, the central government is reluctant to approve electricity charge hikes. However, the government had no choice but to approve gradual increases in electricity charges.[190]

185 "Ozawa to Abolish All Nuclear Power Plants within 10 Years if Elected' (*Japan Today* 2 August 2012) https://japantoday.com/category/politics/ozawa-vows-to-abolish-all-nuclear-power-plants-within-10-years-if-elected accessed 10 January 2018.

186 Andrew Blowers, "The Future Is Not Nuclear: Ethical Choices for Energy after Fukushima," in Richard Hindmarsh (ed), *Nuclear Disaster at Fukushima Daiichi: Social, Political and Environmental Issues* (Routledge 2013) 175.

187 "Despite 2011 Disaster, Pro-Nuclear Party Could Win Power in Japan" (*Reuters* 26 November 2012) www.reuters.com/article/us-japan-election-nuclear/analysis-despite-2011-disaster-pro-nuclear-party-could-win-power-in-japan-idUSBRE8AQ02U20121127 accessed 10 January 2018.

188 "First the iPhone. Now Renewables" (*Wall Street Journal* 18 June 2012) http://online.wsj.com/article/SB10001424052702304371504577404343259051300.html accessed 10 January 2018.

189 "Chuubuden, saishu akaji 600 okuen, genpatsu teishide karyoku nenryouhi zouka [Chubu Electric Reported 60 billion JPY Deficit: Impact of Fuel Cost Increase because of the Stoppage of Nuclear Power]" (*Nihonkeizai Shinbun* 4 September 2012) www.nikkei.com/article/DGXNASGD0402U_U2A900C1TJ0000/ accessed 10 January 2018.

190 The electricity charge is already 40% higher for general customers compared with pre-disaster level. "Genpatsu teishi dakejanai: Denkiryoukin joushouno shinsou [It is Not Only the Nuclear Power Stoppage: Truth behind Constant Electricity Charge Hike]" (*Toyo Keizai* 22 September 2014) http://toyokeizai.net/articles/-/48133 accessed 10 January 2018.

Abolition of nuclear power was one of the central issues in the 2012 election. However, as discussed previously, the LDP won in a landslide victory, securing more than a two-thirds majority in the House of Representatives despite its pro-nuclear stance. Apparently, the people did not want the abolition of nuclear power.[191]

6.2.2 Establishment of the Nuclear Regulatory Authority

As we saw in previous chapters, the most egregious flaw in the regulatory scheme for nuclear safety was the absence of a truly independent regulatory agency.[192] As long as nuclear power subsists in Japan, the government must ensure a truly independent regulatory agency.

The DPJ government indicated its willingness to establish a new agency within the Ministry of Environment (MOE) to safeguard nuclear power.[193] The cabinet approved the decision to submit a bill to establish the Nuclear Regulatory Agency, within the MOE, which would have brought the agency into existence on 1 April 2012.[194] The opposition LDP submitted a different bill to establish a Nuclear Regulatory Commission, an independent commission. Negotiation thereafter between the DPJ and the LDP/Komei Party coalition brought about a compromise and a new bill was submitted to the Diet. The Act to Establish the Nuclear Regulatory Authority was finally passed by the Diet and promulgated on 27 June 2012.[195] The Nuclear Regulatory Authority (NRA) began work on 19 September 2012 with its predecessor, the Nuclear and Industrial Safety Agency (NISA) and the Nuclear Safety Commission (NSC), being abolished on the same day. The NRA was created as an external organ of the MOE with the Nuclear Regulatory Agency as its administrative arm and is granted independence within the MOE.

The NRA's mission is to regulate the safety of nuclear power in order to protect life, health, and property, to preserve the environment, and to contribute to the security of Japan.[196] The NRA was established under the umbrella of the MOE. The NRA is led by a chairperson and four commissioners.[197] The chairperson

191 "A Cautious Return to Nuclear Power" (*Japan Times* 3 January 2013) www.japantimes.co.jp/news/2013/01/03/national/a-cautious-return-to-nuclear-power/#.Uc_Yxz5dbR0 accessed 10 January 2018

192 Chapter 3 n 183.

193 Chief Cabinet Secretary, Press Release (kantei 15 August 2011) www.kantei.go.jp/jp/tyoukanpress/201108/15_a.html accessed 10 January 2018.

194 Cabinet (kantei 31 January 2012) www.kantei.go.jp/jp/kakugi/2012/kakugi-2012013101.html accessed 10 January 2018.

195 Genshiryoku kisei iinkai secchihō [Act to Establish the Nuclear Regulatory Authority], Law no 47 of 2012 (Nuclear Regulatory Authority Act).

196 Ibid art 3.

197 Ibid art 6(1).

and all commissioners are appointed by the prime minister with the consent of both houses in the Diet.[198] To preserve the NRA's independence, the statute excludes nuclear power company executives and employees, other nuclear business operators, and members of associations affiliated with these companies, or operators from becoming NRA commissioners.[199] What is unique about this regulatory agency is its adoption of a no-return rule[200] for officials coming from other governmental departments such as the Ministry of Economy, Trade and Industry (METI) and the Ministry of Education, Culture, Sports, Science and Technology (MEXT). This basically amounts to a total denial of the traditional bureaucratic custom that sees public officials transferring from one department to another and then returning to their previous department after a term of service. The no-return policy was adopted as a measure for securing the independence of NRA officials.[201] Likewise, a policy prohibiting NRA officials from retiring to positions in the nuclear industry was contemplated.[202] This initiative represents an attempt to curb the practice of "amakudari," similar to the western concept of the "revolving door" that sees officials move from positions as regulators into cushy positions in the industries they once regulated. This practice has long been associated with corruption arising from unhealthy relationships between industry and government that undermine regulation. Just how successful the NRA will be at resisting regulatory capture remains to be seen.

Under the new system, the METI will promote nuclear energy, while the NRA, as an independent agency within the MOE, will supervise compliance with safety regulations. Moreover, the Nuclear Reactor Regulation Act was amended to strengthen the safety requirements for power-generating nuclear reactors and to require that pre-existing nuclear reactors be retrofitted so that they satisfy the new safety requirements.[203] Furthermore, the Diet has moved the nuclear power plant regulation in the Electricity Business Act to the Nuclear

198 Ibid art 7(1). However, when the nuclear emergency declaration is issued or when there is a special emergency, the prime minister can appoint the chairperson without Diet consent. Ibid art 7(3). Moreover, when the Diet is adjourned and thus unable to give consent to the appointment, the prime minister can appoint the member temporarily. Ibid. Since consent for the first appointment was not obtained from the Diet and the Diet's session was nearly ending, Prime Minister Noda decided to appoint the first chairperson, Shun-ichi Tanaka, as well as other members using these exceptional clauses.

199 Ibid art 7(7).

200 Ibid addendum, art 6(2).

201 However, a proviso included in the statute allows return if there is a compelling reason in light of the willingness and capacity of particular workers within five years after this Act takes effect. Ibid addendum, art 6(2) proviso. Many suspected that the ban might be practically undermined by this proviso.

202 Ibid addendum art 6(3) (mandating the introduction of a ban on finding a job after retirement in companies which might raise public suspicion or distrust on the fairness of enforcement in an employment capacity). However, it is important to note that the ban was not included in the text of the statute.

203 Chapter 3 n 60.

Reactor Regulation Act,[204] thus making the NRA the sole nuclear safety regulator for nuclear power plants.[205] It is utterly for the NRA to ensure the safety of the nuclear power plants in the future.

6.2.3 New safety standards for nuclear power plants

The NRA adopted new standards in December 2013.[206]

The new standards were the result of sober reflection on the failure to prepare for severe disaster, leaving preparation to the self-regulation of power companies, and the failure to apply the safety standards to pre-existing power plants that needed to be retrofitted. Other primary problems under the previous safety regulations include the failure to introduce new foreign knowledge about how to improve safety and the failure to evaluate overall risks including external factors such as fires or landslides.[207] The standards were also informed by the new legislative mandate for the NRA to consider not only massive natural disasters but also criminal acts such as terrorist attacks, to prepare for severe accidents, to require the power company to periodically evaluate the overall risk, to introduce the "backfit" system to retroactively apply the new safety standards to pre-existing reactors, and to consolidate the nuclear safety regulations into a single statute.[208]

It thus intensified the prevention measures against severe accidents by introducing much stronger countermeasures against natural disasters and to prepare for fire, flooding, and power loss.[209] Especially, it required the much intensified tsunami countermeasures, countermeasures against flooding, measures to

204 Denki jigyohō [Electricity Business Act], Law no 170 of 1964, art 112–13. The Atomic Energy Commission (AEC) still has a jurisdiction on fundamental policy on nuclear power and especially on the use of nuclear power for peaceful purposes. But there has been an on-going discussion on the reconsideration of the status and power of the AEC. Cabinet Office, Genshiryoku iinkai no arikata minaoshi notameno yushikisha kaigi [Expert Conference on the Status of the Atomic Energy Commission], Genshiryoku iinkai no arikata minaoshi nitsuite [On Reconsideration of the Status of the Atomic Energy Commission] (CAS 10 December 2013) www.cas.go.jp/jp/seisaku/genshiryoku_kaigi/pdf/houkoku.pdf accessed 10 January 2018 (proposing to limit the jurisdiction of the AEC or its successor to issues on the use of nuclear power for peaceful purpose, issues on the disposal of nuclear waste, and issues on the fundamental importance of the use of nuclear power and to reorganize the commission as an independent commission inside the Cabinet Office).

205 The Nuclear Reactor Regulation Act was thus revised to create the independent category of "nuclear reactor for power generation" and provided for the permit and regulation of nuclear reactor for power generation. Kakugenryo busshitsu, kakunenryo busshitsu oyobi genshiro no kisei nikansuru hōritsu [Act on Regulation of Nuclear Source Materials, Nuclear Fuel Materials and Nuclear Reactors], Law no 166 of 1957, art 43–3–5–art 43–3–34 (Nuclear Reactor Regulation Act).

206 Nuclear Regulatory Authority, Jitsuyou hatsudenyo genshiro nikakawaru shin kiseikijun nitsuite (gaiyou) [On New Regulatory Standards for Power-Generating Nuclear Reactors (summary)] (NRA) www.nsr.go.jp/data/000070101.pdf accessed 10 January 2018.

207 Ibid 1.

208 Ibid 2.

209 Ibid 6.

improve the reliability of external power supply, and measures to secure multiple internal power sources.[210] It also mandated for the first time specific countermeasures against severe accidents, especially measures to reduce the internal pressure inside the suppression chamber and measures regarding the supply of water into reactors and cooling pools, measures to prevent the destruction of pressure chambers, measures to prevent hydrogen blasts, and measures to prevent the spread of radioactive materials.[211] Moreover, it mandated the establishment of emergency support facilities to implement emergency countermeasures.[212] The concern with the possibility of terrorist attacks or airplane crashes, previously not considered, also necessitated these countermeasures as well.[213]

In order to avoid damages from natural disaster, it specifically banned the construction of essential buildings on the fault surfaced on the ground.[214] If there is no evidence of movement of fault lines within 120,000 to 130,000 years, then it could be assumed that there is no possibility of active fault, but if there is some doubt, then the standards say it is necessary to consider movement within 400,000 years.[215] Also power plants were mandated to consider the possibility of volcanos within 160 km and adopt appropriate countermeasures.[216]

Moreover, in order to secure the external power supply, the new standards require two independent external power supply systems. In order to secure the internal power supply, they require an additional emergency power generator, portable power generators, and sufficient fuel for power generation for seven days.[217]

In order to prevent nuclear meltdown, power companies are mandated to adopt countermeasures such as mobilizing the portable power generator to operate the vent and using a portable water supplier to supply water from outside.[218] In order to secure the pressure chamber, the power company is mandated to adopt countermeasures such as the installment of a filtered vent system or a system to cool down the heated reactor core underneath the chamber.[219] Furthermore, in order to prevent the spread of radioactive materials into the air, the power company is mandated to adopt countermeasures such as the exterior water bubble release system.[220] Finally, in order to prepare for an intentional airplane crash, the power company is mandated to prepare for the emergency control room away from the plant as well as the power supply, portable power generators (together

210 Ibid. More specifically, it mandated the installment of tsunami barrier to prevent tsunami water to enter into the plant and establishment of anti-flooding door to prevent the water entering into the facilities. Ibid 10.

211 Ibid.

212 Ibid.

213 Ibid.

214 Ibid 11.

215 Ibid 12.

216 Ibid 14.

217 Ibid 15.

218 Ibid 17.

219 Ibid 18.

220 Ibid 19.

with multiple connecting switches) and portable water supply system to respond to the attacks.[221]

Are these new safety standards sufficient?

Japanese courts in the past have been reluctant to take issue with the safety of nuclear power or to question plant operations or the government permission process.[222] However, now that the myth of nuclear safety has been completely shattered, the time could be ripe for testing whether judicial treatment of these issues should be changed. Indeed, some courts have come to show much more reluctance in accepting the safety argument of the government and power companies. In a recent case involving an application for preliminary injunction against the restart of the No 3 and No 4 reactors of the Takahama Nuclear Power Plant operated by Kansai Electric, the Otsu District Court granted the preliminary injunction, prohibiting the power company from restarting operation of these two reactors even if they both cleared the new safety standards.[223] The court found that the new safety standards adopted by the NRA are utterly inadequate and there is an immediate danger that the residents might suffer serious damages.

However, the Osaka High Court reversed this decision and adopted a totally different and more deferential attitude, thus rejecting a motion for a preliminary injunction.[224] It looks as though the courts are still reluctant to actively intervene in a battle against the nuclear power plant.[225] However, surely it is debatable whether the new standards are sufficient to ensure the safety of the nuclear power plants when a massive earthquake hits the plant next time.

6.2.4 Evacuation plans and nuclear disaster countermeasures

Even if more vigorous safety standards are imposed and nuclear safety is assured by an independent regulatory agency, the possibility of a serious nuclear accident remains. It is thus necessary to prepare for such events. After the Fukushima disaster, evacuation instructions were issued amid the chaos without adequate preparation or consultation with local government. Local residents had no access to relevant information and were simply told to evacuate without being told where to go. All of this produced tremendous confusion and disorder.

The central government has thus decided to amend the "nuclear disaster countermeasures guideline" (*genshiryoku saigai taisaku shishin*) and require local governments to prepare for nuclear disaster by making adequate evacuation

221 Ibid 20.

222 Shigenori Matsui, "T-Rex, Jurassic Park, and Nuclear Power: Nuclear Power Plants and the Courts after the Fukushima Nuclear Accident," (2017) 42 *William & Mary Environmental Law and Policy Review* 145.

223 Otsu chihō saibansho [Otsu Dist Ct], 9 March 2016, 2290 *Hanrei jihō* 75. See also Fukui chihō saibansho [Fukui Dist Ct], 21 May 2014, 2228 *Hanrei Jihō* 72; Fukui chihō saibansho [Fukui Dist Ct], 14 April 2015, 2290 *Hanrei Jihō* 13.

224 Osaka kōtō saibansho [Osaka High Ct], 28 March 2017, TKC database.

225 Matsui (n 222).

preparations based on the guideline.[226] The guideline created two different zones.[227] The first of these zones is known as a "precautionary action zone" (*yobouteki bougo sochi junbi kuiki*) (PAZ). Within a PAZ, precautionary measures are taken even before an accident, including the distribution of iodine pills in case immediate evacuation is necessary. According to the international standards, PAZ should extend to between 3 km and 5 km of nuclear power plants. The Japanese government opted for the more expansive 5 km radius for PAZ in Japan.[228] The second of these zones is referred to as an "urgent protective planning action zone" (*kinkyu bougo sochi junbi kuiki*) (UPZ). In UPZ, emergency preparations to minimize radiation exposure must be in place. International standards suggest that a UPZ extends out to between 5 km and 30 km from a nuclear power plant. The Japanese government has designated areas within a 30 km radius of nuclear power plants as UPZ.[229]

Evacuation plans are definitely essential and local governments and municipalities must secure shelter in case these plans need to be put into action. Local governments and municipalities must provide residents with necessary information relevant to evacuation and give clear guidance. This is one of the unmistakable lessons learned in the wake of the Fukushima accident. Eventually, all local governments and municipal governments which have nuclear power plants inside their jurisdiction came up with adopting revised plans.

Still, some critics claim that the nuclear disaster countermeasures guideline is utterly defective. Pointing out the fact that the Iitate Village is more than 30 km away from the Fukushima plant and its residents were forced to evacuate, they claim that a 30 km radius is inadequate. Moreover, the worst-case scenario presented to Prime Minister Kan as the Fukushima accident was unfolding mandated evacuation of all residents within 170 km of the plant, and recommended evacuation for those within 250 km. Critics thus argue that the government should expand UPZ far wider than a 30 km radius.[230] However, the NRA, in later revising the guideline once again, maintained its original stance in the revised guideline.

6.2.5 Restarting the nuclear power plants

Nuclear plants operating at the time of the Tohoku Earthquake were automatically shut down after the earthquake. Moreover, as a part of ongoing maintenance, nuclear reactors must be shut down for regular check-ups. As discussed previously, in response to the strong concerns of local residents, the

226 Nuclear Regulatory Authority, Genshiryoku saigai taisaku shishin [Nuclear Disaster Countermeasures Guideline] (NRA 31 October 2012, updated 5 July 2017) www.nsr.go.jp/data/000024441.pdf accessed 10 January 2018.

227 Ibid 52.

228 Ibid.

229 Ibid.

230 Citizen's Commission on Nuclear Energy, Genpatsu zero shakai eno michi [Road to Nuclear Power Zero Society] (CCNE) www.ccnejapan.com/20140412_CCNE.pdf accessed 10 January 2018 167–68.

central government decided to require informal stress testing before restarting nuclear reactors and more robust formal stress testing to make sure that safety standards are observed.[231] If a nuclear reactor fails to satisfy these formal stress tests, the central government will halt its operation.

By requiring these stress tests, the central government claims that the safety of nuclear power can be sufficiently assured. However, many remain unconvinced that nuclear power is safe, even if reactors pass these stress tests, and object to restarting nuclear power plants. When a power company wants to restart a nuclear plant, it requires consent from the local government because of nuclear safety agreements with the power companies and local governments/municipalities.[232] Since the accident at Fukushima, it has become very difficult to obtain this consent in order to restart nuclear power plants after check-ups.

The DPJ government conducted an informal stress test at the No 3 and No 4 reactors of the Kansai Power Company's Ooi Nuclear Plant in Fukui Prefecture and gave the go ahead for operations to restart in August 2012. Fukui's prefectural government also approved the restart. As a result, at the time these two reactors were the only ones operating in Japan after the Fukushima disaster.[233]

The LDP government has shown resolve in restarting nuclear power plants that were shut down after the Tohoku Earthquake. Since the NRA adopted new standards on 19 June 2013,[234] calling for much more demanding requirements at nuclear power plants,[235] it has already received more than 25 applications for review under new standards and granted permission to 12 reactors, and already five reactors are reactivated, including the No 1 and No 2 reactors of the Sendai Nuclear Power Plant of the Kyushu Electric Company, the No 3 and No 4 reactors of the Takahama Nuclear Power Plant of the Kansai Electric Company, and the No 3 reactor of the Ikata Nuclear Power Plant of the Shikoku Electric Company.[236] It is expected that all the power companies applied for safety reviews

231 *See* Chapter 3 n 172.

232 For the nuclear safety agreement of the Fukui Prefecture with power companies, *see* Fukui Prefecture, Genshiryoku hatsudensho shuhen kankyo no anzen kakuhotō ni kansuru kyouteisho [Agreement on Securing the Safety in the Environment of the Nuclear Power Plant] (Fukui Prefecture) www.athome.tsuruga.fukui.jp/nuclear/information/fukui/data/betsu_08.pdf accessed 10 January 2018. Fukui Prefecture is the prefecture that has the largest number of nuclear reactors inside the jurisdiction. For the nuclear administration of the Fukui Prefecture, *see* Fukui Prefecture, Fukuiken no genshiryoku gyousei [Nuclear Administration of the Fukui Prefecture] (Fukui Prefecture) www.athome.tsuruga.fukui.jp/nuclear/information/fukui/data/betsu_03.pdf accessed 10 January 2018.

233 "Regulators to Inspect Japan's Sole Operating Reactors on June 15" (*Japan Times* 10 June 2013) www.japantimes.co.jp/news/2013/06/10/national/regulators-to-inspect-japans-sole-operating-reactors-on-june-15/#.Uc_HJz5dbR0 accessed 10 January 2018.

234 n 206.

235 "Genpatsu shinkijun: Genshiryoku kisei iinkai ni yotte kettei, naiyou wa? [NRA Adopted the New Nuclear Power Plant Standards: What Are the Changes?]" (*Huffington Post* 19 June 2013) www.huffingtonpost.jp/2013/06/19/nuclear_power_n_3463677.html accessed 10 January 2018.

236 Federation of Electric Power Companies of Japan, Kokunai no genshiryoku hatsudensho no saikado nimuketa taiou joukyou [Move to Reactivate the Nuclear Power Plants] (FEPCJ) www.fepc.or.jp/theme/re-operation/ accessed 10 January 2018.

of nuclear reactors at different nuclear power plants.[237] However, even when the safety reviews are completed, the issue of whether or not power companies will be able to receive consent to restart from the local government remains up in the air. The government now estimates that nuclear power will compose roughly 20% of all power generated in 2030.[238]

The new standards generally require decommissioning of a nuclear power plant after 40 years of operation, but allow exceptions of an additional 20 years if safety standards are satisfied.[239] Being a relatively new ministry compared with the METI, whether or not the MOE will be able to effectively regulate the METI-promoted nuclear industry in the midst of the new LDP government's declared commitment to economic development remains uncertain. The LDP government has already hinted that exceptions to the 40-year rule for reactors may be granted more easily than the DPJ had indicated.[240] If the government puts more emphasis on economic development than environmental protection, then the MOE and its NRA could be hard-pressed to adequately supervise and regulate the nuclear power industry.[241]

Moreover, we already saw that some of the courts came to adopt a highly skeptical view on the sufficiency of the new safety standards and are reluctant to allow reactivation of the nuclear reactors that satisfied the new standards.[242] The government and power companies will have a hard time persuading the courts about their safety after the Tohoku Earthquake.

6.2.6 Nuclear power plants above active fault lines

The Fukushima nuclear disaster gave new life to ongoing concerns over the safety of nuclear power plants situated directly above active fault lines. In the past, due to broad safety concerns, the LDP government practically prohibited the construction of nuclear power plants in these areas through construction guidelines. However, skepticism has surfaced over government willingness to find

237 Ibid.

238 Ministry of Economy, Trade and Industry, Chouki energy jukyu mitooshi [Long-term Energy Supply Plan] (METI July 2015) www.meti.go.jp/press/2015/07/20150716004/20150716004_2.pdf accessed 10 January 2018.

239 *Huffington Post* (n 235).

240 "Genpatsu unten, 40nen seigen no minaoshi yousei: Jimin giren [LDP Diet Members Requested Reconsideration of Nuclear Power 40 Years Rule]" (*Nihonkeizai Shimbun* 7 July 2015) www.nikkei.com/article/DGXLASFS07H2X_X00C15A7PP8000/ accessed 10 January 2018.

241 However, due to new demanding standards pronounced by the NRA, many old nuclear power plants are faced with the plight of spending a significant amount of money for improvement to outdated facilities to satisfy the new standards. As a result, an increasing number of power companies have come to believe that upgrading will not make any economic sense and have given up any hope of reactivating some of the old nuclear power plants. "4 genpaysu 5ki hairo e: Kiseii ga ninka [Four Nuclear Power Plants, Five Reactors are Slated to Decommissioning: Nuclear Regulatory Authority Approved]" (*Nihonkeisai Shimbun* 19 April 2017) www.nikkei.com/article/DGXLASGG19H04_Z10C17A4MM0000/ accessed 10 January 2018.

242 n 223.

evidence of active fault lines.[243] Now that the myth of nuclear safety has been totally shattered, the NRA appears poised to prohibit the construction of nuclear power plants above active faults by applying a new safety standard that expands classification of an "active fault" from one that has shifted in the past 120,000 to 130,000 years to one that has shifted within the past 400,000 years.[244] Applying this new standard, there is a distinct possibility that active faults will be found directly below existing nuclear power plants. If active faults are found beneath nuclear reactors, the NRA may be forced to shut them down permanently.

Final determinations on whether nuclear power plants are indeed situated above active fault lines are very controversial, especially if geographic evidence is dated or insufficiently convincing. Since the number of available experts is limited and experts in this field are apt to disagree, the NRA will have a hard time deciding whether or not to abandon nuclear power plants situated above allegedly active fault lines. Power companies and business organizations can be expected to argue that the government should consider the costs and benefits before shutting down existing nuclear power plants. Whether the central government will be able or willing to shut any existing nuclear power plants down remains to be seen.[245]

6.2.7 Promotion of alternative energy

The Fukushima nuclear disaster forced the Japanese government to reduce reliance upon nuclear power even if it was able to maintain nuclear power. It became imperative for the Japanese government to promote alternative energy.[246]

243 "Fukushima Watch: Japan Orders Another Look at Earthquake Faults Under Two Nuclear Plants" (*Wall Street Journal Japan* 18 July 2012) http://blogs.wsj.com/japanrealtime/2012/07/18/fukushima-watch-japan-orders-another-look-at-earthquake-faults-under-two-nuclear-plants/ accessed 10 January 2018.

244 Nuclear Regulatory Authority (n 206) 12. See also "Nuclear Watchdog to Forbid Reactor Construction above Active Faults" (*Asahi Shimbun* 23 January 2013) http://ajw.asahi.com/article/0311disaster/fukushima/AJ201301230064 accessed 10 January 2018.

245 The special focus is now centered on the Tsuruga Nuclear Power Plant, located in Fukui Prefecture. "Fault Under Reactor at Tsuruga Active: NRA" (*Japan Times* 16 May 2013) www.japantimes.co.jp/news/2013/05/16/national/fault-said-active/#.Uc_Stz5dbR0 accessed 10 January 2018. The NRA found the fault underneath the Unit 2 reactor of the Tsuruga Nuclear Power Plant was active in light of the new standard but the Japan Atomic Power Company that operates the reactor submitted a rebuttal arguing that the fault was not active. Now attention is focused on how the NRA decides on this issue and whether the NRA orders the operation of the reactor to stop. The NRA restarted reviewing the application for reactivation. Nuclear Regulatory Authority, Shinkisei kijun tekigosei nikakawaru shinsa [Review on the Satisfaction of New Safety Standards] (NRA) www.nsr.go.jp/activity/regulation/reactor/kisei/shinsa/shinsa1.html accessed 10 January 2018; "Tsuruga 2 gouki, 2 nen teitai no shinsa saikai, genshiryoku kiseii, katsudansou no sonpi shouten [NRA Resumes the Review on Tsuruga Unit 2 Reactor after Suspension for Two Years: Whether the Active Fault Could be Found or Not Is the Focus]" (*Tokyo Shimbun* 22 December 2017) www.tokyo-np.co.jp/s/article/2017122201001873.html accessed 10 January 2018.

246 The Japanese government has also been promoting a reduction in the consumption of energy. Energy no shiyo no gourika nikansuru hōritsu [Act on Rationalization of Energy Consumption], Law no 49 of 1979. In 2015, the Diet has revised this Act to facilitate the shifting use of energy when there is no significant demand. Agency for Natural Resources and Energy, Sho ene seisaku no douko [Progress of Energy Consumption Reduction Policy] (METI February 2017) www.enecho.meti.go.jp/category/saving_and_new/saving/pdf/2017_02_shoueneseisaku.pdf accessed 10 January 2018.

The Diet had already passed the Act to Facilitate the Development and Introduction of Non-Fuel Energy[247] in 1980. In order to promote non-fuel energy, the Diet also passed the Special Measures Act on Facilitation of Use of New Energy.[248] New energy sources included solar, wind, and geothermal energy. The focus of this past legislation was to secure a stable energy supply in light of the vulnerability of relying too much on imported oil, especially since Japan heavily relied upon oil produced and imported from the Middle East. The 2002 Basic Act on Energy Policy[249] outlined Japan's basic energy policy. It committed Japan to finding stable supplies of power and accommodation of energy policy with the needs for prevention of global warming and preservation of the Earth's environment. It also mandated the government to establish a Basic Energy Plan.[250] Mandatory purchase of surplus solar energy generated by solar power companies at a fixed price began in 2009 with the imposition of the "burden to support solar power" (*taiyokou hatsuden sokushin hukakin*) on every consumer.[251] Before the Fukushima nuclear disaster, however, the government did not have any plan on reducing reliance on nuclear power.

Everything changed after Fukushima. The Diet passed the Special Measures Act regarding the Acquisition of Electricity Generated by Renewable Energy by the Power Companies[252] in 2011, mandating power companies to purchase electricity generated by renewable energy sources such as solar, wind, or geothermal generation at a fixed price. This statute was designed to provide security for organizations that want to generate renewable power by ensuring stability and profitability for the renewable energy industry. In order to make the generation of renewable energy profitable, the fixed price is set by the government, and in order to allow power companies to provide financial resources to purchase electricity at fixed prices, all consumers are mandated to pay a "renewable energy facilitation burden" (*saisei kano energy hatsuden sokushin hukakin*) in addition to having a burden to support solar power.

This statute was enthusiastically promoted by Prime Minister Kan as one of the conditions for him to step down. The percentage of electricity

247 Hikaseki energy no kaihatsu oyobi dounyu no sokushin ni kansuru hōritsu [Act to Facilitate Development and Introduction of Non-Fuel Energy], Law no 71 of 1980. The original title of this Act was Sekiyu daitai energy no kaihatsu oyobi dounyu no sokushin nikansuru hōritsu [Act to Facilitate Development and Introduction of Alternative Energy to Oil]. The title was revised in 2009.

248 Shin-energy no riyoutō no sokushin ni kansuru tokubetsu sochihō [Special Measures Act to Facilitate the Use of New Energy], Law no 37 of 1997.

249 Energy seisaku kihonhō [Basic Act on Energy Policy], Law No. 71 of 2002.

250 The government established the first basic energy plan under this Act. Agency for Natural Resources and Energy, Energy kihon keikaku [Basic Energy Policy] (METI October 2003) www.enecho.meti.go.jp/category/others/basic_plan/pdf/0301007energy.pdf accessed 10 January 2018.

251 Energy kyoukyu jigyousha niyoru hikaseki energy gen no riyou oyobi kaseki energy gen no yuukouna riyou no sokushin ni kansuru hōritsu [Act concerning Facilitation of Use of Non-Fuel Energy Sources by the Energy Supply Business Operators and Efficient Use of Fuel Energy], Law no 72 of 2009.

252 Denki jigyousha niyoru saiseikanou energy denki no choutatsu ni kansuru tokubetsu sochihō [Special Measures Act on the Acquisition of Electricity Generated by Renewable Energy by the Power Companies], Law no 108 of 2011.

generated by the renewable energy sources slightly increased but it still only occupied only about 3.2% of all electricity generated in 2014.[253] It will be a long time before electricity generated by such renewable energy will reach the 20% benchmark set for 2030 by the Japanese government.[254] Moreover, the sudden increase in alternative renewable energy has produced unexpected instability and the government has had to introduce measures to contain their development.[255]

6.2.8 Power companies and the electrical supply system

The Fukushima nuclear accident also revealed problems with the electrical supply system in Japan. As previously discussed, electricity used to be provided by a state corporation with a statutory monopoly over the production and supply of electricity. With privatization, power companies became private corporations. With deregulation, some other private companies also gained the right to generate electricity, though such electricity could only be used by those companies alone and could not be sold or directed to other users. These private companies could only sell the electricity they generated to power companies. The power companies were obliged to purchase energy produced by renewable energy sources. Therefore, virtual local monopolies still remained. Such privileged status was viewed as necessary in order to compensate power companies for the responsibility they shouldered for providing electricity to all consumers in their designated areas, including remote islands and rural areas.

Japan is divided into ten regions and each power company is responsible for service in its region. This system has proven to be vulnerable when one company faces a serious problem. We have only to look at the situation TEPCO and its customers were in following the Tohoku Earthquake. The Tohoku Earthquake and the Fukushima nuclear accident showed that some system of interregional cooperation is definitely necessary.[256] Moreover, the Japanese power companies

253 Agency for Natural Resources and Energy, Saisei kanou energy [Renewable Energy] (METI) www.enecho.meti.go.jp/category/saving_and_new/saiene/renewable/family/index.html accessed 10 January 2018.

254 The government revised its Basic Energy Plan in 2014. It still viewed nuclear power as the basic power source and refused to establish a target for renewable energy while keeping the 20% mark for all electricity as a benchmark. Agency for Natural Resources and Energy, Energy kihon keikaku [Basic Energy Plan] (METI April 2014) www.enecho.meti.go.jp/category/others/basic_plan/pdf/140411.pdf accessed 10 January 2018.

255 After the Fukushima accident, a significant number of solar power generators were established and attempted to provide power to the power companies. Faced with the possibility that the power generated by solar power might disrupt the overall balance, the power companies came to suspend the new purchase of solar power. The Ministry of Economy, Trade and Industry was forced to reconsider the mandatory purchase of renewable energy and place a limit on solar power. Agency for Natural Resources and Energy, Koteikakaku kaitori seido no unyo minaoshitō nitsuite [On Reconsideration of Fixed Price Purchase System] (METI 22 January 2017) www.meti.go.jp/press/2014/01/20150122002/20150122002-3.pdf accessed 10 January 2018.

256 Kenji E. Kushida, Japan's Fukushima Nuclear Disaster: Narrative, Analysis, and Recommendations (15 December 2012) https://ssrn.com/abstract=2118876 accessed 10 January 2018.

used to be vertically integrated: power generation, transmission and retail sale were handled by one single power company for each region.[257] Disintegration and liberalization was necessary.

One more serious problem with the electrical supply system in Japan is that the eastern half of Japan uses a different frequency than the western half of Japan. Due to differences in power generators when they were first imported during the Meiji Era, power companies in the east now use 50Hz electricity while those in the west use 60Hz electricity.[258] In the past, this difference became a headache when one moved from the west to the east or vice versa and it also served up a challenge when the government constructed the bullet train connecting Tokyo and Osaka (Japan Rail Tokai now switches the electricity frequency in Shizuoka). When TEPCO lost its Fukushima power plant and was unable to generate sufficient electricity for the needs of consumers in the region, the neighboring Chubu Electric Power Company was tapped to supply additional power to TEPCO. However, in order for Chubu Electric to supply electricity to TEPCO, it had to convert its electricity frequency to correspond with that used by TEPCO. Unfortunately, the facilities and equipment for realizing the necessary conversion were simply inadequate. As a result, there were serious limitations on the degree to which Chubu Electric was able to assist TEPCO.[259] The same problem could happen again in the future.

With this in mind, the government proposed a radical reform of the power supply system and more radical privatization. A fundamental policy for reform was published by the METI. Its three major reform policies were as follows:[260]

(1) First step: Reform for providing electricity

This reform will totally liberalize the retail sale of electricity by lifting the previous restrictions on the sale of electricity and abandoning regional monopolies, thereby providing a choice of power company to all consumers. To encourage competition, the reform will remove regulations on charges and obligations on power companies to provide service to all regional consumers. However, if unregulated, some customers might find it difficult to obtain electricity. Therefore, it might be wise to keep the aspect of the current system that ensures that all customers do have access to power from at least one provider. Also, a surcharge system could be introduced to offset the cost of supplying electricity

257 Ibid.

258 Federation of Electric Power Companies of Japan, Electricity Review Japan (FEPCJ 2015) www.fepc.or.jp/library/pamphlet/pdf/2015ERJ_full.pdf accessed 10 January 2018 4.

259 Agency for Natural Resources and Energy, Energy Whitepaper 2014 (METI) www.enecho.meti.go.jp/about/whitepaper/2014html/1-1-2.html accessed 10 January 2018.

260 Ministry of Economy, Trade and Industry, Denryoku system kaikaku senmon iinkai [Power System Reform Special Committee], Denryoku system kaikaku no kihon houshin [Fundamental Policies for Electrical System Reform] (METI July 2012) www.meti.go.jp/committee/sougouenergy/sougou/denryoku_system_kaikaku/pdf/report_001_00.pdf accessed 10 January 2018.

to consumers on remote islands and to provide them with comparable rates. Also, various measures must be introduced to reduce energy consumption and encourage balance (for instance, charging higher rates during peak times, charging different rates depending on time of use, or charging gradually higher rates depending on time of use).[261]

(2) Second step: Power production reform

In order to promote the generation of electricity and allow other companies to enter the market, this reform will separate power production companies from electricity providers, and eliminate restrictions on selling electricity. The reform will allow the sale of electricity from power producers to any electricity provider and also encourage the sale of electricity in the wholesale market.[262]

(3) Third step: Transmission lines service reform

This reform will preserve fairness and neutrality by allowing power producers to use transmission lines to send electricity, allowing electricity companies to supply power, and allowing customers to receive the electricity they need. The reform will also allow the transmission of electricity beyond the current regions and much broader contingency planning as it relates to electricity distribution. This reform will increase capacity to convert electrical frequency if there is a serious accident.[263]

The creation of such divisions between power production, transmission services, and retail supply could be essential for electrical supply system reform in Japan. However, when the LDP returned to power, it decided to postpone implementation of divisions between power producers and transmission service providers because of strong opposition from within the party. The Diet thus passed an amendment to the Electricity Business Act in 2013[264] to allow the establishment of an organization to provide electricity to other power companies in need. In 2014, another bill was introduced into the Diet to allow the liberalization of electricity retail.[265] Power companies were allowed to sell powers to companies outside of its traditional jurisdiction. Power producers such as solar power companies were allowed to sell power they produced to residents as well as companies regardless of their place of production. After accomplishing the first and second steps, the third and final step was introduced to mandate the legal separation of transmission services, which prohibited transmission service companies from engaging in power production as well as power retail.[266]

261 Ibid 4–7.
262 Ibid 10–12.
263 Ibid 18–22.
264 Denki jigyohō no ichibu wo kaiseisuru hōritsu [Act to Amend Parts of the Electricity Business Act], Law no 74 of 2013.
265 Denki jigyohōtō no ichibu wo kaiseisuru hōritsu [Act to Amend Parts of the Electricity Business Act], Law no 72 of 2014.
266 Denki jigyohōtō no ichibu wo kaiseisuru hōritsu [Act to Amend Parts of the Electricity Business Act], Law no 47 of 2015.

The total liberalization of retail service started in April 2016. A significant number of new power retail companies have been established alongside the traditional power companies.[267] The legal separation of transmission service will start from 2020. The power system in Japan will significantly change. Moreover, as a result of the first reform, the Nation-wide Power Management Authority was established in 2015, which was created to balance supply and demand of power nationwide.[268] Therefore, when one power company is facing a power shortage, it could instruct other power companies to generate more power and supply that surplus power to the power company in need.[269] This system will surely be a help to power companies, which might face an extreme difficulty in supplying power because of the nuclear power accident, such as was the case with TEPCO.

6.3 Future of law and politics in Japan

What about the future of law in Japan? Have there been any legal reforms? Have the Japanese people learned lessons from the miserable experience in the aftermath of the Tohoku Earthquake? What about the future of politics?

6.3.1 Lessons learned

Judging from the sheer volume of legislative response in the wake of the Tohoku Earthquake, the Japanese people seem to have learned many vital lessons. They learned what kinds of legal measures are necessary following a momentous disaster. As we already saw, the Diet has amended the Basic Act on Disaster Countermeasures twice since the Tohoku Earthquake to intensify the preparation for a future powerful earthquake.[270] The government has come to prepare for reconstruction after the serious earthquake as well.[271] The government, in mandating disaster prevention planning, has been cognizant of the need to plan ahead for disaster restoration and reconstruction.[272] It has required local governments to devise disaster response timeline schedules in accordance with projected progressions of events following a disaster.

267 During the first year, 2.4 million households changed to new power providers and the number of registered new power providers reached 390, providing roughly 9% of all power supply. Ministry of Economy, Trade and Industry, Denryoku kouri zenmen jiyuka no shinchoku joukyo [Current Progress of Total Liberalization of Power Supply] (METI 21 April 2017) www.meti.go.jp/committee/sougouenergy/denryoku_gas/denryoku_gas_kihon/pdf/003_03_00.pdf accessed 10 January 2018.

268 Agency for Natural Resources and Energy, Denryoku system kaikaku no genjo to kadai [Current Progress of the Power System Reform] (METI 27 September 2016) www.meti.go.jp/committee/sougouenergy/kihonseisaku/denryoku_system_kaikaku/pdf/01_05_00.pdf accessed 10 January 2018 9.

269 Ibid 10.

270 nn 4, 17.

271 n 53.

272 n 73.

The Japanese government has also introduced the new tsunami preparedness regulations and allowed local governments to designate a "special tsunami disaster hazard zone" to prohibit construction in vulnerable locations.[273] The central government has made many efforts to greatly reduce the potential number of casualties and the scale of damage that would follow any powerful tsunami in the future.

The government must have learned a lot about the necessity of preparing for the evacuation of such a huge number of people, providing them a place to stay, and preparing food, water, and blankets for them, as well as the inevitability of having to provide a tremendous amount of temporary housing and public services for evacuees. It must also have gained a lot of experience in making exceptions for evacuees and providing assistance to them, as well as experience in assisting recovery and reconstruction efforts in the aftermath of such a massive natural disaster.

The Japanese government also revised the Nuclear Reactor Regulation Act in order to establish the NRA, the independent regulatory agency on nuclear safety inside the MOE, and intensify the safety standards.[274] The NRA also adopted revamped safety standards for all power-generating nuclear power stations. Ultimately the government must have learned a lot on what should be done during the time of nuclear emergency.

6.3.2 Any changes following the deeper failures of law?

As for the more fundamental problems inherent in the Japanese legal system, no serious attempt at reform has been made so far. No serious attempt has been made to enact emergency legislation that would grant broad emergency powers to the prime minister. Likewise, no attempt has been made to allow the prime minister to suspend enforcement of regulatory statutes in disaster areas so the government can act more efficiently and be less constrained by red tape.[275] The Basic Act on Disaster Countermeasures remains the single most important piece of legislation pertaining to natural disasters and the legal powers it grants to the government remain quite limited. There is no provision allowing the government to exercise broad discretionary power in times of crisis. No attempt has been made to grant the prime minister the power to order or require necessary measures during a nuclear emergency. The only powers of the prime minister, as the director of the Emergency Disaster Response Headquarters or the Nuclear Disaster Response Headquarters, are the powers of coordination and instruction.

There has been no change to the existence of the vast number of regulatory statutes that grant very broad regulatory power to bureaucrats. Nothing has been

273 Chapter 4 n 60.

274 n 195.

275 Amended Basic Act on Disaster Countermeasures (n 5), art 108–4 automatically triggers the application of various exceptional treatments for the victims when the prime minister declares the "disaster emergency declaration." It also automatically triggers the application of the Rights of Disaster Victim Protection Act. Ibid art 108–5. This is a significant improvement.

done to encourage bureaucrats to be less reluctant to allow prompt and flexible implementation of assistance to disaster victims.

There has been no change in preference of informal powers over formal legal powers. The statutes rely more on recommendation and instruction rather than legal order. There is no mandatory evacuation and there is no legal ban on marketing or consumption of contaminated agricultural products. No legal reform has been introduced to facilitate the redevelopment and relocation by clarifying land ownership and restricting property rights. Moreover, even when the new regulatory power was granted to restrict the construction of houses in tsunami vulnerable areas, the local government has been rather reluctant to use such legal power.

The NRA is established and now it is this independent agency that is supposed to supervise the government's effort to promote nuclear power. But still a question is lingering over whether the NRA could effectively control a government bent on the promotion of nuclear power. This concern was the result of the unwillingness or resistance to creating an independent administrative agency in the government in the past and the long-standing desire to instead establish an "independent agency" as a government department under Cabinet control.

The legislative process, dominated by bureaucrats, was not modified and the legislation passed by the Diet is still filed with bureaucratic language and terms unfriendly for the general public. Since each department is tasked with the preparation of a bill, legislation passed by the Diet still lacks coordination. Almost all disaster legislation still shows the heavy imprint of bureaucratic thinking.

Many of the failures of law manifested by the Tohoku Earthquake, tsunami, and nuclear meltdown are rooted in the fundamental character of law in Japan: "bureaucratic law." Laws are drafted by government bureaucrats and enforced by bureaucrats with the political approval of the legislature. Law in Japan is a law used by the bureaucrats to control the public. The strong power of government bureaucrats in Japan is well noted.[276] Although there has been controversy over whether the bureaucrats have dominant power or are instead working for politicians,[277] the fact remains that the bureaucrats play a

276 John Creighton Campbell, "Democracy and Bureaucracy in Japan," in Takeshi Ishida & Ellis S. Krauss (eds), *Democracy in Japan* (U Pittsburgh 1989) 113; Bradley Richardson, *Japanese Democracy: Power, Coordination, and Performance* (Yale 1997) 110; Michio Muramatsu & Ellis S. Krauss, *Bureaucrats and Politicians in Policymaking: The Case of Japan*, 78 A.P.S.Q. 126 (1984). Moreover, all of the legislative bills to be submitted by the Cabinet need to go through a careful and grilling review by the Cabinet Legislation Bureau, an expert organization on bills and legislation. Cabinet Legislation Bureau, Cabinet Legislation Bureau (CLB) www.clb.go.jp/english/index.html accessed 6 March 2018. This review is supposed to make the bills flawless in light of the Constitution and other related statutes but at the same time it surely makes all the statutes as if they were crafted best for bureaucrats.

277 J. Mark Ramseyer & Frances McCall Rosenbluth, *Japan's Political Marketplace* (Harvard University Press 1993), for instance, argues that the bureaucrats are agents for the LDP politicians. Maurice Wright, "Who Governs Japan? Politicians and Bureaucrats in the Policy-making Processes" (1999) 47 *Political Studies* 939 (1999).

dominant role in enacting and enforcing law; the dispute is only whether the law is serving the interests of the bureaucrats or of the politicians. Most laws in Japan are drafted by government bureaucrats within a respective government department, submitted by the prime minister with cabinet approval, passed by the Diet without significant revision, and are enforced by the government bureaucrats who drafted them. This fact has left significant impacts on the nature of law in Japan.

Even after various legal reforms introduced after the Great East Japan Earthquake Disaster, the law basically still remains "bureaucratic law." It is a tool used by bureaucrats to regulate the public, and by its design it is intended for bureaucrats to exercise broad discretion. After the DPJ's demise, the LDP government came to maintain a good relationship with bureaucrats. The LDP politicians know quite well how to use them and how to enjoy the benefit of their effort. The administrative agencies are allowed to formulate and enforce government policy with the help of LDP politicians. It is no wonder the law in Japan still shows such strong signs of "bureaucratic law."

It thus appears that Japan, for whatever reason, is not prepared to address many of the fundamental problems in its legal system nor do the necessary reforms seem to be on the horizon.

6.3.3 Any changes following the failures of politics?

The Tohoku Earthquake surely taught an important lesson to the Japanese people by forcing them to face the necessity of preparing for another massive natural disaster. Nonetheless, the people seem to place high priority on economic development.

The LDP Abe Cabinet, elected in a landslide victory in 2012 and re-elected again with a convincing victory in 2014 and in 2017, vowed to continue and further promote "Abenomics," a kind of economic development strategy.[278] Apparently his strategy successfully attracted the trust of many voters. Although the LDP government under Abe has introduced various countermeasures against natural disasters, such as the enactment of the National Resilience to Disaster Promotion Basic Act[279] as well as the Nankai Trough Earthquake Special Measures Act[280] and the Special Measures Act concerning Countermeasures against the Earthquake Just Below the Capital,[281] and evaluated the vulnerability of the infrastructure and preparations that are in place for the next massive earthquake, the true motivation of the LDP government might lie in the promotion of construction work. Instead of preparing various strategies against future massive

278 Prime Minister's Office, Abenomics: Seichou senryaku de akarui nihon ni [Abenomics: To Create the Bright Future for Japan by Adopting Development Strategy] (kantei) www.kantei.go.jp/jp/headline/seicho_senryaku2013.html accessed 10 January 2018.

279 n 49.

280 n 117.

281 n 91.

earthquakes and tsunamis, the LDP's policy might end up simply spending huge amounts of public money for infrastructure improvements.[282]

As discussed previously, the Tohoku Earthquake revealed serious political failures in Japan. The Japanese political system, with one major political party and a number of minority opposition parties, is a portrait of instability. Although the DPJ finally succeeded in forcing a change of government in 2009, it now seems unlikely that the DPJ will return to power any time soon.[283] If all opposition parties could unite together to challenge the LDP/Komei coalition, Japan would have two major political parties.[284] However, unless they form a coalition or combine to form a single political party, these minority parties will remain very difficult to win single member districts seats in the House of Representatives. Nevertheless, the proportional representation system allows each political party to retain supporters and win some seats and, as a result, there is little incentive for opposition parties to unite.

Indeed it seems there are no strong calls for major political changes. The Japanese public appears convinced that a two-party system is not appropriate for Japan and that representation in the Diet should reflect the split opinions of the nation. Many are convinced that securing more opportunity for small party representation in the Diet is more important than facilitating a change of government. This absence of strong opposition party to take over the government deprives the incentive for minority oppositions to become realistic and willing to propose more sensible solutions to various issues. It thus reduces the opportunity for cooperation and compromises between the ruling party and opposition parties. As a result, the LDP does not have to worry about the change of government and opposition parties have practically no impact on the policy choice the LDP adopts for the government.

No reforms have been introduced that would allow the public to choose the prime minister. In the 2012 election, voters who cast votes for LDP effectively chose to elect its president, Shinzo Abe, as prime minister. However, who knows what will happen next. If Abe decides to step down, the public will be powerless to choose his successor. Some have argued for constitutional amendments that would allow direct public election of the prime minister, but

282 Koukyou jigyou kaikaku shimin kaigi, Q&A kokoga okashii kokudo kyoujinka [Q&A on National Resilience to Disaster Promotion] (Koukyou jigyou kaikaku shimin kaigi) http://stop-kyoujinka.jp/qa.html accessed 10 January 2018.

283 Kenji Kushida & Phillip Y. Lipscy (eds), *Japan under the DPJ: The Politics of Transition and Governance* (Shorenstein Asia-Pacific Research Center 2013); Yoichi Funabashi & Koichi Nakano (eds), *The Democratic Party of Japan in Power* (Routledge 2016).

284 The Japanese election system for members of both House of Representatives and House of Councilors is a combination of election-district election and proportional representation. Shigenori Matsui, *The Constitution of Japan: A Contextual Analysis* (Hart 2011) 47–50. As to the members of the House of Representatives, the lower House, 289 out of 465 members are elected in single-member election districts with the first-past-the-post rule while 176 will be elected based on proportional representation.

others are strongly opposed.[285] Whether voters chose Abe's LDP because they were convinced that Abe would be well suited to handling a critical crisis also remains uncertain, though one hopes the nation's voters do now fully grasp the importance of having a leader capable of dealing with a major calamity.

As we already saw, strong bureaucratic power over government policy has still remained untamed. Despite the fruitless efforts of the DPJ government to stripe them of their strong power and place politicians ahead of them, such efforts have simply resulted in politicians becoming isolated from the bureaucrats and politicians being miserably unable to control them when needed. The LDP government thus came to build upon their cooperative attitude toward bureaucrats, meaning the bureaucracy continues to dominate the policymaking process.

For sure, there have been some changes under the new LDP government: the LDP government has certainly come to assert more power over the bureaucrats. Especially, with the establishment of the Cabinet Personnel Bureau, the Cabinet have come to have more influence on the choice of vice secretary generals (top bureaucratic positions for each department) and other high-ranking positions.[286] For instance, two female bureaucrats were promoted to department chief of the Human Rights Department of the Ministry of Justice and department chief of the Trade and Economic Cooperation of the METI. These appointments reflected both Prime Minister Abe's wish to increase the number of female appointees comprising higher ranking government positions, as well as increased participation of the Cabinet office in the promotion of high ranking government officials.[287] The LDP government appears to be using the power and wisdom of bureaucrats more cleverly.[288]

No attempt has been made to deprive bureaucrats of the power of preparing bills to the Diet and giving them the power to enforce such legislation. Even during an emergency, each department has retained its power and is allowed to make exceptions. No attempt has been made to enable the prime minister chosen by

285 "Shinsaigo no seiji ni human, 8 wari: Asahi Shimbun yoron chousa [Eighty Percent of People Dissatisfied with Politics after the Disaster: Asahi Newspaper Poll Result]" (*Asahi Shimbun* 26 December 2011) www.asahi.com/special/10005/TKY201112250192.html accessed 10 January 2018 (70% of people favor the public election of the prime minister).

286 "Naikaku jinjikyoku: Kantei shudou jinji ni heigai—kanryogawani sontaku ya human [Cabinet Personnel Bureau: The Vices of Personnel Decision Led by the Cabinet—Conjecture and Disappointment on the Side of Bureaucrats] (*Mainichi Shimbun* 3 June 2017) https://mainichi.jp/articles/20170603/k00/00m/010/128000c accessed 2 February 2018.

287 "Chuou shochoni joseikanbu zokuzoku: Houmu, keisanshode hatsuno kyokuchō [Increasing Female Appointment to High Ranking Officials: First Female Appointment in the Ministry of Justice and METI]" (*Nihonkeizai Shimbun* 4 July 2014) www.nikkei.com/article/DGXNASFS0400I_U4A700C1MM0000/ accessed 10 January 2018.

288 In 2017, the vices from the bureaucrats' tendency to "sontaku" (conjecture) the unexpressed wishes of the prime minister and to act to accomplish those conjectured wishes has become apparent. These were the reflection of the fact now the politicians have come to have a strong impact on the personnel promotion of the bureaucrats.

the public to make a quick and definitive decision in times of emergency.[289] No attempt has been made to enable the politically appointed cabinet or individual cabinet members to make a basic policy decision and simply leave bureaucrats to implement that decision. In most cases, it is still bureaucrats that are supposed to formulate and implement policy decisions, with politicians only required to give approval. Surely bureaucrats need to obtain the approval from the ruling party and the policies they created need to be adopted by the legislation. But they could have a critical impact on the way legislation is crafted and framed. What matters more is the framework of disaster law in Japan to prepare for a massive natural disaster or serious nuclear accident and to provide adequate response to it.

Strong bureaucratic departmentalism within the central government has also remained unchanged. Each department of the central government is still allowed to hire its own employees, and the candidates for management positions are selected from among the graduates of the best universities in Japan who pass the very competitive examinations. Each department has its own vested interest in the industries it are supposed to be regulating and in making sure that its top ranked officials will be secured cushy "amakudari" positions. Each department does not want to lose grip on power or lose any of its budget.

***

Owing to these considerations, it seems that the Japanese people have learned many significant lessons from the Tohoku Earthquake. However, there are significant reasons for doubting whether the Japanese people have really learned any lessons from the underlying problems of law and politics that the Tohoku Earthquake has brought to light.

The fact that the Japanese people have failed to adequately reconsider the nation's legal and political systems, especially in light of the many legal and political failures related to the disaster, is undeniably disappointing.[290] We can only hope that the Japanese people will fare better the next time such a massive disaster is unleashed upon the nation. However, how can the Japanese people realistically expect to fare any better without reforming the ailing legal and political systems in meaningful ways? Inattention to the many legal and political flaws

289 Moreover, in establishing the NRA, the Diet excluded the prime minister's instruction during the time of nuclear disaster on the safety issues of the nuclear power plant, leaving the NRA the sole regulatory agency on the safety of the nuclear power plant. Genshiryoku saigai taisaku tokubetsu sochihō [Special Measures Act on Nuclear Disaster Countermeasures], Law no 156 of 1999, art 20(3). This exclusion of the prime minister's intervention on the safety issues of the nuclear power plant during the nuclear emergency was apparently prompted by the blunders committed by Kan. But this exclusion surely raises a question on the constitutionality since the Constitution of Japan gives the executive power to the Cabinet led by the prime minister.

290 Jeff Kingston, "Introduction," in Jeff Kingston (ed.), *Natural Disaster and Nuclear Crisis in Japan: Response and Recovery after Japan's 3/11* (Routledge 2012) 4.

that exacerbated the effects wrought on the country by the triple disaster suggests little reason for optimism here.

Many observers now feel that the Japanese people are settling back into familiar pre-disaster patterns. People were understandably in a state of shock as they tried to cope in the aftermath of the disaster. In many cases, they found someone to blame and have introduced at least some measures in an attempt to mitigate the effects of future disasters. Satisfied with incremental changes, people tend to eventually forget the disaster, relegating it to a distant memory.[291] Nonetheless, hopefully the lessons of the triple disaster brought by the Tohoku Earthquake will never be entirely forgotten.

291 Peter Dunns, "Dealing with Disaster," in Kingston (n 290) 175.

Conclusion

The Tohoku Earthquake and tsunami inflicted tremendous loss and damage on Japan. Japan is considered by many to be the country most well prepared for massive earthquakes and tsunamis; and this reputation is, perhaps, well deserved. It is for good reason that the Japanese word "tsunami" has come to be the universally accepted term for destructive waves caused by earthquakes. So many earthquakes and tsunamis have struck Japan and the nation's people and government have learned many important lessons every time. Nevertheless, the tsunami caused by the Tohoku Earthquake revealed that the country was, in fact, not prepared to prevent the mass death and destruction brought on by a disaster of this scale.

The Tohoku Earthquake and tsunami revealed that the Japanese legal system failed to anticipate that such devastation could result from an earthquake and tsunami. It was not prepared to provide immediate rescue unfettered by bureaucratic hindrance. It had not contemplated how to deal with such massive casualties nor how to dispose of such vast quantities of debris and waste. It had not anticipated how to assist evacuees by softening regulations during a time of emergency.

The Japanese legal system was, and still is, unsuited to facilitating swift reconstruction in the Tohoku Region. Since there was no government apparatus for facilitating reconstruction, the government had to set one up, and even that took nearly one year. Although this new body was supposed to supervise all reconstruction, in realty, all pivotal powers were retained and are being exercised by other government departments. Rebuilding has been painfully slow and the same can be said for group relocation and the redevelopment project. Bureaucratic hurdles routinely hinder the process for obtaining reconstruction funds and, even when affected local governments do get these funds, the central government attaches cumbersome restrictions on their use.

The nuclear power plant accident in Fukushima also revealed that the Japanese legal system was sorely unprepared for a major nuclear accident. Although the legal system appeared to regulate the safety and security of nuclear power plants and was capable of responding to nuclear accidents, the reality was that the legal system had not anticipated that a serious nuclear accident was even possible. As a result, as the nuclear crisis unfolded, the chain of command was chaotic and the government had to scramble in an ad-hoc fashion to facilitate evacuation and deal with food contamination. In addition, Japan was not prepared for the loss of electricity due to shutdowns of its nuclear power plants.

The aftermath of the nuclear accident further revealed just how unprepared the Japanese legal system was in the face of such a crisis. The legal system hadn't even contemplated the containment of a serious nuclear disaster. Nor had the legal system ever anticipated a need or method for disposing of contaminated waste and de-contaminating the environment. There was no system to facilitate evacuees' return after containment and to make sure that they could live without safety concerns. The government also had to come up with a system for providing damage awards and compensation to local residents and a system to support the power company that has had to pay a huge amount of damages on the fly.

These failures revealed many fundamental problems in Japan's legal system. The absence of emergency power, the excessive bureaucratic regulation, the preference for informal power, the overconfidence in the ability to control technology and a refusal to institute adequate disaster planning, the reluctance to regulate property rights, and blind faith in nuclear safety proved to be catastrophic. These numerous and fundamental failures of law clearly show that something is desperately wrong with the Japanese legal system. All of these failures, I argued, are fundamentally rooted in the character of the Japanese law as a bureaucratic law.

The Tohoku Earthquake also brought several failures of politics into clear view. Japanese politicians failed to safeguard the country against powerful earthquakes and tsunami and had long promoted nuclear power in anticipation of economic reward, without thinking seriously about the potential damage that a nuclear accident could cause. The government, led by Prime Minister Naoto Kan, committed various blunders in attempting to contain the nuclear disaster. The political process also prevented bipartisan support for the people of Fukushima and hampered early and effective reconstruction efforts. These failures of politics also evinced something deeply wrong with Japanese politics. They clearly indicated that the primary focus of Japanese politics on economic development, their inability to choose a reliable leader, the fragmented political parties and inability to form two big parties, and the strong power of the bureaucrats and strong departmentalism are the root causes of these failures of politics.

Japanese people surely learned many significant lessons. They are now preparing for the possibility of another powerful earthquake such as the Kanto Earthquake, Tokai Earthquake, or triple mega earthquake consisting of Tokai, Tohnankai and Nankai Earthquakes (Nankai Trough Megathrust Earthquake). They have revised the disaster prevention plan to prepare for the next one based on more realistic risks and prepare for a more reliable and solid post-disaster protocol. They have amended disaster countermeasures statutes to incorporate many of the lessons, revamped the nuclear power policy, and introduced a new energy policy.

However, when it comes to failure of law and politics, more deeply ingrained problems of Japanese law and politics, not much has been changed. The basic character of Japanese law as bureaucratic law has not changed and the inability of Japanese politics to face an emergency has not altered. Many of the failures of law and politics remain as inherent problems for Japan.

The Tohoku Earthquake brought incredible tragedy. It will be similarly tragic if the lessons learned in the wake of these disasters are not applied to safeguarding the nation's future to the greatest extent possible. Japan must address its legal and political shortcomings in order to adequately prepare for future disasters. As Shakespeare wrote, "what's past is prologue."[1] If Japan fails to apply the lessons of the Tohoku Earthquake and make the legal and political changes that this disaster-prone nation so clearly needs, its citizens are almost certainly going to face future tragedy on a similar scale.

There are so many lessons the people in the other countries could learn from the failures of Japanese disaster law. The Japanese experience could vividly show what should have been prepared and what should have been provided as a rescue and reconstruction. The Fukushima nuclear accident and its aftermath also clearly showed what is needed to ensure the safety of the nuclear power plant and to prepare for a serious nuclear accident. It is tempting to believe that the Japanese experience is so unique and that there is nothing to learn from their experience. But such belief is utterly mistaken.[2] It is easy to find a similar flaw and drawback in other countries as well. Japanese government before the Fukushima disaster insisted that Japan was well prepared and nuclear reactors were safe in contrast to other countries. This overconfidence has been vividly undermined by the Fukushima disaster. Surely, there is a lesson other countries in the world need to learn from this experience. It would be a tragedy if they refused to learn important lessons from Japan based on the same kinds of mistaken belief.

1 William Shakespeare, *The Tempest*, act II, scene I (MIT) http://shakespeare.mit.edu/tempest/full.html accessed 20 January 2018.

2 Phillip Lipscy, Kenji E. Kushida & Trevor Incerti, "Were Japan's Nuclear Plants Uniquely Vulnerable?" in Edward D. Brandford & Scott D. Sagan, *Learning from a Disaster: Improving Nuclear Safety and Security after Fukushima* (Stanford 2016) 157.

Appendices

1 Statutes and regulations

Act against Ocean Pollution and on Prevention of Ocean Disaster, 1970 > Ocean Pollution Prevention Act

Act concerning Basic Policy and Organization for Reconstruction after the Hanshin Awaji Earthquake Disaster, 1995

Act concerning Building Communities to Prevent Tsunami Disaster, 2011 > Tsunami Disaster Prevention Act

Act concerning Earthquake Insurance, 1966 > Earthquake Insurance Act

Act concerning Exceptions to the Land Improvement Act in order to Respond to the Great East Japan Earthquake Disaster, 2011.

Act concerning Exception to the Air Waves Act with Respect to Digital Broadcasting as a Result of the Great East Japan Earthquake Disaster, 2011.

Act concerning Exceptional Construction Limitations in Urban Cities Seriously Damaged by the Great East Japan Earthquake Disaster, 2011

Act concerning Facilitation of Redevelopment to Create Parts with Sufficient Disaster Prevention Capacity within the Highly Clustered Urban Areas, 1997

Act concerning Facilitation of Use of Non-Fuel Energy Sources by the Energy Supply Business Operators and Efficient Use of Fuel Energy, 2009

Act concerning Facilitation of Seismic Upgrades for Buildings, 1995

Act concerning Facilitation of Various Life Support Measures for Evacuees in order to Protect and Assist Residents Including Children Who Suffered from the Disaster Because of TEPCO's Nuclear Accident, 2012

Act concerning Financial Measures of the Government to Facilitate the Group Relocation Program in order to Prevent Disaster, 1972 > Group Relocation Facilitation Act

Act concerning Governmental Substitution with Respect to Disaster Restoration Construction of Public Facilities Damaged by the Great East Japan Earthquake Disaster, 2011

Act concerning Graveyard and Burial, 1948

Act concerning Measures to Accomplish the Prompt and Sufficient Damage Award for Nuclear Damages Caused as a Result of the Nuclear Power Plant Accident during the Great East Japan Earthquake Disaster and Special Treatment of the Statute of Limitations on the Nuclear Damages, 2013

Act concerning Nuclear Damage Liability Indemnity Contract, 1961
Act concerning Ownership of Condominiums, 1962 > Condominium Act
Act concerning Payment of the Disaster Condolence Benefit, 1973 > Disaster Condolence Benefit Act
Act concerning Prohibition of Seizure of Support Money for Victims of the Great East Japan Earthquake Disaster, 2011
Act concerning Promotion of Tsunami Countermeasures, 2011
Act concerning Special Financial Assistance and Support in order to Respond to the Great East Japan Earthquake Disaster, 2011.
Act concerning Special Financial Assistance in order to Cope with Extremely Serious Disaster, 1962 > Extremely Serious Disaster Act
Act concerning Special Treatment of Administrative Matters Relating to Evacuees and Those Who Changed Residence as a Result of the Nuclear Power Plant Accident following the Great East Japan Earthquake, 2011
Act concerning Special Treatment of Local Bonds Issued by Merged Cities and Towns in Light of the Great East Japan Earthquake Disaster, 2011
Act concerning Special Measures to Preserve Rights and Legal Interests of Victims of Specified Emergency Disaster, 1996 > Rights of Disaster Victims Protection Act
Act concerning Special Measures to Secure the Necessary Financial Resources to Cope with the Great East Japan Earthquake Disaster, 2011
Act concerning Special Treatment of Construction Limitations in Urban Cities Seriously Affected by the Great East Japan Earthquake Disaster, 2011
Act concerning Special Treatment of Administrative Matters Relating to Evacuees and Those Who Changed Residence as a Result of the Nuclear Power Plant Accident following the Great East Japan Earthquake Disaster, 2011
Act concerning Special Treatment of Victims of the Great East Japan Earthquake Disaster with Respect to Passport Issuance, 2011
Act concerning Temporary Exception to the Election of Maritime District Fishing Adjustment Commission and Farming Commissioners in Light of the Great East Japan Earthquake Disaster, 2011
Act concerning Temporary Exceptional Treatment for Disaster Victims of the Great East Japan Earthquake Disaster with Respect to National Tax Statutes, 2011
Act on the Great East Japan Earthquake Disaster Affected Business Operators Reconstruction Support Organization, Inc., 2011
Act on Damage Payment for Nuclear Damages, 1961 > Nuclear Damage Award Act
Act on Development of Adjacent Areas of the Electricity Power Generation Facilities, 1974
Act on Disposal and Clean-up of Waste, 1970
Act on Final Disposal of Specified Radioactive Waste, 2000 > Radioactive Waste Final Disposal Act
Act on Protection of Personal Information Held by Administrative Agency, 2003 > Personal Information Protection Act

Act on Rationalization of Energy Consumption, 1979

Act on Regulation of Nuclear Source Materials, Nuclear Fuel Materials and Nuclear Reactors, 1957 > Nuclear Reactor Regulation Act

Act on Resource Recycling of Automobiles No Longer in Use, 2002

Act on Special Financial Accounting, 2007

Act on Special Financial Aids and Subsidies in order to Respond to the Great East Japan Disaster, 2011

Act on Special Financial Arrangement for Measures to Promote Development of Electricity Power, 1974

Act on Special Treatment of Total Amount of Local Distribution Aid in 2011 as a Countermeasure to the Great East Japan Earthquake Disaster, 2011

Act on Special Treatment of Nuclear Damage Awards Dispute Arising from the Great East Japan Earthquake Disaster That are Using the Arbitration Mediation Procedure of the Nuclear Damage Liability Dispute Resolution Commission in order to Suspend the Application of the Statute of Limitations, 2013

Act on Tax to Promote Development of Electricity Power, 1974

Act to Amend Parts of the Act concerning Earthquake Disaster Prevention Countermeasures against Tohnankai/Nankai Earthquakes, 2013 > Nankai Trough Earthquake Special Measures Act

Act to Amend Parts of the Act concerning Special Measures to Strengthen Financial Functions in order to Improve the Financial Foundation of Financial Institutions and the Special Measures Act concerning Advancement of Reorganization of Financial Institutions in order to Respond to the Great East Japan Earthquake Disaster, 2011

Act to Amend Parts of the Act to Provide Temporary Special Treatment on Election Day for Assembly Members of Local Government and Heads of Local Government in response to the 2011 off the Pacific Coast of Tohoku Earthquake, 2011

Act to Amend Parts of the Basic Act on Disaster Countermeasures, 2012

Act to Amend Parts of the Basic Act on Disaster Countermeasures and Others, 2013

Act to Amend Parts of the Condominium Act and the Act concerning Smooth Rebuilding of Condominium, 2002

Act to Amend Parts of the Construction Standard Act, 1998

Act to Amend Parts of the Construction Standards Act in order to Secure the Safety of Buildings, 2006

Act to Amend Parts of the Disaster Condolence Benefit Act, 2011

Act to Amend Parts of the Disaster Condolence Benefit Act and Disaster Victim Life Rebuilding Support Act, 2011

Act to Amend Parts of the Disaster Victim Life Rebuilding Support Act, 2004

Act to Amend Parts of the Disaster Victim Life Rebuilding Support Act, 2007

Act to Amend Parts of the Electricity Business Act, 2013

Act to Amend Parts of the Electricity Business Act, 2014

Act to Amend Parts of the Nuclear Damage Award Support Organization Act, 2014

Act to Amend Parts of the Local Tax Act, 2011
Act to Establish the Nuclear Regulatory Authority, 2012
Act to Establish the Reconstruction Agency, 2011
Act to Facilitate Development and Introduction of Non-Fuel Energy, 1980
Act to Provide for Special Treatment of the Period in the Civil Code for Electing Acknowledgment or Refusal of Succession as a Result of the Great East Japan Earthquake Disaster, 2011
Act to Provide Temporary Special Treatment on Election Day for Assembly Members of Local Government and Heads of Local Government in Response to the 2011 off the Pacific Coast of Tohoku Earthquake, 2011
Atomic Power Basic Act, 1955
Basic Act on Disaster Countermeasures, 1961
Basic Act on Energy Policy, 2002
Basic Act on Reconstruction from the Great East Japan Earthquake Disaster, 2011
Act on Securing the Quality, Efficacy, and Safety of Drugs and Medical Equipment, 2014 > Pharmaceutical Affairs Act
Basic Act on the National Resilience Promotion for the Purpose to Contribute to the Preservation of Disaster/Reduction of Damages to Promote the Strong and Flexible National Life, 2013 > National Resilience Promotion Basic Act
Cabinet Act, 1947
Cabinet Order concerning Declaration of Specified Emergency Disaster and Designation of Measures to be Adopted with respect to Disasters Caused by the off the Pacific Coast of Tohoku Earthquake, 2011
Cabinet Order concerning Designation of the Great East Japan Earthquake Disaster as an Extreme Serious Disaster and Specification of Measures to Be Applied, 2011
Cabinet Order concerning Special Treatment of the Nuclear Reactor of the Fukushima No 1 Nuclear Power Plant of TEPCO for the Act concerning Regulation of Nuclear Source Materials, Nuclear Fuel Materials and Nuclear Reactors, 2013
Cabinet Order to Amend Parts of the Construction Standards Act Enforcement Order, 1980
Civil Code (Code Civil)
Condominium Act > Act concerning Ownership of Condominiums
Constitution of Japan, 1946
Construction Standards Act, 1950
Convention on the Law of the Sea
Convention on the Prevention of Marine Pollution by Dumping of Wastes and Other Matter
Disaster Assistance Act, 1947
Disaster Assistance Act Enforcement Order, 1947
Disaster Condolence Benefit Act, 1973
Disaster Victim Life Rebuilding Support Act, 1998
Disaster Waste Disposal Act, 2011
Earthquake Disaster Prevention Countermeasures Special Measures Act, 1995
Earthquake Insurance Act > Act concerning Earthquake Insurance

Electricity Business Act, 1964

Employment Benefit Act, 1974

Extremely Serious Disaster Act > Act concerning Special Financial Assistance in order to Cope with Extremely Serious Disaster

Family Registration Act, 1947

Fire Department Organization Act, 1947

Fire Fighters Act, 1948

Food Safety Act, 1947

Fukushima Nuclear Accident Victim Support Act > Act concerning Facilitation of Various Life Support Measures for Evacuees in order to Protect and Assist Residents including Children Who Suffered from the Disaster Because of TEPCO's Nuclear Accident

General Special Zone Act, 2011

Government Liability Act, 1947

Great East Japan Earthquake Disaster Affected Business Operators Reconstruction Support Organization, Inc. Act, 2011

Great East Japan Earthquake Disaster Reconstruction Special Zone Act, 2011

Group Relocation Facilitation Act > Act concerning Financial Measures of the Government to Facilitate the Group Relocation Program in order to Prevent Disaster

Hotel Business Act, 1948

Insurance Company Act, 1995

Labor Standards Act, 1947

Large-Scale Disaster Reconstruction Act, 2013

Local Government Act, 1947

Nankai Trough Earthquake Special Measures Act > Act to Amend Parts of Act concerning Earthquake Disaster Prevention Countermeasures against Tohnankai/Nankai Earthquakes

National Pension Act, 1959

National Resilience Promotion Basic Act > Basic Act on the National Resilience Promotion for the Purpose to Contribute to the Preservation of Disaster/ Reduction of Damages to Promote the Strong and Flexible National Life

National Taxation Act, 1962

Nuclear Damage ADR Time Limitation Suspension Act > Act on Special Treatment of Nuclear Damage Awards Arising from the Great East Japan Earthquake Disaster That Are Using the Arbitration Mediation Procedure of the Nuclear Damage Award Dispute Resolution Commission in order to Suspend the Applicability of the Statute of Limitations

Nuclear Damage Award Act >Act on Damage Payment for Nuclear Damages

Nuclear Damage Liability Indemnity Act > Act concerning the Nuclear Damage Liability Indemnity Contract

Nuclear Damage Award Support Organization Act > Nuclear Damage Award and Decommissioning Support Organization Act

Nuclear Damage Award and Decommissioning Support Organization Act, 2011

Nuclear Disaster Special Measures Act > Special Measures Act on Nuclear Disaster Countermeasures

Nuclear Reactor Regulation Act > Act on Regulation of Nuclear Source Materials, Nuclear Fuel Materials and Nuclear Reactors

Nuclear Regulatory Authority Act > Act to Establish the Nuclear Regulatory Authority

Ocean Pollution Prevention Act > Act against Ocean Pollution and on Prevention of Ocean Disaster

Ordinance concerning Standards for Structure, Establishment and Management of the Graveyard, Tokyo Metropolitan Government, 1984

Personal Information Protection Act > Act on Protection of Personal Information Held by the Administrative Agency

Pharmaceutical Affairs Act > Act on Securing the Quality, Efficacy and Safety of Drugs and Medical Equipment

Physicians Act, 1948

Police Act, 1954

Police Officer Job Execution Act, 1948

Public Housing Act, 1951

Public Road Act, 1952

Radioactive Waste Final Disposal Act > Act on the Final Disposal of Specified Radioactive Waste

Reconstruction Agency Act > Act to Establish the Reconstruction Agency

Regulation on Limitation of Electrical Consumption, Ministry of Economy, Trade and Industry, 2011

Regulation to Prevent Radiation Exposure for Workers Engaging in the Clean-up of Soil Contaminated by Radioactive Materials Due to the Great East Japan Earthquake Disaster, Ministry of Health, Labor and Welfare, 2011

Rights of Disaster Victim Protection Act > Act concerning Special Measures to Preserve Rights and Legal Interests of Victims of Specified Emergency Disaster

Road Traffic Act, 1960

Road Transportation and Vehicle Act, 1951

Self Defense Forces Act, 1954

Special Measures Act concerning Countermeasures against Environmental Contamination by Radioactive Materials Released by the Nuclear Power Plant Accident as a Result of the off the Pacific Coast of Tohoku Earthquake of March 11, 2011 > Radioactive Materials Contamination Special Measures Act

Special Measures Act concerning Earthquake Disaster Prevention Countermeasures against the Tohnankai Earthquake/Nankai Earthquake, 2002. Renamed Special Measures Act concerning Promotion of Earthquake Disaster Countermeasures against the Nankai Trough Earthquake

Special Measures Act concerning Promotion of Earthquake Disaster Countermeasures against the Nankai Trough Earthquake, 2002

Special Measures Act on Acquisition of Electricity Generated by Renewable Energy by the Power Companies, 2011

Special Measures Act on Countermeasures against the Earthquake Just Below the Capital, 2013

Special Measures Act on Disposal of Disaster Waste Caused by the Great East Japan Earthquake Disaster, 2011
Special Measures Act on Facilitation of Use of New Energy, 1997
Special Measures Act on Financial Support for Earthquake Countermeasures Facilitation Tasks in the Earthquake Countermeasure Intensification Areas, 1980
Special Measures Act on Large-Scale Earthquake Countermeasures, 1978
Special Measures Act on Nuclear Disaster Countermeasures, 1999 > Nuclear Disaster Special Measures Act
Special Measures Act on Promotion of Earthquake Disaster Prevention Countermeasures against Deep Sea Earthquake in the Vicinity of the Japan Trench and the Chishima Trench, 2004
Special Measures Act on Rebuilding of Condominium Suffering from Damages, 1995
Special Measures Act on Reconstruction and Revival of Fukushima, 2012
Special Measures Act on Securing Necessary Funds to Implement the Revival Plan Following the Great East Japan Earthquake Disaster, 2011
Special Measures Act to Facilitate the Use of New Energy, 1997
Special Measures Act to Promote Reconstruction of Urban Areas Affected by the Disaster, 1995
Specified Home Electronic Devices Recycling Act, 1998
Structural Reform Special Zone Act, 2002
Telecommunication Business Act, 1964
Tsunami Disaster Prevention Act > Act concerning Building Communities to Prevent Tsunami Disaster
Weather Business Act, 1952

2 Court judgments

Supreme Court, 3rd petty bench, 9 December 2003, 57 Minshu 1887
Sendai District Court, 17 September 2013, 2204 Hanrei jihō 57
Sendai District Court, 25 February 2014, 2217 Hanrei jihō 74
Sendai District Court, 24 March 2014, 2223 Hanrei jihō 60
Sendai District Court, 13 January 2015, 2265 Hanrei jihō 69
Morioka District Court, 20 February 2015, 2268 Hanrei jihō 91
Sendai High Court, 20 March 2015, 2256 Hanrei jihō 30
Sendai High Court, 15 April 2016, TKC Database
Sendai High Court, 22 April 2015, 2258 Hanrei jihō 68
Supreme Court, 2nd petty bench, 17 February 2016, TKC Database
Supreme Court, 2nd petty bench, 17 February 2016, TKC Database
Sendai High Court, 26 October 2016, Court judgment online
Maebashi District Court, 17 March 2017, 2339 Hanrei jihō 4
Supreme Court, 26 April 2017, 2nd petty bench, TKC Database
Chiba District Court, 22 September 2017, TKC Database
Fukushima District Court, 10 October 2017, TKC Database

3 Glossary

Atomic Energy Commission (*genshiryoku iinkai*): a commission established in the Cabinet Office for the development of the basic nuclear energy policy

Basic Act on Disaster Countermeasures (*saigai taisaku kihonhō*): a statute providing for the government responses to the serious national disaster

Catastrophic natural disaster or social disturbance (*ijouni kyodaina tensai-chihen matawa shakaiteki douran*): exceptional circumstances to relieve the liability of the nuclear power operators to pay for nuclear damages under the Nuclear Damage Liability Act

Central Disaster Prevention Council (*chuo bousai kaigi*): an organization tasked with adopting the national disaster prevention basic plan

Certificate of damage (*risai shoumeisho*): officiate certificate on the extent of damages issued by the municipal government

Coordinating Committee for Earthquake Prediction (*jishin yochi renrakukai*): an organization to exchange information on prediction of earthquakes and promote the prediction

Compact city: city design to concentrate the residents in much smaller communities to provide efficient city service. Following the Tohoku earthquake, this idea became popular in reconstruction planning

Designated administrative agencies (*shitei gyousei kikan*): agencies of the central government designated by the prime minister in order to carry out the responsibilities of the central government performing its disaster prevention duties under the Basic Act on Disaster Countermeasures

Designated emergency evacuation spot (*shitei kinkyu hinan basho*): places designated as destinations for emergency evacuation according to specific type of disaster

Designated public organization (*shitei koukyou kikan*): national public organizations designated by the prime minister to cooperate with the central government and local government in times of emergency, including independent public corporations such as Bank of Japan, Japan Red Cross, and NHK and major private corporations such as power companies, natural gas providers, transportation companies, or telecommunication service providers under the Basic Act on Disaster Countermeasures. A local public organization designated by the governors is called a "designated local public organization"

Designated shelter (*shitei hinansho*): shelters designated for evacuees to stay in the case of emergency

Designated waste (*shitei haikibutsu*): highly contaminated waste that necessitates the central government to dispose of it outside of the contaminated area

Difficult-to-return zone (*kitaku kon-nan kuiki*): zone closest to the Fukushima nuclear power plant where residents are prohibited from returning for a long time > **no-return zone**

Disaster assistance fund (*saigai kyujo kikin*): fund contributed by prefectures to provide disaster assistance to victims of disaster

Disaster broadcasting station (*rinji saigai housoukyoku*): broadcasting station licensed with informal procedure for fixed period for the reduction of damages following disaster

Disaster condolence benefit (*saigai chouikin*): benefit to be paid to the disaster victims under the Disaster Condolence Benefit Act

Disaster emergency countermeasures (*saigai oukyu taisaku*): emergency countermeasures to be adopted in response to the disaster under the Basic Act on Disaster Countermeasures

Disaster emergency situation (*saigai kinkyu jitai*): the declaration that would allow the prime minister to adopt certain measures by a cabinet order under the Basic Act on Disaster Countermeasures

Disaster hazard zone (*saigai kiken kuiki*): zone designated under the Construction Standard Act to prohibit all new construction because of the vulnerability to disaster

Disaster reconstruction housing loan (*saigai hukkou jutaku yushi*): special loan available to disaster victims through Japan Housing Finance Agency

Disaster reconstruction special tax redistribution grant (*shinsai hukkou tokubetsu kouhuzei kouhukin*): special grant distributed by the central government for the reconstruction from the disaster

Disaster victim life rebuilding support benefit (*hisaisha seikatsu saiken shienkin*): benefit granted to the disaster victims to rebuild their life under the Disaster Victim Life Rebuilding Support Act

Disaster victim life rebuilding supporting organization (*Hisaisha seikatsu saiken shien houjin*): an organization run by each prefecture to pay the disaster victim life rebuilding support benefit through its fund

Disaster waste (*saigai haikibutsu*): waste caused by the Tohoku Earthquake. This designation allowed the government to dispose of all wastes resulting from the Tohoku Earthquake regardless of distinction between ordinary household waste and industrial waste

Double loan (*niju loan*): a situation when a disaster victim has to pay off an existing loan for a house destroyed by the disaster and to secure a new loan to build a new house and pay the additional loan

Earthquake Assessment Committee for Earthquake Disaster Countermeasures Reinforcement Area (*jishin bousai taisaku kyouka chiiki hanteikai*): a committee established in the Japan Meteorological Agency to decide whether a warning for a massive earthquake should be issued

Earthquake disaster countermeasures reinforcement area (*jishin bousai taisaku kyouka chiiki*): area designated by the prime minister under the Special Measures Act on Large-Scale Earthquake Countermeasures to require intensified countermeasures against very powerful earthquakes

Earthquake Disaster Preparation Headquarters (*jishin saigai keikai honbu*): government organization that is supposed to be set up when an earthquake warning is issued

Earthquake Disaster Prevention Countermeasures Special Measures Act (*jishin bosai taisaku tokubetsu sochihō*): a statute enacted after the Hanshin

Awaji Earthquake to supplant the earthquake countermeasures under the Basic Act on Disaster Countermeasures

Earthquake information (*jishin jōhō*): information to be circulated by the Japan Meteorological Agency when a strong earthquake hits

Earthquake insurance (*jishin hoken*): insurance for damages resulting from the earthquake to be bought as an optional choice of fire insurance

Earthquake just below the Capital emergency countermeasures reinforcement zone (*shuto chokka jishin kinkyu taisaku kuiki*): zone where there is a danger that a serious disaster is likely to happen and there is the necessity to adopt emergency countermeasures if the massive earthquake just below the capital happens

Emergency (*kinkyu jitai*): a declaration that would allow the prime minister to take over police organization during an emergency under the Police Act when there is a need to maintain public safety

Emergency earthquake early report (emergency earthquake warning) (*kinkyu jishin sokuhō/kinkyu jishin keihō*): a warning of the main tremor of a very powerful earthquake when an early movement is detected

Emergency evacuation preparation zone (*kinkyuji hinan junbi kuiki*): zone within 30 km radius of the Fukushima nuclear power plant except evacuation instruction area where residents are instructed to prepare for evacuation if needed

Emergency measures (*oukyu taisaku*): specific disaster countermeasures to be adopted in response to disaster under the Basic Act on Disaster Countermeasures

Emergency warning (*keikai sengen*): a warning to be issued by the prime minister under the Large-Scale Earthquake Special Measures Act when a massive earthquake is likely to strike, urging everyone to prepare for the massive earthquake

Emergency disaster (*kinkyu saigai*): more serious disaster that will lead to the establishment of the Extraordinary Emergency Disaster Response Headquarters inside the central government under the Basic Act on Disaster Countermeasures. A somewhat less serious disaster is called an extraordinary disaster, calling for the establishment of the Extraordinary Disaster Response Headquarters

Emergency Disaster Response Headquarters (*kinkyu saigai taisaku honbu*): a government organization to be established in time of emergency disaster to be headed by the prime minister. The first such headquarters was established right after the Tohoku Earthquake

Emergency evacuation preparation zone (*kinkyuji hinan junbbi kuiki*): zone outside of the evacuation instruction zone where the residents are told to be prepared for evacuation in times of emergency

Emergency road (*kinkyu koutsuro*): roads to be used for emergency countermeasures and assistance

Evacuation instruction zone (*hinan shiji kuiki*): zone where instruction for evacuation is issued in response to the Fukushima nuclear power plant accident

Evacuation instruction removal preparation zone (*hinan shiji kaijo junbi kuiki*): zone around the Fukushima nuclear power plant where residents are allowed to return home when environmental decontamination is finished

Extraordinary disaster (*hijo saigai*): serious disaster that will lead to the establishment of Extraordinary Disaster Response Headquarters inside the central government under the Basic Act on Disaster Countermeasures. A more serious disaster is called an emergency disaster calling for Emergency Disaster Response Headquarters

Extraordinary Disaster Response Headquarters (*hijo saigai taisaku honbu*): government organization to be established when there is an extraordinary serious natural disaster

Extremely serious disaster (*gekijin saigai*): extremely serious disaster designated by the central government to allow it to cover the cost of implementing emergency measures by the local governments under the Basic Act on Disaster Countermeasures and the Extremely Serious Disaster Act

Final disposal site (*saishu shobunjō*): site to bury spent nuclear fuel and nuclear waste permanently

Fukushima Nuclear Power Plant (*Fukushima genshiryoku hatsudensho*): nuclear power plant of the Tokyo Electric Power Company (TEPCO) located in Fukushima prefecture that ended up melting down after the Tohoku Earthquake

Fukushima Reconstruction and Revival Basic Policy *(Fukushima hukkou saisei kihon houshin*): the basic policy for the reconstruction and revival of Fukushima after the nuclear accident

General disaster victim support grant (*hisaisha shien sougo kouhukin*): one of the grants distributed to the disaster victims

General Insurance Rating Organization of Japan (*Songai hoken ryouritsu sanshutsu kikō*): a consortium of insurance companies to set the premium rate for earthquake insurance

Great East Japan Earthquake Disaster (*Higashinihhon daishinsai*): official name of the disaster following the Tohoku Earthquake and tsunami

Great East Japan Earthquake Disaster Affected Business Operators Reconstruction Support Organization (*Higashinihon daishinsai jigyousha saisei shien kikō*): an organization established to assist business operators suffering from the Great East Japan Earthquake Disaster to recover from the disaster

Great East Japan Earthquake Disaster Reconstruction Headquarters (*Higashinihon daishinsai hukkou taisaku honbu*): a government organization to lead the reconstruction of Tohoku headed by the prime minister

Great East Japan Earthquake Disaster Reconstruction Basic Act (*Higashinihon daishinsai hukkou kihonhō*): basic act stipulating the policy and organization for reconstruction following the Great East Japan Earthquake Disaster

Great East Japan Earthquake Disaster Reconstruction Basic Policy (*Higashinihon daishinsai karano hukkou no kihon houshin*): basic policy adopted by the government for the reconstruction of the Tohoku region after the Great East Japan Earthquake Disaster

Great East Japan Earthquake Disaster Reconstruction Design Council (*Higashinihon daishinsai hukkou kousou kaigi*): an advisory board established to give advice on fundamental policy for reconstruction of Tohoku

Great East Japan Earthquake Disaster reconstruction special loan (*Higashi-nihon daishinsai hukkou tokubetsu kashitsuke*): special loan available to the business operators affected by the Great East Japan Earthquake Disaster

Group relocation (*bousai shudan iten*): a program that allows local residents as a group to relocate from a disaster area to much safer places

Group relocation promotion zone (*iten sokushin kuiki*): zone to implement the group relocation program

Hanshin Awaji Earthquake (*Hanshin Awaji daishinsai*): strong earthquake that hit Kobe in 1995. It left various lessons for the legal system on earthquake disaster

Hanshin Awaji Earthquake Disaster Reconstruction Headquarters (*Hanshin Awaji daishinsai hukkou honbu*): government organization established to lead the reconstruction work after the Hanshin Awaji Earthquake

Hazard zone (*keikai kuiki*): disaster area designated by the municipal heads to prohibit entry and force evacuation in order to prevent harm to human life and persons with criminal penalty under the Basic Act on Disaster Countermeasures

Highly unusual and extremely serious extraordinary disaster (*ichijirusiku ijo katsu gekijin na hijō saigai*): if so designated, various exceptional treatments are to be allowed under the Rights of Disaster Victim Protection Act or under the 2013 amendment to the Basic Act Disaster Countermeasures

Integrated Response Headquarters (*taisaku tougou honbu*): the organization jointly coordinated between the government and TEPCO to respond to the Fukushima nuclear accident

Intensive decontamination survey area (*osen joukyou juuten chousa chiiki*): area where the central government left the local government to take a lead on decontamination around the Fukushima nuclear power plant. Radiation level is lower than in special decontamination areas

Interim storage site (*chukan chozou shisetsu*): site to store nuclear waste before final disposal for 30 years

Japan Earthquake Reinsurance Co. (*Nihon jishin saihoken kabushiki gaisha*): a company that takes all liability for earthquake insurance based on reinsurance from all the insurance companies and concludes a reinsurance contract with the government

Japan Nuclear Insurance Pool (*Nihon genshiryoku hoken pool*): a pool created by the insurance companies to sustain nuclear damage insurance with power companies

Jogan Earthquake (*Jōgan jishin*): very powerful earthquake that hit the Sanriku region in 869 AD

Kanto Earthquake (*Kanto daishinsai*): massive earthquake that hit the Kanto area, including Tokyo in 1923. It is anticipated another powerful Kanto Earthquake will hit the Kanto area soon. Common name for the earthquake just below the capital

Kumamoto Earthquakes (*Kumamoto jishin*): a series of powerful earthquakes that hit the Kumamoto area in 2016

Large-scale Earthquake Disaster Reconstruction Act (*daikibo jishin saigai hukkouhō*): a statute enacted for the reconstruction following a large-scale earthquake

Local tax distribution grant (*chihō kouhuzei kouhukin*): grant distributed to the local government by the central government from tax revenue in order to supplement local tax revenue

Measures against nuclear damage (*songai baisho sochi*): measures to make sure that nuclear power operators would be able to pay for nuclear damage. The power company is required to conclude nuclear damage insurance with insurance companies plus an indemnity contract with the government or make a deposit for the amount of 120 billion JPY

Nankai Trough Earthquake disaster prevention countermeasures promotion area (*Nankai Trough jishin bousai taisaku suishin chiiki*): area where various countermeasures need to be adopted to prevent disaster resulting from a Nankai Trough Megathrust Earthquake

Nankai Trough Earthquake disaster prevention countermeasures promotion basic plan (*Nankai Trough jishin bousai taisaku suishin kihon keikaku*): the basic plan to be established by the Central Disaster Prevention Council to prevent disaster resulting from a Nankai Trough Megathrust Earthquake

Nankai Trough Earthquake tsunami evacuation countermeasures special reinforcement area (*Nankai Trough jishin tsunami hinan taisaku tokuebtsu kyouka chiiki*): area where intensified countermeasure need to be adopted to facilitate the evacuation from a tsunami caused by a Nankai Trough Megathrust Earthquake

Nankai Trough Megathrust Earthquake (*Nankai Trough jishin*): a triple combination of massive earthquakes of Tokai, Nankai, and Tohnankai Earthquakes that might hit the west part of Japan

National Resilience Promotion Headquarters (*kokudo kyoujinka suishin honbu*): government organization established under the Basic Act for the Strengthening of the Infrastructure

New Tohoku (*atarashii Tohoku*): idea to revitalize the Tohoku region after the Great East Japan Earthquake Disaster

No-return zone (*kitaku konnan kuiki*): common name for difficult-to-return zone, where residents are precluded from returning because of the high radiation around the Fukushima Nuclear Power Plant

Nuclear and Industry Safety Agency (NISA) (*genshiryoku anzen/hoan in*): an agency in the Agency for Natural Resources and Energy of the Ministry of Economy, Trade and Industry that used to have regulatory authority over the nuclear power plant. It was abolished after the Fukushima accident and all of its powers were transferred to the Nuclear Regulatory Authority (NRA)

Nuclear damage (*genshiryoku songai*): damages to be paid by the nuclear power operators under the Nuclear Damage Award Act when a nuclear accident occurs at a power plant

Nuclear Damage Award Act (*genshiryoku songaibaishohō*): a statute on the liability of the power company for the nuclear damage

Nuclear Damage Award Dispute Resolution Center (Arbitration Center) (*genshiryoku songai baisho hunsou kaiketsu center*): an organization established under the Nuclear Damage Liability Conflict Resolution Commission to arbitrate the claims of residents against TEPCO over the nuclear damage

Nuclear Damage Award Support Organization (*Genshiryoku songai baisho shien kikō*): an organization established to support the power company, which is liable to pay damage awards for nuclear damage. Later the name was changed to the Nuclear Damage Award and Decommissioning Support Organization (*genshiryoku songai baisho hairotō shiennkikō*)

Nuclear Damage Award Liability Conflict Resolution Commission (*genshiryoku songai baisho hunsou shinsakai*): a commission established in the Ministry of Education, Culture, Sports, Science and Technology to formulate and handle disputes between the residents and TEPCO over the nuclear damage caused by the Fukushima nuclear accident

Nuclear Disaster Countermeasures Guideline (*genshiryoku saigai taisaku shishin*): a guideline established by NRA on the countermeasures against nuclear disaster

Nuclear Disaster Response Headquarters (*genshiroku saigai taisaku honbu*): a government organization to be established when there is a serious disaster caused by a nuclear accident

Nuclear Disaster Special Measures Act (*genshiryoku saigai tokusohō*): a statute enacted for countermeasures against a nuclear accident

Nuclear emergency (*genshiryoku kinkyu jitai*): a situation in which serious nuclear accident might be caused, necessitating a declaration from the prime minister

Nuclear Reactor Regulation Act (*genshirotō kiseihō*): statute regulating on the permit for construction as well as operation of nuclear reactors

Nuclear Regulatory Authority (NRA) (*genshiryoku kisei iinkai*): agency established in the Ministry of Environment to regulate the safety of nuclear power plants after the Fukushima nuclear accident

Nuclear safety agreement (*genshiryoku anzen kyotei*): agreement between the power company and local government with respect to the safety of the nuclear power plant

Nuclear Safety Commission (*genshiryoku anzen iinkai*): a commission established in the Cabinet Office to develop nuclear safety policy and to supervise safety regulation by the agency. Abolished after the Fukushima accident

Nuclear village (*genshiryoku mura*): group of corporations and people who support the development of nuclear power

Planned evacuation zone (*keikakuteki hinan kuiki*): zone outside of the 30 km radius of the Fukushima nuclear power plant, where the radiation exposure is likely to be high and residents were told to evacuate by the designated date

Precautionary action zone (PAZ) (*yobouteki bougo sochi junbi kuiki*): a zone where precautionary measures need to be adopted against the possibility of nuclear accident

Private renegotiation procedure (*shiteki seiri*): procedure to allow disaster victims to renegotiate with financial institutions to reduce the amount of the outstanding loan or to reduce the interest rate

Reconstruction Agency (*hukkou cho*): a government agency to direct the reconstruction of Tohoku

Reconstruction benefit (*hukkou kyuuhukin*): one of the benefits distributed to the victims of the Great East Japan Earthquake Disaster

Reconstruction bond (*hukkousai*): special government bond to raise money necessary to implement reconstruction measures for Tohoku

Reconstruction development plan (*hukkou seibi keikaku*): one of the reconstruction measures to promote the reconstruction of Tohoku

Reconstruction fund (*hukkou kikin*): special fund available for business operators in Tohoku in order to promote reconstruction

Reconstruction grant (*hukkou kouhukin*): one of the reconstruction measures to promote the reconstruction of Tohoku

Reconstruction grant business plan (*hukkou kouhukin jigyou keikaku*): one of the recnstruction measures using the reconstruction special district

Reconstruction housing (*hukkou jutaku*): public housing that is offered to those who lost homes in the Tohoku Earthquake with a special discount rent and with the possibility of buying out at a special discount price

Reconstruction income tax (*hukkou tokubetsu shotokuzei*): special income tax imposed on taxpayers to raise the money necessary for Tohoku reconstruction

Reconstruction promotion plan (*hukkou suishin keikaku*): one of thc reconstruction measures to promote the reconstruction of Tohoku

Reconstruction special zone (*hukkou tokku*): special zone designated to remove some regulatory red tape and to facilitate reconstruction, and give tax breaks under the Reconstruction Special Zone Act

Residence restriction zone (*kyoju seigen kuiki*): zone close to the Fukushima nuclear power plant where residents must wait for intensified environmental decontamination before returning home

Self Defense Forces (SDF) (*jieitai*): Japanese armed force although it is not officially called an armed force. Established to defend Japan against foreign attacks despite article 9 of the Constitution of Japan, SDF officers are often called on during a time of natural disaster for rescue

Special decontamination area (*josen tokubetsu chiiki*): area where the central government has a primary responsibility to decontaminate around the Fukushima power plant

Special Measures Act on Large-scale Earthquake Countermeasures (*daiki-bojishin taisau tokubetsu sochihō*): special legislation focused on a devastating large-scale earthquake, especially the Tokai Earthquake, allowing the designation of an earthquake disaster countermeasures reinforcement area and prediction of the earthquake in order to issue an emergency warning

Special Measures Act on Reconstruction and Revival of Fukushima (*Fukushima hukkou saisei tokusohō*): The statute to lead the reconstruction of Fukushima after the nuclear accident

Special tsunami disaster hazard zone (*tsunami saigai tokuetsu keikai kuiki*): area within tsunami disaster hazardous areas that is especially vulnerable to tsunami disaster, requiring construction restrictions under the Tsunami Disaster Prevention Act

Specified disaster zone (*tokutei hisai kuiki*): municipalities specified by the cabinet order as falling into this zone would be entitled to apply for the reconstruction zone program

Specified evacuation recommendation spot (*tokutei hinan kanshou chiten*): particular spot outside of evacuation instructed area and planned evacuation area, where the possibility to high radiation exposure is likely. Local residents are practically forced to evacuate if designated

Specified extraordinary disaster (*tokutei hijo saigai*): highly unlikely and extremely serious extraordinary disaster, designated as specified emergency disaster, could trigger various exceptional treatments for victims

Specified nuclear facility (*tokutei genshiryoku shisetsu*): nuclear power plant designated by the Nuclear Regulatory Authority to require special supervision

Specified reconstruction and revival base zone (*tokutei hukkou saisei kyoten kuiki*): zone created in the "no-return zone" to facilitate the decontamination and infrastructure improvement to allow local residents to return within five years. The specified reconstruction and revival base zone reconstruction and revival plan need to be formulated by the municipal government heads and receive approval from the prime minister

Temporary housing (*kasetsu jutaku*): housing constructed temporarily to allow the victims of a natural disaster to stay until permanent housing is provided

Temporary storage site (*ichiji shuseki basho*): site to store nuclear waste temporarily before transferring to interim storage site

Tohoku Earthquake (*Tohoku jishin*): massive earthquake that struck the Tohoku region in Japan on 11 March 2011. Common name for 2011 off the Pacific Coast of Tohoku Earthquake

Tokai Earthquake (*Tokai jishin*): massive earthquake that hit the central Tokai area in 1854. It is anticipated another Tokai Earthquake will hit western Japan soon

Tokyo Electric Power Company (TEPCO) (*Tokyo denryoku*): power company supplying electricity to all the residents in the Kanto area including Tokyo. It is an operator of the Fukushima Nuclear Power Plant, which caused a serious nuclear accident after the Tohoku Earthquake

Tsunami disaster hazard zone (*tsunami saigai keikai kuiki*): zone that is vulnerable to a tsunami disaster, requiring a special emergency evacuation plan under the Tsunami Disaster Prevention Act. An area that is especially susceptible to tsunami disaster is called a special tsunami disaster hazardous area to call for construction restrictions

Tsunami warning (*tsunami keihō*): a warning to be issued when there is a possibility of a strong tsunami after an earthquake. When the tsunami is not likely to be so strong, a tsunami advisory (*tsunami chuihō*) is issued

Urban disaster recovery promotion area (*hisai shigaichi hukkou suishin chiiki*): area seriously destroyed by the disaster and in need of speedy redevelopment under the Special Measures Act to Promote Reconstruction of Urban Cities Affected by Disaster

Urgent protective planning action zone (UPZ) (*kinkyu bougo sochi junbi kuiki*): a zone where emergency preparation needs to be institutionalized against the possibility of nuclear accident to minimalize the exposure to radiation

Waste from contaminated area (*osen haikibutsu taisaku chiki nai no haikibutsu*): highly contaminated waste in the contaminated area, former hazard area, and planned evacuation area

2011 off the Pacific Coast of Tohoku Earthquake (*Heisei23nen Tohoku chihō taiheiyōoki jishin*): official name given by the Japan Meteorological Agency to the Tohoku Earthquake

Index

www.ingramcontent.com/pod-product-compliance
Ingram Content Group UK Ltd.
Pitfield, Milton Keynes, MK11 3LW, UK
UKHW022015180926
475701UK00003B/368
* 9 7 8 0 3 6 7 4 8 1 3 2 2 *